LIMITATION OF LIABILITIES IN INTERNATIONAL AIR LAW

LIMITATION OF LIABILITIES IN INTERNATIONAL AIR LAW

BY

H. DRION

Springer-Science+Business Media, B.V.
1954

Originally published by Matinus Nijhoff, The Hague, Holland in 1954
Softcover reprint of the hardcover 1st edition 1954

ISBN 978-94-017-5751-5 ISBN 978-94-017-6127-7 (eBook)
DOI 10.1007/978-94-017-6127-7

PREFACE

Though the title speaks generally of limitation of liabilities in international air law, this book will only deal with the problems arising in connection with limitation of liability under the Warsaw Convention of 1929 and under the two Rome Conventions of 1933 and of 1952 on surface damage. With respect to the latter Conventions most attention will be devoted to the Convention of 1952, for the practical reason that, whatever may be the future of this more recently signed Convention, the interest of its predecessor, notwithstanding the popularity which it has enjoyed with students of air law, now seems mainly to lie in its past.

Since the limitations of liability provisions are as important for the Warsaw Convention as they are for the Rome Conventions, and since they raise a number of similar problems, it was thought worth while to devote a combined study to the three conventions, in order to bring out the similarities and the differences. For that purpose it was necessary, in stead of dividing this book in two sections, one devoted entirely to the Warsaw Convention and the other to the Rome Conventions, to discuss with respect to each separate problem arising in connection with limitations of liability, how it has been treated in the three Conventions respectively. This has resulted in a somewhat complicated pattern.

Another source of complications was the necessity of frequent references to national laws. International air law, like one of these huge waringin trees of tropical countries, has its aerial roots hanging down in the soil of as many national systems of laws, as there are countries flown over by aircraft. It is not a self-sufficient closed system, but must feed itself on local law. One cannot transplant it to the hot-house of a textbook without taking also parts of these national laws sticking to its roots.

What in other fields might be a more or less superfluous parade of learning, is in a study on international private air law the minimum – or an attempt thereto – for a realistic description of the actual problems arising in this branch of the law. Even to limit the references to the legal systems of England, the U.S.A., France and Germany – as studies in comparative law often do – would be to ignore the fact that civil aviation refuses to be kept within the geographical boundaries of what happen to be the countries with the better known systems of law. The interest of French or English law becomes academical when a flight, say, between Buenos Aires and Amsterdam is involved. Meanwhile it is clearly impossible to deal, be it ever so superficially, with the laws of all or even the majority of countries where aircraft may pass. A choice must be made, and it will be an arbitrary choice, determined by the hazard of available books and of personal preferences. The real purpose of discussing national laws in a study on international air law, therefore, can only be to cultivate a certain awareness as to the existence of possibilities outside the sphere of one's own legal thinking, an awareness which is as essential for the intelligent interpretation of the air law conventions, as it is necessary for the handling of the day-to-day legal problems which arise out of international air transportation. In order not to obscure the international character of the air law conventions which are the subject of this study, matters of national law have generally been relegated to the footnotes.

Since Latin has ceased to be the accepted medium of communication of the learned world, the language problem has become one of the most difficult in international discussions of legal matters. The loss which the disappearance of the Latin language has been to Western civilization is felt most keenly perhaps by those whose mother tongue happens to be one of the less spoken languages. There was a time that Dutch authors would write their books in Latin and would be understood all over the Western world. Authors and readers would have the same handicap, if any. The Dutch author who now wants to write for a public outside the boundaries of the Dutch language, has to choose one of the international languages and will experience – at least this author did – the kind of frustration suffered by the person who attends a formal dinner in borrowed clothes which he knows do not fit too well. Moreover, in legal thinking even more than in other matters, choice of a language implies a choice of approach. The mere using of the English language sets its stamp on the way of one's legal thinking.

The writing of this book has been made possible thanks to the generosity of the Van Vollenhovenfonds of Leiden University, of the Harvard Law School, and of the Institute of Air Law of McGill University, as well as to the kind and generous co-operation of the Koninklijke Luchtvaart Maatschappij N.V. (K.L.M./ Royal Dutch Airlines). Though it is the direct result of work done at the Institute of Air Law of McGill University, under the inspiring guidance of its Director Professor John Cobb Cooper, much of the materials relating to comparative law were already collected during the author's stay in 1946/1947 (repeated in May 1953) at the Harvard Law School, that paradise for students in comparative law. To work at these institutes and to enjoy the hospitality so liberally offered, was a unique experience. I should also like at this place to express my gratitude for having enjoyed through a number of years the privilege to make use of the fine collections of international law and comparative law at the Library of the Palace of Peace at The Hague, and especially for the never failing helpfulness of the members of the Library Staff.

The writing of this book was completed by the 1st of March, 1954, so that publications and decisions which have appeared after that date could not be taken into account.

August, 1954. H. DRION

TABLE OF CONTENTS

References are to pages

TABLE OF CASES *

The numbers refer to paragraphs and the footnotes thereto

*) For a chronological list per country of the cases which are only referred to by their date (civil law countries) see the end of this Table.

France *(continued)*

France (*continued*)

Germany

Netherlands (*continued*)

Norway

Spain

Sweden

LIST OF BOOKS AND ARTICLES WHICH HAVE BEEN CITED BY THE NAME OF THE AUTHOR ONLY

Ambrosini (1928): A. Ambrosini, Limitazione legale della responsabilità aeronautica, in 5 Il Diritto Aeronautico (1928) 1 sq.

Charlesworth (1947): Charlesworth, On Negligence, 2d ed. London, 1947.

Chauveau (1951): P. Chauveau, Droit aérien. Paris, 1951.

Cleveringa (1946): R. P. Cleveringa, Het nieuwe zeerecht, 4e druk. Zwolle, 1946.

Coquoz (1938): R. Coquoz, Le droit privé international aérien. Paris, 1938.

A. de Cupis (1946): A. de Cupis, Il Danno. Milano, 1946.

Gay de Montellá (1950): R. Gay de Montellá, Principios de derecho aeronáutico. Buenos Aires, 1950.

Goedhuis (1933): D. Goedhuis, La Convention de Varsovie. La Haye, 1933.

Goedhuis (1937): D. Goedhuis, National Airlegislations and the Warsaw Convention. The Hague, 1937.

Goedhuis (1943): D. Goedhuis, Handboek van het luchtrecht. 's-Gravenhage, 1943.

Van Houtte (1940): J. Van Houtte, La responsabilité civile dans les transports aériens intérieurs et internationaux. Louvain-Paris, 1940.

Joerges (1933): H. Joerges, Die rechtliche Behandlung der Freizeichnungsklauseln im deutschen und französischen Recht. Inaugural-Dissertation Göttingen. Quakenbrück, 1933.

Juglart (1952): M. de Juglart, Traité élémentaire de droit aérien. Paris, 1952.

Kamminga (1953): M.S. Kamminga, The Aircraft Commander in Commercial Air Transportation. The Hague, 1953.

Knauth (1935): A. W. Knauth, Aviation and Admiralty, in 6 A.L. R. (1935) 226 sq. and 309 sq.

Knauth (1953): A. W. Knauth, American Law of Ocean Bills of Lading, 4th ed. Baltimore, 1953.

Koffka (1937): O. Koffka, H. G. Bodenstein and E. Koffka, Luftverkehrsgesetz und Warschauer Abkommen. Berlin, 1937.

Lefebvre d'Ovidio and *Pescatore* (1949): A. Lefebvre d' Ovidio and G. Pescatore, Manuale di diritto della navigazione. Milano, 1950.

Lemoine (1947): M. Lemoine, Traité de droit aérien. Paris, 1947.

Litvine (1953): M. Litvine, Précis élémentaire de droit aérien. Bruxelles, 1953 (Extrait du Répertoire du droit belge, vol. XIV).

Losecaat Vermeer (1939): C. Asser, Handleiding tot de beoefening van het Nederlandsch burgerlijk recht. 3e Deel: Verbintenissenrecht, 1e Stuk, bewerkt door P. A. J. Losecaat Vermeer. Zwolle, 1939.

Mayne (1946): Mayne, On Damages, 11th ed. by W. G. Earengey. London, 1946.

Mazeaud I (1948), II (1949), III (1950): H. and L. Mazeaud, Traité théorique et pratique de responsabilité civile délictuelle et contractuelle, 4e éd. Paris, 1948–1950, 3 vols.

McNair (1953): A. D. McNair, The Law of the Air, 2d ed. by M. R. E. Kerr and R. A. MacGrindle. London, 1953.

Mechem (1952): F. R. Mechem, Outlines of the Law of Agency, 4th ed. by Ph. Mechem. Chicago, 1952.

Müller (1932): H. Müller, Das internationale Privatrecht der Luftfahrt. Inaugural-Dissertation Kiel. Dortmund, 1932.

Nánássy (1946): B. de Nánássy, Le droit international des transports par chemins de fer. Commentaire à la Convention internationale concernant le transport des marchandises par chemins de fer (C.I.M.) du 23 novembre 1933. Trad. de l'allemand par E. Ruffy. Bâle, 1946.

Neuner (1941): R. Neuner, Respondeat Superior in the Light of Comparative Law, in 4 Louisiana Law Rev. (1941), 1 sq.

Planiol-Ripert (1947): M. Planiol, Traité élémentaire de droit civil, revu et complété par G. Ripert. II (2e éd.). Paris, 1947.

Prosser (1941): W .L. Prosser, Handbook of the Law of Torts. St. Paul, Minn., 1941.

Riese (1949): O. Riese, Luftrecht; das internationale Recht der zivilen Luftfahrt unter besonderer Berücksichtigung des schweizerischen Rechts. Stuttgart, 1949.

Ripert (1952): G. Ripert, Traité de droit maritime. Vol. II (4e éd.) Paris, 1952.

Robinson (1939): G. H. Robinson, Admiralty Law. St. Paul, Minn., 1939.

Salmond (1945): Law of Torts. 10th ed. by W. T. Stallybrass. London, 1945.

Schleicher-Reymann (1937): Schleicher and F. Reymann, Recht der Luftfahrt; Kommentar zur deutschen Luftfahrtgesetzgebung. 2. erw. Aufl. Berlin, 1937.

Scrutton (1948): Th. E. Scrutton, The Contract of Affreightment as expressed in Charterparties and Bills of Lading, 15th ed. by W. L. McNair and A. A. Mocatta. London, 1948.

Shawcross and Beaumont (1951): C. N. Shawcross, K. M. Beaumont and P. R. E. Browne, On Air Law, 2d. ed. London, 1951. With Suppl. 1952.

Stanesco (1951): P. Stanesco, La responsabilité dans la navigation aérienne (dommages causés aux tiers à la surface). Paris, 1951.

Ussing (1939): H. Ussing, Responsabilité en droit danois, in: Premier Congrès International de l'Association Henri Capitant. Montreal, 1939, pp. 109 sq.

Williams (1951): G. L. Williams, Joint Torts and Contributory Negligence. London, 1951.

Williston (1936): S. Williston, Treatise on the Law of Contracts. Revised edition. New York, 1936. 8 vols.

Winfield (1950): P. H. Winfield, Textbook of the Law of Torts, 5th. ed. London, 1950.

Wolfsbergen (1946): A. Wolfsbergen, Onrechtmatige daad. Leiden, 1946.

Woltman (1936): J. J. Woltman, De beperkte aansprakelijkheid van den reeder. Proefschrift-Leiden, 1936.

LIST OF ABBREVIATIONS

Air L. Rev. = Air Law Review, 1930 sq. (U.S.A.).
A.L. = Archiv für Luftrecht (Germany).
A.L.R. = American Law Reports, Annotated (U.S.A.).
Am. Dec. = American Decisions.
Am. J. Comp. Law = American Journal of Comparative Law.
Appel = Cour d'Appel (French and Belgian Court of Appeal).
B.G.B. = Bürgerliches Gesetzbuch (German Civil Code).
B.G.H. = Bundesgerichtshof (Supreme Court of postwar Western Germany).
B.T.I. = Bulletin des Transports Internationaux par Chemins de Fer publié par l'Office Central à Berne (French and German texts.)
Cal. L. Rev. = California Law Review (U.S.A.).
Cass. = Cour de Cassation (French, Belgian and Egyptian Court of highest Jurisdiction) or Corte di Cassazione (Italian).
C.I.T.E.J.A. = Comité international technique d'experts juridiques aériens. Constituted by the Paris Conference 1925.
C.J.S. = Corpus Juris Secundum (U.S.A.).
Cod. Nav. = Codice della Navigazione, 1942 (Italy).
Col. L. Rev. = Columbia Law Review (U.S.A.).
D. = Recueil Dalloz (France).
D.L.R. = Dominion Law Reports (Canada).
D.M.F. = Droit Maritime Français.
E.R. = English Reports.
Giur. Ital. = Giurisprudenza italiana.
GIUnF = Entscheidungen des K.K. Obersten Gerichtshofes, Neue Folge (Austria).
G.P. = Gazette du Palais (France).
Harv. L. Rev. = Harvard Law Review (U.S.A.).
H.G.B. = Handelsgesetzbuch (German Code of Commerce).
I.A.T.A. = International Air Transport Association. The post-

war organization of the world's large scheduled airlines, replacing the prewar International Air Traffic Association, comprising only the European airlines.

I.C.A.O. = International Civil Aviation Organization (created by the International Civil Aviation Conference of Chicago, 1944).

Ill. L. Rev. = Illinois Law Review (U.S.A.)

Ir. Jur. = Irish Jurist.

I.U.A.I. = International Union of Aviation Insurers.

J.A.L. = Journal of Air Law. After 1945 continued as J.A.L.C. (U.S.A.).

J.A.L.C. = Journal of Air Law and Commerce, 1946 sq. (U.S.A.).

Journ. Comp. Law. = Journal of Comparative Law and Jurisprudence (England).

J.W. = Juristisches Wochenschrift (Germany).

L.C. = Legal Committee.

L.R.Q.B. = Law Reports — Queens Bench (England).

L.T. = Law Times (England).

Minn. L. Rev. = Minnesota Law Review. (U.S.A.).

N.J. = Nederlandse Jurisprudentie (Netherlands).

N.J.B. = Nederlands Juristenblad (Netherlands).

R.B.D.A. = Revista brasileiro de direito aeronautico (Rio de Janeiro) 1951 sq. (Brazil).

R.C. 1933 (1952) = Rome Conference 1933 (1952).

Rd. = Railroad.

R.D.N. = Rivista di diritto della navigazione (Italy).

Resp. civ. = Responsabilità civile (Italy).

Rev. crit. = Revue critique de jurisprudence belge.

Rev. for. = Revista forense (Brazil).

Rev. Jur. Arg. = Revista de Jurisprudencia Argentina.

R.F.D.A. = Revue française de droit aérien (France).

R.G. = Reichsgericht (German Supreme Court).

R.G.A. = Revue générale de l'air (France).

R.G.D.A. = Revue générale de droit aérien, 1932 sq. Continuation of *Droit Aérien* (France).

R.G.Z. = Entscheidungen des Reichsgerichts in Zivilsachen (Germany).

Ry. = Railway.

S. = Recueil Sirey (France).

Transport = Internazionales Transport Zeitschrift (also published as Revue internationale de Transport).

U.S. Av. R. = United States Aviation Reports (Baltimore) since 1952 as: U.S. & C.Av.R.

U.S. & C.Av.R. = United States and Canadian Aviation Reports.

W. = Weekblad van het Recht (Netherlands).

W.C. = Second Conference of International Private Air Law at Warsaw 1929 (published: Warsaw, 1930).

W.v.K. = Wetboek van Koophandel (Netherlands Code of Commerce).

Z.G.L. = Zeitschrift für das gesamte Luftrecht, 1930 sq. (Germany).

Z.L. = Zeitschrift für Luftrecht (Germany).

Chapter I

THE GROUNDS FOR LIMITATION OF LIABILITY IN PRIVATE AIR LAW

§ 1. INTRODUCTORY REMARKS

> 'It matters little what profession [...] a man may make, provided only he follows it out with charitable inconsistency'. SAMUEL BUTLER.

1. The global limitation of the shipowner's liability has been called the 'clé de voûte', the 'keystone', of maritime law. International air law does not have a global limitation of liability, and if one had to characterize the importance of limitation of liability in the field of aviation it would be more appropriate to compare it with the 'leitmotiv' of some unfinished symphony. It certainly is not the only theme, but it is one that comes back every now and then and which makes international private air law, as it has developed in the last 25 years, unthinkable without a limitation of the carrier's or operator's liability.

It is therefore that the principle of limitation of liabilities has been aptly called 'the governing principle in the legislation on air navigation' [1]. In the Warsaw Convention it largely determines the interest of the scope of application of that Convention (Articles 1 and 34); it lends force to the provisions dealing with the form of traffic documents, and it enhances the importance of the period of the carrier's liability. In the Rome Conventions it has led to provisions on the liability of servants and agents and it has set its stamp – perhaps too much so – on the solution of the intricate problems of jurisdiction and enforcement of foreign judgments.

---

1. [1]) Apel. Rio de Janeiro 28.1.1947, 1 R.B. D.A. (1951) No. 1, 217, at 223.

2. It is logical to start a study on limitation of liability with an examination of the question why the liability of the air carrier or aircraft operator should be limited at all: logical, but not without danger, for naturally the answer to that question will easily, and with reason, influence the interpretation which one attaches to the various legal provisions dealing with limitation of liability. If the answer to the question were obvious and would not allow much difference of views, the interpretation of the legal provisions clearly should be as much as possible determined by their purpose. But, unfortunately, this is not the case with the aims of limitation of liability in civil aviation. A large number of reasons for limiting the air carrier's and operator's liability have been brought forward, each as 'the' reason for such limitation of liability. Which of the grounds one prefers in this respect will largely depend on one's personal views, determined by psychological, economical and geographical factors. Moreover, we enter here the field of legal philosophy with all its dangers of easy generalizations. It would not be the first time that logical consequences would be drawn from such broad generalizations with an appearance of scientific necessity, and that at the end logic, instead of the deficiency of the premises, would be blamed for any untenable results. For in legal matters every generalization is a deficient premise for logical reasoning; the difficulty is that we cannot work without generalizations, nor without logic. The question of limiting liability cannot be avoided, and to postpone its treatment until the end of this study has disadvantages which seem to outweigh the dangers just mentioned. In order to reduce these dangers it is necessary to keep in mind the tentative nature which any answer to such questions as these should possess.

3. Before entering into a discussion of the problem it is essential to examine the various forms of limitation of liability which exist, as well as the different types of liability involved, for it is evident that the rationale of limitation of liability needs not be the same for every kind of liability and for every form of limitation.

This study will deal only with the liabilities envisaged by the Warsaw Convention of 1929 concerning the air carrier's liability for passengers and goods carried, and with the two Rome Conventions of 1933 and 1952 respectively, concerning the aircraft operator's liability for damage caused on the surface. It does not deal with the limitation provisions contained in the Brussels Convention for the Unification of Certain Rules Concerning the Assistance and Salvage of Aircraft at Sea, which was signed in 1938 but has not been ratified by any State and has never come into effect [1]).

The Warsaw Convention governs liabilities arising from the performance of contracts of carriage, even though these liabilities need not always be contractual in nature; the liability to which the Rome Conventions apply is strictly delictual, no contractual tie whatsoever existing between the party suffering damage and the party liable. It is clear that the existence of a contractual relationship between the parties may have a direct bearing on the question of whether and how liability should be limited.

Another element which can affect the desirability of limiting liability is the commercial character of the operation. Both the Warsaw Convention and the Rome Conventions apply not only to commercial aviation, but also to private flyers, though the Warsaw Convention does contain an important restriction in this respect, in so far as, according to Article 1, carriage by private flyers is only governed by the Convention if it is performed for remuneration.

Moreover, the rationale for limiting liability may well vary as to the different forms of limitation which are possible. In fact the difference in form will often be motivated by a difference in rationale.

4. The following forms of limitation are of interest for this discussion:

1. The *global limitation* of all kinds of liabilities, contractual and delictual, arising in the course of a journey or, more limited, arising out of one accident. This kind of limitation of liability is known in the maritime laws of most countries and has also been the subject of international legislation in the Brussels

3. [1]) On this Convention see I. H. Ph. Verschoor, *Het verdrag van Brussel van 1938 betreffende hulp en berging van of door luchtvaartuigen op zee*, 's-Gravenhage 1943, especially pp. 34 sq. (on limitation).

Convention for the Limitation of the Shipowner's Liability of 1924. It is closely related with, and has been developed from, the right to abandon the ship to those claiming damages [1]. A right to abandon the aircraft together with the earned freight instead of paying damages was provided by Article 43 of the old Italian law of 1923. The obvious objection to such a system in air law is that, in most cases where damages are claimed by persons on the surface, nothing more than a wreck is left of the aircraft, so that the victims actually will not get any compensation. Though introduction of this institute of maritime law has been strongly advocated by Professor Ambrosini as a Reporter for CITEJA on the global limitation of liability [2], it was never adopted and it has even been relinquished by the Italian legislator in the 1942 Code of Navigation.

The general problem of global limitation of liability in air law has received much attention in the CITEJA where it was for a long time a standing item on the agenda [3]. The need for such overall limitation was especially felt when the aircraft operator's liability in case of salvage at sea became a subject of discussion [4]. But after the question had been fully considered in the 11th Session of CITEJA in 1936, the interest of the aviation world appears to have faded, and in its decision of 15 May 1953 the Council of ICAO listed the question of global limitation under the 'subjects on which no work should be undertaken or directed by the Legal Committee unless and until a report has been submitted to the Council indicating the need for such work'.

5. 2. *Limitation per accident, of liabilities belonging to one category.* This form of limitation of liability has been adopted in

4. [1] On the system of abandon see i.a. Ripert (1952), II, nos. 1228 sq. Apart from the maritime law of France, the system seems to be still in force in Spain, Portugal, Rumania, Turkey and a number of South and Central American countries. See also the Note in 35 Col. L. Rev. (1935) 246, at 261. On the connection with the Roman law *dedito noxalis* see Mazeaud, III No. 2347: Brittany seems to have been one of the few provinces where the institute was taken over (Art. 640 of the *Coutume de Bretagne*). Comp. Art. 4 of the Greek motorvehicle act of 1911, which allowed the car-owner to escape liability by abandoning his car.

[2] CITEJA, Doc. 305 (1936). See also his studies in Il Diritto Aeron. 4 (1927) 241, at 249 sq. and 4 (1928) 1 sq.

[3] CITEJA, 3d Commission (1936), Doc. 321 (entirely devoted to global limitation). See also CITEJA Docs. 18, 247, 270, 290 (pp. 169–176), 296 (pp. 8–21), 305, 312, and 314.

[4] See Ripert in CITEJA Doc. 321, pp. 18/19.

the Rome Conventions, which both base the limits on the weight of the aircraft. A number of national air laws follow the same system, which is also known outside the field of aviation e.g. in automobile accident law [1]).

6. 3. *Limitation per person killed, injured or delayed, or per object damaged, lost or delayed.* This is the only form of limitation provided in the Warsaw Convention. Though the Rome Conventions also have this form of limitation with respect to death or personal injuries, it can be said that this way of limiting liabilities is more typical for contractual liability. As fas as goods are concerned, it is related to the generally accepted requirement that damages should be foreseeable, and that carriers may ask for a declaration of value in order to determine their risk. Limitation of liability for death or personal injuries per person killed or injured is most generally known in the field of Workmen's Compensation Acts. In the case of purely delictual liability it is more rare, the USA offering the most notable examples of such limitation outside the sphere of contractual liability in the death statutes of a number of its States [1]).

7. Apart from the various existing forms of limitation of liability, attention should be given (a) to the variety of situations in which limitation of liability may be invoked in international air law, (b) to the different kinds of damages to which they apply, and (c) to the different classes of persons who find their claims limited thereby. Too often general conclusions are drawn with a view to only one of the various possible situations or categories

---

5. [1]) See e.g. Art. 31 (4) of the Dutch *Wegenverkeerswet*, 1935 (Road Traffic Act), limiting the total liability for property damage caused by an automobile, and Paragraph 12 of the German *Kraftfahrzeuggesetz*, 1909 (Motor Vehicle Act), containing separate global limits for personal injuries and for property damage. Similarly § 10 of the Finnish motorvehicle act. Art. 4 of the old Greek Act of 1911 gave a right of abandon to the car-owner. Both the Dutch and German Acts leave the liability for proven negligence unaffected.

6. [1]) According to ICAO–LC/Working Draft No. 402 (see Rio Session (1953) II, p. 149), 17 individual States in the U.S.A. have statutory liability limitations ranging from $ 5.000 to $ 20.000, the average of these limits being somewhat less than $ 13.000. S.N. Rittenberg in his study on *Limitation of Airline Passenger Liability*, 6 J.A.L. (1935), 365 at 390, lists the following 15 States: Colorado, Connecticut, Illinois, Indiana, Kansas, Maine, Massachusetts, Minnesota, Missouri, New Hampshire, Oregon, South Dakota, Virginia, West-Virginia and Wisconsin.

of damages. When speaking of limitation of liability under the Warsaw Convention one is apt to forget that the limitation provisions do not envisage aircraft accidents and cases of death or injury to passengers only. The majority of claims where they are applied are concerned with loss or damage to baggage or freight, without any aircraft accident being involved. The same is true with respect to delays generally. Though most of the cases contemplated by the Rome Conventions will involve some accident of an aircraft, even there the situation may be less spectacular e.g. in the event of claims for noise caused by low flying aircraft.

Again, apart from the distinction between injured persons having a contractual relationship with the carrier, and those who have not (Warsaw as against Rome Conventions), differences exist between the classes of claimants, which may be relevant in determining the rationale of limitation of liability. The shipper of goods, more often than not, is a businessman for whom the contract of carriage which he concludes with the carrier is no less a commercial transaction than it is for the carrier. Generally he will insure the shipment, which means that it is the insurer who has the main interest in the amount of the carrier's liability in case of loss or damage. Carrier versus insurer! Or better: insurer of the carrier against insurer of the goods. How far away are we from the poor widow asking compensation from the big airline for the death of her husband!

§ 2. RATIONALES OF THE VARIOUS FORMS OF LIABILITY

8. Having briefly reviewed the different forms of limitation of liability and the variety of situations to which they apply, it is time to revert to our question: Why must the liability of the air carrier or operator be limited? But should we not first consider that primary question: Why liability? For how is it possible to give an intelligent opinion on the former problem, as long as one has not formed some view on the grounds for making the carrier or operator liable for certain damages? It is with legal questions as with some waterplants. One innocently intends to pick just one waterlily, and one finds oneself dragging half the vegetation of the pond out of the water.

To discuss, even cursorily, all theories which have been developed on the rationale for imposing delictual and contractual liability, would require at least one special volume. The only thing which the author can do in the scope of this study is to state briefly his own views as far as they are relevant to the discussion of the limitation of liability in air law.

The important thing to start with is that there does not exist one single ground which could cover the various liabilities for damages, not even when limited to the field of aviation. For practical purposes – though there may be objections of a dogmatical nature – the liabilities in our field can be distinguished in the following three main classes: (1) liability for one's own negligence, (2) liability for the negligence of one's servants or agents, and (3) liability for a risk-creating activity which in itself is not considered blameworthy. The first and second group of liabilities are embodied in the Warsaw Convention, the second and third in the Rome Conventions.

9. It is believed that at the root of all liability for negligence lies the idea of prevention, whether or not combined with the principle – which is not necessarily limited to liability for negligence – that if one of two parties has to bear the consequences of an accident, it is reasonable that it should be the person whose negligence caused the accident rather than the victim. As long as most liabilities were based on negligence, the aim of prevention was generally emphasized, and anything which would reduce the preventive effect of liability was frowned upon as contrary to the public interest. Thus it is not surprising to see that when liability insurance was introduced it met with strong opposition from all those who feared that now an important, if not the most important, incentive for the prevention of damages would be taken away. And when the practical need for liability insurance appeared to be such that its introduction could no longer be stopped, and when it became more and more a general feature of our modern liability system, it seemed a logical consequence to hold that the rationale of prevention had devaluated to an outmoded dogma of an older era. It is only in recent years that successful attempts have been made to save the old idea of prevention without banning the device of liability insurance which has become an indispensable part of our economic life. Liability insurance, far from taking away the incentive of avoiding damage, has only changed the person who has a direct interest in the avoidance of damages. Since it is now the insurer who has to pay, it is he who will be primarily interested in all measures of accident prevention. And since the insurer is in the position to exercise the necessary pressure on the person through whose activity liabilities can arise, either by increasing the premium or by threatening to terminate the insurance, the preventive effect of imposing liability is maintained through the medium of insurers.

10. It can even be said that the development of liability insurance has strengthened the effect of accident prevention. It has done so in two ways. In the first place it has taken away the chance of insolvency on the side of the person liable. By thus increasing the number of cases where it will make sense to bring an action for compensation, it has indirectly strengthened the preventive effect of the liability principle. The insolvent person has in practice not much to fear from claims for damages, but if he is insured, his insurer *will* have a clear interest in preventing such claims, and will bring appropriate pressure on the insured to take the necessary measures. In other words: liability insurance has created guardians with a financial interest in the prudent behaviour of persons who by their own insolvency are invulnerable to the sanction of civil actions. The effect is not much different from that arrived at by the rule of *respondeat superior*, under which the financial interest in the avoidance of claims is also placed in a person (the employer) who has the necessary influence on the persons (his servants) whose carelessness could create damage, to make them take the necessary measures for the prevention thereof.

In the second place, through liability-insurance the financial interest in the prevention of claims has been centralized in a limited number of liability insurers who are often in a better position to work out programs of accident prevention and to perform the necessary research in that field. Thus liability insurance has perhaps even extended the preventive effect of liability for negligence beyond the lines of prevention of individual negligence, because it has created the possibility of coordinated measures which could not reasonably be asked from the insured individuals.

11. It was stated above, that the liability of the Warsaw Convention is a liability for negligence (combined with a liability for the negligence of servants and agents). In fact, Article 20 of the Convention allows the carrier to disclaim liability if he can prove that he has taken all necessary measures to prevent the damages, or that it was impossible for him to take such measures. If it is true that the rationale of liability for negligence is prevention, this must also be the rationale for the liability established by the Convention. As long as no aircraft accident is involved – that means in the majority of baggage and freight claims, as well as nearly all claims for delay – a strong case can be made for basing the carrier's liability on the principle of prevention. But with respect to aircraft accidents – which includes the large majority of passenger claims – the practical need for preventive liability seems highly doubtful. To think that a carrier, without fear for passenger claims, would become careless in the operation of his aircraft, clearly neglects the fact that in case of an accident the loss of his aircraft will be a financial blow more certain and more severe than his possible liability for claims, not to mention the adverse publicity aspects attached to aircraft accidents [1]). If the expectancy of claims, in case of accidents, could have any preventive effect, it would not be from the financial loss which they may bring upon the carrier, but rather from the possibility that a keen plaintiffs' counsel might dig out some flaw in the safety system of the carrier or in his flight operation instructions, with the undesirable publicity resulting from such discovery.

Assuming that the main rationale for negligence-liability is prevention, and that civil liability is a poor means of prevention as far as aircraft accidents are concerned, it follows that limitation of liability under the Warsaw Convention for the consequences of aircraft accidents does not as gravely affect principles of public policy as is often assumed. This is of special importance for the passenger claims since they nearly always arise from

11. [1]) Cf. T.C.Giannini in 12 R.G.A. (1949) 334, at 345.

aircraft accidents. As the Rome Conventions are not based on negligence, the above reasoning does not apply to them.

12. We now have come to the second class of liability, i.e. the liability of the master or principal for his servants or agents. Where liability is imposed irrespective of negligence for the risks involved in certain activities, such as is the case in the Rome Conventions, the liability for the acts of servants or agents, when performing these activities, is a consequence of the primary liability, and it is impossible not to base it on the same rationale. But with the Warsaw Convention we are in a different situation. Though based on the principle of negligence (with shifting of the burden of proof), the carrier is made liable for the negligence of his servants or agents whether or not he can in any way be blamed for such negligence. This system of liability, apart from the question of burden of proof, coincides with the common law principles of Anglosaxon countries as well as of a great number of civil law countries [1]). But the seeming contradiction of an absolute liability on the part of the master for the acts of his servants, with the added limitation that such absolute liability should be restricted to the *negligent* acts or omissions of his servants, has always offered a crux for those interested in the rationale of the rule [2]). The theory which in later years has probably received most support in one form or another, the so-called 'entrepreneur theory', according to which damages caused by servants should be considered as 'costs of the business', insufficiently explains why these damages are only to be considered costs of the business when they were caused by the *negligence* of the servants.

---

12. [1]) I.a. France, Italy, Netherlands, Belgium, Luxembourg, Portugal, Egypt, Argentine, Peru, Venezuela, Quebec, Louisiana (Art. 2299 as construed by the courts), Siam. In a number of countries the master is permitted to disculpate himself in one way or another for the acts of his servants: i.a. Germany, Switzerland, Poland, Spain, China, Japan, Brazil, Chili, Ecuador, Guatamala, Mexico, San Salvador, Uruguay. In some countries the burden of proof as to negligence of the master in the choice or supervision of his servant seems, at least theoretically, to rest upon the plaintiff: Austria, Hungary, Sweden, Costa Rica.

[2]) Among the more recent discussions of the rationale of the master's liability for the acts of his servants see i.a. T.B. Barlow, *South African Law of Vicarious Liability in Delict, etc.* Capetown, 1939, pp. 177 sq.; B. Starck, *Essai d'une théorie générale de la responsabilité civile, etc.* Paris, 1947, pp. 204 sq.; W. J. Slagter, *Rechtsgrond van de schadevergoeding bij onrechtmatige daad*, 's-Gravenhage, 1952, pp. 80 sq.; Mechem (1952) § 359; G. J. Hughes and A. H. Hudson, *The Nature of a Master's Liability in the Law of Tort*, 31 Can. Bar Rev. (1953) 17 sq.

The most acceptable justification seems to be that offered by Professor Clarence Morris, who has supplemented the 'entrepreneur theory' with the idea of prevention [3]). Because of their general insolvency, servants have little to fear for direct actions brought against them for damages caused by their negligence. By imposing liability upon their employer, who is not immune against actions, one creates a financial interest in the prevention of negligence in a person who is in the best position to take the necessary preventive and repressive measures against the guilty but insolvent employees. To the extent that the carrier's liability for his servants and agents is, therefore, also motivated by the principle of prevention, the same that has been said with respect to the liability for his own negligence applies here: the actual need for prevention will not be very great as far as aircraft accidents are concerned, since quite apart from his liability as a carrier he has such a clear financial interest in preventing such accidents, that his possible liability towards passengers or shippers will hardly offer an additional incentive to take appropriate measures against negligent servants.

13. The third form of liability, the absolute or strict liability, has found its expression in both Rome Conventions. Whether or not one wants to consider aviation as a dangerous activity, it is difficult to deny that the fact of having an aircraft in the air above third persons or their property, creates certain unique risks towards these persons or their property which cannot be argued away by the rhetorical question whether aircraft should be considered 'dangerous animals'. Speaking of dangerous activities generally, it has been said that 'as a matter of social economics the damages caused by such activities should be considered as general costs of the activity concerned, and that they should be taken into consideration as such when one wants to evaluate the part of such activity in society':

> 'That result is obtained automatically if one connects the liability with the activity. If the liability rule would not exist, it could arrive that an industry is continued during a number of years, though it does not produce a value superior to the damages it causes, so that, from a social point of view, its

12. [3]) *Torts of an Independent Contractor*, 29 Ill. L. Rev. (1934) 339, at 341.

interest would be negative. If, however, the rule of liability comes into play, the industry concerned is compelled to keep its accounts with society balanced' [1]).

In fact it is a sound principle of economics that the costs arising from any industry be borne by that industry. If it is felt desirable to support an industry, the way to do so is by subsidizing it, not by burdening incidental victims with the damages caused by it. 'This serves to gauge the economic value of the activity and at the same time to keep the entire loss from falling on one unprepared to meet it' [2]).

The situation is of course clearly different from that contemplated by the Warsaw Convention. There, carrier, passengers and shippers are more or less participating in a joint venture, and the costs of the industry are finally paid by its users. In the situations to which the Rome Conventions apply the injured parties have nothing to do with the operation of the aircraft, and there ought to be a strong reason before requiring them to pay even a part of their damages. The general public should not 'assume the economic burdens incident to the operation of air transportation' [3]).

§ 3. RATIONALES OF LIMITATION OF LIABILITY

14. After this brief survey of the main reasons for imposing liability on the air carrier or aircraft operator, we come back to the principal question: On what grounds should that liability be limited? Before discussing the validity of the various answers given to this question, it may be useful to emphasize once more that limitation of liability may be justified by more than one rationale, and in the second place, that the rationale for limiting liability may vary according to the nature of the liability and the form of limitation.

The following grounds have been brought forward in justification of the limitation of the air carrier's or operator's liability:

(*a*) Analogy with maritime law with its global limitation of the shipowner's liability;

(*b*) necessary protection of a financially weak industry;

---

13. [1]) H. Ussing (1939) p. 117.

[2]) Note in 61 Harv. L. Rev. (1948), 515, at 521.

[3]) Nunneley (USA) at R.C. 1952, I, 149.

(*c*) catastrophical risks should not be borne by aviation alone;
(*d*) necessity of the carrier's or operator's being able to insure against these risks;
(*e*) possibility for the potential claimants to take insurance themselves;
(*f*) limitation of liability as a counterpart to the aggravated system of liability imposed upon the carrier and operator ('quid pro quo').
(*g*) avoidance of litigation by facilitating quick settlements;
(*h*) unification of the law with respect to the amount of damages to be paid.

(*a*) *Analogy with maritime law.*

15. With the strong influence exercised by maritime law, especially in the first stages of the development of air law, it is not surprising that the institution of the limitation of the shipowner's liability with its old history was a source of inspiration, when the desirability of limiting the air carrier's or aircraft operator's liability came to be discussed [1]. This was especially the case when the possibility of a global limitation of liability in air law was being considered by CITEJA. It brought the Italian legislator to extend the maritime system of abandonment to aircraft.

The similarity of ships and aircraft for the purpose of limitation of liability has been stated in the following terms by an eminent expert of maritime law:

> 'Ships and aircraft are peculiarly liable to total loss involving large cargo values and extensive life claims under circumstances over which the managers have only remote control. Railroading is quite different: it is rare for a freight wreck to destroy more than six or eight comparatively small cars, although trains in collision may each have been 100 cars long with cargoes of great aggregate value'. [2]

Whatever is the value of these arguments (they will be discussed under (c) below), the simple statement that maritime law also has its limitation of liability can never in itself be a sufficient ground for limiting the carrier's or operator's liability

15. [1]) See i.a. Ambrosini (1928) at p. 3; Knauth (1935) pp. 310/311; G. R. Sullivan in 7 J.A.L. (1936) 1 at 28; A. N. Sack in 4 A.L.R. (1933), 345 at 354.

[2]) Knauth (1935) at 310.

in air law. In order to have any significance, it should be proven (1) that the limitation of liability is a sound principle in maritime law, and (2) that the reasons why it is a sound principle apply also to aviation.

In an excellent study on the 'logical foundations of the principle of limitation of the shipowner's liability', Spasiano has criticized the various justifications which have been proposed in defence of that principle [3]). Since we are not dealing with maritime law, this is not the place to repeat his arguments; most of them will come up when the other grounds are discussed which can or have been invoked for limitation of liability in air law [4]). His conclusion, however, deserves to be mentioned: according to him the only tenable argument for the limitation of the shipowner's liability is to offer to national shipowners the same protection which shipowners of foreign ships enjoy under their own law. Already in the beginning of the 19th century competition with foreign (Dutch) ships had been invoked by English courts as main justification for the limitation of the shipowner's liability [5]). Whatever the value of this argument – it tastes a little like the childish 'the others started' excuse – it certainly cannot be invoked by the international legislator when introducing a convention for the unification of the law. As far as is known, the argument has never been used for justifying the limitation provisions in the air law conventions [6]).

(*b*) *Protection of a financially weak industry.*

16. The first English Act to limit the shipowner's liability [1])

15. [3]) E. Spasiano, *Il Fondamento Logico del Principio Limitativo della Responsabilità Armatoriale*, 9/14 R.D.N. (1943/48), 125–159.

[4]) The justification based on the special position of the master of the ship who in some (exceptional) cases is not even chosen by the shipowner, does not seem to have been relied on in the field of air law.

[5]) *The Dundee* (1823) 2 Hag. Ad. 137, *per* Stowell L. J.

[6]) When the Legal Section of the 4e Congrès International de Navigation Aérienne at Rome, 1927, recognized 'la nécessité de régler la matière [de la limitation légale de responsabilité des transporteurs aériens] suivant des prescriptions uniformes adoptées par les divers Etats afin que les transporteurs aériens puissent se trouver dans des conditions d'égalité pour la concurrence internationale', it invoked the desirability of equal chances in the international competition as an argument for unification of the law, not for the principle of limitation of liability itself (the Resolution can be found as Annex A–2 in the Minutes of the 3d Session of CITEJA Madrid, 1928, p. 85).

16. [1]) 7 Geo. II, c. 15 (1734).

contained in its preamble the consideration that 'it is of the greatest consequence and importance to this Kingdom to promote the increase of the number of ships and to prevent any discouragement to merchants and others from being interested and concerned therein' [2]). From the start, the idea of helping an industry in its infancy – the public interest in which far exceeding its financial outlooks – has been a major factor in the limitation of liability in air law. It was felt – without much foundation, as the later history of aviation, especially within the USA, would prove – that with unlimited liability for the carrier 'all commercial aviation would be impossible' [3]). Since nearly all airlines were at that time either owned or heavily subsidized by the State, limitation of liability could be seen as a desirable alleviation of the Government budget [4]). In 1935 Ambrosini expressed the opinion that 'the liability of the operator should be limited as much as possible for the benefit of aviation' [5]). In the same year Knauth wrote that in the event of the accident curves moving adversely 'limitation of liability statutes will be indicated as a remedy to keep down the losses as an expression of the public inteiest in making aviation enterprises economically possible' [6]).

Twelve years later a Brazilian judge seemed to echo the words of his English colleague of more than a century ago, by explaining the principle as follows:

'...the limitation of liability was adopted as an incentive for air navigation to prevent that the risk of their entire fortune becoming absorbed [by claims] would discourage people from putting their activity and capital in the service of communications and transportation, which are of an undeniable utility to society' [7]). Another judge in the same case justified limitation of liability as 'furthering the creation and development of an economical, political and social instrument for communications,

---

16. [2]) Cf. Bradley J. in *Norwich Co.* v. *Wright*, 80 U.S. 1871, who described the purpose of the American Limitation of Liability Act as 'to encourage shipbuilding and to induce capitalists to invest money in this branch of industry' (quoted in 35 Col. L. Rev. (1935) 251).

[3]) The Belgian Delegate De Vos (who played such a preponderant part in the history of the Warsaw Convention) in the R.C. 1933, I, 132.

[4]) Cf. M. Maschino in 14 Droit Aérien (1930), 4 at 23/24.

[5]) 10th Session of CITEJA 1935, Doc. 290, p. 138.

[6]) Knauth (1935) p. 322.

[7]) Apel. Rio de Janeiro 28.1.1947, 1 R.B.D.A. (1951) No. 1, 217 at 223.

relations and defence, of an incomparable utility and value for Brazil' [8]). Finally, the Diplomatic Conference, which in 1952 established a new Rome Convention on surface damage caused by aircraft, stated in the Preamble to the Convention that the extent of the liabilities should be limited 'in order not to hinder the development of international civil air transport'.

It is submitted that protection of the aviation industry is never a good ground for limitation of liability. If society wants to maintain air services although they cannot pay their own costs (including the damages they cause), it should frankly subsidize such services. 'Otherwise, one could as well take the view that a railway working at a loss, should not be obliged to pay for the expropriations effected as a consequence of its exploitation' [9]).

17. The idea that aviation would be impossible without limitation of liability is flatly contradicted by the facts. Though USA law has no limitation of liability of the air carrier or aircraft operator, neither with respect to passenger or cargo claims nor to surface damage, there is no country in the world where civil aviation has developed to a comparative level. And not only does American law not know of special limitations of liability for the protection of aviation, but the claims awarded there against carriers and operators are avowedly higher than anywhere else. As far as international aviation is concerned, the airlines have continued to operate their services over countries the majority of which have no limitation of liability for surface damage. The commercial operator who would even hesitate to fly over some country merely because of the risk of unlimited liability only lives in the thin air of legal theory. Nevertheless it has been contended as recently as 1952 that 'if the limits [in the Rome Convention] were considerably increased [...], the practical result would be the prevention of the development of international aviation for countries which did not have sufficient financial means in comparison with other countries' [1]). A 'practical result' which is belied by the actual practice of aviation.

16. [8]) Dissenting opinion of Judge A. Vieira Braga in the decision of the *Cameras Civeis reunidas* of 23.9.1948, ibidem at p. 237.
[9]) H. Ussing (1939) p. 117.

17. [1]) Loaeza (Mexico) in R.C. 1952, I, 123.

In recent years the argument of protection has been more frequently heard with respect to private aviation. Liability insurance represents a much larger part of the operating costs of the private flyer than the large airline [2]), and many governments are interested in developing private aviation. But here again it has been rightly said that 'if the Governments wanted to give special support to flying clubs, [...] the best course would be to use subsidies' [3]). The incidental victims on the ground should not be made financial supporters of private aviation against their own wish!

18. Though we have made more mention of the limitation of liability for surface damage, the criticism against this argument also applies to the liabilities under the Warsaw Convention. An additional criticism can be made here: that it is of little sense to protect the industry at the expense of its users, i.e. of those for whose sake the protection presumably would be chiefly extended. The question as to what extent limitation of liability can be defended to avoid having the passenger with relatively small claim risks pay higher fares in order that the damages of the passenger with big claim risks may be fully compensated, is something different from protection of the aviation business, and will be discussed later.

(c) *Catastrophical risks should not be borne by aviation alone.*

19. The idea that liability for aircraft accidents should not extend to catastrophical risks has played a part chiefly in the discussions on the limitation per aircraft provided in the Rome Conventions [1]). Where it was invoked, it was nearly always in the sense that the operator's liability should not be limited further than to apply to the exceptional catastrophical damages only. But even in its negative way the argument implies that it is

17. [2]) According to M. Bouché (France) at the R.C. 1952 (I, 130) the cost of public liability insurance for the big airline would be 1/6000 of its operating costs, whereas for the private flyer it would represent one sixth of his operating costs. These figures were called 'misleading' by the Observer for IUAI, Mr. Goodfellow (I, 131).

[3]) Steenstra Toussaint (Netherlands) at R.C. 1952, I, 128.

19. [1]) See i.a. Observations of the German Delegate to the CITEJA, Doc. 31 (1930), p. 2; R.C. 1952, I, 119/120 (IUAI), 120 (U.S.A.), 128 (Netherlands), 129 (Mexico), 132 (Portugal), 134 (Canada).

reasonable not to let aviation bear the full consequences of catastrophical accidents caused by it.

The argument that the legislator should not try to deal with the exceptional cases [2]) does not seem a very sound one for limiting a liability which generally would be unlimited. Yet it is believed that there does exist a valid ground for not imposing the full burden of air catastrophies on aviation. When discussing the absolute liability for surface damages caused by aircraft, we have based it on the principle that the costs arising from an industry should be borne by that industry and should not be shifted to the shoulders of incidental victims. The principle can also be expressed thus: damages caused by aviation are aviation costs, and should as such be borne by aviation. If that is the true rationale for the operator's absolute liability, any limitation of that liability can only be justified if it tends to exempt the operator from liability for such damages as cannot reasonably be considered to remain within the scope of typical aviation costs. The fire started by a crashing aircraft, which destroys part of a city, is as little a typical aviation risk, as it would be a typical automobile risk, when started by a traffic accident. Similarly, the explosion of a gastank caused by a falling aircraft is as much or more a risk inherent to the gas industry, than to aviation. True, to define the field of aviation risks, which should be borne by aviation, by the amount of damages involved, may seem a rather inaccurate method, but it has at least the advantage of being simple, and though the size of the damages is not necessarily a correct criterion for the nature of the risk, there is much to be said for having aircraft accidents with catastrophical consequences dealt with as national or regional emergencies rather than as mere aviation accidents.

20. As far as surface damages are concerned, the typical aviation risk is the damage caused by the direct impact of the falling aircraft. It might be asked whether the criterion for determining the catastrophical damages could not better be stated in terms of causation, rather than in maximum amounts of money. The requirement contained in Article 1 of the Rome Convention, 1952, that the damage must be the 'direct conse-

19. [2]) CITEJA (1930), Doc. 31, p. 2; R.C. 1952, I, 129 (Mexico).

quence of the incident giving rise thereto', does not go so far as to exclude all damages not directly caused by the impact.

The fire started by the falling aircraft may still be considered a direct consequence of the accident even if it spreads to neighbouring houses. The minor success of the New York rule of causation which refuses compensation to the owner of the second house burnt down by a fire [1]), illustrates the difficulty of solving these problems in terms of causation. In an international convention which is to be applied in a number of countries with a large variety of concepts and theories on the problem of causation, that difficulty becomes insurmountable.

21. If this is the rationale of the global limitation of the operator's liability for surface damage, does it justify the limits of liability provided in the Rome Convention? The Convention of 1933 provides for a limit per aircraft varying from 600.000 gold francs (ab. D. fl. 150.000, or US $ 40,000) to 2,000,000 gold francs (ab. D. fl. 500,000 or US $ 130,000) according to the maximum take-off weight of the aircraft, the limit for all aircraft having a weight in excess of 8,000 kilogram (which includes all commercial aircraft now in use) being 2,000,000 gold francs. It is plainly impossible to justify these figures with the argument that any damage in excess of them would be of such a catastrophical character that it could not longer be considered a typical aviation risk.

The Convention of 1952 has lowered a little the ceiling for the small private aircraft (500,000 instead of 600,000 gold francs), but has taken away the maximum ceiling for the large type aircraft, the increase in the limit for heavier weight aircraft degressing from 400 francs per kilogram (for aircraft from 1,000 to 6,000 kilograms) to 100 francs per kilogram (for aircraft weighing more than 50,000 kilogram) which makes a limit of 11,964,000 gold francs (ab. D. fl. 3,000,000 or ab. US $ 794,000) for a Boeing Stratocruiser and a limit of 18,654,000 gold francs (ab. D. fl. 4,700,000 or US $ 1,234,000) for the Bristol Brabazon. For the Lockheed Constellation the limit comes to 10,276,000 gold francs (ab. D. fl. 2,586,000 or ab. US $ 680,000).

---

20. [1]) *Ryan* v. *New York Cent. Railway Co.* (1866) 35 N.Y. 210, 91 Am. Dec. 49. Cf. Prosser (1941) p. 349.

Though for the large type aircraft the limits of the latest Rome Convention could, at least for a number of countries, be rationalized as not burdening the operator with the catastrophical 'atypical' risks, this explanation fails for the smaller aircraft. To say that damages exceeding US $ 40,000 would give to an accident caused by a small aircraft the character of a catastrophy, which would take it out of the sphere of typical aviation risks, is difficult to defend, even in countries with a considerably lower standard of living than that of the USA. An automobile accident might easily reach such an amount of damages.

It should be observed that when speaking of catastrophical risks, which should not be borne solely by aviation, the catastrophical nature must be determined by objective standards outside aviation. The fact that a private flyer may well be ruined by a liability amounting to US $ 40,000 or more, is, of course, quite a different matter. The possibility of being ruined by claims arising from one's activities is not at all uniquely characteristic of aviation. Perhaps the probability of big claims in aviation is greater than in the day to day activities of a normal citizen, but that is only an argument for considering these bigger claims as typical aviation risks to be borne by aviation.

(*d*) *Desirability that the carrier or operator be able to insure his liability risks.*

22. Except for theological reasons, it is difficult to deny the advantage to both the aviation industry and the general public of having the aviation risks covered as much as possible by insurance. To the industry, insurance means the spreading of exceptional losses over a number of years and a number of carriers; to the general public it means having a solvent person from whom to claim compensation for its damages. As the technique of insurance makes it necessary to have some limits of coverage in every policy, unlimited liability for the carrier or operator almost necessarily results in part of the liability being uncovered by insurance. So far, so good. But for the following – and essential – step in the reasoning a logical jump has to be made. If one assumes the desirability of the carrier or operator insuring his liability, and also that such insurance is only possible within limits, does that mean that the uninsurable part of the risk should be borne by the victim? This would be a sound conclusion only if the victim could reasonably and more easily have insured that part of the risk. But then the reason is not so much that the carrier could not insure himself against unlimited liability, but rather that the victim was in a better position to insure against that risk. The latter consideration will be discussed below (under e).

Meanwhile the argument has also been stated differently: It is better for the victim to have a limited claim which he can be sure will be paid, than to have an unlimited claim on an insolvent person [1]). The practical value of this argument can hardly be denied, but it only holds good if the limitation of liability is conditioned upon the carrier or operator having insured his liability. This is in fact the system under the Rome Convention of 1933, which in Article 14 (b) sets aside the limitation of liability if the operator has failed to take out the necessary insurance. It proved to be one of the main obstacles for many countries to the ratification of this Convention. The national legislations which have introduced compulsory insurance for the air carrier or operator do not generally seem to have made compliance with the legal insurance requirements a condition for the application of the limitation provisions [2]). The new Rome Convention of 1952 also has disconnected the limitation of liability from the existence of liability insurance.

The conclusion must be that the desirability of the carrier or operator being able to insure their liabilities is no sound reason for limiting these liabilities, if one does not accept the system of the Rome Convention 1933 to the effect that the limits cannot be invoked by the carrier or operator who has failed to insure his liability.

(e) Possibility for the potential claimants to take insurance themselves.

23. 'If the limitation of liability of shipowners is so easily

---

22. [1]) Cf. CITEJA Doc. 31 (1930), p. 2.

[2]) See e.g. the **German** Act of 1943 (RGBl. I, 69) 'zur Aenderung des Luftverkehrsgesetzes'; and the **Spanish** *Ley de Bases* 1947. But the **Italian** Cod. Nav. 1942 for surface damage followed the system of the Rome Convention of 1933 (see Art. 971); for claims from passengers, however, the limitation of liability has been made independent from compliance with the legal insurance requirements (see Art. 941 and 943).

accepted by modern legislators, it is because the potential victims, shipowners and shippers, are insured [...] Everything after all comes down to a settlement between underwriters', wrote Ripert already in 1926 [1]). It has become common knowledge that with the enormous growth of insurance on both sides of the fence – on the side of the potential victim and on the side of the person who may become liable – our general principles of liability can no longer be studied without regard to insurance practices. The impact of insurance on the law of tort and the rules of contractual liability is certain, but how far it goes and how far it should go, are still problems which are far from being settled [2]).

There can be little doubt that if liability insurance had not become the normal thing instead of the exception, at least in such fields as automobile accidents, jury verdicts in the USA would not be as generous as they are now. Curiously, because jury verdicts became more liberal, more and more people have decided to take out liability insurance. Whether one wants to call this a vicious circle or a beneficial one, depends upon one's personal views, but the fact of the influence exercised by insurance cannot be denied. Another often quoted example is that of the development of French law with respect to automobile collisions. When it had to be decided whether the presumption of liability for damages caused by objects under one's control, provided by Article 1384 (1) of the Code Civil, should also apply between the owners of colliding cars, French courts finally decided – in spite of much criticism from the authors – to apply the presumption, because it would mean that in practice each owner would have to pay the damage to the other car. Since in France motor car-

23. [1]) *Traité de Droit Maritime. 2e éd.* Paris, 1926 (4e ed. 1952) II, Nos. 1231–32. But he added that passengers generally are not insured, so that for them it was shocking to see all right of recourse disappear, this being in practice often the result of the limitation of the shipowner's liability.

[2]) Cf. H. Ussing, *Scandinavian Law of Torts, Impact of Insurance on Tort Law,* in 1 Am. J. Comp. Law (1952) 359 at 363: 'I think that in tort law the most important problem of the near future is that of determining whether, or rather, how, tort law will be influenced by the growth of insurance'. See also the excellent study by F. James Jr, *Accident Liability Reconsidered: The Impact of Liability Insurance,* 57 Yale L. Journ. (1948) 549–570; and the observations by P. Chauveau in *Le Droit Privé Français au Milieu du XXe Siècle. Etudes Offertes à G. Ripert,* Paris, 1950, II, 398 sq. at 404/405, and by L. Vučina in 62 B.T.I. (1954) 42 sq. Of special importance to aviation is the study by J. L. François, *Incidence des Assurances sur la Responsabilité du Transporteur Aérien* (*Exposé à la Chambre de Commerce Internat.*) 6 R.F.D.A. (1952), 450–456.

owners are generally insured against liability but not against damage to their own cars, the rule of liability worked out by the courts tends to have the damages paid by the party normally insured [3]).

As the development of liability insurance has been favourable to a general increase of liabilities, so the growth of insurance on the side of potential claimants – either in the form of accident insurance or workmens' compensation schemes, or in the form of insurance by shippers against loss or damage, fire insurance etc. – may lead to restrictions on accepted liability rules [4]). Insurance against insurance. If the insurance aspects were the only important ones – which they are not – all problems of liability (including limitation of liability) could be reduced to the question how the various risks can best be insured.

24. Insurance presupposes a grouping of risks, and apart from historical causes and from the practical needs of the moment, the main criterion for determining the various groups seems to be the requirement of equal spreading of risk within each group. Where the risk is not equally spread over the various members of the group, those carrying the smaller risk will have to pay for the bigger risk carried by the other members of the group. Now the size of the risks to be insured is composed of two factors: the incidence of the occurrence, and the amount of damages involved in each occurrence. This creates a difficult problem with respect to the impact of insurance on principles of liability: according to incidence, risks can better be grouped around the point of the

23. [3]) Cf. i.a. R. Savatier in Rev. gén. ass. terr. 1933, 501 and Chauveau (1951) No. 562 (4).

[4]) In his article quoted in No. 23(2), Prof. Ussing mentions (at p. 367) a Danish Act on Insurance Contracts of 1930, which allows the judge to deny or reduce a claim for compensation, if the damaged property for which compensation is claimed were insured against such damage (fire insurance or insurance against other kinds of damages), in the absence of wilful misconduct or gross negligence, and in case the liability were based on the *respondeat superior* rule. Especially in the latter case Danish courts generally seem to reject liability. Equally interesting are some recent developments in fire insurance practices in the Netherlands, where fire insurers have decided to waive in advance — through advertisements — any rights of recourse against the party having caused the fire — except against the military authorities — (see Nieuwe Rotterdamsche Courant of February 16, 1954) and where moreover damages caused by falling aircraft can be included at an additional premium. The result will be that in case of damage caused to insured property on the surface, no claim will be brought against the liable operator.

risk-creating activity because at that point more of the factors determining the incidence can be ascertained, such as quality of equipment, know-how of staff, carelessness, and surrounding circumstances, whereas according to the amount of damages involved in each occurence, they can better be calculated at the point of the object of the risk (be it persons or property). The difference is a relative one only. The liability insurer of an American domestic carrier knows very well in advance that the average claim which he will have to pay will be higher than the average claim to be paid by the liability insurer of a domestic carrier in a less developed country. Conversely, the accident insurer of a person living very close to an airport or to an ammunition factory might take into account the greater possibility of an aircraft- or explosion-accident involving such person.

But the problem can not be solved with the purely theoretical statement that a certain risk can, in abstract, better be ascertained for the purpose of insurance in one way than in another. What is more important is that insurance in a certain form is actually available and readily available, which means that it should not be an abnormal step to take out the insurance.

25. It is time now to apply these observations to the types of risk envisaged in the Warsaw and Rome Conventions, keeping in mind that actually there exist other aspects to the question than the insurance aspects only. With respect to the Warsaw Convention the risks coming within the ambit of that Convention can be grouped, inside the category of aviation risks, as easily from the side of the passenger or shipper (through air travel accident insurance or shipper's insurance), as they can be from the side of the carrier (through liability insurance). But for a further determination of the chance, that an occurrence insured against might happen, liability insurance has the advantage over passenger or shipper's insurance in that, by means of the loss experience of the carrier, such factors as efficiency, safety and organization can also be taken into account, whereby the risk can be more narrowly defined as far as the probable incidence is concerned. On the other hand, the amount of damages involved in every individual passenger accident, or in every case of loss or damage to baggage or goods, can only be estimated in advance –

and the risk accordingly classified as far as the amount involved is concerned – on the part of the passenger or shipper.

It follows that if the compensation to be paid for every passenger or for every shipment were the same, or were to vary only in accordance with easily ascertainable factors such as weight, the risk could better be insured by the carrier by way of liability insurance. By calculating the average claim and limiting the carrier's liability thereto, one roughly arrives at that situation. As far as the transportation of a passenger or shipment involves a risk in excess of the average, that special risk can better be classified as such, i.e. by the passenger in the form of a travel accident or baggage insurance, and by the shipper in the form of a normal insurance of his shipment.

26. The average value per kilogram has actually been an important factor in determining the liability limit for baggage and goods in the Warsaw Convention. The Draft Convention submitted to the Warsaw Conference of 1929 contained a limit of 100 old francs or 500 Poincaré gold francs per kilogram. IATA raised the objection that a calculation, made on the basis of a great number of shipments, had shown the average value of goods carried by air to be 130 Poincaré gold francs per kilogram. The limit was then lowered from 500 to 250 Poincaré gold francs. This episode in the drafting history is interesting both in that it shows the interest attached to the average value, and for the limited influence allowed to that value: instead of 130 francs the limit was fixed at 250 francs per kilogram.

To what extent the average 'value' of the passenger's life has been a factor in determining the limit of the carrier's liability for death or injuries to passengers it is impossible to say, for the drafting history of this provision of the Convention, as far as it can be traced, fails to disclose on what basis the framers of the Convention placed themselves when fixing the limit at 125,000 Poincaré gold francs. At the First Conference of International Private Air Law which was held at Paris in 1925 and which established the first draft on the air carrier's liability which later was to become the Warsaw Convention, the limit for death or injuries to passengers had been fixed at 10,000 old gold francs (i.e. 50,000 Poincaré gold francs). It does not appear how that figure was reached. The amount was later increased to 25,000 old gold francs (i.e. the present limit of 125,000 Poincaré gold francs) in view of the special defence as to pilot's error which at that stage was also given to the carrier, also, with respect to passengers. That amount was retained, apparently without much discussion, even when the defence as to pilot's error was limited to the carrier's liability for baggage and goods (Article 20 (2) of the present Convention) [1]).

27. If we consider the limitation of liabilities in the Rome Conventions from the insurance angle as stated above, we find a different situation. In the first place it is clear that the global limit per aircraft can never be explained by the argument that any claims in excess of the global limit could better be classified as insurance risks from the side of the victims. For the amount of damages to which each individual claim will be limited depends upon the weight of the aircraft and the number of the other claimants, and is therefore entirely unascertainable in advance for the potential victim, which means that the difference between his full damages and that amount – i.e. his claim as far as it would exceed the operator's limited liability – is also as unascertainable for him as it is for the operator.

But with respect to the individual limit per person killed or injured (200,000 Poincaré gold francs in the Convention of 1933, 500,000 in the Convention of 1952) a similar reasoning can be followed as for the Warsaw Convention, with the one important difference however, that on the side of the potential victims it is difficult to make any risk classification, selecting the aviation risks, such as is automatically made when passengers or shippers are insuring themselves or their property against the risks arising from air transportation. That the importance of this difference should not be exaggerated – and this also illustrates the somewhat theoretical character of this discussion on insurance – appears from the fact that most modern accident insurance policies no longer make an exception for accidents suffered in

---

26. [1]) The drafting history of the liability limit for passengers has been retold by Prof. J. C. Cooper in a statement to the Air Transport Committee of ICAO (see Rio Session (1953) II, 213 sq.).

normal air transportation [1]). But a number of factors, foreign to the problem, have played a part in that development.

28. So far we have considered the subject from a purely technical angle, and we have neglected the more practical problem: to what extent present day insurance practices make it reasonable – apart from considerations of prevention and moral responsibility – to rely on the potential claimants as well as on the carrier or operator for the insurance of the risks involved. If insurance were equally customary – and absence of it the exception – on both sides of the fence, it would perhaps be permissible to abstract from this aspect. Actually, however, only a small minority of mankind who might suffer injuries from falling aircraft have insured themselves against the risk of accidental death. With respect to passengers travelling by air this is much less true. Though no statistical data are known to this author, it is probably correct to say that a fair proportion of the travelling public, at least in countries with the most developed air transportation, carry insurance against the risk of accidental death or injuries. This is even more true with respect to the shippers of goods, for whom it is normal practice to have their shipments insured. It is not surprising, therefore, that the possibility for the potential claimant to insure the risk himself, has been more frequently emphasized with respect to the Warsaw Convention than to the Rome Conventions. In *Pauwels* v. *Sabena* [1]) the Brussels Tribunal pointed to the fact that 'for that part of the risk which the passenger is willing to run [i.e. the amount in excess of the limit], the passenger can either be his own insurer, or else take out insurance, as he will generally do in case of air transportation' [2]).

But even with respect to persons on the ground killed or injured

27. [1]) Cf. Shawcross-Beaumont (1951), No. 627: 'whilst being carried as a passenger on a regular air-line'. Art. 114 of the Brazilian *Codigo do Ar*, 1938, forbids the exclusion in life or accident insurance policies on the risks resulting from the carriage on regular air services ('linhas regulares de navegaçao aérea').

28. [1]) 4 R.F.D.A. (1950) 411, at 425; Pas. 1950, III, 96; 1950 U.S.Av.R. 367.

[2]) The possibility of insurance for passengers has also been mentioned in the valuable report of the Air Transport Committee on the limitation of liability towards passengers (Rio Session (1953) II, 127 sq. at 131) and during the discussions of the Legal Committee at Rio (I, p. 106).

by falling aircraft, the possibility of insuring themselves for amounts in excess of the average damages involved in death or injury cases has been frequently invoked as a ground for limiting the operator's liability to a certain amount per person killed or injured. When the individual limit was first proposed during the prolonged discussions on the new Rome Convention, the Swedish Delegate who made the proposal pointed to the fact that 'the persons who considered themselves more valuable than 200,000 francs could take out insurance themselves' [3]). One author, speaking of property damage, has even ventured the supposition that 'it might be socially easier to spread the risk, at a trifling cost per unit, over the property exposed on the earth's surface' [4]).

(f) Limitation of liability as a counterpart of the aggravated system of liability imposed upon the carrier and operator.

29. The validity of this 'quid-pro-quo' argument, perhaps the most invoked justification for the limitation of liability in international air law, depends upon the answers given to two questions:

(1) Assuming that private air law conventions have made the liability of the carrier and/or operator more stringent than it would have been without them, is it reasonable, by way of consideration, to limit the compensation of all those claiming under the Convention?

(2) To what extent have the private air law conventions made the liability of the carrier and/or operator more stringent than it would have been without them?

30. In order to answer the first of the two questions it is necessary to distinguish between the situation in which the claimant actually benefits from the more stringent system of liability imposed upon the carrier or operator, and the situation in which he does not draw any advantage from it. In the first case there is certainly nothing unreasonable in limiting the claim, which is offered to him only by virtue of the Convention, to a certain

28. [3]) Mexico Session (1951) p. 129. See also the English and Australian Delegates at the R.C. 1952, I, 122 and 144. But comp. the protest by the American Delegate at p. 149.

[4]) A. W. Knauth (1935) p. 237. Similarly P. de La Pradelle in his Preface to Stanesco (1951) pp. V/VI. Comp. also No. 23 (4).

amount. But where the victim, in the circumstances of the case, would also have had a claim without the more advantageous system of liability created by the Convention, it is open to serious doubt, whether the fact that *other claimants* have profited from that more advantageous system, is a sound justification for limiting also *his* claim. And that is what the Warsaw Convention and both Rome Conventions do by not only limiting compensation in case the claimant is relying on the provisions of the Conventions which shift the burden of proof or which impose absolute liability, but also in case he is able to prove the carrier's or operator's negligence. Since the general legal principles of almost all countries make a carrier or operator liable for his negligence, a limitation of liability which includes cases of proven negligence can only be justified by the quid-pro-quo argument in those cases where the more advantageous liability system would, even for such claimants, strengthen the bargaining position and thus favourably influence the amount of settlement. But the argument would not apply to cases where there is clear evidence of negligence [1]).

Or could it be said that even if a claimant in a specific case might not profit from the principles of aggravated liability, the limitation of his compensation could be justified by the fact that in a majority of claims those principles do offer a benefit to claimants? This would only be true if the existence of some collective interest of claimants could be assumed, or to put it in other words, if the claimants could be considered as an economic unity. The way such collective interest or such economic unity could be construed is again that of insurance. If it were so that all claimants would normally take out insurance and that the insurance premium to be paid by them would be favourably influenced as a result of the liability system laid down in the Conventions, they would all profit from it, even those who in a specific case would have had no need of the special liability rules, since they too would have had to pay less premium.

It is believed that only with respect to the carrier's liability

30. [1]) It is true that in these cases the plaintiff will also try to avoid the limitation of liability under the present Warsaw Convention by alleging a fault which is to be considered equivalent to 'dol'. Especially those French Courts which hold the '*faute caractérisée*' to amount to '*faute lourde*' might be inclined to apply Art. 25 of the Convention in cases of clear negligence.

towards shippers of goods under the Warsaw Convention has this reasoning a certain merit. As has been said before, shippers are accustomed to insure their goods, and a more favourable system of liability might well affect the premium, since it would enable insurers to recoup a greater portion of their losses from the carriers. To less extent this also applies to the liability for baggage.

But no such collective interest through insurance can be construed with respect to the liability for passengers under the Warsaw Convention, and with respect to the liability for surface damage under the Rome Conventions. Since life and accident insurers are generally [2]) not subrogated into the rights of the persons insured, the chances of the latter being entitled to compensation from the person who caused the accident will have no influence on the amount of the premium. This applies equally to passenger claims under the Warsaw Convention and to death and injury claims under the Rome Conventions.

As to claims for property damage under the Rome Conventions, it is true that insurers would generally benefit from better claim rights, but at least at this time it would be impossible to speak of a collective interest through insurance of all persons whose goods might be destroyed by falling aircraft since no general custom of insurance exists and since, moreover, the incidence of damages caused by aircraft is infinitely too small to have any influence whatsoever on insurance premiums.

Summarizing, it can be said that the first question has to be answered in the negative, except for the liability under the Warsaw Convention for goods carried. It remains to be seen whether the 'quid-pro-quo' argument, even with its scope thus limited, can be upheld when we have answered the second question, which must be discussed now.

31. Have the air law conventions actually made the liabilities of the carrier and operator more stringent than they are under general legal principles? There can be little doubt that the Rome Conventions with their system of absolute liability have created a liability which does not exist under general principles of law

30. [2]) Except that workmen's compensation insurers are often subrogated by statute, but it is obvious that a better subrogation right in case of aviation accidents will in no way affect the premium to be paid for such insurance.

in the majority of legal systems. In view of the negative answer to the first question it is not necessary, however, to go further into this matter [1]).

As to the Warsaw Convention, it has been said that the position of passengers and shippers has been substantially improved in two ways:

1) by shifting the burden of proof as to negligence to the carrier, and

(2) by nullifying all contractual clauses which would exempt a carrier from liability or would limit his liability below the limits of the Convention.

These two improvements would justify a limitation of the carrier's liability.

32. The improvement most frequently referred to in this respect is that of the burden of proof as to negligence which the Convention imposes on the carrier by the combined effect of Articles 17, 18 and 19 on the one hand, and Article 20 on the other hand. Actually in most legal systems the position of the carrier in this respect is not better, and often much worse, than it is under the Convention. As far as the carriage of goods is concerned, both the civil law and the common law systems hold the carrier liable unless he can prove force majeure. At common law the liability of the common carrier is often described as that of an insurer of the goods carried, and his defences are limited to acts of God or of the King's Enemies, inherent vice of the goods, or negligence of the shipper. His defences under civil law systems are a little broader, in so far that they include any unforeseeable and unpreventible outside cause, but in both groups of countries the carrier cannot relieve himself of liability by simply proving absence of negligence. Any loss or damage due to a defect of the carrying vehicle, be it ship or car, is at his risk. The Warsaw Convention, therefore, has in no way aggravated, but has only ameliorated his position, even apart from the second paragraph of Article 20 which relieves the carrier from liability for negligent pilotage by his crew [1]).

31. [1]) The quid-pro-quo argument has nevertheless also been frequently invoked for the Rome Conventions, see i.a. the R.C. 1933, I, 131 and 132, and the R.C. 1952, I, 127.

32. [1]) The Carriage by Air Act, 1932, has broadened the scope of this defence

33. Those who want to justify the limitation of liability by pointing to an allegedly more stringent rule of liability laid down in the Convention, are probably thinking of the carriage of persons rather than that of goods. Even with respect to passengers, however, the shifting of the onus of proof to the carrier can be considered an aggravation of the carrier's position solely in countries adhering to the common law, and even there only to a limited extent. In nearly all civil law countries, carriage of passengers is dealt with in the same way as carriage of goods: i.e. the passenger – or his dependants – has only to prove the contract of carriage as well as the fact that he has not safely arrived at the point of destination, whereupon the carrier must prove force majeure or exclusive negligence of the passenger in order to escape liability [1]). Absence of negligence again will generally not be sufficient to relieve him from liability.

But at common law a carrier of persons is liable only for the

---

by translating the French 'conduite de l'aéronef' (steering of the aircraft) into 'handling of the aircraft', which could be read to include groundhandling, maintenance and repairs. Cf. Kamminga (1953) p. 103. This drafting history of the term is ignored by McNair (1953) pp. 197/198. See also No. 168 (6). In the earlier Drafts of the Convention the defence was extended to the carrier of passengers. Only in the 3rd Session of CITEJA (Minutes p. 50) was it limited to baggage and goods. Art. 20 (2) is now generally felt to offer an unjust defence and the General Conditions of Carriage of IATA (Art. 11 (3) (a)) have set it aside, as far as transportation by the vast majority of the scheduled airlines is concerned. Omission of this defence was unanimously adopted by the L.C. of ICAO at its Rio meeting (1953), see Art. X of the Draft Protocol adopted there. By para. 14 of the First Schedule of the *English* Carriage by Air (Non-International Carriage) Order, 1952 (S.I. 1952, No. 158), which Order made the majority of the provisions of the Convention applicable to 'non-Warsaw' traffic, Art. 20 (2) has been also expressly omitted.

33. [1]) In **France** the Cour de Cassation reversed its previous decisions (in which the carrier's liability was considered a quasi-delictual liability requiring proof of negligence) by its decision of 21.11.1911, D. 1913.1.149, S. 1912.1173. Cf. for other continental countries: Premier Congrès de l'Association Henri Capitant, 1939 (Montreal, 1940), 315–450 (reports from Belgium, Quebec, France, Greece, Japan, Lebanon and Syria, Rumania, Yugoslavia). Only Quebec seems to have had a contrary development of the law, probably under influence of the common law (l.c. 327). Similar to France the **Netherlands** (Hof 's-Gravenhage 13.1.1938, N.J. 1938, No. 369); in **Argentine** the majority of the courts and authors seem to agree that art. 184 Cod. com., though speaking only of railroad transportation, is to be applied also to other forms of transportation. (See J. A. Leña Paz in Rev. Jur. Arg. 1947–III, pp. 82 sq., at 92 sq. and cf. *T. P. de Fontania* v. *FAMA*, 203 Gaceta del Foro (1951) 134, also related in 15 R. G.A. (1952) 251); **Brazil** (cf. Supr. Trib. Fed. 3.9.1948, Rev. for. 121, 455); **Italy** T. C. Giannini, *Il passeggero marittimo istruito*, Milano, 1939, pp. 192–193 (with decisions) and Lefebvre d'Ovidio and Pescatore (1949), pp. 245 sq. For other (especially South American) countries see also the extensive comparative survey in Rio Session (1953) II, pp. 221 sq.

consequences of his negligence or that of his servants or agents, and such negligence generally has to be proven by the passenger. Thus in common law countries the Convention could be truly said to have shifted the burden of proof, which ordinarily would rest on the plaintiff, onto the shoulders of the carrier. But even here the sacrifice of the carrier, which should justify his limitation of liability, is less important than it would appear to be, in view of the fact that in a great number of cases the res ipsa loquitur rule can be invoked. This will at least mean that the carrier must be able to offer some acceptable explanation for the accident having happened without his negligence, more or less substantiated by the facts, and at most that the carrier has the burden of proof that the accident was not caused by his negligence. It would be beyond the scope of this study to go into the many intricate problems connected with the applicability and the effect of the res ipsa loquitur rule in air passenger accident cases [2]). It seems fair to say, however, that in those situations in which the known facts in no way point to negligence of the carrier, the legal position of the latter has been weakened by the Convention in comparison with his position in many if not most of the common law jurisdictions [3]), though in one category of cases the contrary is true.

---

33. [2]) Cf. Shawcross and Beaumont (1951) No. 345 with a survey of the cases where the rule was held to apply and where it was not. For a general discussion of the problem involved see Prosser (1941), pp. 291–310.

[3]) Though the difference is slight for those who construe Art. 20 (1) so as to relieve an air carrier from liability when, in accidents due to an undiscovered cause, he is able to prove that he has taken all general measures as to airworthiness of the aircraft and ability of the crew to prevent the accident, without it being necessary for him to prove that up to the last moment before the accident happened his crew did not commit any negligent act. Thus O. Schreiber in 1 Z.G.L. (1930), 22, at 43; Müller (1932) p. 95; Goedhuis (1937) p. 239; Van Houtte (1940) No. 46; Lemoine (1947) No. 821; J. Lacombe in 12 R.G.A. (1949) 822, 823; T. C. Giannini in 12 R.G.A. (1949) 334 at 342; (probably) Gay de Montellá (1950), pp. 544/546; Lefebvre d'Ovidio and Pescatore (1949), p. 277 ('a carico del caricatore i danni [. . .] da causa ignota'); Chauveau (1951) No. 333. But most, if not all, of the court decisions, and a number of authors have construed Art. 20 (1) to mean that the carrier bears the risk of the cause of an accident remaining unknown. Thus Landgericht Frankfort/Main, 8.3. 1939, 9 A.L. (1939), 180, 187; *Wyman and Bartlett* v. *Pan American Airways*, 43 N.Y.S. 2d 420, 1943 U.S.Av.R. 1, 3; Trib. civ. Brussels, 6.5.1950, 4 R.F.D.A. (1950) 411, 424 (*Pauwels* v. *Sabena*). In the same sense Koffka (1937) p. 326, Riese, (1949), p. 459, Abraham in 2 Z.L. (1953), 75 at 85. See also the discussion on Article 20 (1) at the Rio Session (1953) of the Legal Committee of ICAO, I, pp. 80 sq. The whole problem has been extensively discussed by J. G. H. Sauveplanne, *De onopgehelderde oorzaak in het luchtvervoersrecht* in Rechtskundige Opstellen aangeboden aan R.P. Cleveringa. Zwolle, 1952, pp. 363 sq.

34. When an accident is caused by an inherent defect of the vehicle for which the carrier cannot be blamed in any way, but which could have been avoided by the manufacturer if he had exercised due diligence and reasonable skill, a number of jurisdictions adhering to the common law will hold the carrier liable [1]). Under Article 20 of the Warsaw Convention the carrier can also deny liability for such accidents by merely proving that he or his servants had taken all measures to avoid such accidents. Whilst the last Draft established by CITEJA contained a proviso to the effect that the carrier would be liable for damages arising from the inherent defect of the aircraft, that phrase was deleted at the Warsaw Conference [2]).

35. Summarizing our observations on the 'quid-pro-quo' argument with respect to the limitation of liability under the Warsaw Convention, we arrive at the result that as far as the carrier's liability for goods is concerned, that argument could in principle have had a certain validity, but actually the liability system provided by the Convention only ameliorated the position of the carrier; so the argument fails for that reason. As far as passengers are concerned, on the other hand, the Convention has in certain respects actually somewhat aggravated the carrier's liability in a number of common law jurisdictions, whilst in civil law countries its provisions are in these cases also more favourable than the prevailing systems of liability. But here the 'quid-pro-quo' argument is *basically* unsound, since there does not exist a collective interest of passengers which would justify a *general* reduction of their claim in consideration of an aggravation of

---

34. [1]) **Ireland**: *Burns v. Cork and Bandon Ry. Co.* (1863), 13 I.C.L.R. 543, 15 Ir. Jur. 71, and *Ryan v. Clarkin*, Ir. Rep. (1935), 1. **Canada**: *Nystad* v. *Wings. Ltd etc.* [1942] 3 D.L.R. 336, 1942 U.S.Av.R. 120. **USA** (*New York*): *De Vito Admx.* v. *United Air Lines* 1951 U.S.Av.R., 181 (quotes *Curtiss* v. *The Rochester and Syracuse Rd. Co.* 18 N.Y. 534: '(it is) well settled that the carrier is responsible for the negligence or want of skill of everyone who has been concerned in the manufacture of any portion of its apparatus').

In the leading **English** case *Readhead* v. *The Midland Ry. Comp.* (1869) L.R. 4 Q.B. 379, 393 the question 'to what extent and under what circumstances they [carriers] may be liable for the want of care on the part of those they employ to construct works or to make or furnish the carriages and other things they use', was left unanswered. In the earlier case of *Grote* v. *Chester and HolyheadRy.* (1848) 2 Ex. 251, Pollock C.B. had answered that question in the affirmative.

[2]) For the drafting history of the question of inherent defects of aircraft see Goedhuis, (1937) pp. 249 sq.

carrier's liability from which only *part* of the passengers would benefit.

36. The second improvement of the position of passengers and shippers in the Warsaw Convention, which has been invoked as a justification for the limitation of his liability, is that laid down by Article 23 which invalidates any contractual clauses relieving a carrier of liability or fixing a lower limit than that which is established in the Convention [1]).

It is submitted that this is a much sounder argument in justification of the carrier's limitation of liability than the alleged aggravation of his liability resulting from Article 20 (1). Especially with respect to goods and baggage many national laws permit a carrier to exempt himself from liability or at least to limit the amount of his liability by appropriate clauses in the document issued to the shipper or passenger [2]). Sometimes the limitation of liability is only allowed if the carrier has offered a choice of rates to his customer, thereby enabling the latter to have the goods carried at a higher limit of liability (declaration of value) [3]). But there appears to exist a growing tendency with legislators to lay down mandatory rules of liability for the carrier, which the carrier cannot avoid by contractual clauses. This is especially true with respect to shipping law, where the Brussels Bills of Lading Convention of 1924 has set the pattern by providing in which cases the carrier shall be liable and in which cases he shall not, and by generally nullifying 'any clause, covenant or agreement in a contract of carriage relieving the carrier or the ship from liability for loss or damage to or in connection with goods arising from negligence, fault or failure in the duties and obligations provided in this Article or lessening such liability otherwise than as provided in this Convention' (Article III (8)) [4]).

---

36. [1]) Comp. the Reporter Pittard in the Paris Conference, 1925 (edition of 1936, at p. 64) and the Reporter De Vos in the W.C. 1929, at p. 165.

[2]) See No. 247.

[3]) See No. 247 (3).

[4]) The Brussels Convention on bills of lading has been ratified by nearly all important shipping countries including Great-Britain, the U.S.A. France, Germany, Scandinavian countries. The Netherlands have not yet ratified the Convention though most of its principles have been incorporated in its national legislation, but the Government has announced its intention to submit to Parliament a Bill for ratification in the parliamentary year 1953/1954. See for a full list of ratifications Knauth (1953) p. 73.

Though few legislations make a formal distinction between liability for property damage and personal injuries [5]), there seems to be a tendency of the courts to look less favourably upon clauses which involve the integrity of human life [6]). Moreover, in many jurisdictions the dependants of a killed person, suing for the loss suffered by them as a consequence of the death, are considered to have independent rights which, as such, are not affected by any contract which may have existed between the carrier and the killed passenger [7]).

Outside the Warsaw Convention, therefore, the possibilities of a carrier contracting out of his liability or limiting his liability have become more and more restricted. Still it seems fair to say that the provision of Article 23 offers an advantage to the passengers and especially to the shippers of goods by protecting them against exoneration clauses which in many cases, even if their validity were subject to doubt, would mean a serious menace to their right of compensation. It is not unreasonable that such advantage be offset by a legal limitation of carrier's liability.

(g) *Avoidance of litigation by facilitating quick settlements.*

37. In 1932 there appeared the somewhat revolutionary Report by the Committee To Study Compensation For Automobile Accidents, to the Columbia University Council For Research and Social Sciences. The report was based on extensive case work. It found that the larger claims were rarely paid within 6 months from the accident, and in most cases even more than a year later.

36. [5]) Such distinction is made by Art. 139 of the **Lebanese** Code of Obligations of 1932, no doubt under influence of the teachings of Josserand (see his *Transports 2e éd.* Paris, 1926, No. 627).

[6]) See for **U.S.A.**: Williston (1936) IV, p. 3051, and Note in 37 Col. L. Rev. (1937) 248 at 255. Compare also the **Dutch** decision of the Hoge Raad 14. 4.1950, N.J. 1951, No. 17 (setting aside a contractual exemption clause by which a Health Fund tried to escape liability for the consequences of careless medical treatment) with Hoge Raad 3.6.1938, N.J. 1938, No. 920 (in which the court upheld a clause exempting a garage-holder from liability for damage caused to the car of a customer). For **France** see e.g. Trib. civ. Bordeaux 29.6.1953, 7 R.F.D.A. (1953) 381, D. 1954, Jur. 83, Note G. Ripert. (*Vizioz* v. *Air France*).

[7]) Thus i.a.: in France, Belgium, the Netherlands, and also in England, as far as clauses limiting the amount of the carrier's liability are concerned. In the U.S.A. the situation does not seem quite clear. See also No. 248. Article 24 of the Warsaw Convention makes it clear that the limits of liability of the Convention also apply to delictual actions brought by dependants of the killed passenger in their own name. See No. 64 (1).

It was felt that victims are better helped by quick payments of limited amounts than by a right to unlimited compensation for which they would have to fight through one or more court instances, with the result that in case of success they might receive some 50% of the award, the rest being paid to their lawyers. Following the example of the Workmen's Compensation Acts, which at that time had been adopted by most if not all of the States of the U.S.A. and by most civilized countries generally, the Report proposed a Compensation Plan which would give a right to fixed amounts along the lines of the Workmen's Compensation Acts, this right being the exclusive remedy offered to the victim. These proposals do not seem to have been followed by the legislators of any of the States of the U.S.A., but they have inspired Saskatchewan when drafting its Automobile Accident Insurance Act, 1945 [1]). Similar proposals had already been made in 1925 at the Genoa Conference of the Comité Maritime International, with respect to the sea-carrier's liability towards his passengers. These proposals, meanwhile, were never adopted.

During the preliminary discussions on the first Rome Convention, Ripert expressed himself in the following terms to defend the proposed individual limit per person killed or injured:

> 'People seem to believe that with respect to these damages the limitation of liability may result in depriving a person from the right to integral compensation. Everybody knows, however, that as to death or injuries, it is left to the discretion of the judge to decide on the amount of what is called the compensation for the damage. Nobody is able to say what is the value of a limb; the damages allowed will differ from country to country and from court to court [...] One will render a service to the courts by saying: the damages to be paid for death or injuries inflicted to a person shall not exceed a certain amount per person. The service thus rendered will be much greater than by fixing a global amount and saying: find your own way [...] Everybody will prefer to know that in case of

37. [1]) Comp. J. Green, *Automobile Accident Insurance Legislation in the Province of Saskatchewan*, 3d Series, XXXI Journ. Comp. Law, 39–53 (reprinted in Lawson, *Negligence in Civil Law*, Oxford, 1950, pp. 315–335). It is to be observed that in one important point the Saskatchewan Act does not follow the Report of 1932 by allowing the victim additional damages, to be claimed from the negligent owner or operator, to the extent his actual damages would exceed the insurance amount collected under the Act (Sec. 48).

an accident caused by an aircraft he may obtain e.g. 100,000 francs as he cannot calculate the damage suffered, whether it be material or moral damage [...] By fixing for every case of injuries the damage caused by the aircraft at an amount of x [...] the Experts would, it is suggested, accomplish something extremely useful' [2]).

In his explication to the President of the basic principles of the Warsaw Convention, when that Convention was going to be submitted to the Senate of the U.S.A. for ratification, the Secretary of State Cordell Hull mentioned as one of the beneficial effects of the limitation of liability, that it would 'tend to lessen litigation' [3]).

38. It is clear that avoidance of litigation through limitation of liability can only be invoked as a rationale for the individual limit per person killed, injured or delayed (in the Warsaw and Rome Conventions), or per baggage or shipment lost, damaged or delayed (in the Warsaw Convention). The reason why litigation can be reduced by these limits must be sought in the fact that they tend to reduce disputes on the amount of damages to be paid. The global limit based on the weight of the aircraft as provided in the Rome Convention could never be invoked as a means for this purpose, for the very reason that it has no connection at all with the objects of the damage, persons or goods.

Especially in case of death or wounding of a person so much is left to the appreciation of the Court in determining the damages, that the difficulty in agreeing on the amount of damages is often, if not generally, a more serious obstacle to a quick settlement than the question of liability. By limiting the carrier's liability to the amount of the average claim, one has an easy basis for agreeing on the compensation to be paid. Unless the actual damages are far below the amount of the limit, the carrier will generally be prepared to offer the limit without much discussion. If reducing litigation were the only justification for limiting the carrier's or operator's liability, it would be logical and equitable to make it at the same time a minimum. Thus one would

37. [2]) 3d Commission of CITEJA (1930), Doc. 36, p. 29 (translated from French).
[3]) Senate Doc., Executive G., 73d Congres 2d Session, p. 3, quoted in *Ross* v. *P.A.A.* 1949 U.S.Av.R. 168, 177.

come close to a kind of accident insurance, such as the Saskatchewan legislator has adopted for automobile accidents, and such as is now generally accepted for workmen's compensation. But the setting of a minimum has the disadvantage that it bestows benefits upon persons who do not need them at the expense of others. Especially in death cases it might lead to the situation of far relatives receiving damages for the death of a person from whom they never could expect any financial support. This result could only be avoided by limiting the circle of persons entitled to compensation, as the workmen's compensation laws use to do. But in an international convention it would be extremely difficult, if not impossible, to determine the persons to whom a right to automatic compensation should be given. In some countries the circle of persons usually supported is much larger than in more urbanized countries.

39. It has been suggested above that according to this rationale the limitation of liability should be based on the average claim of the persons who would suffer damages. If the limit were to exceed substantially the average claim, the carrier or operator would often try to pay less than the limit with resulting chance of litigation. It is, therefore, believed that the individual limit of 500,000 gold francs (ab. Dutch fl. 126,000 or ab. U.S. $ 33,200) cannot really be justified by this rationale. The actual damages will remain below the limit in too many cases.

But the Warsaw limit for passengers of 125,000 gold francs (Dutch fl. 31,500 or U.S. $ 8293) is such that the carrier will in most cases not go to the trouble of a law suit in order to prove that that amount would exceed the actual damages, even if he might have a good chance of winning the suit. This does not mean, of course, that there could not exist other reasons for increasing the limit, but only that a too substantial increase will result in an increase of litigation, the costs of which should be deducted, at least partially, from the amounts recovered by the claimants before one tries to evaluate the advantage derived from the increase by the potential victims.

Though the limitation of liability for cargo and baggage has been calculated on the basis of the average value of goods carried at the time the Convention was drafted, it seems doubtful whether avoidance of litigation can be considered as one of the rationales for the 250 gold francs limit of the Warsaw Convention. The standards for determining damages in case of loss or damage to goods are better and more uniformly defined than those which determine compensation for death or injuries. Difficulty in ascertaining damages, therefore, is a less frequent source of litigation, where loss or damage to goods is involved, than it is in case of death or injuries to persons. Most legal systems refer to the market value of the goods at the place of destination and that is generally not too difficult to determine [1]).

40. So far we have only spoken of death or injuries on the one hand, and loss or damage on the other hand. Limitation of liability for delay deserves special mention. If any damage is difficult to determine, it is the damage arising from delay. Here, more than anywhere else, limitation of liability could serve the purpose of avoiding litigation. But Article 22 of the Warsaw Convention, by providing the same limit for delay as it does for death or injuries and for loss or damage to baggage or goods, apparently cannot be explained by this rationale as far as delay is concerned. For a limit equal to that applicable to cases of death or injuries, or of total loss, will seldom offer a sound basis for settlement in cases of delay. The Berne Railroad Conventions for goods (C.I.M.) and for passengers and baggage (C.I.V.) contain special limits for delay, distinguishing between cases in which the actual damage can be proven by the passenger or shipper, and those in which it cannot. These limits are considerably lower than those for loss or damage to the goods or baggage; as far as goods are concerned, the limit is based on the freight paid for the transportation [1]).

---

39. [1]) See No. 105 (3).

40. [1]) Some national legislations have also special limits for delay. See i.a. Para. 13 of the First Schedule of the **English** Carriage by Air (Non-International Carriage) Order, 1952, establishing a limit to the amount representing double the sum paid for the carriage, and Artt. 345 and 349 of the **Mexican** *Ley de Aviación Civil* of 1949, limiting the liability for delay to the passage fare, or the freight. The curious limitation of liability for delay, provided in Art. 87 of the **Brazilian** *Codigo do Ar*, and in Art. 151 of the **Uruguayan** *Código de Legislación Aeronautica*, to 10% of the damages sustained, hardly offers a solution for the avoidance of litigation.

(h) Unification of the law with respect to the amount of damages to be paid.

41. During the discussions at Rome in 1952 various delegates to the conference pointed to the need of unification when defending an individual limit of liability per person killed or injured.

> 'The Conference was achieving unification in regard to property since in all countries there were the same bases for estimating loss of a material nature. But, when it came to human life, there was the greatest variety in the various legislations. The bases of evaluation were absolutely different, both as to the value of human life and as to the concept of the moral damage which the personal representatives might suffer as a consequence of that death. Sometimes it was considered, that it was not good to take moral damage into account while, in other countries, it was considered that moral damage gave a right to considerable compensation.
> 'It would constitute a position exactly opposite to the unification which everyone wished to carry out within the scope of the Convention if the Convention permitted a person who had suffered slight damage but a certain incapacity for work to obtain, in certain cases and according to the court where the case was brought, the absolute limit without specifically establishing an individual limit [1])'.

It is believed that unification of the law can hardly be considered a goal in itself. It needs an explanation itself. Why is it desirable to unify the law with respect to the liability of the air carrier or aircraft operator for damages to persons or goods carried by the aircraft or on the surface, more than it would be desirable to do so in any other field of the law? Clearly it is because aviation is by its very character international, and thus suffers more from the multiformity of national laws than many other activities which usually remain within the boundaries of one state. A multitude of possibly applicable laws means uncertainty for those concerned, especially for the operator or carrier who cannot calculate in advance the risks which he runs. The rationale of 'unification of the law', therefore, could seem to have some affinity with the rationale that the carrier or operator should be able to insure his liability risks [2]).

41. [1]) Golstein (Belgium) in Minutes, p. 145. Also the delegates of Argentine (p. 147) and Egypt (p. 151).
[2]) See No. 22.

But actually the necessity of limits in insurance coverages has little to do with the aim of foreseeability and certainty served by unification of the law. The possibility for the carrier or operator to determine in advance the extent of his liability is the necessary counterpart of any liability which would, at least partially, be based on the principle of prevention. In the beginning of this Chapter it has been argued that the negligence liability (with a reversal of the burden of proof) provided by the Warsaw Convention can only be based on that principle. Can it be said that, by unifying the law as to the carrier's liability and by thus enabling the carrier to determine in advance the extent of his liability, the limitation of liability provided by Article 22 of the Warsaw Convention, far from weakening the foundation of the liability principles of the Convention, is in harmony with these principles? It is submitted that this would be an excess of logic. For though it is true that some certainty in the law is a prerequisite for prevention, uncertainty as to the extent to which the amount of liability may rise in a specific case does not weaken the preventive effect of possible liability, and if it would do so, then only by the possibility of low liabilities, not by the possibility of high claims.

If there is any field in which unification of the law on a world wide basis would be inappropriate, it is the field of the amount of damages to be paid in case of death or injuries. For in few areas local views and circumstances of a social and economic character are of such importance. Unification of the law as a ground for limitation of liability, therefore, should be rejected.

42. This closes the discussion of the more important justifications which have been invoked for the limitation of liability of the air carrier or operator. By way of summary, it may be useful to state briefly with respect to the Warsaw and Rome Conventions separately, and with respect to each of the limits contained therein, by what valid grounds they can be justified.

For the limitation of liability in case of *death or injury of passengers*, provided by the Warsaw Convention, the only sound rationales have been found to be (a) the better position of the passenger in insuring the risk of his death or injury in excess of the average passenger accident risk, and (b) reduction of litigation by offering an easy basis for settlement.

The same rationales can be invoked for the 250 gold francs per kilogram limit for the passenger's *registered baggage*, and the 5,000 gold francs for his *handbaggage* to which should probably be added the argument that limitation of the carrier's liability is a reasonable quid pro quo for the prohibition of contractual exoneration clauses.

With respect to *goods* the limitation of the carrier's liability can best be justified by (a) the better position of the shipper in insuring the excess value of his goods, and (b) the quid-pro-quo argument. It seems doubtful whether reduction of litigation can be invoked as a third rationale. The air waybill generally contains sufficient information to determine the amount of damages in case of loss. Moreover, there is probably more uniformity in the laws of most countries as to the rule of damages to be applied in case of carriage of goods than in case of death or injuries to persons.

It is believed that the limitation of liability for *delay* – whether of passenger, baggage or goods – should be based on the same grounds. Since the limits are the same as for death or injuries to passengers, or respectively for total loss of baggage and goods, they are not suited to serve the purpose of avoiding litigation, in the way the limits provided in the Berne Conventions on international railroad transportation do.

As to the *Rome Conventions* the only acceptable justification of the *global limit* per aircraft would seem to be the argument that catastrophical risks should not be borne by aviation alone. It has been pointed out, however, that the limits laid down in the Convention – even the higher ones of the Convention of 1952 – can only be said to approach the level of catastrophical risks as far as the larger types of aircraft are concerned. For the relatively low limits for the smaller type aircraft no valid ground can be invoked. With respect to the Rome Convention of 1933, the limitation of the operator's liability can be defended, moreover, as a consideration of the advantage to the victim that the liability will be covered by insurance.

It seems doubtful whether avoidance of litigation – the only discussed justification which could be invoked here – offers a sound reason for the individual limit per person killed or injured as provided by the Rome Convention, at least as far as the latest

Rome Convention with its 500,000 gold francs limit is concerned. The better justification is probably that the individual limit offers an equitable basis for distribution of the global limit per aircraft in case of different persons of greatly varying incomes being killed or injured by an aircraft. Without an individual limit per person the death of one very rich person could reduce the claims of a person with a small income killed by the same aircraft practically to zero. Especially with respect to the new Convention of 1952 this rationale for the individual limit has been stressed by various delegates [1]).

§ 4. EXCEPTIONS TO LIMITATION OF LIABILITY: WILFUL MISCONDUCT

43. Once the principle of limited liability has been accepted for one reason or another, the question remains whether there should be added certain exceptions to that principle, and if so, why. The Draft Convention which was established by the First Conference on International Private Air Law of Paris, 1925, did not contain any exception to the limited liability of the carrier. The first proposal thereto was made by the Second Commission of CITEJA. It added a provision which would set aside the limitation of liability in case of 'intentional illicit acts' of the carrier [1]). After lengthy discussions especially dealing with extension of the carrier's unlimited liability to intentional and grossly negligent acts of his personnel [2]), the Diplomatic Conference of Warsaw 1929 finally adopted the much litigated and most unhappily phrased Article 25, which deprives the carrier of the limitation of his liability in case of 'dol' (intentional misconduct) or of faults equivalent thereto, as well as for such acts of his servants acting within the scope of their employment. The Rome Convention of 1933 changed both the terminology and the principle of the exception by simply speaking of 'dol' or 'faute lourde' (gross negligence), and by permitting the carrier to limit his liability in case of such acts of his servants by proving that he

42. [1]) R.C. 1952, I, pp. 143/44, 146, 148.

43. [1]) Report of De Vos in the 2d Session of CITEJA (1927) p. 65.
[2]) 3d Session CITEJA (1928) pp. 52–54, W.C. 1929, pp. 40 sq. and 139 sq.

had taken all proper steps to prevent the damage (Article 14). The Rome Convention of 1952, has further limited the scope of the exception, in the first place by requiring 'a deliberate act or omission done with intent to cause damage', and in the second place by requiring proof that in case of such acts committed by servants or agents the latter were acting in the course of their employment and within the scope of their authority.

44. For a discussion of the rationale of this exception in the various Conventions it is necessary to distinguish between acts of the carrier or operator himself, and those of his personnel. But first, a preliminary observation must be made which applies to both aspects of the exception. Though there can be little doubt that the existing principles as to the effect of contractual liability clauses in case of wilful misconduct or gross negligence haunted the minds of the framers of the Warsaw Convention and probably also of the Rome Convention of 1933, it is submitted that a sharp distinction should be made between legal limitation of liability and contractual limitation of liability, especially if the latter is laid down in standard conditions printed on tickets or consignment notes. The rule that forbids a party, unilaterally (for any fiction of an implied agreement notwithstanding, that isho w it happens in practice), to limit or exclude its liability for the more serious forms of misconduct, is not necessarily based on the same rationale as that which limits the scope of legal limitation provisions which it must be assumed are drafted with due regard to the interest of all concerned [1]). If the carrier limits his liability in his contract of carriage, it is only because limited liability is better for him than unlimited liability. But the considerations of a legislator, whether national or international, are not so one-sided. His decision to limit the carrier's liability is the result of a balancing of the conflicting interests of carriers and customers. The argument of the unequal bargaining position of

44. [1]) The distinction has been ignored by the French Cour de Cassation in Civ. (sect. com.) 31.5.1949, D. Jur. 1950, 157, with note by Ripert, involving application of the limit of 8.000 francs per package provided by Art. 5 of the Act of 1936 on carriage of goods by sea. Though the Act does not make an exception for gross negligence, the Court held the limit not applicable in case of gross negligence. But in a case governed by the Brussels Convention on bills of lading, the Paris Court of Appeal has held the carrier's gross negligence not to set aside the limitation of his liability: 6.6.1952, 4 D.M.F. (1952) 421, with note by F. Sauvage.

the carrier and his customer, as far as liability clauses are concerned (which, consciously or unconsciously, makes the courts especially reluctant to accept such clauses), has no value where the limitation of liability is provided by the legislator.

45. The reasons which are brought forward for excluding the limitation of liability of the carrier or operator suffer from lack of clarity. It is often said that it would be shocking if the intentional wrongdoer were entitled to limit his liability for the consequences of his conduct. This is a moral postulate about which it is difficult to argue, but the value of which cannot easily be denied. If the argument is extended to non-intentional acts, it becomes less convincing. But as long as a conscious disregard of the other's interests is required, the objections against unlimited liability can very well be based on principles of ethics.

It is possible to go a step further – a very important step indeed – by extending the 'exception' to acts of gross negligence not involving any recklessness, or even to acts of simple negligence. In fact, that is what was done in the Brussels Convention on the limitation of the shipowner's liability in conformity with the national legislations of Great Britain and the U.S.A.: Article 2 of this Convention excludes the limitation of liability i.a. with respect to obligations arising from the actual fault or privity ('faits ou fautes') of the shipowners [1]). It has been pointed out before that the main rationale for the liability for negligence is prevention. Limitation of liability might, at least theoretically, reduce the preventive effect [2]). But as has been pointed out before, the factor of prevention in liability for air accidents actually does not play as important a part as is sometimes believed, in view of the fact that, apart from any liability, the operator or carrier generally will have a sufficiently strong incentive to prevent accidents in the fact that accidents most often also involve

45. [1]) The 'without his actual fault or privity' formula has also been used in Sec. 42 (1) of the Civil Aviation Act, 1949, to render the words 'qu'il a pris toutes les mesures utiles pour empêcher le dommage' of Article 14 (a) of the Rome Convention, 1933. This section has not come into effect (Sec. 50 of the Act, and comp. Shawcross and Beaumont (1951) No. 2298).

[2]) It is possible that to a certain extent it does reduce the preventive effect, but not so much by limiting the amount to be paid in case of liability, but indirectly by limiting the danger of litigation. Danger of litigation may focus the attention of carriers and operators on problems of safety and supervision.

loss of his aircraft, and perhaps of his life. The social need for unlimited liability in case of negligence, therefore, is subject to serious doubt. This would seem to apply both to simple negligence and gross negligence. For it is difficult to make any clear distinction between the two forms of negligence as far as prevention is concerned. This means that it is also difficult to find a sound reason of public policy to set aside the limits of liability for either degree of negligence, as long as no conscious recklessness is involved.

46. From a practical point of view, the exception to the limitation of liability based on wilful misconduct, or some other qualified form of misconduct of the servants or agents of the carrier or operator, is of more importance than that based on the personal misconduct of the carrier or operator. Most activities in connection with the operation of, or the transportation by, aircraft are performed by servants or agents of the operator or carrier, not by the operator or carrier himself. For this reason there has been frequent objection to restricting the cases of unlimited liability to cases of personal wilful misconduct of the operator or carrier, on the ground that with such a restriction there would be very few cases of unlimited liability, especially if one requires intentional wrongdoing. This argument reminds one of the story of that barbarian king who, in order to keep his full weekly ration of executions, decided to extend the death penalty to less serious crimes, when his people started to show distressing signs of declining criminality. To say that, with the exception of unlimited liability restricted to the personal conduct of the carrier or operator, there would remain very few cases of unlimited liability, is only a good argument against such a restriction, if it is felt desirable to have a minimum number of cases with unlimited liability. But that seems hardly a rational approach to the problem. The reason for the exception to the limitation of liability is not that from time to time there should be cases of unlimited liability [1]), but that in certain cases limitation of the carrier's or operator's liability would shock our moral

46. [1]) Comp. Garnault in R.C. 1952, I, 426: 'It could not be admitted that the operator could be placed in a situation where one could imagine that he would never have unlimited liability'.

sense. If these cases are rare, so much the better ... unless one is opposed to the principle of limitation of liability itself; but thèn one should frankly say so, and do away with that principle. It is believed that those who are fighting against the non-applicability of the unlimited liability clause in case of misconduct of servants or agents, are driven by an emotional dissatisfaction with the principle of limitation of liability, rather than by the motives for unlimited liability openly invoked by them [2]).

Article 25 of the Warsaw Convention provides in its second paragraph that 'the carrier shall not be entitled to avail himself of [the provisions which exclude or limit his liability] if the damage is caused as aforesaid [i.e. by intentional misconduct or such a fault as, in accordance with the law of the Court seized of the case, is considered to be equivalent to intentional misconduct] by any servant or agent of the carrier acting within the scope of his employment'. Article 14 of the Rome Convention of 1933 speaks of 'intentional misconduct or gross negligence of the operator, or his servants or agents, except when the operator proves [...] where his servants or agents are concerned, that he has taken all proper steps to prevent the damage'. Finally, Article 12 of the Convention of 1952 extends the unlimited liability of the operator to the deliberate acts or omissions of his servants or agents, 'provided that in the case of such act or omission of such servant or agent it is also proved that he was acting in the course of his employment and within the scope of his authority'.

Thus the carrier is burdened with unlimited liability under the Warsaw Convention, without it being necessary that he is in any way to blame for the occurrence, if only his servant has been guilty of wilful misconduct. It is even of no importance how much care he has used in chosing and supervising his servants. Under the Rome Convention of 1933, the operator may become liable without limit for the slightest degree of negligence, provided one of his servants or agents has been guilty of gross negligence; and the burden is on him to prove that the damage can in no way be imputed to his negligence. But under the Rome Conven-

46. [2]) The same is probably true with respect to arguments brought forward for the retention of the sanction of unlimited liability in the case of passengers or goods being carried without a ticket or air waybill having been issued or without these documents containing the necessary particulars.

tion of 1952 the plaintiff who wants to escape the limits of liability must prove that the servant or agent, who has been found guilty of a deliberate act done with the intent to cause damage, was acting in the course of his employment and within the scope of his authority. In most, but not all, cases this will mean that the servant or agent was acting with the authority of the operator, so that a deliberate wrongdoing of the latter is also involved [3]).

The unlimited liability of the carrier for the wilful misconduct of his servants under the Warsaw Convention has not been adopted without discussion. At the Confeıence of 1929 Ripert remarked that in his opinion it was an 'excess of logic' to add to the intentional illegal acts of the carrier the intentional illegal acts of his servants and agents [4]). 'Excess of logic' indeed if one tries to justify the deviation from the rule of limited liability in the cases of wilful misconduct of the carrier's servants by the maxim that the acts of one's servants should be considered one's own acts. A legal maxim seldom, if ever, explains or justifies anything; it merely offers a simplified form of stating certain legal principles. Only if the rationale of the maxim, that one is liable for the acts of one's servants as for one's own acts, were the same as that for setting aside the limits of liability in case of the wilful misconduct of the carrier oı operator, would it be permissible to apply the maxim to the latter rule. Actually, however, the rationale of the vicarious liability of the master or servant, whatever it may be, has nothing to do with the reason for holding a carrier or operator not entitled to the protection of the limits, whenever he has himself intentionally or recklessly caused the damages. It is difficult to see how the limitation of one's liability for the intentional acts of another person could be qualified as 'shocking to the moral sense' [5]). It rather would seem shocking to allow an operator, who had been grossly negligent in appointing an unexperienced pilot or one inclined to drinking, to limit his liability for the accidents resulting from the inexperience or the drinking of his pilot, but to set aside the limits of liability for the operator who could in no way be blamed, neither as to the choice nor as to the supervision

46. [3]) See Nos. 214–215.
[4]) W.C. 1929, p. 42.
[5]) Stanesco (1951) p. 233, citing Garnault with approval.

of his servants, if e.g. some member of the local groundpersonnel in a far away country were suddenly to commit an act of sabotage.

47. A more practical objection which has been raised against not extending the unlimited liability provision to the misconduct of the carrier's or operator's servants is that in the majority of cases where the carrier or operator is a corporation, it is difficult, if not impossible, to draw any sharp line between the acts of the carrier or operator himself and those of his servants or agents. That is certainly true, but it could hardly be a reason to make the carrier or operator unlimitedly liable for all these acts. Nobody will deny that it is often difficult to draw the line where negligence ends and force majeure begins, but that does not mean that negligence should be dropped as a criterion in the law of tort. Anyhow, the difficulty has not prevented a great number of national legislators and the international legislator from distinguishing between the personal faults of the shipowner and those of his servants for the purpose of limiting the shipowner's liability, though from time to time it is causing difficulties to the courts [1]).

47a. To the extent limitation of liability is carried by the rationale of reducing litigation, it is weakened by any exception, but especially if that exception, apart from reopening the question of damages, introduces the new question as to the nature of the act which caused the damage. Most of the litigation under the Warsaw Convention has turned around the application of Article 25. But litigation is not the only result of a broad escape clause such as Article 25. Since most claims are settled out of court, the effect of the possibility of unlimited liability on the amount of settlements is perhaps more important. It may work out as a hidden increase of the liability limits, but it does so in a rather haphazard way, thereby destroying the unification of the law which was the aim of the Convention. If an increase in the limits of liability would be felt desirable, the limitation provisions should be changed, and the desired increase should not be left to the more or less liberal application of the escape clause by courts or juries, or to the fears of the airlines for litigation.

---

47. [1]) See Ripert (1952) II, No. 1279, G. H. Robinson, *Admiralty*, St. Paul, Minn. 1939, § 124, Scrutton (1948) p. 511, and Note in 35 Col. L. Rev. (1935), 246 sq. See also No. 212 (1).

CHAPTER II

SCOPE OF APPLICATION OF THE LIMITATION OF LIABILITY PROVISIONS

48. The scope of application of the provisions for limitation of liability contained in the Warsaw and Rome Conventions is determined by at least two circles. The first and largest circle is the one defining the cases to which the Conventions will apply. The second circle encloses the liabilities which are limited by the limitation provisions of each Convention. In the following observations we shall first deal with the Warsaw Convention, thereafter with the two Rome Conventions, in order to conclude with two paragraphs in which some specific problems common to all three Conventions will be discussed: the applicability of the limits to recourse actions and to legal interests and legal costs.

§ 1. WARSAW CONVENTION

A. Scope of Application of the Convention.

49. Article 1 of the Warsaw Convention limits the applicability of its provisions to certain, geographically restricted, cases of international carriage of persons, baggage or goods performed by aircraft by an air transport undertaking, or by any person if the carriage is performed for reward. Article 34 excludes, however, all carriage performed by way of experimental trial by air transport undertakings with a view to the establishment of a regular line of air navigation, as well as carriage performed in extraordinary circumstances outside the normal activities of air commerce ('en dehors de toute opération normale de l'exploitation aérienne') [1].

49. [1]) The French words were inexactly translated by the English legislator into 'outside the normal scope of an air carrier's business', which translation was taken over in the official, though not binding, American translation of the Convention. The Draft Protocol to the Warsaw Convention established by the Legal Committee of ICAO at its 9th Session at Rio de Janeiro, 1953, has taken over the English wording: 'an air carrier's business' and has changed the French text accordingly.

The geographical restriction referred to above is contained in para. 2 of Article 1, and limits the international carriage governed by the Convention to carriage in which, according to the stipulations [2]) made by the parties, the points of departure and destination are situated within the territory of two Contracting States, or within the territory of one Contracting State, if it was contemplated that a landing would be made [3]) in the territory of another State. The provision is worked out in paragraph 3 in the sense that carriage performed by successive air carriers which was regarded by the parties as a single operation [5]) must be considered one and the same carriage for the purpose of determining the places of departure and destination, irrespective of whether it was contracted for in the form of one contract or a series of contracts.

The provisions of paragraphs 2 and 3 of Article 1 raise some difficult problems, a full discussion of which would go beyond the scope of this study. Suffice it to mention the more important questions:

(*a*) whether High Contracting Parties in Article 1 include these signatory States which never ratified the Convention [6]).

---

49. [2]) The English and American texts speak of 'the contract' made by the parties, but the original French text has 'stipulations'.

[3]) The English and American texts have: 'if there is an *agreed* stopping place', which does not seem to be exactly the same as the French' si une escale est prévue'. The difference is small but might be of importance in some cases, e.g. where a misunderstanding would appear to have existed as to where the stop would be made, both parties having in mind a landing in another country, but at different places. In such situation the existence of an *agreed* stopping place could be well denied, but it would be difficult to hold that no landing in another State was contemplated ('prévue'). See also infra No. 265.

[4]) It is believed that air carriers performing two stretches of carriage, interrupted by a stretch of surface transportation, cannot be considered *successive* carriers, at least not when the surface transportation is not also performed by one of them. A contrary view is apparently taken by G. R. Sullivan in 7 J.A.L. (1936) 1, 12.

[5]) It is to be observed that the *carriage* must have been regarded by the parties as a single operation, not the execution of the contract or contracts of carriage. One contract of carriage may cover more than one operation of carriage. Whether or not one operation was involved in the contemplation of the parties will depend upon the circumstances of each case. The form in which the document of carriage has been made will be an important indication but not necessarily a decisive one. A domestic carrier selling much interline traffic partly on other carriers and to other countries, could not avoid applicability of the Convention by printing a clause in his tickets or air waybills that the carriage on his own line is to be regarded as a separate operation.

[6]) The question was raised in *Philippson* v. *Imperial Airways Ltd.* [1939] A.C. 332, 1939 U.S.Av.R. 63, which is some times quoted as construing the word High Contracting Parties in Article 1 to include also the signatory States which did not

(*b*) whether round trip tickets should be considered to involve only one carriage or two operations of carriage each having its own points of departure and destination. British and American Courts have adopted the former view [7]).

(*c*) whether two stretches of air carriage interrupted by surface carriage can be considered as one single operation in the sense of paragraph 3 of Article 1.

(*d*) whether carriage between two Contracting States, between whom a state of war exists, is governed by the Convention [8]).

(*e*) whether applicability of the Convention to baggage follows its applicability to the carriage of the passenger, or whether both questions should be considered separately [9]).

(*f*) whether carriage performed in deviation from a contract of carriage, which itself would fall within the scope of the Convention, is also governed by the Convention (passengers, baggage

---

ratify the Convention. Actually this problem does not pose itself for British Courts since, by Section 1 (2) of the Carriage by Air Act, 1932, they are bound only to consider High Contracting Parties, for the purpose of applying the Convention, those States listed in the latest Order in Council. The Philippson Case only indirectly affects the interpretation of Article 1, as it turned upon the question how a clause of the applicable Conditions of Carriage, which reproduced the wording of Art. 1 (2), should be construed. Only Lord Atkin expressed himself on the interpretation of Article 1 of the Convention itself (in the sense that H.C.P. would include the signatory States which did not ratify). Two other Lords limited themselves to the view that the words as used in the Conditions of Carriage were not clear beyond doubt, and should therefore be construed against the party by whom they were used. Lord Russell of Killowen thought that the words clearly were meant to include only the States having ratified the Convention.

[7]) *Grein* v. *Imperial Airways Ltd.* [1937] 1 K.B. 50, 1936 U.S.Av.R., 211 at 235; *Garcia* v. *P.A.A.* 55 N.Y.S. (2d) 317, cert. denied 329 U.S. 741, 1945 U.S.Av.R., 39 at 42 and 1946 U.S.Av.R. 496. The latter case involved a circular trip, and the court emphasized the fact that the ticket expressly called the point where the journey was eventually to end (being the same as the point of departure) the (only) point of destination, all stopover-points being indicated as intermediate stops. This element does not seem to have played a part in the Grein Case. See also *Glenn* v. *Cia. Cubana de Aviación and P.A.A.* 1952 U.S.C.Av.R. 182 (applicability of the Convention to round trip Miami–Havana assumed without discussion). *Atlantic Fish and Oyster Co.* v. *P.A.A.* 1950 U.S.Av.R. 23 does not seem to offer a clear authority on this point (the headnote in U.S.Av.R. is confusing).

[8]) The problem has been discussed by H. Achtnich in 1 Z.L. (1952) 323, at 325–331, holding the Convention not applicable to transportation between countries at war. A contrary view has been defended in the same review by the present author 1953, 303 sq., and by M. Bodenschatz 1954, pp. 13 sq.

[9]) This problem has not received much attention from the authors. Though on the one hand it is obviously desirable that the liability for a passenger's baggage be not governed by a different set of rules from the liability for the passenger, there are serious difficulties in having the applicability as to baggage always follow the applicability as to the passenger, especially if one accepts the English and American view with respect to roundtrip tickets (cf. note 7). See also Rio Session (1953) I, pp. 36/37.

or goods, put on the wrong plane, or goods or baggage which are not offloaded at the place of destination).

(*g*) whether carriage performed pursuant to shipper's instructions given in accordance with Article 12 will be governed by the Convention, if the carriage envisaged in the original contract is governed by its provisions.

Only the last two questions will be considered in more detail below. As to the other questions arising from the geographical restrictions on the applicability of the Convention, it will be assumed in the following pages that the carriage was 'international carriage' as defined in Article 1.

50. Thus the extent of the first and largest circle is determined by the following conditions:

(1). The carriage must be by *aircraft*. As will be pointed out below, the scope of applicability, as far as the carriage of baggage and goods are concerned, has been expressly extended somewhat beyond the period during which they are in the aircraft (Article 18 (2));

(2). the carriage must be pursuant to some *agreement* since the points of departure and destination must be determined by the 'stipulations' made by the parties. (Article 1 (2)).

From the other provisions of the Convention, especially those dealing with traffic documents, it is clear that the agreement envisaged by the drafters is a *contract of carriage* [1]). Article 3 (2), to mention only one example, provides that 'the absence, irregularity or loss of the passenger ticket does not affect the existence or the validity of *the contract of carriage*, which shall none the less be subject to the rules of this Convention' [2]). In his Report to the Warsaw Conference of 1929, De Vos characterized the Draft prepared by CITEJA by the following words: 'the text is therefore solely applicable to the contract of carriage with respect to its exterior aspects, and to the legal relations which are established between the carrier and the persons carried etc.' [3]).

50. [1]) Cf. i.a. Riese (1949) p. 406.

[2]) Similarly Art. 3 (4) and 5 (2) for the baggage check and consignmentnote respectively. Other express references to a contract of carriage in Art. 11–14, 28, 30 and 32.

[3]) W.C. 1929, p. 160. Cf. CITEJA, 3e Session, Compte Rendu, p. 19.

The question of whether the Convention presupposes a contract of carriage should not be confused, of course, with the question of whether the liabilities which it deals with are only contractual or include delictual liabilities [4]).

51. Since some contract of carriage is necessary, the carriage of a *stowaway* is certainly not governed by the Convention, but by national law. This may result in the carrier becoming liable without limit in case some accident happens due to the proven negligence of the pilot after the stowaway has been discovered. In order to avoid the curious situation of the regular passenger being entitled only to limited compensation and the stowaway receiving unlimited damages, it has been proposed that the Convention be amended to the effect that a stowaway would never have better rights than the normal passenger [1]).

But the difficulty arises not only in the case of stowaways. Whenever a person is carried without a contract of carriage, the situation exists of a carrier who does not enjoy the protection of the limitation provisions which would protect him if a contract of carriage had been made. Thus the carrier would not be protected by the limitation provisions if the pilot, without consent of the carrier, were to take a friend with him on the plane for a free ride. It may be, of course, that the applicable law will

---

50. [4]) See No. 64.

51. [1]) Cf. Art. 2 (5) (e) of the Draft prepared by the 'Warsaw' Sub-Committee of the L.C. of ICAO at its meeting of 1952 at Paris (LC/Working Draft 391). Riese (1949, p. 407) thinks (probably with respect to Swiss law) that the carrier could by way of the *exceptio doli* reach already now the same result. A similar view is taken by Koffka (1937) p. 104. It must be doubted whether the courts would be easily prepared to go that far in replacing the legislator. It is suggested that they would rather try to find a way to deny all liability, either by (a) invoking the carrier's immunity towards trespassers (Anglosaxon rule, but at least in the U.S.A. generally held not applicable in case of discovered trespassers, cf. Prosser (1941) p. 613 – but comp. also Mechem (1952) § 387); or (b) by extending the concept of contributory negligence; or (c) by denying the necessary duty-relationship between carrier and stowaway; or (d) by holding stowaways not included within the class of persons protected by the safety regulation, the violation of which would have caused the accident.

Finally, there may be some specific provision of national law which can be invoked either directly or by way of analogy, such as Art. 414 (in connection with Art. 949) of the **Italian** Cod. Nav., excluding all liability of the carrier with respect to persons carried purely as a matter of courtesy or friendliness, except in case of wilful misconduct or gross negligence. Similarly Art. 100 of the **Guatemalan** *Ley de Aviación Civil* of 1949, and Art. 153 of the **Uruguayan** *Código de Legislación Aeronautica*, 1942.

completely exclude the carrier's liability, at least as far as the pilot's negligence is concerned, for the reason that the person carried knew that the pilot was acting beyond the scope of his authority [2]). But the latter defence would probably not be possible if the pilot had the express or implied permission to give a free ride to his friend or if the latter could reasonably have assumed such permission. Still less would it be possible where the carrier himself were to offer such a free ride. This situation might not easily arise with the large scheduled airlines, but the term 'air transport undertaking" includes the smallest air-taxi service with aircraft operated by the manager himself. In such cases the manager may very well take some friends on a flight without any contract of carriage having been made [3]).

Since it will depend upon all circumstances whether the existence of a contract of carriage is to be assumed or not, the Courts will have great latitude in deciding on the applicability of the Convention, so that often the equity of the case will play a preponderant part. Where the carrier's negligence is established they may, in order to avoid the free passenger enjoying better treatment than the paying passenger who receives only limited compensation, more easily assume the applicability of the Con-

---

51. [2]) See i.a. for the **Netherlands**: H.R. 6.3.1924, N.J. 1924, 507, W. 11192; for **France**: Cass. crim. 12.3.1903.D.1904. 1.70, Cass. crim. 22.6.1933. S. 1933. 1.359, and comp. Cass. crim. 18.10.1946. S. 1947. 1.39; the **English** decisions *Lygo* v. *Newbold* (1854) 23 L.J.Ex. 108, 156 E.R. 129, *Twine* v. *Bean's Express Ltd.* (1946) 175 L.T. 131; the **U.S.A.** decisions in Annotation in 2 A.L.R. (2d) 406, 421 sq. and cf. Mechem (1952) §§ 386 sq.; **Italy** see Cass. civ. 21.6.1940, n. 2905, Resp. civ. 1941, p. 148 (with note by Gentile); **Belgium** see Note by Dabin–Lagasse in 3 Rev. crit. (1949) 50, at 69.

[3]) The somewhat artificial construction of a contract of carriage in the case of a free ride being offered to a friend has been fairly generally rejected. **Italy** seems to be an exception, holding the liability of the automobile owner towards his guests a contractual one. Cf. Cass. civ. 2.8.1935. Settimana di Cass. 1935. col. 446 (No. 3179), Peretti-Griva in Rassegna giur. circol. stradale 1939, col. 680. But with respect to carriage by sea and air, even Italian law admits the possibility of free transportation without a contract of carriage ('trasporto amichevole') as distinguished from gratuitous transportation based on a contract of carriage ('trasporto gratuito'): Cod. Nav., Artt. 414 and 413 respectively, in connection with Art. 949 (on the different treatment of ground transportation and sea and air transportation cf. Cass. civ. III, 29.3.1950, n. 848, Giur. Ital. 1950, I, 1, 646). For a comparative survey of the civil law principles and theories with respect to free rides see J. C. Arrosa in Revista de derecho, jurisprud. y admin. (Montevideo) 1939, pp. 224 sq., 260 sq. and 292 sq., and D. Hoogenraad, *Kosteloos mederijden*, Zwolle, 1945. For the **U.S.A.** see M.V. Malcom, *Automobile Guest Law Statutes and Decisions*, Chicago, 1937, the Annotation in 155 A.L.R., 575, and especially R.S. Rice in 27 Minn. L. Rev. 323–382 and 429–467 (also discussing English decisions).

vention than they would do in the event of an accident which cannot be imputed to any fault of the carrier. For if the Convention would be applied to the latter case, the passenger would be entitled to unlimited compensation, and, in view of the fact that no ticket was issued, the carrier would not even have the defence of force majeure (Article 3).

52. It is not essential that the contract of carriage be concluded with the passenger or the owner of the goods [1]). The contract may be made with any person, employer, husband, father or friend of the passenger, and with the forwarding agent of the owner of the goods, provided the contract includes the points oi departure and destination of the passenger or goods concerned. This is important also for the question, who should be considered the 'carrier', entitled to invoke the limits of liability, as will be discussed later when the meaning of the term 'carrier' will be examined [2]).

53. But the contract should be a contract of *carriage*, and one of carriage between agreed points. This excludes contracts by which one person *hires* his aircraft to an other person as well as a *time-charter* agreement by which aircraft with crew is put at the disposal of someone for a certain time [1]). But the time-charterer may in such a case conclude contracts for the carriage of passengers or goods to be carried by the chartered aircraft, and such carriage would again be governed by the Convention provided the other conditions were fulfilled. How far the operator of the aircraft would in such case be entitled to the defences and limits of the Convention is a problem which will be discussed later [2]).

A *voyage charter*, however, by which one person assumes the

---

52. [1]) This question is distinct from that of whether the passenger ticket should be delivered to the passenger himself in order to enable the carrier to invoke the defences and limits of the Convention. The latter problem was discussed in *Ross.* v. *P.A.A.* 1949 U.S.Av.R. 168.

[2]) See Nos. 119–121.

53. [1]) Cf. D. Goedhuis in Revue de Droit International et de Législation Comparée 1932, 687 sq., Hürzeler, *Probleme des Chartervertrags nach Luftrecht.* Zürich, 1948, and A. Ambrosini in 5 Nuova Rivista di Diritto Commerciale, Diritto dell' Economia, etc. (1952) 224 sq. See also infra No. 120.

[2]) See Nos. 136 sq.

obligation to carry with his aircraft and crew, from one point to another, certain persons or goods agreed upon or to be indicated by the charterer, would be a contract of carriage governed by the Convention, even if not all persons or goods were to be embarked or offloaded at the same points, since nothing prevents persons from agreeing in one contract on the carriage of passengers or goods over various stretches [3]). The only result of the fact that the charterer may conclude in his own name contracts of carriage with the passengers or shippers for the transportation to be performed by the chartered aircraft will be to deprive the party whose aircraft was chartered of the quality of a carrier as regards the rights and liabilities of the passengers or shippers [4]).

54. Is the existence of a contract of carriage compatible with a *contract of employment* between the same parties? The majority of authors seem to reject this possiblity, at least as far as employees travelling on duty are concerned [1]). No difference of opinion

---

53. [3]) Similarly Goedhuis l.c. (note 1 supra) and Goedhuis (1937) p. 134, Ambrosini l.c. (note 1) at 236/237.

[4]) On the question of whether, as an agent of the carrier, he will be entitled to the defences and limits provided in the Convention, see Nos. 136 sq.

54. [1]) Riese in 4 A.L. (1934) 46 and Luftrecht (1949) p. 406; Kaiser, Personenbeförderungsvertrag im Luftverkehr, Erlangen, 1936, p. 94; Koffka (1937) p. 268; Coquoz (1938) p. 86; W. L. P. A. Molengraaff, Leidraad bij de beoefening van het Nederlandsche Handelsrecht, 8e druk, Haarlem, 1948, II, p. 601; H. Achtnich in 1 Z.L. (1952) 323, at 343 sq; A. Schweickhardt in 3 Z.L. (1954) 7. See also Art. 12 (12) of the **Spanish** *Ley de Bases de la Navegación Aerea* of 1947: 'to damages suffered in an accident by personnel bound by a labour contract to the owner or operator of the aircraft, the provisions of the labour legislation will apply'.

Contra Goedhuis (1933) p. 89, and (1937) p. 129 and (hesitating:) (1943) p. 205; Von Rieben, *Haftung des Luftfrachtführers nach dem Warschauer Abkommen*, 1937, p. 11; Litvine (1953) No. 201; also the discussion of the article of Achtnich by the present author in 2 Z.L. (1953) 303, at 308 sq. Comp. Article 32 of the **Czech** Air Navigation Act, 1925, providing that the provisions of the Act as to liability shall apply to 'persons carried by the aircraft, provided that the aircraft was used: (a) against payment, or in the course of carriage of persons or goods performed as a commercial enterprise; (b) whilst in service or following the orders of the person liable, to the extent the damage is not fully covered by the accident insurance (Article 48)',

See also the decision of the **U.S.** Supreme Court in *Spencer Kellog and Sons* v. *Hicks. Adm'x et al.* (*'The Linseed King'*) 10 A. M. C. (1932) 503, 510 *per* Roberts J.: 'Kellog and Sons sustained toward employees injured or killed the dual relationship of a carrier by water and a general employer at its Edgewater plant'. For this reason the court allowed compensation in admiralty under the applicable Death Statute, notwithstanding the New Jersey Workmen's Compensation Act. In this case the carrier was not even a common carrier, but a contractor who maintained a ferry service for the transportation of his employees. The case was distinguished in *Carlin Construction Comp. et al.* v. *Heaney and State Industrial Board.* 1936 A.M.C. I, 6 at 10 and II, 1677 exists with respect to members of the crew, who are exercising their functions on board the aircraft, or more broadly with respect to any employee of the carrier who has his work on the aircraft [2]). The difficulty starts where a servant of the carrier boards an aircraft for the purpose of being carried to some place where he has to do some business for his employer.

The argument of those who deny the applicability of the Convention to the carriage of such persons is that they do not fly pursuant to a contract of carriage, but for the performance of their obligations under the contract of employment with the carrier. These authors apparently assume that an employee who is performing his duties under a contract of employment cannot at the same time have a contract of carriage with the employer for the furthering of these activities.

It is submitted that this assumption is unfounded. The situation of a passenger travelling on duty for his employer is a normal one. In fact, the majority of air passengers might belong to this class. Of all these passengers it can be said that they are travelling

---

at 1679, on the ground that there the claim had only been brought against the defendant in his quality as employer.

With respect to *railroad accidents* the **American** courts seem to have followed the view that an employee who is travelling in the service of his employee cannot be considered the passenger of his employer. See decisions in 13 Corpus Juris Secundum s.v. *Carriers* § 546, but employees travelling to or from their work on the lines of their employer have been held to be passengers, i.a. *Sassaman* v. *Pennsylvania Railway Co.* 144 F. 2d., 950, 955. It is to be observed that the American railroad cases are largely based on the interpretation of Statutes dealing with employer's liability or interstate transportation, so that it is doubtful whether and to what extent they could be invoked with respect to the interpretation of the Warsaw Convention.

The **Brazilian** Supremo Tribunal Federal held in its decision of August 1, 1944, Rev. for. 102 (1945) 466 that an engineer employed by a railway company and travelling on service should enjoy the same protection as a passenger: 'Good justice requires the assimilation of the employee who runs the risk with every person who voluntarily contracts with the carrier for his transportation' and 'the fact that one is an employee does not deprive one from the quality of passenger, with a right to bodily integrity [...] He is not a passenger, undoubtedly, and has no contract, but in the service which he performs, the employee has a right to the protection (guarantees) which the Company offers to every person'. The last two statements seem somewhat contradictory.

For **Argentine** cf. R. C. Fernandez, *Codigo de Comercio comentado*, Buenos Aires, 1943, I p. 303, note (36), refusing the status of passenger to railway employees for the purpose of Article 184 C. com.

54. [2]) Cf. the Brussels Convention of 1924 on the limitation of shipowner's liability, Article 2 (3) and 7 (3) excluding the shipowner's obligations 'arising from the engagement of persons in the service of the vessel'. On the universal acceptance of this exception cf. Note in 35 Col. L. Rev. (1935) 246, 253(40). It is to be observed that the exception is limited to persons engaged in the service of the vessel, and does not comprise the shipowner's groundpersonnel travelling on service.

for the performance of their obligations under a contract of employment. The only difference between these passengers and those to whom the status of passenger has been denied, is that for the latter the contract of employment happens to be a contract concluded with the same person who is performing the carriage. It is not contended that this difference is not a real one, but only that it does not prevent the latter persons from entering also into a contract of carriage with the carrier (their employer).

The weakness of the contrary view is revealed if one thinks of the case of a member of the carrier's groundstaff being transferred to a branch office in another country, taking his family and furniture with him. How about the carriage of his wife and children and the carriage of his belongings? Would the authors who refuse the status of passenger to the employee himself, do the same with respect to his family? It would be a difficult thing to do. The same can be said with regard to the transportation of his goods, with the additional difficulty that, assuming the carriage of his wife and children being governed by the Convention, one could hardly hold a different regime applicable to the transportation of their belongings, so that it would become essential to determine to which of the spouses the goods belong.

It was said that there does exist a real difference between an employee being carried by his own employer's service, and one carried by the service of another. With respect to the latter the fact of the carriage by an air transport undertaking will in normal circumstances be sufficient to prove the existence of a contract of carriage. As far as transportation of the carrier's own employees is concerned, there must be found additional evidence that the parties intended to enter into a contractual carrier-passenger relationship. The issuance of a ticket will not necessarily be sufficient, as this could well be mere compliance with some public regulation. But as often as a ticket is issued and the carrier is *in fact* performing the normal duties of a carrier with respect to the carried employee, it would be unrealistic to deny a carrier-passenger relationship and to construe the performance of the transportation in terms of the contract of employment, which would imply that the aircraft would be his temporary 'workshop' or 'office' and that the operation of the aircraft by the carrier would, as far as the travelling employee is concerned, be the performance of his obligations 'as an employer'! [3])

Another argument can be made against the majority view. Almost everybody agrees that when a carrier allows his employees to travel on his aircraft with a free ticket for their own pleasure or business, a contract of carriage exists and the Convention is applicable provided its other conditions are fulfilled [4]). This means that it will depend upon what the employee is going to do *after completion of the carriage*, whether the carriage may be based on a contract of carriage or not! The situation becomes extremely difficult when the trip has a combined purpose: vacation and some business of the carrier. The weakness of the refuted theory also becomes clear in case of pooled services when the employee does not know in advance whether he will be carried by an aircraft of his own company or by one of the poolpartner. For in the latter case nobody would deny the existence of a contract of carriage.

Could it be said that as a matter of equity it would be undesirable to allow the employee an action under the Convention? It is difficult to see why. Thousands of employees are travelling daily for the business of their employer, and will have an action under the Convention in case of an accident. These employees will generally also be entitled to recovery under some workmen's compensation scheme, as will the employees of the carrier.
Why discriminate between the two classes of employees. To base such discrimination on an assumption of risks by the carrier's employees would be to ignore the fact that a number of officers

---

54. [3]) Cf. the **Dutch** decision of the Kantonrechter 's-Gravenhage 21.1.1953, N.J. 1954, No. 134, concerning the claim of the widow of a deceased employee, killed as a passenger on defendant's aircraft, when travelling on duty from Indonesia to the Netherlands. The claim was founded on the contract of employment (Art. 1638x B.W.): '... it is not denied that the aircraft 'Roermond' at said time was flying on a normal line service, and, as a public means of conveyance, was carrying on board also a number of co-passengers. Defendant, in operating this service, therefore, was acting as carrier, and the circumstance that I., as a passenger in the aircraft, at the same time was in the employment of defendant, must be considered a combination of circumstances which could not have any special legal effect, since I.'s employment fell within the scope of defendant's Personnel Department and had no connection with any of the activities which were performed on board the 'Roermond' by other personnel of defendant. [...] under these circumstances said aircraft cannot be considered to come within the notion of 'locals, tools and instruments' [referred to in Art. 1638x B.W.], in or with which the employer [...] made I. perform his work'.

[4]) Contra only A. Schweickhardt in 3 Z.L. (1954) 7 sq.

of big companies have to travel as much by air as the ground-personnel of an air carrier.

It has been said that application of the Convention to the transportation of the carrier's employees would be unfair on the carrier as it would impose upon him the double liability of carrier and employer [5]). This objection does not take into account the effect of Article 24, which provides that actions for damage by a passenger or his dependants, however founded, can only be brought subject to the limits set out in the Convention. Whether the actions be based upon the contract of employment or upon the contract of carriage, the carrier shall be entitled to invoke the defences and limits established by the Convention. This may bring hardship upon the employee in those cases in which the applicable workmen's compensation law does not give him a direct action against the compensation insurer but only an action against the employer. It is sumbitted, however, that this is a matter for the national legislator to deal with, and that it should not influence the interpretation of an international Convention such as the Warsaw Convention.

(3)

55. The carriage must be one of persons, baggage or goods (Article 1 (1)), excluding carriage performed pursuant to international postal conventions (Article 2 (2)). The first part does not seem to import any real limitation. There can be no doubt that the French 'marchandises' includes livestock. The wording for the exclusion of mail (by reference to the international postal Conventions) was chosen to avoid the necessity of defining what should be considered mail and to make sure that no conflict between the Warsaw Convention and the postal Conventions could arise.

(4)

56. The carriage must be for remuneration if it is not performed by an air transport undertaking. The requirement of remuneration should be taken in a strict sense, since the whole tenor of the Convention makes it clear that it purports to deal with commercial

---

54. [5]) Goedhuis (1933) p. 90.

transportation only. This is especially evidenced by the provisions prescribing the traffic documents to be used. Only such remuneration which makes the contract of carriage itself a commercial transaction will be sufficient to bring the carriage within the scope of the Convention. A share expenses flight by a couple of friends would not be carriage for remuneration [1]). Analogies with national laws or other international conventions using the same or a similar criterion should be considered with the greatest caution, as often they are based on different grounds, and involve different interests [2]).

(5)

57. The carriage should not be performed by air navigation undertakings by way of experimental trial with a view to the establishment of a regular line of air navigation, nor should it be performed in extraordinary circumstances outside the normal scope of air commerce (Article 34). The provision only envisages truly exceptional situations in which it would be unfair to burden the carrier with the responsibilities of a normal carrier. It is to be observed that the last past of the Article applies to both air transport undertakings and private fliers. In the text adopted in the British Carriage by Air Act the applicability to the latter group has been largely taken away by the translation of the broad words 'exploitation aérienne' into 'an air carrier's business' [1]).

---

56. [1]) Similarly Riese (1949) p. 140.

[2]) It is submitted that the French concept of 'transport bénévole' (transportation for reasons of courtesy or friendliness) is much narrower than carriage without remuneration, in the sense of the Convention; it was developed by the French courts only to avoid the man who out of pure kindness would offer a free ride being burdened with the heavy responsibility of Article 1384 (1) of the Civil Code, and it has been restricted by the courts in order to grant the protection of 1384 (1) to as many persons as possible. It is even to be doubted whether 'transport interessé', as this notion has been developed by French courts and authors (cf. P. Georgiadès, in 6 R.F.D.A. (1952) 91 sq.), is always carriage against remuneration in the sense of Article 1 of the Convention, if it were only for the fact that 'transport interessé' does not require a contract of carriage. Similarly it would be dangerous to think that the concept of carriage for remuneration, as used in Articles 5 and 7 of the Chicago Convention, is necessarily the same as that in the Warsaw Convention. The confusion has not always been completely avoided by the authors, cf. Riese (1949) p. 410 (14), A. Meyer, *Cabotage aérien*, Paris, 1948, p. 58.

Cf. also the English cases of summary jurisdiction mentioned by Shawcross and Beaumont (1951) No. 358, sub (f) *in fine*, construing the words 'for hire or reward' for the purpose of certain Air Navigation Orders to mean that such carriage includes carriage on a share expenses basis.

57. [1]) See No. 49 (1).

58. Supposing that all the above conditions are fulfilled, that there is carriage by aircraft between two Contracting States, and that there is a contract of carriage; in such cases will all carriage by air performed in connection with the contract be governed by the Convention, even if such carriage was not originally foreseen by the parties? The question can arise in two ways:

(1) regularly, in case of shipper's instructions to stop or to return the goods in accordance with Article 12 or in case of changing of route by the carrier in the exercise of rights reserved in the Conditions of Carriage, and

(2) in an irregular way, where passenger, baggage or goods are being embarked or loaded by error into a wrong plane, or where they are not disembarked or offloaded at the place of destination.

59. The problems as to the applicability of the Convention arising from the rights given to the shipper by Article 12 do not seem to have received much attention [1]). They are twofold: What is the effect of a shipper's instruction to stop the goods at some intermediate point on the route if that is situated in a non-Contracting State, the original point of destination being in a Contracting State, or conversely? How should the applicability of the Convention be determined with respect to the transportation back to the shipper, pursuant to instructions given by him in accordance with Article 12?

The answer to the first question depends upon the character which one attaches to the right of disposition granted by Article 12. The Article was largely drawn from the provisions of Article 21 and 22 of the Berne Convention on carriage of goods by railroad (C.I.M.), which governs almost all international railroad transportation in continental Europe. Article 21 of that convention is entitled 'Right to modify the contract of carriage' and Article 22 'Performance of the modifications made in the contract of carriage'. The text of Article 21 also speaks of 'modifying the contract of carriage', and in line with this idea Article 22 provides, otherwise than Article 12 of the Warsaw Convention, that when the shipper has the goods stopped at an intermediate point, the

59. [1]) See however Koffka (1937) p. 270.

payable freight will be that applicable up to such intermediate point.

Article 12 of the Warsaw Convention, though derived from the C.I.M., seems to be based on a different principle. It does not speak of a right to modify the contract of carriage, but of a right to dispose of the goods, and it makes it clear that this right can only be exercised 'subject to the shipper's liability to carry out all his obligations under *the* contract of carriage'. The contract of carriage to which this refers is apparently the orginal contract of carriage. The right of disposition described in Article 12 is, therefore, a right attached to the contract of carriage which remains the same whether that right be exercised or not.

Since the contract of carriage is not changed by the exercise of the right of Article 12, the applicability of the Convention cannot be affected by the shipper's decision to have the goods delivered at an intermediate point in another country than where the agreed place of destination is situated. If the shipper directs the goods to be returned to the place of departure, such transportation is performed by the carrier pursuant to his obligations under the contract of carriage, and will therefore be governed by the Convention, if the original carriage was governed by the Convention.

Article 12 does not, of course, prevent the parties from modifying the contract of carriage by common agreement. In that case it is believed that any modification as to the point of destination or as to an agreed stopping place will be determinative for the applicability of the Convention, though it is doubtful whether it will also affect the part of the transportation already completed [2]).

It may therefore be vital to find out whether the change in the place of delivery was made pursuant to a unilateral shipper's instruction in accordance with Article 12, or pursuant to a contract of novation. Any changes permissible in the exercise of the shipper's right of disposition under Article 12 – or of a similar provision in the municipal law in case the transportation originally agreed upon were not governed by the Convention – should be

59. [2]) Koffka (1937), p. 270 expresses a somewhat different view, to the effect that only the agreed points of departure and destination at the time of the conclusion of the contract of carriage are relevant.

presumed to have been thus made and not to involve a modification of the contract of carriage. The same applies to changes in routing which the carrier, in his conditions of carriage, would have reserved the right to make. By exercising such right, the carrier could not affect the applicability of the Convention [3]).

60. How is the situation in the event of *irregular deviations*? 'Irregular deviations' should be taken to comprise all cases in which passenger, baggage or goods are carried on the wrong route due to some mistake either by the carrier (which will be the most frequent case) or by the passenger or shipper. Taken in this sense, irregular deviations of passengers will be rare in the present stage of civil aviation. But the cases of baggage or goods being put on the wrong plane or not being offloaded at the place of destination are more frequent. What if the goods or baggage get lost during such transportation? It is believed that this still would be transportation in which 'according to the stipulations made by the parties' the places of departure and destination would be those which brought the agreed carriage within the scope of the Convention. Article 1 does not require that each phase of the carriage must be in accordance with the contract of carriage, in order to be governed by the Convention, but it only assumes that there exists a case of international carriage by air based upon a contract of carriage. This interpretation finds support in Article 18 (2) defining the period of carriage for which the carrier is liable as 'the period during which the baggage or goods are in charge of the carrier, etc.' There can be no doubt that in the event of overshipping or involuntary deviations the goods remain in charge of the carrier.

61. It remains to be considered to what extent the problem

59. [3]) Cf. Article 8 (c): 'the agreed stopping places ('arrets prévus'), provided that the carrier may reserve the right to alter them in case of necessity, and that if he exercises that right the alteration shall not have the effect of depriving the carriage of its international character'. It is to be observed, however, that this rather inappropriately placed provision, which was added at the request of the British Delegate (W.C. p. 100), only deals with deviations from agreed stopping places in case of necessity, and not with changes made by the carrier in the exercise of a right reserved by him in the contract of carriage. Article 8 (c) would not seem to forbid such reservation. Meanwhile the IATA carriers have limited their right to change the agreed stopping places to the cases of necessity. See Art. 13 (2) (3) of the IATA General Conditions of Carriage for Goods (1953).

of the application of the Warsaw Convention in the case of deviation is affected in England and the U.S.A. by the rule as to the effect of deviation on the contract of carriage of goods. In English law the result of deviation is said to be that 'the carrier cannot claim the benefit of any special contract covering the carriage, and so cannot rely on any provisions contained in it which exclude or limit his liability', on the assumption that 'such a special contract will be construed as applicable only to the performance by the carrier of the actual service contracted for' [1]). A similar rule seems to be applied in the U.S.A. [2]). The principle has been extended by the House of Lords to the application of the limitation of liability provisions of the Carriage of Goods by Sea Act, on the ground that there is 'nothing in the Act which makes its statutory exceptions apply to a voyage which is not the subject of "the contract of carriage of goods by sea" to which the Act applies' [3]).

In a recent textbook on air law the effect of deviation on the applicability of the provisions of the Carriage of Goods by Sea Act has been called 'indistinguishable in principle' from the situation under the Warsaw Convention [4]). It is respectfully submitted that the two Acts can well be distinguished on this point, in fact that they should be. Article II of the Rules of the Carriage of Goods by Sea Act provides that *'under every contract of carriage* of goods by sea the carrier [...] shall be subject to the responsibilities and liabilities and entitled to the rights and immunities hereinafter set forth'. The title of the Schedule containing this provision is called 'Rules Relating To Bills of Lading'. The Warsaw Convention is entitled a 'Convention For the Unification of Certain Rules Relating To International

---

61. [1]) Shawcross and Beaumont (1951) No. 354. See also No. 243.

[2]) But limited to maritime law, see the statement by Judge Learned Hand quoted by Knauth (1953) p. 240. See also Williston (1936) IV § 1096. In *Lichten* v. *Eastern Airlines Inc.* 1949 U.S. Av.R. 80, 88, the New York District Court speaks of an 'archaic theory'. This case however, was concerned with the application of Tariff Rules filed with the C.A.B.

[3]) *Stag Line Ltd.* v. *Foscolo, Mango and Co.* [1932] A.C. 328, 340, *per* Lord Atkin. It is to be observed that this case did not deal with the £ 100 limit of the Act but with the general defences. Scrutton (1948) pp. 470/71, takes the view that 'probably the carrier could still rely on [...] Art. IV, Rule 5 [£ 100 limit] in view of the words 'in any event". In the U.S.A. the question of whether the $ 500 limitation of the American Carriage of Goods by Sea Act, 1936 is affected by deviation, seems not to have been decided yet; see Knauth (1953) p. 243.

[4]) McNair (1953) p. 227.

Carriage by Air'. Article 1 (1) of this Convention provides that it 'applies to all international carriage of persons, luggage or goods, performed by aircraft for reward' etc. There is a striking difference between the bills of lading Convention which is drafted in a way so as to regulate the *contract* of carriage by sea, and the Warsaw Convention which applies to *international carriage* by air. That difference is further stressed by Article 24 of the latter Convention, which makes it clear that the Warsaw Convention does not only purport to deal with contractual liabilities, but that 'in the cases covered by Articles 18 and 19 any action for damages, *however founded,* can only be brought subject to the conditions and limits set out in the Convention'. The cases referred to in Article 18 are those of 'destruction or loss of, or damage to, any registered baggage or goods, if the occurrence which caused the damage so sustained took place *during the carriage by air'*, that means during the period in which the goods are in charge of the carrier.

Indeed, there are such important differences between the two Conventions and the two Acts by which the Conventions were introduced, that the holding of the *Stag Line* case is of little interest when determining the applicability of the Warsaw Convention. This could not be better illustrated than by the rephrasing of the words of Lord Atkin ventured by the learned authors of the quoted textbook: 'there is nothing in the Carriage by Air Act which makes its statutory exceptions apply to a journey which is not the journey the subject of the contract of carriage by air to which the Act applies'. In fact there is nothing in the Act which makes its provisions inapplicable to such a journey, as – contrary to the Carriage of Goods by Sea Act – the Warsaw Convention does not apply to *contracts* of carriage but to *carriage.*

The deviation rule of English law has been developed as a rule of interpretation of contractual clauses. In the leading case of *Gibaud* v. *Great Eastern Railway* it was said that in cases of deviation 'you cannot rely on the conditions which were only intended to protect you if you carried out the contract in the way in which you had contracted to do it' [5]). That being so, the deviat-

61. [5]) [1921] 2 K.B. 426,435 per Scrutton L.J. See also *L. & N.W. Ry. Co.* v. *Neilson.* [1922] 2 A.C. 263 and comp. the rule as formulated by Shawcross and Beaumont quoted in the text.

ion rule should only be applied to the Warsaw Convention if a reasonable construction of that Convention leads to such a rule. Neither the drafting history – the Convention was mainly drafted by civil law experts for whom the deviation rule as a general principle had little if any significance – nor the wording of the Convention offers any support for reading into it a principle devised by anglosaxon courts to restrict the scope of contractual liability clauses. The only case which seems to have dealt with the problem has rightly held the provisions of the Warsaw Convention applicable, notwithstanding that the goods were lost during deviation:

> 'Even assuming that the doctrine of deviation, as known in maritime law, applies to air carriage, and assuming that the overcarriage or miscarriage, which here occurred, [the shipment had not been duly offloaded at Asmara for transshipment to another plane and was wrongly carried on by the first plane to Aden] amounted to an unjustifiable deviation from the contractual voyage, I can find nothing in the 1932 Act or the Convention which justifies the conclusion that what occurred in this case served to remove the carriage from the ambit of the Convention' [6]).

B. Scope of Application of Article 22.

62. So far the borders of applicability of the Convention as a whole have been outlined. The following pages will deal with the smaller circle enclosing the liabilities coming within the limitation provisions of Article 22.

The first question to be answered is whether Article 22 refers only to the liabilities defined in the Articles 17, 18 and 19, or to all carrier's liabilities arising under the Convention. The more

61. [6]) *Rotterdamsche Bank N.V.* v. *British Overseas Airways Corp.* [1953] 1 W.L.R. 493, 1953 U.S. & C. Av. R. 163, 170. The case was concerned with the jurisdiction provision (Art. 28) of the Convention, but it seems difficult to distinguish it on that account (as suggested by McNair, l.c.). See also *Morritt* v. *N.E. Railway Comp.* (1876) 1 Q.B.D. 302 (involving a case of registered baggage which had not been transloaded at the point where the passenger had to change trains, and was damaged whilst carried on by the first train) where the Court of Appeal held the Carrier's Act, 1830, including the provision limiting the railway's liability, applicable to the on-carriage. The older deviation cases invoked by plaintiff, in which the carrier had been denied his contractual defences, as far as the deviatory carriage was concerned, were distinguished by Blackburn J. on the ground that they all involved intentional deviations. For the same reason it is believed that, whatever is the significance of the *Stag Line Case* for the application of the Carriage by Air Act, that case could not be invoked with respect to involuntary deviations, such as envisaged in the text.

important liabilities of the carrier outside those of Articles 17, 18 and 19 would seem to be [1]:

(i) the liability for non-performance or the carriage;
(ii) the obligation to refund the fare or the freight in case of incomplete performance of the contract;
(iii) the liability for damages arising from incompleteness of documents (Article 3, 4 and 8);
(iv) the liability for any failure in complying with the shipper's instructions under Article 12;
(v) the liability imposed by Article 12 (3).
(vi) the liabilities arising out of the collision of two aircraft operated by the same carrier.

63. It is difficult to construe Article 22 otherwise than as referring only to the liabilities referred to in Chapter III dealing with the 'liability of the Carrier'. This follows not only from the placing of Article 22 in Chapter III, but also from the fact that, pursuant to Article 24, in the cases mentioned in Articles 17, 18 and 19 any action can be lodged only within the limits established by the Convention.

This does not, however, mean that Article 22 limits only the liabilities imposed by Article 17, 18 and 19, so that the carrier's liability for cases not covered by these articles would be unlimited. The better construction would seem to be that Chapter III deals with all liabilities connected with the carrier's obligations as to the safety, preservation and speedy transportation of passengers, baggage and goods carried. For the most frequent cases in which such liabilities arise, Articles 17 to 21 establish a system of liability. In the cases not covered by these Articles, in which the carrier would nonetheless have fallen short of his obligations as to safety or preservation, his liability will be governed by national law [1], but will be limited by Article 22. Thus the carrier's liability for the consequences arising from insufficient disinfection of the aircraft, or from flying at an unwarranted altitude without a

62. [1]) Liabilities arising from special obligations under the contract of carriage, not provided for in the Convention such as c.o.d. arrangements, evidently are not governed by it.

63. [1]) Cf. Lemoine (1947) No. 812. Contrary Riese (1949) p. 443.

pressurized cabin, would be determined by the applicable national law (whatever that might be) since there would be no accident which would bring the claim within the scope of Article 17, but such a liability would be subject to the limitation provisions of Article 22.

64. Could it be said that Article 24 strictly confines the scope of the limitation provisions to the liabilities imposed by Articles 17, 18 and 19 by providing that *in the cases covered by* these articles any action, however founded, can only be brought subject to the conditions and limits set out in the Convention? It is believed that this would be overestimating the logical consistency of an international Convention such as the Warsaw Convention with a drafting history of almost five years. The Convention itself offers a strong argument against such a grammatical interpretation. Article 22 (3) provides for a limitation of the carrier's liability for objects of which the passenger takes charges himself. If Article 24 were to be construèd to allow claims beyond the limits provided in Article 22 with respect to any liabilities not mentioned in Articles 17, 18 and 1 9, the limitation of the carrier's liability for handbaggage, which is not dealt with in either of these articles, would have no significance.

The purpose of Article 24 was to prevent a plaintiff from avoiding the defences and limits of the Convention by not founding his claims on the contract of carriage e.g. by suing in tort. A typical case of actions which may be brought outside the contract of carriage is, of course, the action by the dependant of a killed passenger for recovery of his loss of support. In many legal systems the dependant's right of recovery is independent of the right to damages of the passenger or his estate. Article 24 was inserted to prevent that such and similar claims could be brought outside the sphere of the Convention [1]). It certainly was not

---

64. [1]) Cf. O. Riese in Droit Aérien 1930, p. 216, Goedhuis (1933) p. 219, In view of the clear wording of Article 24 which is fully confirmed by the drafting history (see 3d Session CITEJA (1928) p. 55) it is the more surprising that a few French authors have expressed doubt with respect to the applicability of Article 22 to actions in tort instituted by the dependants of a killed passenger. Cf. Juglart (1952) p. 349 (but see also his later view in 16 R.G.A. (1953) 282 sq.), and Mazeaud in 51 Revue trimestrielle de droit civil (1952), pp. 365/66. The courts have not hesitated to draw the consequences of Article 24 and to apply Article 22 also to such actions of dependants: cf. Trib. Bruxelles 6.5.1950 (*Pauwels* v. *Sabena*) 4 R.F.D.A. (1950) p. 411 U.S.Av.R.

meant to restrict the scope of the defences and limits provided by the Convention.

Liabilities not connected with the carrier's obligations as to the safety of passengers and the preservation of baggage and goods, or with their speedy transportation, are, however, outside the sphere of Chapter III, and therefore also outside the scope of Article 22. It may be useful briefly to consider the consequences hereof on the earlier mentioned six categories of liabilities of such different nature.

65. (i) *non-performance of the carriage* due to the carrier can occur in various ways. An individual flight for which a passenger or a consignment was booked may be cancelled and the passenger or shipper may have no interest in seeing the carriage performed at a later occasion, or the flight may have been overbooked due to some error by the reservation department of the carrier. In such cases, where the carriage has not yet started, it is impossible to speak of delay in the carriage, so that they do not fall within the scope of Article 19, and therefore neither within the limits of Article 22. But the Convention does not prevent the parties from agreeing on a contractual limitation of liability or a complete exemption [1]). It is the applicable national law, whatever it may be, which will determine the validity of such clauses. The same would seem to apply in case of partial non-performance insofar as damages other than those dealt with in the Articles 17, 18 and 19 are concerned. So, where a carrier would not carry a passenger or goods beyond some intermediate stopping place, any expenses made by the passenger or shipper for the last part

---

1950, 367, 374; Trib, Seine 24.4.1952 (*Broche-Hennessy* v. *Comp. Air France*) D. 1952, J. 514, Note Ripert, G.P. 1952.1.339, R.F.D.A. 1952, p. 199. See also the decision by the Court of Appeal of Turin of 23.1.1952, Giurispr.ital. 1952, I, 2,81 sq. in the much discussed case of *Associazione Calcio di Torino* v. *Società Flotte Riunite A.L.I.*, turning i.a. upon the application of Artt. 942 sq. of the Cod. Nav. (similar to Art. 17, 20, and 22 of the Warsaw Convention). The case has been discussed i.a. by F. Vassalli in Riv. dir. nav. XVIII (1952), 161–179. Curiously his argument centers on the question of whether any extra-contractual liability towards third parties (in this case an association had sent out a professional football-team engaged by that association) could exist in case of death of a passenger, apparently assuming that in artt. 942 sq. Cod. Nav. only contractual liability is envisaged. See also infra Nos. 118 sq.

65. [1]) The IATA Conditions of Carriage (1953) have, in Art. 10 (Passengers) and 6 (3) (Goods), reserved the right for the carrier to cancel a flight or the further right to carriage in a certain number of broadly defined force majeure situations.

of the transportation would have to be reimbursed by the carrier who would not be allowed to invoke Article 22, subject, of course, to the defence of force majeure or any similar defence, and subject also to possible clauses in the contract of carrier exempting him from liability or allowing him to discontinue the transportation.

66. (ii) Whether the passenger or his estate, or whether the shipper will be entitled to a *refund* of the fare or freight will depend primarily on the terms of the contract of carriage, subject to possible mandatory rules of some applicable municipal law [1]. Since the obligation of the carrier to make a refund is not a liability falling within the scope of Articles 17 to 21 of the Convention, the validity of contractual clauses, defining or limiting this obligation, are not affected by Article 23 [2]. The IATA Conditions of Carriage for Goods expressly provide that the full freight is earned by the carrier whether or not the goods are lost or damaged [3]. The passenger's right to refund in case of any accident happening to him which would interrupt the voyage has not been expressly dealt with in the IATA Conditions of Carriage [4]. In the absence of a contractual clause it can be argued, under those legal systems which impose a contractual obligation upon the carrier to bring the passenger safely to his place of destination, that when that result has not been reached, the carrier must refund any money paid by the passenger in consideration of the promised result.

In case the passenger or shipper is entitled to a refund of the fare or freight, this right will not be limited by Article 22, since

66. [1]) E.g. Artt. 405, 406, 429 in connection with Artt. 949 and 955 of the **Italian** Cod. Nav. Cf. art. 82 of the **Mexican** *Ley de Vias Generales de Comunicación* of 1939 (not in aviation section).

[2]) Litvine, in his analysis of the different refund situations (Nos. 220 sq.), does not mention the possibility of contractual stipulations.

[3]) Article 4 (7) (b) reads as follows: 'Full applicable charges, whether prepaid or collect, fees, duties, taxes, charges, advances and payments, made or incurred or to be incurred by Carrier and any other sums payable to Carrier, will be deemed fully earned, whether or not the cargo is lost or damaged, or fails to arrive at the destination specified in the air waybill. All such charges, sums and advances will be due and payable upon receipt of the cargo by Carrier, except that they may be collected by Carrier at any stage of the service performed under the air waybill'.

[4]) The cases of 'involuntary refund' (i.e. refund in cases of non-completion of the carriage due to causes arising on the side of the carrier) are enumeraetd in Art. 10 (2) which do not mention the case of accidents to the passenger. See also Art. 8.

such refund would not be a compensation for damages [5]). This does not mean, of course, that the amount of damages could not be affected by a refund. Whenever the goods lost have a market value, the damages will generally be calculated on the basis of the market value at the place of destination [6]). In that case the amount refunded by the carrier should be deducted since otherwise the shipper would have the benefit of getting the value of the goods at the place of destination without having paid for their transportation [7]). But this would still be better for him than if the carrier's liability to make refund had been excluded, for in that case the result would be that the part of the value of the goods at destination which would represent the expenses of their carriage, would also fall within the limit provided by Article 22 of the Convention.

67. (iii) the liability for *damages resulting from non-compliance with the form requirements as to traffic documents* contained in Articles 3 and 4 and 8, must not be confused with the sanction of unlimited liability and loss of defences provided in the Conven-

---

66. [5]) Similarly Litvine (1953), No. 223. Contrary Shawcross and Beaumont (1951), No. 407, footnote (c), suggesting that the damages in case of death would often include the return of the fare paid, as the passenger would have sustained damage by losing the benefit for which the fare was paid viz. safe carriage to his destination. It is submitted that the damage so sustained by the passenger is something entirely different from his payment of the fare. Though the result (of the refund falling outside the limitation of liability) is the same, as when one would hold damages recovered under the Law Reform (Miscellaneous Provisions) Act 1934 to come in addition to any damages claimed under the Carriage by Air Act 1932 (cf. Shawcross and Beaumont (1951) No. 408 note (f) but *contra* McNair (1953) pp. 215/216), the reasoning is quite different, and the difference is of vital importance for other items of 'damages'.

[6]) Article 26 of the **Netherlands** Air Transportation Act, 1936 (*Wet op het Luchtvervoer*, 1936, Stb. no. 523) reads: 'Damages to be paid by the carrier for total or partial loss of goods shall be calculated on the basis of the value of goods of the same nature and quality at the place of destination and at the moment that the goods or baggage should have been delivered, after deducting the amount of freight and other expenses saved because of the non-delivery'. Comp. § 430 HGB (**Germany**), Art. 1696 of the **Italian** Cod. Civ., Art. 363 of the **Spanish** and Art. 179 of the **Argentine** Cod. com. For **English** law see Mayne (1946) pp. 331/332. For **USA** see *Sanib* v. *United Fruit Co.* (1947) 74 F. supp. 64, A.M.C. 419, and S. Williston (1936) IV, § 1111 (p. 3160). For **French** law Ripert, (1952) II, No. 1695. But contrary Art. 9 of the **Swiss** *Lufttransportreglement* (Air Carriage Regulation) of 1952, which takes the value of the goods at the place of departure as criterion for the damages. Similarly Art. 29 of the Berne Convention for Carriage of Goods by Railway (CIM) and Art. 13 of the Arrangement Concerning Letters and Parcels With Declared Value, attached to the Universal Postal Convention of Brussels, 1952.

[7]) Thus expressly Art. 26 (final phrase) of the Netherlands Air Transportation Act, 1936 (see previous note): cf. Williston, l.c. (previous note).

tion [1]). The latter sanction is imposed irrespective of whether the claiming party suffered any damage because of the absence of the prescribed particulars. On the other hand, the damages arising from the incompleteness of the documents need not necessarily be connected with the kind of accidents or occurrences envisaged in Articles 17, 18 or 19 [2]). But in many cases they will be connected. A good example, though highly theoretical, would be the case of the passenger alleging that he had failed to take out an accident insurance because he had not seen an indication on the ticket that the carriage would be governed by the rules relating to liability established by the Warsaw Convention, as prescribed by Article 3 sub (e) of the Convention. That the example is highly theoretical is the natural consequence of the purely theoretical character of the protection which Article 3 was intended to offer. But assuming that the passenger would have a real interest in being able to know by the ticket whether the transportation would be governed by the Convention – and it is on that assumption that Article 3 is based – it is clear that he could also suffer real damages, if the ticket should fail to contain the prescribed particulars. To recover such damages the passenger must prove (1) that he would have taken out insurance had he known about the applicability of the Convention, (2) that a clause on the ticket stating the carriage to be governed by the Convention would in effect have been sufficient to make him take out such insurance, and (3) that his failure to take out such

---

67. [1]) See on that sanction Nos. 222 sq.

[2]) Goedhuis (1933), p. 110 mentions the example of the carrier delivering a ticket without indicating an agreed stopping-place situated outside the normal route, which might bring the passenger into difficulties if that stopping-place were in a country from which the passenger had been expelled. It must be doubted, however, whether the carrier could be accused of any violation of his obligations in such a case. For only the stopping-places envisaged by the *parties* must be mentioned on the ticket, as clearly appears from the drafting history (De Vos at W.C. p. 100: ,,ce qui importe, pour l'application de la convention internationale, c'est de maintenir les arrêts prévus *d'un commun accord*). Comp. also the English and American translations into '*agreed* stopping-places'. In the example given by Goedhuis the passenger apparently had not envisaged this stopping-place. How far a carrier is permitted to make any stops outside the agreed stopping-places is, of course, a different question. The case of Goedhuis could be a good example, however, if the contract of carriage would have been concluded by another person than the passenger. With respect to air waybills it is easier to find examples of incompleteness resulting in damages other than loss of, damage to, or delay of the goods. But for such damages the carrier could not be liable as such (as he is not responsible for preparing the air waybill) but only as an agent of the shipper.

insurance was the direct or reasonably foreseeable consequence of the carrier's failure to insert the clause on the ticket. It is hard to see how a judge or jury could be brought to believe such flagrant fictions, but the drafters of this part of the Convention must have been guided by them and they are still influencing the minds of some members of the Legal Committee of ICAO in the discussions on the revision of the Warsaw Convention.

The situation with respect to air waybills is somewhat different, as here the obligation to issue the document is not laid on the carrier but on the consignor. A failure to mention any of the particulars prescribed by Article 8 could, therefore, in principle, only create a liability of the consignor. On this point the Convention is not entirely consistent as it limits the shipper's liability for such damages to those suffered by reason of the irregularity, incorrectness or incompleteness of *the particulars and statements relating to the goods* (Article 10). For the omission of any other particulars the consignor would not be liable, so that apart from the provision of Article 9 (loss by the carrier of his defences under the Convention), the failure to comply with the form requirements contained in Article 8, not dealing with particulars as to the goods carried, would not create any liability. It is believed that the drafters of the Convention did not fully realize the consequences of the air waybill being issued by the consignor. A number of the particulars listed in Article 8 in practice have to be filled in by the carrier [3]). Though the carrier cannot be liable as such for the damages arising from the incompleteness of the air waybill, he may be liable as agent of the shipper if he had expressly or impliedly accepted the making out of the air waybill on behalf of the shipper. It is clear that such a liability does not fall within the scope of the limitation provision of Article 22.

68. (iv) Is carrier's liability for non-compliance with shipper's instructions for disposition or for faults committed in the compliance therewith governed by the provisions of Chapter III, including Article 22? A distinction should be made between losses, damages or delays, occurring during transportation per-

---

67. [3]) E.g. those under (e), (k) and (p) and probably also the agreed stopping-places under (c). Cf. also Article 12 (3) speaking of 'the part of the air waybill *delivered to the latter*' (i.e. the shipper).

formed pursuant to shipper's instructions, and other forms of non-compliance or faulty compliance. As has been said above, any transportation performed in compliance with shipper's instructions must be considered transportation performed under the contract of carriage and is therefore governed by the provisions of Chapter III. The problem is different if damages are caused by the fact that the carrier failed to follow some instruction for stopping the goods at an intermediate point or for delivering them to somebody other than the consignee. It is believed that such damages should be treated in the same way as damages arising from complete or partial non-performance of the contract of carriage, discussed above.

69. (v) The third paragraph of Article 12 makes the carrier liable towards any person who in a regular way [1]) has obtained possession of the air waybill, for damages, resulting from the fact that he would have followed the shipper's instructions under paragraph 1 of Article 12 (stopping of goods or having them returned or delivered to another person than the consignee) without having required the production by the shipper of his part of the air waybill. The purpose of this provision is to allow the air waybill being used in a limited way as a surety in credit transactions. By holding the shipper's copy of the air waybill, the Bank or any other person having paid on the assumption that the goods would be delivered to the consignee named in the air waybill, can be sure that such delivery will not be prevented by the shipper exercising his right of disposition. Though possession of the shipper's copy of the air waybill does not give any rights under the contract of carriage nor any title to the goods, it is a bar to the shipper's interference with regular delivery in accordance with the air waybill. To limit the protection of the lawful holder to a possible action against the shipper would be obviously insufficient, as the need for protection against such interference by the shipper arises mainly in cases in which an action against him would prove futile.

---

69. [1]) The original French text has 'celui qui est *régulièrement* en possession de la lettre de transport aérien', which has been translated in the British Carriage by Air Act, 1932 into 'any person who is *lawfully* in possession of that part of the air consignment note' (similar to the American translation). It may be questioned whether the term 'lawfully' renders exactly the French 'régulièrement'.

The right of recovery established by Article 12 (3) is given to any person who in a regular way has obtained possession of shipper's part of the air waybill [2]). This may be the consignee, who received the document either direct or through a Bank at the place of departure acting as his agent. But it may also be a third party, in most cases a Bank, who has extended credit on the air waybill (accompanied by invoice and insurance policy) by discounting a draft drawn by the shipper (vendor) on the consignee (purchasor).

The damages which may be recovered under this provision are those caused by the carrier complying with the shipper's instructions of disposition without having required production of his part of the air waybill. These would seem to comprise the cases of non-delivery, misdelivery and delay. Now, such occurrences, when happening during the period of liability provided in Articles 18 and 19, are also governed by these Articles. It is therefore the more important to know whether the provisions of Chapter III (Articles 17 to 30) apply to the liability established by Article 12 (3). If one were to hold that the liability of Article 12 (3) is not limited by Article 22, the amount of liability for non-delivery, misdelivery or delay may depend upon whether these occurrences were a consequence of compliance with a shipper's instruction or not. The same problem has also arisen under Article 21 of the Berne Convention on railroad transportation of goods. Though this article has been the model for Article 12 of the Warsaw Convention, the relevant paragraph 2 contains various differences, the more important of which are (1) that shipper's instructions have to be made in a certain prescribed form and have to be written on the shipper's copy of the consignment-note, (2) that only the consignee is given an action for damages, and (3) that any 'modification' madc by the shipper in other than the prescribed form is null and void.

One of the greatest modern authorities on the Berne Convention, is very definite in his opinion that this liability of the carrier is one outside the contract of carriage and therefore not governed

69. [2]) The Convention does not say that it should be the shipper's copy, but this was clearly the intention as appears from the earlier part of the paragraph which does speak of 'the production of the part of the air waybill delivered to the shipper'. The British legislator has on this point amended the Convention in the Carriage by Air Act, 1932 (similarly the American translation).

by the provisions of Chapter III (parallel to Chapter III of the Warsaw Convention) [3]. He bases his view on the fact that this right is given to the consignee before he has become a party to the contract of carriage.

On the other hand, there can be little doubt that the consignee could recover damages arising from delay or misdelivery under the liability provisions of Chapter III (and only under those) if the carrier had wrongly followed the instructions from some third person having no authority to give such instructions. Could it not be argued, then, that as far as the consignee is concerned, the shipper who cannot produce his part of the air waybill, is in the same situation as such a third person? The argument does not hold, it is true, where the lawful possessor of the air waybill (to whom Article 12 (3) gives the right of action) is a person other than the consignee. But why not have the right of such a person being governed by the provisions of Chapter III, in the same way as, in case of loss or damage, the right of any other third person having an interest in the goods (e.g. the owner who would neither be consignor or consignee) is subject to those provisions, since Article 24 provides that in cases of loss or damage any action for damages, however founded, can only be brought subject to the conditions and limits set out in the Convention?

This does not mean that the carrier can always invoke the limits of Article 22 when he has followed shipper's instructions for disposition without having required production of the air waybill. It may be that the Court would hold such an act to amount to wilful misconduct or a fault considered equivalent thereto. Especially French Courts have often assumed gross negligence in cases of misdelivery by railways [4], and since in France gross negligence is generally considered to be equivalent to '*dol*', the air carrier who would have delivered a consignment to another person than the consignee, following instructions from a shipper who failed to produce his part of the air waybill, could also be refused under Article 25 the right to invoke the limits of Article 22 or other provisions excluding the carrier's liability. Even then, however, there remains an important difference with

69. [3]) Nánássy (1946) pp. 377/379.

[4]) Cass. 20.1.1925, G.P. 1925.2.721 and Cass. 12.6.1950. Bull. de Transports, 1950, p. 624 note Durand. See also Nánássy (1946) p. 612, and P. Durand in 51 B.T.I. 1943) 354, 363 sq.

holding the provisions of Chapter III generally not applicable to the liability of Article 12 (3), as in the latter view claims under Article 12 (3) would not even be governed by the provision forbidding exoneration clauses (Article 23), nor by those dealing with time limitation on actions and jurisdiction [5]).

70. The validity of contractual exemption of this liability raises a special problem. Article 15 (2) provides that any clause derogating from the provisions of Articles 12, 13 and 14 must be written on the air waybill [1]) which clearly implies that parties are left free to deviate from said provisions. This means that Article 15 (2) would permit the carrier to exclude the liability imposed by Article 12 (3) [2]). If, however, in accordance with

---

69. [5]) It is a controversial point, which Articles are included within 'the provisions of this Convention which exclude or limit his [carrier's] liability', referred to in Articles 3, 4, 9 and 25. With respect to Articles 20 and 22 there can be little doubt that they are. As to Article 21 (contributory negligence) the views of the authors are divided. *For inclusion*: Koffka (1937) p. 335, Shawcross and Beaumont (1951) No. 382 (e); *against inclusion*: Coquoz (1938), p. 146, Schleicher-Reymann (1937) p. 360, Sullivan in 7 J.A.L. (1937) 37 and 43, Riese (1949) p. 467 (citing other authors), Lemoine (1947) No. 834, Chauveau (1951) No. 232, and Litvine, No. 380. But most authors seem to consider Articles 26, 28 en 29 not included (cf. besides the last mentioned authors: Shawcross and Beaumont (1951) No. 382 and strongly with respect to Article 28: Lacombe in 12 R.G.A. (1949) 823). The view that only the defences offered by Article 20 were in the contemplation of the drafters finds strong support in the drafting history of the Convention: when the Reporter De Vos explained in the Second Session of the CITEJA (Compte-rendu, p. 25) the sanction of Articles 3, 4 and 9, he described this sanction in the following words (translation): 'the carrier shall lose the advantages *which are given to him by Articles 5, 6 and 7 of the preliminary Draft* of the Convention on Liability (without, however, affecting the other provisions of said preliminary Draft) and such contract will be governed by the common law ('droit commun') with respect to the matters dealt with in said Articles'. Articles 5, 6 and 7 of the preliminary draft (i.e. the Paris Draft of 1925) were later to become Articles 20 and 22 of the present Convention, so that there would seem to exist a strong historical argument for limiting the provisions which *exclude* the carrier's liability to the provisions of the first and second paragraph of Article 20 (Articles 5 and 6 of the Paris 1925 Draft). The view that in case of wilful misconduct Article 28 (extinction of action) would not apply has apparently been rejected, without arguments, in *Wanderer* v. *Sabena and P.A.A.* 1949 U.S.Av.R. 25.

70. [1]) The paragraph reads: 'Toute clause *dérogeant* aux stipulations des articles 12, 13 et 14 doit être inscrite dans la lettre de transport aérien'. The British legislator has translated this text somewhat loosely into: 'The provisions of Articles 12, 13 and 14 can only be *varied* by express provision in the air consignment note' (similarly the American translation). This translation has raised the question whether under the Carriage by Air Act the parties are free *to set aside entirely* the provisions of Articles 12, 13 and 14, as would be necessary in case of the issuance of a negotiable air waybill. Cf. the present author's report in Rio Session (1953) II, 51 sq. at 59.

[2]) Curiously the current IATA air waybill does not contain such an exclusion, nor does it even make clear that the limitation of liability to 250 gold francs per kilogram also affects the liability envisaged by Article 12 (3).

the above expounded view, this liability would be governed by the provisions of Chapter III, any clause tending to relieve the carrier of such liability or to fix a lower limit as the limit provided in Article 22 of the Convention would be null and void (Article 23). But it is suggested that that would not prevent the parties from agreeing to make the shipper's right of disposition independent from his producing his part of the air waybill, in which case the carrier evidently could not become liable in complying with any such instructions for disposition. Said agreement should be stated in the air waybill so that a third party obtaining possession of the air waybill could know that possession of the document would offer no security. The practical difference between such a clause and a clause which would merely exclude the carrier's liability for having followed the shipper's instructions without requiring production of his part of the air waybill, is that the former clause would make it a *duty* for the carrier to comply with the shipper's instructions without asking for the air waybill.

71. (vi) *Liability for accident caused by negligence of a colliding aircraft also operated by the carrier.* Courts of different countries have held that in case of collision of ships belonging to the same company and caused or contributed to by the fault of the non-carrying ship, the carrier can not invoke any clause in the contract with the shipper or passenger which excludes or limits his liability [1]). It is believed that these decisions, which were based on the interpretation of contractual clauses, cannot be invoked when answering the question of whether Article 22 comprises such kind of liability. In the first place Article 24, as has been

---

71. [1]) *Chartered Mercantile Bank of India, London and China* v. *The Netherlands India Steam Navigation Comp. Ltd.* 10 Q.B.D. 521, 533. In this case Brett J. denied in unambiguous words the existence of any contractual liability of the shipowner of the two colliding ships 'Crown Prince' and 'Atjeh' towards the owners of cargo on board the 'Crown Prince' for damage caused by the 'Atjeh'. Cf. *Wilkie* v. *L.P.T.B.* [1946] 1 All E.R. 650, [1947] 1 All. E.R. 258 (exemption clause on travelpass cannot be invoked if holder is overrun by bus on which he is not a passenger). See also the **Netherlands** decision Gerechtshof Leeuwarden, 8.3.1950, N.J. 1950, No. 725 ('*Lemmerboot*') deciding that a carrier cannot invoke against a passenger an exemption clause in his conditions of carriage with respect to an accident caused by another ship also owned by the carrier. See also the **German** decision R.G. 24.9.1910, J.W. 1910, 952, and comp. R.G. 9.12.1913, RGZ 83, 343, distinguishing between railways and tramways on the one hand, and collision of ships belonging to one owner on the other hand ('ihre Zusammengehörigkeit ist, wenn sie Schiffe derselben Unternehmer sind, nur eine wirtschaftliche').

pointed out before, was meant to bring both contractual and delictual liabilities within the ambit of the Convention, and there is nothing, either in the wording of Articles 17 and 18, or in that of Article 24, to justify an exception for the case of collisions between aircraft. Moreover, the contrary view would lead to the result that the carrier would not be liable under the Convention for such occurrences, so that he would be allowed fully to exclude this liability in the contract of carriage, without being hampered by Article 23 of the Convention.

Moreover, as will be discussed later [2]), Article 20, which makes the carrier liable for the negligence of his 'préposés', does not only apply to persons who are performing activities connected with the transportation concerned, but to all servants acting within the scope of their employment, even if their work had nothing to do with the specific transportation giving rise to the claim. If that is true, the limitation provisions of Article 22 must necessarily also apply to this liability.

72. Before ending this discussion of the liabilities wich are limited by Article 22 of the Warsaw Convention, something must be said on the *period of liability* governed by the provisions of Chapter III. Article 1 states generally that the Convention applies to carriage by aircraft, and Article 31 elaborates this by providing that 'in the case of combined carriage performed partly by air and partly by any other mode of carriage, the provisions of this Convention apply only to the carriage by air'. Neither of these provisions, however, purport to fix a *period* of applicability. Thus the carrier's obligation to issue a ticket will generally arise long before the commencement of the actual carriage by air. Similarly, the presumption of receipt of the goods laid down in Article 11 (1) may apply before the goods have arrived at the airport.

But with respect to liability for death, wounding or delay of passengers, and for loss, damage or dealy of baggage or goods, it was necessary to establish a period within which such mishaps must have occurred, in order to avoid that liability rules being established with a view to the special nature of air transporta-

---

71. [2]) See No. 196.

tion be extended to other risks and other modes of transport, with the danger of conflicting rules. Article 31 has a somewhat hybrid nature in that it probably also was intended to deal with the period of liability besides stating a principle of applicability.

73. Article 17 limits the period of liability for death, wounding or bodily injury by speaking of accidents taking place 'on board the aircraft or in the course of any of the operations of embarking or disembarking'. The exact meaning of 'operations of embarking or disembarking' has probably correctly been construed to include the passenger's walking from the final gate to the aircraft and vice versa [1]). The period to which the limitation of liability for hand baggage applies should probably be taken to be the same as the period of liability applying to death or wounding of passengers, though the Convention fails to offer any indication on this point [2]).

74. With respect to goods and registered baggage the period of liability has been defined in Article 18 (2) as 'the period during which the baggage or goods are in the charge of the carrier, whether in an aerodrome or on board an aircraft, or, in the case of a landing outside an aerodrome, in any place whatsoever'. The period of liability has thus been limited in two ways: (1) the baggage or goods must be in the charge of the carrier, (2) they must be in an airport or on board an aircraft (leaving aside the exceptional case of a landing outside an airport).

The first limitation does not seem to have received the attention it deserves. Two constructions are possible: (a) baggage and goods must be considered in the charge of the carrier from the moment they have been delivered to him till the moment they have again been put at the disposal of the passenger or consignee (or the consignor in case of return to the consignor), or (b) they must be deemed to be in the charge of the carrier as long as they are in his custody. The difference is mainly of importance for the period that goods remain in the custody of the customs or other authorities. Under the first interpretation the period of the car-

73. [1]) Cf. Goedhuis (1933) p. 158 and (1937) pp. 192 sq., Koffka (1937) pp. 315/16, Lemoine (1947) No. 811, Riese (1949) p. 445/46. But the **Scandinavian** Acts, implementing the Convention, have limited the period of liability to the mounting into and alighting from the aircraft; similarly the **German** Government translation.

[2]) Also Goedhuis (1937) p. 259.

rier's liability would continue to run subject to carrier's defences under Article 20 and 21. Under the second interpretation, however, the period of liability would be suspended and carrier's liability would be governed by the applicable national law, without his being entitled to invoke the limitation of liability provided in Article 22, except to the extent that limitation had been made a part of the contract and would be held valid as such by the applicable national law. The first interpretation should probably be preferred. The element that the baggage or goods must be in charge of the carrier was only introduced in the last phase of drafting by the Drafting Committee of the Warsaw Conference, and cannot have been intended to bring about the more far-reaching consequence which would result from the second interpretation [1].

It is worth-while to compare the system adopted in the Berne Convention on railroad transportation of goods (C.I.M). In Article 27 (1) the period of liability is stated to run from the moment the goods have been accepted for carriage until their delivery by the carrier, which is construed to include the period that the goods are being handled by the administrative authorities [2]. The same system was adopted in the Draft established by the Paris Conference of 1925 (Article 1 (2)). The Second Commission of the CITEJA limited the period by providing that it would commence at the time the goods entered the airport of departure and end at the time the goods left the airport of destination. At Warsaw the Drafting Committee split the Article of the Draft establishing the period of liability for the carriage of passengers, baggage and goods, into the three different articles 17, 18 and 19. The Chairman of the Drafting Committee explained in his report that the situation had not been changed, that no new articles were added, but that there was only a new numbering of articles [3]. The addition of the words 'during which the baggage

74. [1]) Cf. De Vos (Reporter) in W.C. p. 164: 'Il va de soi que le transporteur pourra établir qu'il était nullement en faute et qu'il a pris toutes les mesures utiles pour éviter le dommage ou qu'il lui était impossible de les prendre, *notammant parce que l'aérodrome se trouvait sous une autre autorité que la sienne*' (italics supplied). De Vos apparently held that the fact of something happening at an airport which would not be under the carrier's control, might be a defence *under* the Convention (Article 20 (1)), and consequently would not exclude applicability of the Convention.

[2]) Cf. De Nánássy (1946), p. 463.

[3]) W.C. 1929 ,p. 135. See on the drafting history Goedhuis (1933) pp. 148 sq, and the decision of the Court of Appeal of Brussels of 10.6.1950, 1950 U.S.Av.R. 392. (*Favre* v. *Etat Belgique and SABENA*).

or goods are in charge of the carrier' can, therefore, not have been meant to import a change of principle, and the provisions of Chapter III must be considered applicable to losses occurring whilst the goods were temporarily in charge of the customs.

75. Article 19, providing that the carrier is liable for damage occasioned by *delay* in the carriage by air of passengers, baggage or goods, has raised a difficult problem of interpretation as to the meaning of 'carriage by air' in this connection. At least three different opinions have been defended. According to some authors the words must be read in a restricted sense so that only a delay occurring whilst the passengers, baggage or goods are airborne, would be a delay in the carriage by air [1]. A second view would hold the provision of Article 18 (2) – which defines the period of liability for loss of or damage to baggage or goods – applicable to the liability for delay imposed by Article 19, with the argument that otherwise the liability for delay would be a mere fiction [2]. Against this view it has rightly been pointed out that the Drafting Committee of the Warsaw Conference had decided to split the provision dealing with the period of liability into three different Articles for the very reason that there were three different groups of cases involved [3]. Finally there are those who think that 'carriage by air' in Article 19 should be deemed to comprise the entire carriage, as a delay exists whenever the passengers or goods do not arrive on time at the point of destination, irrespective of the cause [4].

It is believed that, different from Articles 17 and 18, Article 19 does not at all deal with a *period* of liability. Part of the difficulties which have arisen in construing the Article stem from the attempt to read a period of liability into the words 'in the carriage by air'. But it is to be noted that the provision speaks of a 'delay *in* [French: '*dans*'] the carriage by air', not of a 'delay *during* [French: '*pendant*'] the carriage by air'. Now a delay *in* the carriage

---

75. [1]) Goedhuis (1933) p. 166, J. van Houtte (1940) p. 85, cf. H. A. Wulff, ***Haftung des Lufttransporteurs in nationalen und internationalen Privatrecht***, Diss. Wurzburg, 1938, p. 16.

[2]) Coquoz (1938) pp. 130/131, Lemoine (1947) No. 843, Litvine (1953) No. 248, Shawcross and Beaumont (1951) No. 330 (c).

[3]) Goedhuis (1933) p. 166.

[4]) Riese (1949) p. 449, Koffka (1937) p. 320; cf. Sullivan in 7 J.A.L. (1937) p. 27.

does not imply that the incident causing the delay must have occurred *during* the carriage by air. Nor does it mean that the aircraft should have suffered delay in its flight. 'Delay in the carriage by air of passengers, baggage or goods' simply refers to any situation in which the carriage by air of the passenger or the goods is completed at a later time than it ought to have been completed under the contract of carriage. It is indifferent at what time the occurence took place which caused the passengers to disembark too late (or the baggage or goods to be offloaded too late) at the place of destination. For that reason the provision dealing with delay has correctly been separated by the Warsaw Conference from those dealing with death or wounding of passengers, or loss of and damages to, baggage and goods.

Whenever the passengers or goods arrive too late by air at the place of destination there is a delay in the air carriage, since in that case the air carriage has been wholly or partly completed too late. Once the passengers have disembarked or the goods have been offloaded in time at the airport of destination, there can no longer be a question of delay in *air carriage*. Any delays occurring after that moment are not governed by Article 19, nor by the other provisions of Chapter III (including Article 22). This applies to delays which a passenger suffers through the customs, or when having his baggage cleared, as well as any delay suffered in getting transportation from the airport to the town. It also applies to delays in the delivery of goods which had arrived already, either because the goods went astray at the airport of destination or because of a failure by the carrier to give notice of arrival to the consignee in accordance with Article 13 (2), or because of delay in the delivery service to the town.

76. How about delays in the air carriage caused by delays in the ground transportation from the town to the airport of departure? It is believed that Article 31, dealing with 'combined carriage', does not apply to these situations [1]). The combined carriage governed by this Article was certainly not meant to include the cases of ground transportation purely incidental to the carriage by air, the kind of ground transportation envisaged by Article 18 (3) being 'for the purpose of loading, delivery or

76. [1]) Similarly Koffka (1937) p. 320.

trans-shipment' [2]). It may not always be easy to draw the line where surface transport incidental to air carriage ends, and genuine 'combined carriage' starts. Generally the concept of combined carriage should not be construed in a restrictive way. The fact that the ground transportation is performed by the air carrier may be an indication that the parties considered it as something incidental to the air transportation, but is by itself not sufficient to take the carriage out of the sphere of Article 31.

To say that Article 31 does not apply to town-airport transportation does not mean that the carrier will be liable for delay in such transportation as if it were carriage by air, but only that if such delay were to result in a delay in the carriage by air, the latter delay would be governed by Article 19, whereas Article 31 seems to imply that in case of combined carriage, any delays occurring in the other parts of the transportation, even if they necessarily were to result in a delay in the air carriage, would not be governed by the Convention. Where a delay in the carriage by air is caused by a delay in accessory ground transportation, the carrier will have to prove that he and his agents had taken all necessary measures to prevent the delay in the air carriage or that it was impossible for him and them to do so (Article 20). If there had been negligence in the delay of the ground transportation, the case would turn upon the question of whether the ground transportation was performed by agents of the carrier. In such an event the carrier would fail in his defence under Article 20. The carrier's liability would, of course, be limited by Article 22 of the Convention.

§ 2. THE ROME CONVENTIONS

77. The scope of applicability of the *Rome Conventions* of 1933 and 1952 on surface damage raises less difficulties. Article 20 (1) of the former and Article 23 (1) of the latter both embody the principle that the Convention shall apply whenever surface damage is caused in the territory of one Contracting State by aircraft registered in another Contracting State.

Only in case of damage caused by two aircraft, one of them being registered in another Contracting State, the other not

76. [2]) Goedhuis (1933) p. 247.

(being either an aircraft of a non-contracting state or of the state where the damage is caused) does a serious problem arise. According to the quoted provisions it is sufficient that damage is caused in a Contracting State by an aircraft of another Contracting State for the Conventions to apply. Taken liberally, this would result in the Conventions also being applicable to the liability of the aircraft of the Non-Contracting State. In earlier drafts of the Rome 1952 Convention the applicability of the Convention was related to the liability of the operator of the aircraft of another Contracting State, which excluded the possibility of having the Convention also govern in collision cases the liability of aircraft of a Non-Contracting State or of the State where the damage occurred [1]). In Mexico it was decided to return to the principle of the Rome 1933 Convention for the reason that by limiting the applicability to liability of the operator, all provisions in the Convention dealing with the liability of other persons than the operator would become senseless [2]). The change was certainly not intended to bring the liability for the aircraft of Non-Contracting States or of the State where the damage was caused within the scope of the Convention. Does this mean that such an interpretation must be rejected? Certainly not, as the whole problem was simply not considered.

The answer must rather be sought in the rationale of the principle that limits the applicability of the Conventions to damages caused in one Contracting State by aircraft of another Contracting State. The reason for requiring that the damage be caused by aircraft of *another* state was to exclude the cases having no international aspect. For the need for unification of the law is felt in international cases, not in domestic ones [3]). The reason

77. [1]) Article 17 of the Taormina Draft of January 1950 (ICAO Doc. 6028 of 31/1/50) and of the Montreal Draft of June 1950 (ICAO Doc. 7015 of 18/6/50).

[2]) Mexico Session (1951) p. 186.

[3]) Need for unification was the only purpose mentioned in the preamble of the Rome 1933 Convention. Curiously the Rome 1952 Convention mentions as the first motive 'a desire to ensure adequate compensation for persons who suffer damage caused on the surface by foreign aircraft, while limiting in a reasonable manner the extent of the liabilities incurred for such damage in order not to hinder the development of international civil air transport'. (It could be questioned why persons on the surface who suffer damage are more entitled to adequate compensation when the damage was caused by foreign aircraft than when it was caused by domestic aircraft). But on the other hand, the 1952 Convention emphasized the limitation to international cases by naming it a Convention On Damage Caused By ***Foreign*** Aircraft etc. (Cf. the American proposal to this effect in Mexico Session (1951) at p. 238).

why that other State should be also a *Contracting* State was probably to prevent non-contracting states from enjoying the benefit of the limited liability for their aircraft without granting such benefit to the aircraft of the other country when that aircraft would cause damage in the territory of the non-contracting state.

Do these reasons prevent a construction of Articles 20 (or 23) to the effect that the Convention shall apply to aircraft not registered in another Contracting State in collision cases involving at least one aircraft registered in another Contracting State? The first mentioned reason (need of unification in international cases) certainly does not. It is more doubtful whether the second reason should not preclude applying the Convention to liability of aircraft of *non-contracting* States even if the damage were caused jointly with aircraft of a Contracting State. For by applying the Convention, the aircraft of the non-contracting states would have the protection of the limitation provisions which protection the non-contracting State might not offer to, foreign aircraft. But if the reason was to induce as many states as possible to adhere to the Convention, that purpose would hardly be frustrated by granting to aircraft of non-contracting States the benefit of the Convention in the rare collision cases.

The consequence of different liability rules becoming applicable to two aircraft having jointly caused some damage, on the other hand, creates certain difficult problems with respect to recourse actions, and clearly does not satisfy one's sense of justice. Therefore, it is suggested that the literal interpretation of Articles 20 (23) is to be preferred, making the Conventions applicable to the liability of aircraft which are registered either in the state where the damage occurred, or in another Non-Contracting State, if such aircraft caused the damage jointly with aircraft of another Contracting State [4]).

78. In addition to the general limitation to damages caused by foreign aircraft of contracting states the Conventions contain

77. [4]) See also the additional argument offered in No. 97 *in fine*.

some special restrictions on the scope of their applicability [1].

In the first place, they are not applicable to damage caused by military, customs or police aircraft [2]. This exception is not to be found in the Warsaw Convention, where it was less necessary in view of the general limitation to carriage by air transport undertakings or carriage for remuneration [3]. It is interesting to compare the analogous provision of the Chicago Convention excluding aircraft *used in military, customs and police services* [4]. A similar wording was used in an earlier Draft of the 1952 Convention [5]. From the history of the Rome Convention of 1933 it appears that it was the intention to comprise by 'military aircraft', as used in Article 31 of that Convention, civil aircraft used exclusively for military purposes [6].

79. In the second place, the applicability of the Conventions has been excluded as between persons who are in certain contractual relationships. It is worth-while to quote the full relevant provisions. Article 22 of the 1933 Convention reads:

> 'The present Convention shall not apply to damages caused on the surface, the compensation for which is regulated by a contract of carriage or a contract of employment concluded between the person suffering damage and the person liable under the terms of this Convention'.

---

78. [1]) It does not seem necessary to discuss in the text the new Article 24 of the 1952 Convention excluding 'damages caused to an aircraft in flight or to persons or goods on board such aircraft'. The provision seems only important for the period that the damaged aircraft is still (or yet) on the surface, though already (or still) in flight in accordance with Article 1 (1).

[2]) Article 21 of the 1933 Convention and Article 26 of the 1952 Convention.

[3]) But see the Additional Protocol of the Warsaw Convention, giving the right to the States, when ratifying or adhering to the Convention, to exclude carriage performed directly by the State. The USA, Argentine and Japan have availed themselves of this right when adhering. Cf. the Draft Protocol established by the Legal Committee of ICAO at its Rio meeting of 1953, which excludes in article 2: 'Carriage by military aircraft and carriage of persons, cargo and baggage for military authorities by aircraft the whole capacity of which has been reserved by such authorities'.

[4]) Article 3 (b). The text of the Chicago Convention is rather ambiguous on the points of (1) whether only aircraft used in military, customs and police services should be deemed state aircraft (affirmed by Shawcross and Beaumont (1951) No. 208 (a) and J. C. Cooper in 17 J.A.L.C. (1950) 292 at 309), and (2) whether the Convention applies to all aircraft which are not state aircraft (Article 3 (a)). Article 30 of the Paris Convention (1919) was much clearer on both points. See also Article 1 (2) of the American Draft submitted at the Chicago Conference 1944 (Proceedings I, 555).

[5]) Article 20 of the Montreal Draft (ICAO Doc. 7015 of 18/6/50).

[6]) The British Delegate at the Rome Conference (I, 263) was only willing to accept the present formula when it was agreed that 'military aircraft' would include 'aéronefs privés affectés exclusivement au service militaire'.

Article 25 of the 1952 Convention reads:

> 'This Convention shall not apply to damage on the surface if liability for such damage is regulated either by a contract between the person who suffers such damage and the operator or the person entitled to use the aircraft at the time the damage occurred, or by the law relating to workmen's compensation applicable to a contract of employment between such persons'.

There exist some notable differences between the two provisions [1]). The most important one is that the new Convention excludes all cases in which the liability is governed by a contract, *whatever that contract may be,* whereas the old Convention only excludes the liabilities governed by a contract of carriage or of employment [2]). Under the 1952 Convention it would seem permissible to set entirely aside the Convention by contract [3]). In the Rome Conference of 1933 the question had been discussed at the occasion of a British proposal to include a provision which expressly would permit contractual deviations from the provisions of the Convention. It was agreed that the validity of such contracts would depend on national law, and that nothing in the Convention itself would forbid them [4]).

Though the new Convention allows the setting aside of the Convention by contract, it does not permit contractual deviations from certain provisions only, for such agreement would automatically result in the non-applicability of the entire Convention, which would be replaced by national law. Of course this national law might allow the parties to make the provisions of the Convention applicable by a contractual choice of law.

80. Both Conventions require for excluding applicability

79. [1]) See also Sec. 42 (6) of the **English** Civil Aviation Act, 1949, which speaks only of contracts of carriage, and Art. 972 of the **Italian** Cod. Nav., which includes all contracts.

[2]) But see the broad interpretation of Article 22 of the 1933 Convention defended by H. Oppikofer (German delegate to the Rome Conference) in 3 Z.L. (1933) 211, at 223/24.

[3]) Though it could be argued by those who consider the Convention to be mandatory law, that such a liability clause would be null and void and, therefore, would not be a 'contract regulating the damage' as referred to in Article 25. If this were a correct interpretation, the applicability of the Convention would be made still more dependent upon the whims or wisdom of national laws.

[4]) R.C. 1933, I, 264. Cf. Goedhuis in Rev. de droit int. et législ. comp. 1935, p. 579. The contrary view of Stanesco (1951), p. 197, seems in conflict with the clear intention of the drafters.

that liability for the damage be regulated by a contract between the persons suffering the damage ('personne lésée' in the 1933 Convention) and the person liable under the terms of the Convention. It is subject to serious doubt whether a contract of carriage between a carrier and a passenger or shipper (the kind of contract which in the Rome Convention of 1933 was the only one envisaged apart from contracts of employment) can be said to regulate the liability for damage caused by an aircraft not engaged in the performance of the contract, but which happens to be operated by the carrier. In maritime law the Courts of more than one country have denied the applicability of the contract of carriage to the action for damages caused by a colliding vessel owned by the same company which operates the carrying ship [1]). The situation does not seem to be different from that of a second aircraft operated by the carrier causing damage to passengers or goods carried by the latter. Nevertheless, this was the very situation for which Article 22 of the 1933 Convention was written. One would, therefore, deprive that Article of its meaning by construing it otherwise than as merely requiring the existence of a contract of carriage between the operator and the person killed or injured or the owner of the goods. Whether the Courts will be prepared to accept such free interpretation of Article 25 of the Convention of 1952 is more doubtful, as that provision, even under a strict interpretation, would retain significance with respect to indemnity agreements expressly aimed at this kind of damages. If they would not, one would have the curious situation that instead of having broadened the scope of the Article (and thus limited the scope of the Convention) the Conference of 1952 would have practically limited it to the agreements specifically written to cover surface damages caused by aircraft of the operator.

81. The wording of both Article 22 of the Convention of 1933 and Article 25 of the Convention of 1952, moreover, raises a serious problem with respect to the purely delictual actions of the dependants of a person killed by aircraft. Since they are suing for their own damages, and not for the damages suffered by the

---

80. [1]) See decisions in No. 71 (1).

person killed (or his estate), a literal interpretation of the above quoted Articles would lead to their action being still governed by the Convention, even if it would not be applicable to the liability towards the estate. Let us take a case envisaged by both Conventions: that of an aircraft crashing into another aircraft of the same operator stationed on the ground and having passengers on board. The next of kin of killed passengers could sue the operator under the Convention whenever the local law would give them an independent action, and the carrier (operator) would have no other defences than those of the Convention; but whenever the action would be given to the estate [1]), their action would not be governed by the Convention and the carrier (operator) would have all the normal defences of a carrier. The same would be true in those legal systems in which the dependants of the passenger are considered third party beneficiaries to whom an independent contractual action is given [2]). It is clear that the

81. [1]) This is the situation in nearly all States of the **USA** which (except Connecticut) have, in addition to such Survival Statutes, Death Acts similar to the English Fatal Accidents Act, 1846, giving an independent action to the close relatives. See the elaborate Note on the rather intricate pattern created by these Statutes in 61 Harv. L. Rev. (1947) 113, at 166 sq. See also W. H. Rose in 33 Mich. L. Rev. (1935), 545, at 587 sq. and Wettach in 16 N. Carolina L. Rev. (1938) 211, at 221. In **England** the Law Reform (Miscellaneous Provisions) Act, 1934, has also made possible an action for damages on behalf of the estate, which does not include, however, any loss to the estate consequent on the death (loss of future earnings) (Sec. 1 (2)). A similar situation seems now to exist in **France** where the later decisions of the *Cour de Cassation* have limited the damages to the estate to loss of earnings suffered between the accident and the death, apart from compensation for moral damages and medical and funeral expenses. See R. Savatier, *Traité de responsabilité civile,* 2e éd., Paris, 1953, II Nos. 543 sq. esp. 546.

Also in **Spain** the *Tribunal Supremo* has granted an action to the heirs under Art. 105 Cod. penal, irrespective of the degree of kinship. See Trib. Supr. 4.3.1944, R. 355, also 30.11.1932, Vol. 127, p. 237. For the similar rule in **Argentine** see Cam., 2a civ. y com. de La Plata (2a Inst.) 26.7.1949, 56 La Ley 444 (*Corti* v. *El Condor*). In **Mexico** the question whether dependants have an independent action or whether they can only sue as heirs of the deceased, seems to be controversial: Comp. Supr. Corte (5a Sala) 19.8.1942, 73 Seman. Jud. III, 4203 and 27.8.1943, 77 Seman. Jud. VI, 5528, with Trib. Supr. (3a Sala) 14.2.1942, 37 Anales de Jurisp. 37.In these countries it would seem that the courts may also take into account loss of future earnings, the action thus replacing the independent action of the next of kin. A similar confusion is also to be found in some French decisions (cf. Savatier, l.c. No. 546 and Mazeaud (1949) II No. 1912, especially note 4). For **Quebec** see *Green e.a.* v. *Elmhurst Dairy Ltd.* (1953) B.R. 85, annotated by A. Mayrand in 31 Can. B. Rev. (1953) 559, (damages granted to the heirs of a killed person for the pain and loss of life expectancy suffered by the deceased).

[2]) Cass. civ. **(French)** 6.12.1932 and 24.3.1933, D.P. 1933.1.140 with note Josserand, and S. 1934.1.81; Cass. req. 19.6.1933, D.H. 1933. 429. The fiction of an implied stipulation on behalf of the dependants of the passenger in each contract of carriage was adopted (against much criticism from the authors) in order to give the dependants

scope of applicability of the Conventions in these cases would thus be largely determined by national law, which is obviously undesirable. Any interpretation of Article 25 (or Article 22) which avoids this consequence deserves preference.

It is suggested that when a person is killed by an aircraft, his death is the 'damage' referred to in Article 25. With respect to Article 24 of the 1952 Convention [3]), another (perhaps more logical) view would lead to the still more absurd and clearly undesired consequence that the next of kin of a passenger killed in a collision of two aircraft could sue the operator of the other aircraft under the Convention, because *their* damage (i.e. loss of support) would have been suffered on the surface. Similarly, when Article 23 (Article 20 of the 1933 Convention) speaks of damage caused in the territory of a Contracting State, it would obviously be an excess of logical subtlety to argue that with respect to actions by dependants, not the place of death but the place where the loss of support is suffered would be the dominating factor [4]). In all these cases the only acceptable interpretation in the event of a person being killed by aircraft is to consider the word 'damage' as referring to the death of that person.

But this construction does not give an answer to another problem. In those countries where the liability for death or injuries to passengers – or to persons who have some other contractual relation with the wrongdoer which creates certain duties of

the benefit of the reversal of the burden of proof connected in French law with the contractual liability arising from the contract of carriage. Now that the Cour de Cassation in the Lamoricière Case (Cass. com. 19.6. 1951. D.1951, J. 717, and J.C.P. 1951.II.5729, discussed i.a. by Juglart in 4 D.M.F. (1952) 281 sq.) has allowed the next of kin of a passenger to sue a sea carrier under Art. 1384 (1) of the Code Civil (delictual liability with burden of proof on defendant) it remains to be seen whether the courts will find it necessary to stick to their rather artificial construction of an implied third party beneficiary stipulation. But in Appel Paris 11.12.1952, 7 R.F.D.A. (1953) 99, 101 (*Jeantelot-Pilleboue* v. *C.A.M.A.T.*, *Michelson et Cie e.a.*) the Court still rejected a claim by dependants of a killed air passenger, based on Art. 1384 (1) C.c., because of the fact that they had also invoked the stipulation on their behalf implied in the contract of carriage, so that they could not anymore ignore the contract by claiming also in tort. The fiction of an implied stipulation on behalf of dependants has been rejected by **Belgian** Courts, cf. Crt. Appeal of Ghent 9.3.1950, Rev. gén. ass. resp. (1950), 4679, Rev. crit. jur. belge 1951, 26 with extensive note by R.V.Dekkers.

81. [3]) 'The Convention shall not apply to damage caused to an aircraft in flight, or to persons or goods on board such aircraft'.

[4]) The same argument could be made when determining the applicable law in case of wrongful death. It has been, quite sensibly, rejected as a 'metaphysical subtlety' by the Scottish Court in *Longworth* v. *Hope & Cook* (1865) 37 Scot. Journ. 552, 556.

care – is considered to be a delictual liability and not a contractual one, the wording of Article 25 of the 1952 Convention (Article 22 of the 1933 Convention) makes it rather difficult to bring the actions arising from such personal injury or death cases within its scope, though it must certainly have been the intention that the Convention would not be applicable to them. It is to be hoped that the English or American Courts – for it is in these countries that death or personal injury claims, even when arising out of a contractual relationship, are often, if not generally, considered to be of a tortious nature [5]) – will not feel themselves so strongly bound to the letter of the provision as to be compelled to ignore the apparent intention of the drafters, or else that they will be ready to accept some contractual liability sufficient to set aside the applicability of the Convention [6]).

82. But although this might give a satisfactory solution in the clear cases of contractual relationship implying some special duty of care such as those arising from a contract of carriage, there will always remain a great number of borderline cases in which the local law and the inventiveness of plaintiff or defendant will determine whether the liability will be construed as a contractual one, which would exclude application of the Conven-

81. [5]) See for **U.S.A.**: Williston (1936) IV, § 1113 (see also § 1071), but comp. the older American cases mentioned by Prosser (1941) p. 305, note 49. **English** Courts are perhaps more inclined to speak in terms of contractual duties. Cf. *Tomlinson* v. *Railway Executive* [1953] All E.R. 1, in which all three judges held that the duty, owed by a railway to a passenger in respect of possible injury from snow on that part of the platform on which a passenger alights from a train, arises under the contract of carriage rather than in tort. For the civil law countries see No. 33 (1).

[6]) In *Salamon* v. *K.L.M.* 1951 U.S.Av.R. 378, Hecht J. admitted the possibility of an action in contract for a passenger who would have suffered injuries because of a failure of pressurization, if the carrier would have assumed the obligation to carry the passenger in a pressurized cabin. 'There appears to be no good reason for denying to a carrier the right, by special agreement, to assume liabilities greater than or additional to those provided for in the (Warsaw) Convention'.

Comp. for maritime law *The Satanita* [1897] A.C. 59, where a contract by which a yacht-owner assumed liability for 'all damages' arising from disobedience with certain sailing rules of a Yachting club was held to waive the right to invoke the limitation of liability provided by the Merchant Shipping Act. See also the Dutch decision of Hoge Raad 12.3.1954, N.J.B. 1954, p. 257 which held Art. 541 W.v.K., limiting the shipowner's liability for collisions, not applicable to the liability arising from a towage contract in case of collision. But the limitation of liability provided by the Merchant Shipping Act, 1894, has been held to apply to liability for damage caused to a vessel in tow by her tug in *Wahlberg* v. *Young* (1876), 4 Asp. M.C. 27, 45 L.J.C.P. 783; contrary the Canadian decision in *British Columbia Towage and Transport Co.* v. *Sewell*, 9 Duval's Rep. 527 (both cases cited by Marsden on Collisions, 9th. ed. 1934, p. 178).

tion. In a number of airports the terminal buildings and restaurants are owned by the airline having the most frequent services at that airport. Since the majority of air accidents occur during the operations of landing or take-off, the possibility of an aircraft of the local airline crashing into its own airport buildings is not an imaginary one. In such a case it will have to be established with respect to every single person on those premises, killed or injured by the accident, whether the liability for his death or injuries is regulated by a contract with the operator. We have here the entire gamma of passengers, invitees, licencees and trespassers, and we have the rich variety of views as to the nature of the liability existing towards such persons, changing from country to country, and within each country from author to author. The Courts generally prefer not to worry themselves about this more dogmatical question of labelling, but here they could not escape the necessity of making their choice. The probability that uniformity will be the result, does not seem much greater than the probability of a monkey, hammering on a piano, turning out to play a Toccata by Bach. The comparison does not reflect any lack of respect for the work of the courts. But in view of the great number of considerations which may be taken into account and which vary from country to country, it is simply impossible for different courts always to come to the same conclusions. There seems to be a good chance that continental courts will more easily accept contractual liabilities than Anglosaxon courts, so that the scope of applicability of the Convention on the Continent and in other civil law countries might be more restricted than in countries with common law.

Not only is the lack of uniformity from country to country, which will result from Article 25, regrettable. It will be very hard for any layman, and in fact for any lawyer having the common sense of a layman, to appreciate why the operator of an aircraft having crashed on an airport due to a reason beyond his control, will be able to invoke force majeure with respect to those persons towards whom he happened to carry some special contractual obligation of care, but not with respect to persons towards whom he did not owe any contractual obligation. The basic weakness of the Article is that it assumes a rather artificial tie between the accident of an aircraft operated by a person who has a contract with the victim, and such contract between operator and victim. This still would not create any serious difficulties if the absolute liability under the Convention were not much heavier than a contractual liability generally is. If it had been the purpose of the Article to permit any agreements purporting to set aside the provisions of the Convention, the wording would be still less succesful.

83. With respect to contracts of employment, Article 25 of the 1952 Convention has the special provision that the Convention shall not be applicable, not only if the liability is regulated by the contract, but also if it is regulated by 'the law relating to workmen's compensation' applicable to the contract of employment. The addition was thought desirable to provide for the cases of workmen's compensation by accident insurance, in which the liability to pay could be said to arise rather under the insurance prescribed by the law than under the contract of employment itself. The 1933 Convention did not contain this provision, nor did the Mexico Draft, and it is to be doubted whether it serves any useful purpose. For even when a workmen's insurance scheme exists, the liability can still be said to be regulated by the contract of employment, if it were only that the employer's liability would be excluded by the existence of such contract. The special addition for the employment cases might even create confusion if a similar compulsory insurance scheme were to be introduced with respect to passengers. One could make a nice argument *a contrario* out of the fact that Article 25 only provides for regulation by law relating to workmen's compensation, so that the operator's liability towards his passengers, when covered by a compulsory insurance, could be held not to be covered by Article 25, and therefore to be governed by the Convention.

Another question which arises in this connection is whether the words 'if liability for such damage is regulated etc' in the beginning of the Article should be read to mean *'to the extent liability etc'*. The question becomes important if the workmens' compensation legislation has not taken away the employee's delictual action against his employer for the difference recovered under the compensation scheme and his real damages. It would be reasonable to apply the Convention to such excess damages rather than the local law governing damages caused by aircraft. On the other hand this interpretation might frustrate the probable intention of the drafters of the Convention by also affecting the cases in which the municipal law recognizes the existence of a delictual liability in addition to a contractual liability arising from the contractual relation between passenger and operator. As was pointed out above, in order to give the intended effect to the provision as applying to contracts of carriage or similar contractual relationships, it is necessary to include all cases (and exclude applicability of the Convention thereto) in which the liability in some way arises from the contract, even though the contractual liability would be coupled with a delictual one.

84. Summarizing the above remarks on Article 25 of the 1952 Convention and Article 22 of the 1933 Convention, it can be said that they create certain intricate problems, and that in a number of situations they make the applicability of the Convention depend upon the divergent views and concepts existing in the various national legal systems.

85. The smaller circle which determines the sphere of applicability of the limitation of liability in the Rome Conventions does not pose any difficult problems. In fact, since the entire Convention deals with liability only (differing from the Warsaw Convention, which also contains provisions on traffic documents), the field of applicability of the Convention itself practically coincides with the sphere of applicability of the limitation provisions contained in it. The latter sphere is defined in Articles 1 and 9 of the 1952 Convention, the first establishing liability for damages on the surface caused by aircraft in flight or by any person or thing falling therefrom, and the latter stating that the person upon whom the Convention imposes liability, as well as their servants and agents, shall be liable for such damage only to the extent expressly provided in the Convention [1]).

---

85. [1]) The Rome Convention of 1933 does not contain a provision similar to Article 9 of the 1952 Convention. The analogous Article in the Warsaw Convention is Article 24, which does not, however, enumerate the persons protected by the Convention. Cf. Chapter IV, especially Nos. 136 sq.

Article 1 (2) defines when an aircraft should be deemed in flight, to-wit 'from the moment when power is applied for the purpose of actual take-off until the moment when the landing run ends'. This wording is much more precise and more restrictive than that contained in the 1933 Convention, which provides that the aircraft is deemed in flight 'from the beginning of the operations of departure until the end of the operations of arrival'.

§ 3. RECOURSE ACTIONS

86. Before completing this Chapter, some special categories of damages should be considered, which raise problems both under the Warsaw and under the Rome Conventions. The most important of those is the question of whether a carrier's or operator's liability to contribute to or pay for any claims satisfied by a third party, should be considered 'damages' with respect to which his liability is limited. The problem may be explained by an example. In a collision of two aircraft operated by carriers A and B, damage is caused to the surface, and passengers carried in A's aircraft are killed. After investigation the accident appears to have been caused by a coincidence of several irregularities, to-wit (1) a mechanical failure in the aircraft of A due to negligence of the manufacturer, (2) a wrong instruction from the Traffic Control and (3) errors committed by the pilots of both aircraft. The dependants of the passengers and the persons suffering damage on the surface may sue A and B and the negligent manufacturer of A and the Traffic Control. If any of the latter three persons should have to pay full compensation for either the killed passenger or the damages suffered on the surface, there is a good chance that he may recover part of this claim from the other persons liable, including A. Will A in such a case have a right to invoke the provisions limiting his liability contained in either the Warsaw Convention or the Rome Conventions? The problem will be discussed first for the Warsaw Convention, thereafter for the Rome Conventions.

A. Warsaw Convention.

87. Who are the persons from whom the carrier could expect a recourse action? This could be anybody causing or contributing to the occurrence of an accident as envisaged in Article 17, or of a loss or damage to goods as envisaged in Article 18 or of a delay as referred to in Article 19, either by his wilful misconduct or negligence [1]), or by any activity with respect to which the law has imposed absolute liability. It may be worthwile to mention briefly here the various categories of persons who may so become liable: (1) the servants of the carrier, (2) the agents of the carrier [2]), (3) the manufacturer of the aircraft or aircraft parts, (4) agencies not falling within categories (1) or (2) whose services are used in the course of the transportation, such as Air Traffic Control Agencies or Telecommunications and Meteorological Services [3]), and finally (5) any person who, without any contractual or statutory duties towards the carrier, has caused or contributed to the damage. Examples of the last category are: the operator of a colliding aircraft, a person (not acting as servant or agent of the carrier) committing some act of sabotage, a person on the ground who has created an obstacle in the neighbourhood of an airport in violation of some regulation. A somewhat special group of recourse actions is that of actions between successive carriers.

88. Whenever an accident to a passenger, or loss of or damage to baggage or goods or a delay [1]) is wholly or partly due to an act of negligence or a negligent omission, or to a wilful wrong committed by any of these persons, the passenger will generally have a right of action against such a person (and if he was acting in the course of his employment, also against his employer) for recovery of damages. If the carrier has also committed a fault, the person who had to pay compensation might have the right to claim contribution from the carrier either on the basis of the contract

87. [1]) Cf. Shawcross and Beaumont (1951) No. 370.

[2]) On the question who should be considered agents of the carrier cf. Nos. 197 sq.

[3]) It is suggested that such agencies cannot be considered agents of the carrier, since they are not *engaged* by the carrier. Cf. J. Lacombe in 12 R.G.A. (1949) 821.

88. [1]) An action in tort against a third party for delay may arise when the delay is caused by an accident due to the negligence of the third party. But when the delay is caused by a booking error, or by a failure to load goods or baggage on the plane in time, or to offload them at the place of destination, it is suggested that no action in tort would lie against the person committing the fault, since there would not seem to exist a general duty for anybody, apart from contractual obligations, to ensure that goods or baggage are loaded or offloaded from an aircraft.

existing between the carrier and himself (categories 1, 2 and 3), or by way of contribution between joint or concurrent tortfeasors. The recourse action may also arise from a special indemnity agreement by which the carrier has agreed to hold the other person harmless from any claims [2]). Whether a recourse action is given, will depend upon the contract between the person sued and the carrier, and its implications under the law governing the contract. In the absence of a contract, the law to be applied will probably be the law applicable to tortious liability [3]). This may even be true where a contract does exist. Thus the recourse action of the person who is held vicariously liable against the person whose negligence caused the damage, is often considered to lie in the sphere of tortious liability rather than to arise from contract [4]).

89. The question whether and under what circumstances an employee would have a recourse action against his employer, if he were sued in respect of damages arising from his negligence committed in the course of his employment, is a problem which does not seem to have received much attention [1]), obviously because of the fact that actions will be seldom brought against the employee. The problem, of course, is closely related to the reverse question of whether and when the principal will have a recourse action against his servants. The general view seems to be that in principle the employer may recover from his employee

---

88. [2]) Such indemnity clauses are imposed by some airport authorities on operators who want to use the airports, e.g. by the U.S. Government with respect to the U.S. Air Force bases outside the U.S.A. See Air Force Regulation 87–7, para. 11.

[3]) Cf. E. Rabel, *Conflict of Laws*. Ann Arbor, 1947, II, p. 263, and Williams (1951) pp. 135/136, who correctly makes an exception for the case where the claim for contribution arises out of some special relation, where the law governing that relation should apply.

[4]) Cf. for **English** law: *Jones* v. *Manchester Corp. et al.* [1952] All. E. R. 125, 131 sq.; for **USA** Prosser (1941), p. 1114; for **France:** Mazeaud, I, No. 728, Planiol-Ripert-Esmein, Traité, VI, No. 656; for **German** law: § 840 BGB but see also § 426 BGB as construed by the *Reichsgericht* i.a. R.G. 22.12.1910, RGZ. 75,251; for **Italy**: De Cupis (1946), pp. 318–320.

89. [1]) But see the exhaustive study by Williams (1951) at p. 162. An action for contribution against the master was held possible under the 'Tortfeasors Act' 1935 in the Jones Case (sea previous note). See also following note. Such action was rejected by a **Canadian** Court in *Johnston* v. *Elmslie* [1939] O.W.N. 84, [1939] 2 D.L.R. 411, and by the **New York** Court in *Kennedy* v. *Travelers Ins. Co.* 217 N.Y.S. 261 (1926). Other American decisions in 45 Harv. L. Rev. (1931/32) 349 at 351.

any claim which he had to pay because of the latter's negligence [2]). It is believed that the construction of master and servant as being joint tortfeasors, and the application of the rules as to contribution between joint tortfeasors has confused the issues, and has obscured the contractual relationship between master and servant. As it was said by an English judge in a recent case: 'The master's claim against the servant, if it exists at all, must [...] be based not on a promise of indemnity, but on damages for breach of contract' [3]). Since the contractual obligation of an employee is to work for his employer, not to work faultless, occasional errors or faults committed by an employee do not necessarily imply a breach of contract which would make him liable towards his employer [4]). Whether this argument can be extended to allow an employee to recover from his employer sums he had to pay as a consequence of his negligence, is a question the discussion of which would go beyond the scope of this study [5]).

---

89. [2]) See besides the authorities cited in no. 88 (4) (but excluding the Jones Case) Williams (1951) pp. 162 sq. and **English** sources quoted by him at p. 164. For **USA** *adde* note in 45 Harv. L. Rev. (1931/32) 349, 351 and Mechem (1952) § 532. Since the liability of master and servant is considered in England as the liability of joint tortfeasors, the Law Reform (Married Women and Joint Tortfeasors) Act, 1935, is applicable to the contribution between them, and this Act gives full discretion to the judge as to whether and how much each party should contribute.

For the **Netherlands** see Wolfsbergen (1946), pp. 262/63,and the reports of P.W. Kamphuisen and F.M. Westerouen van Meeteren to the Nederlandsche Juristen-vereeniging (Handelingen 1939, I at pp. 22 sq. and 38 sq. respectively).

Though the majority of the **French** decisions seem to allow full recovery from the servant for claims paid by the employer, some decisions have required gross negligence or '*abus de fonctions*' on the side of the servant in order that the employer may take recourse: Appel Paris, 14.3.1930. D. 1930.2.115 with critical note A. Besson, aff'd by Cass. req. 18.4.1932 D.H. 1932, 282; Trib. Seine 2.4.49 G.P. 25/28.6.1949, 48 Rev. trim. dr. civ. (1949) 416, with critical note by Mazeaud. See also R. Demogue, *Traité des obligations en général*. Pàris, 1925, V, No. 954, Philonenko in G.P. 1941. Doct. 38, and cf. Planiol-Ripert (1947) II, No. 1141. It is to be observed that the cases which go to the courts will nearly always be cases of clearcut negligence, involving more than the normal error, which even the good employee will occasionally commit.

See also Art. 1123 of the **Argentina** Civil Code; Art. 147 of the **Polish** Code of Obligations; Art. 174 of the new **Egyptian** Civil Code, 1948; Art. 715 (3) of the **Japanese** Civil Code; Art. 1904 **Spanish** Civil Code; Art. 238 of the **Brazilian** Codigo de Commercio; and expressly for the operator's recourse against his crew Art. 44 of the **Chinese** Aviation Act of 1941.

[3]) Dennis J. in *Jones* v. *Manchester Corp.* [1952] All E.R. 125,131, adding, however: 'the difficulty about that way of putting it is that, although the servant is alone negligent, nevertheless in the eye of the law the master and the servant are both tortfeasors. They are, indeed, joint tortfeasors'. The contractual character of the recourse rights between employer and employee under **Dutch** law has been stressed by Wolfsbergen (1946), p. 262.

[4]) Similarly Kamphuisen, l.c. (supra note 2) at p. 28. Contra Williams (1951) p. 163.

[5]) See note 1 supra.

90. Similarly, the recourse action of the agent against the carrier is governed by his contract with the carrier. The difference in regard to the servants would seem to be that the agent has greater independency and, therefore, greater responsibilities in the absence of specific contractual stipulations. Also, there is a greater chance that the matter of recourse will have been expressly dealt with in the agency contract. The contract may contain an indemnity agreement by which the carrier is to take any claim against the agent for his account, in which case the only question arising would be the validity of such an indemnity clause [1]). The same applies to recourse actions by manufacturers.

91. If no contractual relationship nor a specific indemnity agreement exists between the carrier and the person sued, the latter must base his recourse action on the principle of contribution between joint tortfeasors. When the party taking recourse has not been liable for any intentional or criminal act, the majority of legal systems would seem to allow him an action against the concurrent tortfeasor for contribution [1]), but in case of intentional or criminal wrongs the action is often, if not generally, denied [2]). In some countries the law goes much farther in denying contribution. The USA offers the most notable example, with the majority of states still generally forbidding any action between joint tortfeasors [3]), though important inroads have been made in this principle either by statute or by the courts [4]). In France the courts, though generally allowing contribution between joint

---

90. [1]) See on this question No. 248 (9).

91. [1]) For **English** law before the Act of 1935 see Williams (1951) p. 83. **France**: see i.a. Cass. civ. 16.3.1943 and 21.12.1943, D. 1944, 38; **Belgium** cf. Cass. 2.4.1936, Belgique jud. 1936, 392, 426; **Netherlands**: H.R. 30.10.1925, N.J. 1926, 157, W. 11444; **Germany**: BGB § 840; **Switzerland**: Art. 50 Obl.; **Austria** ABGB § 1302; **Italy** Cod. civ. Art. 2055; **Poland** Obl. Art. 137 (2); **USSR**: Gsovski, Sovjet Civil Law. Ann Arbor, 1948 I, 531.; **Spain**: Cod. penal. Art. 109 (3); **Portugal**: Cod. civ. Art. 2372; **Argentina**: decision of Apel. Rosario, 18 La Ley 42 (holding Art. 1082 of the Civil Code, which forbids contribution, not applicable to quasi-delictual torts) and cf. note by Spota in Jurisprud. Argent. 1942 II 255; **Peru**: Cod.civ.Art. 1147; **Venezuela**: Cod. civ. Art. 1195. Cf. Art. 4 (3) of the Brussels Collisions Convention of 1910.

[2]) **Great Britian**: *Merryweather* v. *Nixan* (1799) 8 Term. Rep. 186, and see also Williams (1951) pp. 87 sq; **France** see infra note 5; **Netherlands** cf. Wolfsbergen (1946) p. 241; **Argentina**: Cod. civ. 1082.

[3]) Cf. Prosser (1941), pp. 1113 sq. and the extensive literature there cited.

[4]) Survey in Note in 45 Harv. Law Rev. (1931) 369.

tortfeasors, have refused recourse action to persons who have been found guilty of a criminal offence, even if no intentional wrong but only some minor misdemeanour such as a violation of a regulation were involved [5]).

92. The problem of whether the payment of a claim (in respect of which the party who paid the claim tries to get recovery from the carrier) should be considered damage for which the carrier's liability is limited under Article 22, is only important if the party taking recourse is not also protected himself by said Article. What the position of servants and agents of the carrier is in this respect, is a question which will be discussed later. But apart from them, there will always remain a number of cases in which the original action is not brought against a servant or agent but against some third party joint tortfeasor, whom it would be impossible to consider protected by Article 22. The liability of the operator of the other aircraft in collision cases offers a clear example.

93. It is submitted that nothing prevents the carrier from invoking the limits of Article 22 in case of recourse actions arising from the death or injuries of passengers, or loss or damage of baggage or goods, or in case of delay, provided these occurrences fall within the scope of Articles 17, 18 or 19.

Article 24 provides that 'in the cases covered by [Article 17 and] Articles 18 and 19 any action for damages, *however founded*, can only be brought subject to the conditions and limits set out in this Convention'. This clearly brings delictual recourse actions under the limits and conditions of the Convention. But the wording of Article 24 is sufficiently broad to include also actions based on a contract other than the contract of carriage between the carrier and passenger or shipper. However, since the Convention does not forbid the carrier to accept a contractual liability in excess of the Warsaw limits, it will depend on the interpretation of the contract on which the recourse action is founded, whether it was intended to set aside any limitation of liability provided by the Convention. Indemnity agreements between a carrier and

91. [5]) Cass. civ. 15.12.1948, S. 1949.1.141 with extensive note by R. Meurisse. Contra Planiol-Ripert (1947) II, No. 1040.

his agent or another person, which purport to deal with claims from passengers and shippers arising out of the transportation by the carrier, generally should be construed to prevent the carrier from relying any more on the limits of liability of Article 22, in recourse actions brought under such agreements. Whether such unlimited recourse action will affect the shares of the amount of the limit to be apportioned to the persons whose claims are limited by Article 22, will be discussed in Chapter VIII.

94. It is believed that the provision of Article 24 – which has no parallel in the Brussels Convention of 1924 on bills of lading – gives the carrier the right to invoke the limits of liability in case of a recourse action brought by the operator of a colliding aircraft who would have paid damages for passengers or cargo carried on the carrier's aircraft [1]).

The matter of recourse claims between operators in case of collision has been the subject of long discussions in the CITEJA when the draft Convention on collisions was being debated [2]). In the course of these discussions Professor Ripert, who played such an important part in the drafting of the Warsaw Convention, made the following remark: 'One thing is certain, that is that one may not destroy the Convention of Warsaw. The Convention of Warsaw says, that the carrier cannot be held liable in excess of 125.000 francs per person. The Convention does not distinguish whether there is only one party at fault, or joint negligence, or collision' [3]). For this reason he proposed to exclude all recourse

---

94. [1]) In *The Chattahoochee* (1899) 173 U.S. 540, 549 sq. the shipowner of 'The Golden Rule' was denied the right to invoke the provisions of the Harter Act, limiting his liability for goods carried, against a recourse action of the Chattahoochee for half the amount the latter had to pay to the shippers of these goods. The decision was based on the principle of *The North Star* 106 U.S. 173, which did not, however, deal with a limitation of liability for goods carried, but only held that in case of collision causing damages to both ships there do not arise two independent actions, each limited according to the rest value of the liable ship, but only one action for half of the difference between the damages suffered by both ships, so that the limitation of liability will only be applied to this one action. The Court *per* Brown J. held that from the doctrine of the North Star 'it would seem to follow that the sunken vessel is not entitled to the benefit of any statute tending to lessen its liability to the other vessel, or to an increase of the burden of such vessel, until the amount of such liability has been fixed upon the principle of an equal division of damages'. See also No. 95 (2), and comp. No. 248 (9).

[2]) CITEJA, Third Commission (October 1936) Doc. 321, pp. 61–99 and full session of CITEJA (Berne 1936) Doc. 324, pp. 124 sq. and 188 sq.

[3]) Translation from Doc. 324, p. 131.

between operators of colliding aircraft. In opposition to this opinion the German Delegate Riese held it to be an 'error in logic' to say that it would be irreconcilable with the Warsaw Convention to allow the operator recourse against the carrier to the effect that the latter's total liability would exceed the Warsaw limit, because, in his view (neglecting the effect of Article 24), such recourse action would not be based on the Warsaw Convention [4]).

95. So far we have assumed that the claim for contribution allowed by the applicable municipal law would exceed the limit of the carrier's liability under Warsaw. Some legal systems, however, only grant a right of contribution to the extent the person from whom contribution is sought was himself liable toward the original claimant. This seems to be the principle adopted by the German courts for contribution between concurrent tortfeasors generally [1]). It was also incorporated in the English Maritime Conventions Act, 1911 [2]). Where such a rule applies it is clear that the question of interpretation of Article 22 and 24 of the Warsaw Convention does not even arise.

---

94. [4]) Doc. 324, p. 134.

95. [1]) RG 24.9.1910, J.W. 1910, 952, involving a case of damage to cargo of defendant's ship caused by plaintiff's ship. The latter was sued in tort by the cargo owners, and took recourse against the carrier of the cargo concerned, who had however excluded his liability in the bill of lading for this type of losses, which exemption was construed also to apply to his tortious liability towards the shippers. Under these circumstances the *Reichsgericht* refused to allow contribution under § 426 or § 840 BGB, because of the absence of a concurrent liability. Similarly RG 30.4.1914, RGZ 75, 415.

[2]) 1 & 2 Geo. 5, c. 57, Sec. 3 (1) (2). Cf. Williams (1951) p. 112. The Law Reform (Married Women and Tortfeasors) Act, 1935, also requires in Sec. 6 (1) that a claim for contribution is only possible against a person 'who is, or would if sued have been, liable in respect of the same damages', but it is doubtful whether that would give a right to the person from whom contribution is sought, to invoke a *limitation* of his liability towards the original claimant, since such limitation would still leave him a person liable in respect of the same damages, unless one would attach special significance to the word 'same' in 'the same damages'. It seems more in conformity with the probable intention of the legislator to accord a similar effect to provisions limiting liability as to those excluding liability. It has also been pointed out that the Act gives full discretion to the Courts to decide whether and to what extent contribution should be allowed, so that on that basis alone the Court might refuse contribution in excess of the limits. See arguments pro and contra in Williams l.c. pp. 167/168 (it is to be observed that the author only speaks of contractual limitation of liability and derives some of his arguments from the contractual character of the limitation).

B. Rome Conventions.

96. The problems arising under the Rome Conventions are not greatly different. But it is nevertheless necessary to give special attention to them because of certain differences in their provisions.

Article 9 of the Rome Convention of 1952 (an analogous provision is not contained in the Convention of 1933 [1])) reads:

> 'Neither the operator, the owner, any person liable under Article 3 or Article 4, nor their respective servants or agents, shall be liable for damage on the surface caused by an aircraft in flight or any person or thing falling therefrom otherwise than as expressly provided in this Convention. This rule shall not apply to any such person, who is guilty of a deliberate act or omission done with intent to cause damage'.

It is believed that the words 'liable for damage on the surface' [2]) should be construed to comprise any liability arising from such surface damage, including recourse actions from jointly liable third parties [3]). This means that such recourse actions may also not be brought 'otherwise than as expressly provided in the Convention', so that the operator is under an absolute liability with respect to these actions, subject only to the defences of Articles 5 and 6.

In the majority of cases the liability of the third party for which it tries to take recourse will be based on negligence, so that the operator will be in a position to invoke Article 6, which excludes or reduces the operator's liability if the damage was caused or contributed to by the negligence of the person claiming damages [4]). But the situation becomes rather difficult when the third party's liability for which recourse is taken is also an absolute liability. This case could easily arise if one rejected the earlier adopted view that in case of a collision between a foreign aircraft of a non-contracting State on the one hand and a domestic

---

96. [1]) Cf. No. 126 (2).

[2]) Curiously neither the French nor the Spanish texts have the words 'on the surface', but the difference does not seem to be of any consequence since Article 23 makes it clear that the Convention only applies to surface damage.

[3]) The French text has: 'responsabilité, *en ce qui concerne* les dommages etc.' which perhaps is even broader than the English 'liable *for* damage'.

[4]) For an analogous application of the rule as to contributory negligence or contribution between concurrent tortfeasors, see *The Cairnbahn* [1914] P. 25, and the discussion of this case by Williams (1951) pp. 113 sq.

aircraft of a non-contracting State on the other hand, the liability of both operators would be governed by the Convention. For if such a collision were to occur in a contracting State whose national law would also impose absolute liability upon operators of aircraft for surface damages, the domestic operator might be held liable without proof of negligence, and could in his turn lodge a claim against the foreign operator, which claim – following the here adopted line of thought – would be governed by the Convention, so that the domestic operator need only prove the causal relation between the surface damage and the collision in order to be entitled to full recovery, subject to the limitation provisions of Article 11. The foreign operator would in this case not be able to have the other party bear part of the claim, since the defence of Article 6 is only given to him if he can prove negligence of the person claiming damages.

97. Could it be said that Article 10 of the Convention of 1952 excludes applicability of the provisions of the Convention to such recourse claims? This Article reads:

> 'Nothing in this Convention shall prejudice the question whether a person liable for damage in accordance with its provisions has a right of recourse against any other person'.

The analogous provision of the 1933 Convention (Article 7) reads:

> 'The preceding provisions are without prejudice to the question whether or not the operator of the aircraft may have a right of recourse against the author of the damage'.

It is believed that these provisions in no way affect the application of the Conventional limitation provisions to recourse actions *against* the persons upon whom the Conventions impose liability. They only speak about the right of recourse to be exercised *by* such persons. For this reason Article 10 (Article 7) could become important when a recourse action against a person liable under the Convention would also be brought *by* such a person. The provision, therefore, would seem to prevent application of Articles 1 to 9 of the Convention to recourse actions between operators of aircraft, if both are liable under the Convention.

The question of whether in case of collision between a foreign aircraft of a Contracting State and a domestic aircraft (or a foreign aircraft of a non-contracting State) the latter's liability will also be governed by the Convention, is thus not only of interest with a view to determining the liability of the domestic operator towards the injured parties on the surface, but also in order to know whether the recourse claim of said operator against the foreign operator will be governed by the Convention. If the domestic operator's liability towards persons on the surface comes within the scope of the Convention, his recourse claim does nòt, and reversely, if the domestic operator's liability is outside the Convention, his recourse claim against the foreign operator (of an aircraft of a contracting State) will be governed by it. Since it is obviously desirable that recourse actions between operators be not based on the principle of absolute liability established by the Convention, the previously stated alternative would appear to offer another strong argument in favour of having the Convention apply to the operators of both aircraft, if only one of them were a foreign aircraft of a Contracting State [1]).

98. Meanwhile, the statement that the recourse claim of an operator whose liability is governed by the Convention does not itself come within the scope of the Convention, needs qualification. The problem has still to be faced whether the limitation provisions of Article 11 (Article 8 respectively) apply to recourse claims between operators of colliding aircraft. The importance of this question needs hardly to be emphasized. If the limits could not be invoked with respect to these actions the protection offered by them would have little value as far as surface damage caused by collisions is concerned. The private flyer whose Piper Cub would collide with a stratocruiser would have to bear the liability for the surface damage up to the combined limits applying to his own aircraft and to the stratocruiser! It could be said that the limits do not in any case protect him against the other operator's claim for the loss of the stratocruiser, and for the death of passengers and loss of goods carried therein. But this gap in his protection is due to the absence of a Convention on collisions. Had it been decided at Rome that the convention

97. [1]) See No. 77.

on surface damage was not to deal with liability for damage caused by colliding aircraft, the argument would be a sound one. It was felt, however, that the Rome Convention should also deal with such damages, and prolonged discussions have been devoted to this subject. That being so, the limitation of liability for surface damage should certainly not give way in case of damage caused by collisions.

It remains to be seen whether the texts of the Conventions compel to a conclusion which, as far as recourse claims between operators are concerned, would set aside not only the provisions of Article 1 and those following, but also the limit of Article 11 (resp. Article 8). This is certainly not true with respect to the Convention of 1933. Not only is Article 8 itself very generally worded ('the operator is liable for each accident up to an amount etc.') but the only other article (Article 7) which could be invoked to exclude application of Article 8, is expressly limited to Articles 1 to 6. ('The *preceding* provisions are without prejudice etc.') [1]).

In the Convention of 1952 the situation is less clear. Article 11 limits 'the liability for damage giving a right to compensation under Article 1'. This would not seem to exclude recourse claims. But Article 10 does not – as Article 7 of the 1933 Convention does – only refer to the *preceding* provisions. It provides generally that *'nothing in this Convention* shall prejudice the question whether a person liable for damage in accordance with its provisions has a right of recourse against any other person'. Nevertheless, it is suggested that this provision, by speaking of 'the question *whether* a person [...] has a right of recourse', only refers to the principles which determine the *existence* of liability (such as dealt with in Article 1) not those which *limit* liability, once liability is established.

99. Could it be said that paragraph 1 of Article 1 itself would exclude any recourse claims because these would deal with damage which is not 'a direct consequence of the incident giving rise thereto'? That would be giving by far too restrictive an interpretation to the notion of 'direct consequence'.

---

98. [1]) A proposal at the Rome Conference to take away the word 'preceding' (but not intended to deal with the situation envisaged in the text) was withdrawn (I,, 302 303).

It has been said in a maritime collision case that 'the liability [...] for all the damage to cargo [is ...] one of the consequences plainly to be foreseen', one of the 'manifest consequences', for which the other ship could be held liable [1]). Evidently the same applies to collisions of aircraft. Any other solution would, moreover, lead to absurd consequences. For the result of such an interpretation would be, not that Article 1 would not apply to the recourse claim, but rather that it would be a *complete bar* to any such claims! Either the liabilities created by surface damages, for which recourse could otherwise be taken, are indirect consequences of 'the incident giving rise' to the damage, in which case the third party tortfeasors would always be precluded from taking recourse against the operator of an aircraft causing damage on the surface; or else, they should not be considered indirect consequences, and in that case recourse claims could be based on Article 1 (except when Article 10 sets aside application of Article 1, i.e. with respect to claims lodged by persons liable under the Convention). The choice between these two possibilities is not difficult [2]).

Summarizing it can be said that the limits of Article 11 (re-

---

99) [1]) Holmes J. in *Erie R. Co* v. *Erie Western Transport Co.* 204 U.S. 220, 226 (1907). Cf. *Aktieselskabet Cuzco* v. *Steamship Sucarseco,* 294 U.S. 394, 401 (1934) and *Morrison Steamship Co.* v. *Owners etc. Cargo on Board Greystoke Castle,* 63 T.L.R. 11, 18 (1946), both dealing with the action of cargo owners against the non-carrying ship for recovery of their contribution in general average. Especially the latter (House of Lords) decision is important as it deals extensively with the effect of the rule in the Polemis Case (liability for all *direct* consequences).

[2]) Applicability of the limits on surface damage liability to the recourse claims between operators of colliding aircraft was also accepted by CITEJA in its Draft Convention For the Unification of Rules Relating to Aerial Collision, established at its 11th Session, Berne 1936 (Doc. 324, p. 266). See Article 7 (3) of this Draft, reading: 'Si, à cause de la solidarité, l'exploitant d'un aéronef a payé aux victimes des dommages à la surface une somme que, d'après l'alinéa 2 du présent article, il ne devait pas supporter, le recours que cet exploitant exercera contre l'autre ou les autres aéronefs ne pourra jamais être exercé, que dans les limites de la responsabilité de chaque aéronef envers les tiers'. The Draft was submitted to the IVth Conference on International Private Air Law at Brussels, 1938, but following an American proposal it was not discussed and referred back to CITEJA (Minutes of the Conference, p. 160). This Draft, meanwhile, has inspired various national legislators, such as the **Italian** (Artt. 974 sq, Cod. Nav.; cf. Lefebvre d'Ovidio and Pescatore (1949) No. 513) and the **Brazilian** (Art. 127 sq. of the *Codigo Brasileiro do Ar*; cf. Judge N. de Queiros in *Cameras civeis reunidas* Rio de Janeiro 23.9.1948, 1 R.B.D.A. (1951) 232).

Art. 980 of the Italian Code, however, refers for the limitation of recourse actions between operators of colliding aircraft not to Art. 967 (limiting the liability for surface damage) but to Art. 975, which limits the liability for damage to aircraft and persons or goods aboard the aircraft. The problem, unfortunately, did not arise in the interspectively Article 8) also apply to recourse claims between operators of colliding aircraft, but that Article 10 (resp. Article 7) sets aside the provisions of Article 1 and those following for the purpose of determining *whether* a recourse action exists.

100. If the recourse action is based on contract, it would seem to fall entirely outside the scope of the Convention of 1952 in view of the principle of Article 25 providing that 'the Convention shall apply to damage on the surface if liability for such damage is regulated [...] by a contract between the person who suffers such damage and the operator etc.', though it could be argued that a person who takes recourse for a claim which he has paid as a result of surface damage, is not a 'person who suffers damage on the surface' in the sense of the Article. It is believed, however, that this would be too restrictive an interpretation and that one thus would ignore the underlying principle. The Convention of 1933 does not contain an equally broad provision as Article 25 of the 1952 Convention. Its Article 22 excludes contracts of carriage and of employment, which takes only the recourse actions of employees of the operator outside the scope of the Convention. Other recourse actions on a contractual basis are not excluded, but to the extent they arise from express indemnity or hold harmless agreements, such agreements must be deemed to have set aside the limitation of liability provided by the Convention. The resulting rights to unlimited compensation may, however, affect the share to be apportioned to the other persons claiming damages [1]).

§ 4. LEGAL INTERESTS AND LEGAL EXPENSES

101. Before closing this Chapter on the scope of application of the limitation provisions, some attention should be given to two special items on damages, which will be generally included within

---

esting Brazilian collision case (*supra*), since only the non-carrying aircraft was held at fault. But the possibility of the recourse action against the carrying aircraft being limited by the limitation of carrier's liability does not seem to have been envisaged by Judge Vieira Braga in his long dissenting opinion (l.c. 232 sq. at 236).

100. [1]) Comp. No. 299.

any claim for damages when brought into court: legal interests and legal expenses.

The applicability of the limitation provisions to the legal interests due on the amount of liability arising under the Conventions might be denied on the ground that legal interests are not a compensation for the damages to which the Conventions apply but are the legally fixed compensation for the delay in paying an amount of money which has become due. In maritime law some countries actually do exclude legal interests from the liability limits which apply there [1]). But in other countries they are included [2]). It is to be observed that most if not all of these holdings deal with the global limitation of the shipowner's liability. This is also true of the Italian Codice della Navigazione which has extended the relevant provision of its maritime law section to the global limitation of the aircraft operator's liability for surface and collision damages [3]).

None of the air law conventions contain an express provision on legal interests. Closest to it comes the Rome Convention of 1952, which in paragraph 11 of Article 20 provides that 'interest not exceeding 4% per annum may be allowed on the judgement debt from the date of the judgement in respect of which execution is granted', but this clause deals with the binding force of foreign judgements and it would go too far to read into it an argument *a contrario* that no interests may be awarded in an original judgement on top of the maximum amount fixed by the Convention.

Article 24 of the Warsaw Convention provides that in the cases covered by Articles 17, 18 and 19 any action for damages ('action en responsabilité'), however founded, can only be brought subject to the conditions and limits set out in the Convention. If the claim for legal interests is to be considered an action for damages or part of it, it would seem that Article 24 brings it within the scope of the limitation provisions of the Convention. It is to be observed that Article 24 speaks not only of the limits

---

101. [1]) See for **England** i.a. Scrutton (1948) p. 513 footnote (f).

[2]) Cf. for the **Netherlands** the Opinion by R.P. Cleveringa of 21.10.1943, Arbitrale Rechtspraak 1943, p. 301.

[3]) Artt. 1046 and 625 of the Cod. Nav. See also Art. 37 of the Berne Conventions on Railroad Transportation (C.I.M. and C.I.V.).

but also of 'conditions' set out in the Convention, thereby referring i.a. to the provisions on jurisdiction and on time limitations on actions (Articles 28 and 29). There can be little doubt that a claim for legal interests can only be brought before one of the courts indicated in Article 28 and within the two year period fixed by Article 29. That being so, it seems difficult to hold otherwise with respect to the limitation provisions of Article 22. Either one considers the obligation to pay legal interests on the amount of liability something so different from the carrier's liability envisaged in Articles 17, 18 and 19, that it is not governed by the Convention, in which case none of the provisions of the Convention would apply to it, or one holds that the claim for legal interests, as incidental to the primary claim for compensation, is also governed by the Convention, in which case Article 24 makes it clear that the limitation provisions apply to it. The latter alternative seems the better one [4]).

102. It is believed that *legal expenses* awarded by a court against a carrier who loses a lawsuit, are no part of the damages limited by the limitation provisions of the Conventions. They are not damages arising from the conduct or the fact for which liability is imposed by the Conventions but expenses caused by the lawsuit itself. This is expressly provided by Article 20 (10) of the Rome Convention, 1952: 'the limits of liability prescribed by this Convention shall be exclusive of costs' [1]). It appears also to be the constant practice of the courts when applying the limitation provisions of the Warsaw Convention, and in conformity with what seems to be the general practice in respect to limitations of liability in maritime law [2]).

---

101. [4]) *Contra* Trib. civ. Brussels 30.6.1950, Rev. gén. ass. resp. (1951) 4723, awarding an interest of 5% on top of the Warsaw limit. Also impliedly Appel Paris 28.2.1953, 7 R.F.D.A. (1953) 105 at 120 (*Comp. Air France* v. *Nordisk Transport*).

102. [1]) Also Art. 1049 Cod. Nav. (**Italy**), both for surface damage and for collision claims.

[2]) Sec. 504 of the **English** Merchant Shipping Act, 1894, gives full discretion to the court to award legal expenses in excess of the amount to which the shipowner's liability is limited. This seems to be the actual practice of the courts. Cf. D. Maclachlan, *Treatise on the Law of Merchant Shipping, 7th ed.* London, 1932, p. 97: 'A vexatious resistance of just claims would be encouraged by any other rule'. Similarly Art. 320p of the **Dutch** *Wetboek van Burgerlijke Regtsvordering* (Code of Civil Procedure); for **France** Cass. civ. 4.2.1947, S. 1948.1.105 note Houin, D. 1947. J. 437 note Ripert, and Ripert (1952), II, no. 1281, and see also Cass. civ. 14.10.1953, 6 D.M.F..

A curious exception is offered by a Brazilian decision which held Article 87 of the *Codigo do Air* (Air Code) – limiting the air carrier's liability in case of delay – applicable to the lawyer's salary to be paid by the losing defendant pursuant to Article 64 of the Code of Civil Procedure, on the ground that the latter provision which purports to make the compensation for damage as complete as possible, is overruled by the basic principle of limitation of liability laid down in Article 87 of the Air Code [3]).

To say that, in principle, legal expenses to be paid by the carrier or operator are not limited by the limitation provisions of the Conventions, does not necessarily mean that these expenses could never be an item of damages to which the limits might apply. When legal expenses are included in a recourse claim brought by a carrier or operator against another carrier or operator, there seems to be no reason not to hold the latter entitled to invoke the limitation of his liability also with respect to that part of the claim [4]). Often, of course, a claim for compensation of the legal expenses incurred by the party bringing the recourse action in the original law suit, may be completely rejected, whenever such expenses could have been avoided.

(1954) 80, where the Court held the limitation of the sea carrier's liability under the Act of 1936 inapplicable to the additional damages awarded against the carrier because of his 'injustified resistance' against the claim of the shipper. For **Argentina**: Trib. Supr. 24.6.1936 in Dor 1936, 94 (also comparative survey).

102. [3]) Apel. civel n. 3.603, Rio de Janeiro 10.12.1948, 1 R.B.D.A. (1951) no. 2, p. 203 (summary in 16 R.G.A. (1953) 56).

[4]) Cf. *Hoge Raad* (**Dutch**) 8.1.1954, N.J. 1954, No. 82: for the purpose of determining the possibility of appeal in case of a recourse claim, the legal expenses and interests to be paid by the party taking recourse should be considered part of the recourse claim.

Chapter III

EXTENT OF DAMAGES FOR WHICH LIABILITY IS TO BE LIMITED

103. Before determining the effect of the limitation provisions in the private air law conventions on the liability for damages, it is necessary to study the extent of damages for which liability is imposed. The questions which will be considered in this connection are (1) the question of remoteness or unforeseeability of damages, especially in relation to the question of compensation for exceptionally valuable goods, (2) the influence of contributory negligence, and (3) the question posed by national laws establishing limits of liability in case of death or personal injuries.

Generally it can be said that, insofar as the Conventions do not provide for the extent of damages to be compensated, the matter is governed by national law, which may be the law of the place where the contract was made, the law of the place of destination, the law of the place where the accident occurred, or the *lex fori*. It would go beyond the scope of this study to discuss the intricate problems of conflict of laws involved. Suffice it to say that under the Rome Convention, 1952, a problem will not easily arise, because of the fact that only the courts of the country where the accident occurred will be competent (Article 20). Thus the *lex fori* and the *lex loci delicti* (almost the only laws between which a choice could be made in these cases [1])) will be the same. This

103. [1]) Only when the injured party would happen to be a citizen of the same country to which the aircraft belonged, could application of the national law of both parties be considered. In the cases in which the courts have done so, this national law generally coincided, however, with the lex fori. Cf. Cass. (**Belgium**) 26.11.1908 .Pas. 1909 1.25; Højesterett (**Norway**) 22.10.1921 N.R. 1921, 751 and 25.9.1923 N.R. 1923 II 58; **Canada**: *Assad* v. *Latendresse* 79 Que. S.C. 286 (1941) but comp. *McLean* v. *Pettigrew*, S.C.R. 62 (1945) 2 DLR 65 with note Falconbridge; Hof 's-Hertogenbosch (**Netherlands**) N.J. 1933, 361. See also the **German** Decree of 7.12.1942, Reichsgesetzblatt I, 706, and Art. 12 (2) of the Brussels Maritime Collisions Convention of 1910. Even in such situations the majority of courts on the European Continent and in the U.S.A. seem to have applied the *lex loci delicti*, rather than the law of the common nationality or domicile of the parties (being also *lex fori*). See RG (**Germany**) 14.6.

is not true insofar as the Rome Convention of 1933 and the Warsaw Convention are concerned. Article 16 of the former provides for two competent courts (place of accident and domicile of defendant), and Article 28 of the latter allows for the choice among three *fora* (place where contract concluded, place of destination and country where carrier has his domicile or principal place of business).

§ 1. REMOTENESS OR UNFORESEEABILITY OF DAMAGES

104. Only the Rome Convention of 1952 contains a provision dealing with remoteness of damages. Article 1 (1) states that 'there shall be no right to compensation if the damage is not a direct consequence of the incident giving rise thereto' [1]). The provision is the result of long discussions, some delegates thinking that the matter could be better left to the common sense of the courts, others feeling that without some express limitation courts might feel bound to allow recovery with respect to the

1915, Leipziger Zeitung für das Recht 1915, Kol. 1443, nr. 16 (motor accident in Austria, both parties domiciled in Germany); *Oberste Gerichtshof* (**Austria**) 2.11.1910 G.I.U.n.F. 5219 (accident of Austrian train in Bavaria); *Hof 's-Gravenhage* (**Netherlands**) 28.12.1934, N.J. 1937, No. 108 (collision of two Dutch ships in Argentine waters); *K.M.'s Dom* (**Sweden**) 20.9.1933 Nytt jur. Arkif 1933,365, Zts. Rabel 1933, 931 (motoraccident of two Swedish motorcars in Norway); *Smith* v. *Condry*, (**USA**) 42 U.S. (1 How.) 28 (collision of two American ships in British waters);

104. [1]) It is to be observed that the operator has the burden of proof that the damage is only an indirect consequence of the incident. Since some courts are reluctant to accept proof of direct causation, the question of burden of proof may be of vital importance, e.g. in case of injuries resulting in death, when the carrier would allege intervening negligence in the medical treatment. Cf. on the reluctance of **French** Courts: A. Joly, *Essai sur la distinction du préjudice direct et du préjudice indirect. Caen*, 1939, pp. 310. sq. On medical error *as novus actus interveniens* see *Hogan* v. *Bentinck West Hartley Colleries Ltd.* [1948] 1 All. E.R. 129 (Note in 64 L.Q.R. 1948, 163), where the Court of Appeal felt bound to its earlier decision ruling medical errors to break the line of causation, contrary to the view accepted by the **American** Courts (Prosser (1941), p. 362), and by the **German** *Reichsgericht* 29.11.1909, RGZ. 72, 219, and 3.6.1921 RGZ 102, 130.

In the Rome Convention of 1933 the plaintiff needs not even to prove causal relation, but only that the damage 'provient de l'aéronef' (a proposal to have this changed into 'caused by the aircraft', failed). It will be up to the operator to prove that there was no causal relation (whatever the applicable national law may consider necessary for the existence of sufficient causal relation) between the damage and the incident. Cf. H. Oppikofer in 3 Z.L. (1933) 211, at 222. An interesting parallel of this allocation of the burden of proof can be found in connection with the quasi-absolute liability under Article 1384 (1) of the French Civil Code as construed by the Courts: the plaintiff has only to prove that the object of which defendant had custody played a part in the realization of the damage ('qu'elle est intervenue dans sa réalisation'), in order to make the defendant liable unless – apart from some other defences – he proves that the object played only a '*passive*' part. See Cass. civ. 23.1.1945 S. 1946. 1.57 with long annotation by P. Hébraud; cf. Ch. Blaevoet in J.C.P. 1946 I, 560.

most remote consequences [2]). It would be optimistic to think that the express restriction to direct consequences will greatly facilitate the task of the courts. A similar limitation is accepted by the majority of legal systems both common law and civil law, with varying results [3]). In fact, it is suggested that the circumstances in every case, even where logically they would have nothing to do with causal relation, may often be of greater importance in leading the courts to their final decisions than the wording of the principle of causality, whether it has been phrased in terms of directness, 'proximateness', 'natural or probable consequences' or 'foreseeability'. For the purpose of this study it is not necessary, however, to go into this complicated problem which seems to be one of the 'attractive nuisances' of most legal systems, nor into the related problem posed by the 'duty-concept' of the common law and the analogous concepts of some continental countries [4]).

---

[2]) Montreal Session (1950) pp. 64–65, 168–170, Mexico Session (1951) pp. 143–145, R.C. 1952, I, pp. 19–25.

[3]) Some extreme cases: *Bracket* v. *Bellows Falls Hydro. Electric Corp.* 175 A. 822 (S. Crt. N.H. 1934): Defendant, by damming a river had caused a raise of water on the land of plaintiff. The resulting pools attracted muskrats, who built their dens underground. When mowing his land plaintiff's horse tumbled in such a hole and threw plaintiff from the mowing machine, by which plaintiff was injured. He was entitled to recovery since his fall was considered a direct consequence of the flooding of plaintiff's ground. In the case of *Rasmussen Adm'x* v. *Benson.* 275 N.W. 674 (Neb. 1937), aff'd on rehearing 280 N.W. 890 (1938) defendant negligently and in violation of a statute sold to plaintiff's intestate a sack of unlabeled poisoned bran. This he innocently fed to his livestock causing their death as well as the loss of his laboriously built up dairy business. The consequent mental shock produced a decompensation of his heart which resulted in his death. The claim of his wife was granted.

The **French** case of Cass. civ. 9.12.1902. S.1903.1.95 would seem to stretch the notion of causal relation very far: a schoolgirl who used to pass a railway crossing just after a train had passed, was injured by an irregular train which was delayed of 5 minutes. She was allowed to recover damages because, 'without the delay the accident would not have happened'. The Court, apparently required here only that the negligence was a *conditio sine qua non.*

[4]) Prof. Winfield has expressed the view (34 Col. L. Rev. (1934) 41, at 58) that 'there is no trace in the modern Continental systems' of the Anglosaxon duty-concept. See also Prosser (1941), p. 179. It is submitted that this is too general a statement, as a similar notion is known and accepted by the courts in the **Netherlands** (cf. i.a. Wolfsbergen (1946) pp. 93 sq.), and to a certain extent also in **German** and **Austrian** law (cf. E.Rabel in *Deutsche Landesreferate zum Int. Kongress für Rechtsvergleichung im Haag* 1932, Berlin–Leipzig, 1932, pp. 11 sq. at 16).

The question could be raised whether the use of the word 'any' in Article 1 of the Rome Convention of 1952 ('Any person who suffers damage') precludes application of the duty principle. It is felt that this would be too litteral an interpretation of the Article. There can be no doubt that the word 'any' was used without any such intention. It is interesting to note that the Spanish text of the Convention simply speaks of '*La persona* que sufra daños.'

105. One of the curious instances of parallel development of the law in common law and civil law countries is offered by the rule for recoverable damages for breach of contract. Both common law and civil law countries seem to have accepted fairly generally the principle that in contracts only those damages can be recovered which were foreseeable or were in the contemplation of the parties at the time the contract was concluded [1]). What is curious is not so much the similarity in legal development, as the fact that the principle has been criticized in both systems [2]). In its general form the principle has its most frequent application to cases of delay. But the generally accepted limitation of damages in case of loss of goods to the market value at the place of destination [3]) is probably also to be considered an application of the idea that only foreseeable damages are to be recovered.

106. Of special interest to our problem is the application which the principle has received in some civil law countries with respect to declaration of value by shippers of goods or by passengers with respect to baggage. French courts have held that shippers should not recover more damages for loss of a shipment than the value declared by them when shipping the goods, even when the declaration of value was made for customs purpose only [1]). The basis for such a limitation is found in Article 1150 of the Civil Code which states the principle that in case of breach of contract only the damages foreseeable when the contract was

---

105. [1]) **England**: *Hadley* v. *Baxendale*, 1854, 9 Ex. 341; for **U.S.A.** cf. T. McCormick, On Damages, St. Paul, 1935, Ch. 22; **France**: Art. 1150 Cod. civ.; **Netherlands**: Art. 1283 B.W. (Civil Code); **Italy**: Art. 1225 Cod. civ.: **Roman-Dutch** law (S. Africa): G.A. Mulligan in 71 S. Afr. Law J. (1954) 44 sq. But **German** law does not limit contractual liability to foreseeable damages, see §§ 249 and 252 BGB, and comp. also **Swiss** Code of Oblig. Art. 99 in connection with Art. 43.

[2]) For **England** see Mayne (1946) p. 10. For **France** see i.a. Planiol–Ripert (1947) II, No. 749; Mazeaud (1950) III. No. 2391. For **Italy** cf. A. de Cupis (1946) p. 146. For the **Netherlands** see Losecaat Vermeer (1939) p. 211.

[3]) See No. 66 (6).

106. [1]) Cass. civ. 17.5.1892. S. 1893.1.94. See also Cass Civ. com. 2.12.1947. G.P. 1948.1.84 in which case the court reversed the lower court's decision allowing full damages (1.500 fr.), notwithstanding the fact that the goods had been carried under the tariff, applicable only to goods not exceeding 200 fr. The Lower Court had followed the principle that limitation of liability to a ridiculously low sum amounts to a full exemption forbidden by Art. 102 Code com. Recognizing the validity of that principle, the *Cour de Cassation* held, however, that that did not prevent parties from agreeing in advance on the value of the goods and being bound thereby.

made may be claimed [2]). Since the Warsaw Convention does not state any rule as to remoteness of damages or foreseeability, it must be assumed that these questions are governed by national law. It is believed, therefore, that Article 1150 of the French Civil Code will generally apply to claims brought under the Warsaw Convention, whenever French law would be applicable. If this is true, the question arises whether Article 22 of the Convention would allow the courts to exclude compensation beyond the declared value, even if such value were below the limit fixed in Article 22. It is suggested that this question must be answered by interpretation of the relevant part of Article 22, rather than by some construction of Article 1150 of the Code. Whenever the Convention offers a guidance, that guidance should be followed rather than that of any national law in order to safeguard the uniformity aimed at by the Convention. The significance of Article 22 with respect to declaration of value will be discussed in another chapter [3]).

107. Closely related to the question of declaration of value in connection with foreseeability of damages is the question of whether and when, in the absence of any declared value, the value of a piece of baggage or cargo can be considered to be such as could not reasonably be expected by the carrier [1]). As long as the value remains below the limits established for registered baggage or cargo, it would be difficult to hold so. These limits have been fixed on the basis of the average value of goods carried at the time the Convention was drafted [2]). A value below these limits could never be something unforeseeable for the carrier. But the situation is somewhat different with respect to the special limit

106. [2]) The principle is not applied to delictual liability, and since the borderline between contractual and delictual liability is far from clear, especially in French law, the consequences of the principle can easily be evaded. Cf. Cass. civ. 21.10.1946. Sem. jur. 1946.2.4348, note P.L.P., in which case the *Cour de Cassation* reversed the lower court's decision which had held a janitor's liability, for loss of a package checked by him, limited to the declared value of fr. 1,000, whereas the real value was fr. 30,000. The *Cour de Cassation* assumed here delictual liability to which Art. 1150 does not apply.

[3]) See Nos. 274 sq.

107. [1]) Cass. req. 2.1.1912. D. 1912.1.223 and other decisions in Planiol-Ripert (1947) II, No. 747.

[2]) Cf. Goedhuis (1933) p. 210: After the carriers had proven that the average value of goods carried amounted to 130 french francs per kilogram, the limit was lowered from 500 french francs to 250.

of 5.000 gold francs for the personal effects which the passenger takes charge of himself. If a passenger were to give his raincoat to the stewardess in the plane and it appeared afterwards that he left something valuable in the pocket so that his loss amounted to $ 300 (i.e. less than 5.000 gold francs or 1240 guilders or $ 350), it would not be so unreasonable for the carrier to claim that such damage was unforeseeable [3]).

108. In such cases there may often be a possibility of invoking the plaintiff's contributory negligence [1]). In fact, the relation between the problem of causality and that of contributory negligence is a very close one, and frequently the latter is phrased in terms of the former, especially at common law [2]). In those countries, however, where the defence of contributory negligence is not considered a complete bar to recovery by the plaintiff, but only a factor reducing the damages [3]), it is important, at

---

[3]) Comp. *Gerechtshof* (Court of Appeal) 's-Gravenhage, 5.12.1946 N.J. 1947, No. 476 concerning the liability for valuable things left in a dressing-room.

108. [1]) Cf. *Oberste Gerichtshof Britische Zone* (Cologne) 22.9.1950, Transport 1951, p. 4449· a passenger who, in the confused postwar years, had entrusted baggage containing exceptionally valuable goods to the railway, held guilty of contributory negligence.

[2]) Winfield (1950) pp. 419/20; F. H. Bohlen, *Contributory Negligence*, 21 Harv. L. Rev. (1908) 233, at 234 sq.; L. Green, *Contributory Negligence and Proximate Cause*, 6 N. Car. L. Rev. (1927) 1. See also Holdsworth, *History of the Common Law*. VIII (2d ed.) 460 sq. Also in the civil law countries the issue of causality has been of great influence in the development of the rule as to the influence of plaintiff's negligence on his right to recovery. But as the principle of distribution of loss between plaintiff and defendant (instead of complete denial of plaintiff's claim) was developed by the courts of most civil law countries at an earlier date, the decline of the causality aspect also came earlier here, though the relation between the two issues could not fail to appear from time to time, especially in the 'last clear chance' cases. That the adoption of the distribution of loss principle has not completely severed the relation with the causality issue is well illustrated by the following consideration of the *Cour de Cassation* of **Belgium** (decision of 4.1.1926, Pas. I, 151) :'If the causal relation between the act of the victim and the damage is not complete, the negligence of the party suffering the damage does not exclude the liability of the negligent person (i.e. defendant)'. Cf. also Planiol-Ripert (1947) II No. 1027: 'il ne s'agit plus ici d'une question d'imputabilité de la faute, mais d'une question de la causalité'.

[3]) This is true for all or nearly all civil law countries, the Scandinavian countries, and those common law countries which have abolished the common law rule as to contributory negligence by statute, such as the United Kingdom, the provinces of Canada, and a few states of the U.S.A. (Wisconsin, Nebraska, Mississippi) as well as the American federal legislator in a number of statutes.

In some common law jurisdictions the courts have found the courage, under the impact of social necessities, to arrive at the same result without statute. This seems to be the case in Georgia (cf. i.a. *Georgia Ry. and Banking Co.* v. *Auchinachie* (1914) 83 S.E. 127, 131). See also the recent **South-African** decision in *Union and National* least theoretically, to decide separately the two questions of causal relation and contributory negligence. For, to the extent that there does not exist a sufficient causal connection between the negligence (or other liability-creating fact) and the damages, the carrier will not be liable at all for such damages or such part of the damages, whereas the carrier would remain partly liable for those damages caused by him, of which the plaintiff's negligence would have been a contributory cause.

109. Before entering into a general discussion of the influence of contributory negligence, something should be said on the problem of unforeseeability of damages in connection with loss of registered baggage or cargo when the carrier is not allowed to invoke Article 22 because of some omission in the baggage check or air waybill [1]. There can be no doubt that even in those cases the requirements as to sufficient causal relation remain applicable [2]. It is submitted that if the applicable law were to reject liability for unforeseeable damages and were to consider unforeseeable the damage arising from the loss of exceptionally valuable goods – assuming that the carrier had not been informed about the value – such 'unforeseeable' damages could not be claimed under the Convention, even though the limits of Article 22 could not be invoked (pursuant to Articles 4 or 9) [3].

Assurance Co. of S. Africa Ltd v. *Mate*, 1952 (2) S.A. 109 (N) (commented on in 69 S.A.L.J. (1952) 263).

Moreover, it is well known that, where the courts do not have that courage, the juries very often dò. Cf. for the **U.S.A.** the often cited statement by Holt J. in *Haeg* v. *Sprague, Warner and Co.* (1938) 202 Minn. 425, 430, 281 N.W. 261, and J. N. Ulman, *A Judge Takes the Stand*, New York, 1933 pp. 31 sq. and 65/66; for **England**; Lord Chancellor Sankey in the House of Lords (1932), 84 Hansard (Lords), 554; for **Australia** and **New Zealand**: O. C. Mazengarb, *The Law Relating to Negligence on the Highway*, Wellington, 1942, pp. 180/181.

109. [1]) The problem has less importance, at least in most civil law countries, as far as the cases of '*dol*' or '*faute lourde*' (wilful misconduct) are concerned, since the limitation to foreseeable damages does not apply to damages caused by '*dol*' or '*faute lourde*'. See the Code provisions mentioned in No. 105 (1). But comp. note 3 infra.

[2]) Whatever may be the significance of the sanctions provided in Articles 3, 4 and 9 of the Convention. See on that problem Nos. 221 sq.

[3]) In the February 1950 Draft of the Reporter Major K. M. Beaumont a provision was contained which would limit the liability of goods valuing more than 2500 gold francs per kilogram to the normal limit of 250 gold francs per kilogram *even in case of wilful misconduct*, unless the value would have been declared (article 8, para. 8). This exception to the unlimited liability in case of wilful misconduct was omitted by the 'Warsaw' Subcommittee in Jan. 1952, after the notion of wilful misconduct had been narrowed down.

Can the same be said for a declared value, which afterwards were to appear to be less than the actual value? Since Article 22 (2) expressly deals with the possibility of a declaration of value, the question must be answered by interpretation of that Article rather than by applying some rule of a municipal law concerning remoteness or unforeseeability of damages. The construction of Article 22 (2) will be discussed in Chapter VII.

§ 2. CONTRIBUTORY NEGLIGENCE

110. The Warsaw and the two Rome Conventions all contain provisions dealing with the influence of the plaintiff's negligence on his right to recovery. But the provisions differ greatly and reveal an interesting development which is in conformity with the general development of the law on this question [1]). Whereas Article 21 refers to the *lex fori* for deciding whether the plaintiff's negligence shall be a complete bar to this recovery or shall only result in a mitigation of damages, Article 3 of the Convention of 1933 has omitted the reference to the *lex fori*, thereby leaving the choice of law (which in most cases [2]) would be the *lex loci delicti*) to the court seized of the claim. The Rome Conference of 1952 finally took the natural step of adopting the principle of mitigation of damages without any reference to national laws [3]).

It is not the place here to enter into a discussion of the numerous problems which can arise in the event of negligence or other faults [4]) on the part of the plaintiff. The only point to be consid-

---

110. [1]) See No. 108 (3).

[2]) English law is the notable exception. See i.a. Cheshire, *Private International Law, 4th ed.*, Oxford, 1952, pp. 257 sq. and M. Hancock, *Torts in the Conflict of Laws*, Ann Arbor, 1942, pp. 1 sq. A general comparative survey in E. Rabel, *Conflicts of Laws*, Ann Arbor, 1947, II, 247 sq., C. W. Dubbink, *De onrechtmatige daad in het Nederlandse internationale privaatrecht*, 's-Gravenhage, 1947, and the present author in Rechtsgeleerd Magazijn Themis, 1949, pp. 3 sq., especially 37 sq.

[3]) Article 6 of the 1952 Convention, in a rather detailed way, also provides for the imputation of the negligence of plaintiff's servants or agents, or of the person killed.

[4]) The Warsaw Convention and the Rome Convention 1933 use the general French word 'faute' which includes both negligent and intentional acts. The same word is used in the official French text of the Rome Convention 1952 (the Spanish text has 'culpa'). But where the English text of the latter correctly speaks of 'negligence or other wrongful act or omission', the English translation of the Warsaw Convention in the Carriage by Air Act 1932 has merely 'negligence' for the French 'faute', which is too narrow. It is believed, however, that no court would reject a carrier's defence based on an intentional wrongful act because that would not be negligence. Generally, the right to recovery will be entirely denied to a plaintiff who has been guilty of

ered is that of the relationship between the provisions dealing with the influence of the plaintiff's negligence on the amount of damages, and the provisions which set a ceiling to the carrier's or operator's liability.

Which of these provisions should be applied first and which last? Or to put it otherwise, do the limitation provisions of the respective Conventions apply to the operator's or carrier's liability after taking into account the plaintiff's contributory negligence, or is the reduction of damages because of contributory negligence to be made on the basis of the amounts established by the limitation provisions?

The answer is not difficult. Both the rationale of the limitation provisions enabling the operator or carrier to calculate in advance the extent of his risk, and the system of the Conventions, make it clear beyond doubt that the limits are to be applied only after all the facts which determine the existence and the extent of the liability have been established [5]). In all three conventions the limitation provisions, therefore, come at the end of the substantial rules for the carrier's or operator's liability, after the various defences including the defence of plaintiff's own negligence.

The alternative solution, moreover, would lead to impossible consequences in the case of one total limit applying to a number of claims, which is a frequent situation under both the Warsaw Convention and the Rome Conventions. Under the Warsaw Convention the carrier's liability for the death of a passenger is limited to 125,000, irrespective of how many actions are brought in connection with the death. Suppose the accident were found to have been 50% due to the negligence of the passenger and suppose there were two claimants. The procedure would be that the full damages of each claimant would first be established in order to fix the share of each in the limit. If A were thus entitled to $\frac{1}{2}$ of the limit, the final compensation would be $\frac{1}{4}$ of the limit

wilful misconduct or 'dol', either because the necessary causal relation between defendant's negligence and the damage is then said to be lacking, or because the less serious fault of the defendant is said to have been 'absorbed' by the wilful misconduct of plaintiff, or else for the reason that the plaintiff is said to have assumed the risk of the damage.

110. [5]) Nevertheless, some delegates at the Madrid Session of the Legal Committee of ICAO (September 1951) were more hesitant about the problem. They may have been influenced by the fact that the provision on contributory negligence in the draft then discussed came after the article on limitation of liability.

after mitigation for the passenger's contributory negligence. That would leave $\frac{3}{4}$ for the other claimant, assuming he would sue after the other had received $\frac{1}{4}$ of the limit. The remaining $\frac{3}{4}$, however, would have to be halved because of the passenger's contributory negligence, which would make B's share $\frac{3}{8}$! The situation would become still more inextricable if there were contributory negligence on the side of only one claimant, which does not frequently occur in passenger cases, but may easily happen in cases of damages to the surface.

The question does not seem to have created serious doubt in respect to maritime cases, where both the principle of distribution of loss in case of contributory negligence and that of the limitation of liability had developed at a much earlier date [6]).

§ 3. EFFECT OF CONVENTIONAL LIMITS ON LOWER LIMITS IN APPLICABLE MUNICIPAL LAWS

111. There can, of course, be no doubt that the Conventions set aside all municipal laws regulating the subject matter covered by the Conventions. Any limitation of the air carrier's or operator's liability which might be provided by national legislations are overruled by the limitation provisions of the Conventions, whether the national limits are higher or lower than the limits of the Conventions. A real problem arises only when the Conventions have left it to the national laws to determine the measure of damages up to the limits established by them. This is especially true of damages for death or personal injuries.

Article 24 (2) of the Warsaw Convention expressly provides that the Convention does not prejudice the question 'who are the persons who have the right to bring suit and what are their respective rights'. Though the two Rome Conventions do not contain such specific language, it is certain that the matter of measure of damages for death or injuries was intended to be left to the

110. [6]) It is submitted that the English decision in *Kelly* v. *Stockport Corporation* [1947] 1 All E.R. 893, referred to in this connection by Shawcross and Beaumont (1951) No. 390 note (e), has no application to the subject problem. That case involved the entirely different question of whether, for the purpose of determining the jurisdiction of a country court to take cognizance of a claim, the amount of the claim as brought by plaintiff should be taken into account, or the amount of the liability after mitigation of the damages under the Law Reform (Contributory Negligence) Act, 1945. The lower court had adopted the first solution, which decision was reversed on appeal. Clearly the rationale for limiting a lower court's jurisdiction to claims not exceeding £ 200 has nothing to do with the rationale for limiting a carrier's or operator's liability.

applicable law. Attempts to insert a conflict of laws rule into these Conventions failed twice, so that even the question as to which law shall apply is governed by municipal law [1]).

112. The criteria determining the categories of recoverable damages and the measure of damages vary greatly from country to country. A number of laws allow compensation for grief, others do not [1]). In most countries funeral expenses may be recovered, in some they cannot [2]). Often the right to compensation is given to the decedent's estate, more often the next of kin have an independent right for damages which they themselves have suffered in the form of loss of support from the deceased [3]). The majority forbid the deduction of insurance moneys, collected as a consequence of the death, from the compensation, but some do deduct such amounts [4]). On the other hand, any benefits by

---

111. [1]) Both times it was a Dutch proposal to insert a conflict of laws rule referring to the *lex loci delicti*. Cf. R.C. 1933, I, pp. 71 sq., and Mexico Session (1951), p. 190.

112. [1]) The majority of states would seem to allow compensation for the grief suffered by the next of kin, though sometimes this right is limited to cases involving a criminal act (**Argentina, Italy, Mexico**), but no such damages are granted in **England**, the great majority of states of the **U.S.A.** (except Florida, Louisiana, Virginia and West-Virginia), **Denmark, Germany, Hungary, Netherlands** and the **U.S.S.R.**

[2]) Funeral expenses are not recoverable in the **Netherlands** and a minority of the states of the **U.S.A.** (and in **England** before the Law Reform (Miscellaneous Provisions) Act, 1934).

[3]) An action is given to the estate in those states of the **U.S.A.** where the claim is based on survival Statutes; in nearly all these states, howevei, there are also Death Statutes giving an independent action to the next of kin.

Since the Law Reform (Miscellaneous Provisions) Act, 1934 has provided for the survival of the deceased's rights, a similar situation exists in **England.** Though the language of Sec. 1 (5) of the Act might seem to allow cumulation of damages under this Act and the Fatal Accident Acts, as well as the Carriage by Air Act, 1932, it has been held that the Act does not lead to duplication of damages. *Rose* v. *Ford* [1937] A.C. 826, at 835 and 852. With respect to the other problem created by the Law Reform Act of 1934, viz. whether any damages recovered under that act would come in addition to thc 125.000 gold francs, which could be claimed under the Carriage by Air Act, 1932, it has been suggested (Shawcross and Beaumont (1951) No. 408, note (f)) that 'it is unlikely that the legislature intended to enlarge, by such a side-wind, the carrier's liability in England under an International Convention to which it had previously given full statutory effect'. Similarly McNair (1953) p. 215.

In many, if not most, **civil law countries** the action is given to the next of kin for the loss of support suffered by them, but often there exists some confusion with the courts as to whether the next of kin recover in their quality of heirs or independently. See also No. 81 (1).

[4]) Examples of the latter are offered by **India**, and to a certain extent by the **Netherlands.** In **England** it seems doubtful whether insurance moneys should not be taken into account with respect to death claims arising under the Carriage by Air Act, 1932: see Shawcross and Beaumont (1951) No. 408 (c) and McNair (1953), p. 216.

inheritance are generally deducted, but not always [5]. Sometimes the financial circumstances of both parties have to be taken into account [6] and in at least one country damages are only allowed in the event that the claimant would, due to the loss of support, no longer be able to maintain the same standard of living [7].

113. None of these variations, however, offer a serious problem, as far as the limitations of liabilities of the private air law conventions are concerned [1]. The real difficulty starts where the applicable national law provides for a limited amount of compensation for death or injuries. This is provided by the statutes of a number of American States in regard to death claims [2], and in the Federal District of Mexico the Civil Code contains since 1940 a general reference to the Workmen's Compensation Act for the amounts of compensation to be recovered in case of claims for death or injuries [3].

Can it be said that such limitation provisions in national laws are overruled by the limits contained in the Warsaw Convention (125,000 gold francs) and the two Rome Conventions (200,000 and 500,000 gold francs respectively)? As far as the national limitation specifically applies to liabilities arising from aviation accidents there can be no doubt that they are overruled [4]. But what if the limitation applies generally to all cases of wrongful death or injuries such as is the case in the above mentioned states? The rationale of such a limitation in the USA would seem to be, to keep the natural generosity of juries within reasonable bounds [5]. A similar motive influenced the Legal Committee of ICAO to adopt the special limit per person killed

---

112. [5]) Benefits from inheritance are not taken into account e.g. in **Germany** and **New-Zealand.**

[6]) See the comparative study of A. E. Salas, *Indemnización debida a la victima de un acto ilicito.* 20 Revista Colegio de Abogados de Buenos Aires (1942) 3, 9 sq.

[7]) In the **Netherlands** under Art. 1406 of the Civil Code as construed by the *Hoge Raad.*

113. [1]) For a discussion of the difficulties which may arise in distributing the amount of the limit under the various claimants see Chapter VIII.

[2]) For the States having a limitation of liability see No. 6 (1).

[3]) Art. 1915 (as amended in 1940) of the *Código Civil del Districto Federal,* which refers to the *Ley Federal del Trabajo.*

[4]) But see also No. 159 on the effect of the conversion clause of the Warsaw Convention (Art. 22 (4)) and the Rome Convention 1933 (Art. 19).

[5]) Cf. Prosser (1941), p. 965.

or injured in the new Rome Convention [6]), which is an argument for holding that the latter limit prevails over any lower limits in municipal law. That this would be the effect of incorporating a special limit in the Convention was clearly the general understanding at the Diplomatic Conference of 1952 [7]). The argument has not the same force when applied to the Warsaw Convention since the main motive for the limitation of liability for death or injuries in that Convention was to enable the carrier to calculate the extent of his risks in advance, and to protect a new industry [8]). As far as the Rome Conventions are concerned, these two aims have been taken care of by the total limit per aircraft, rather than by the limit per person killed or injured.

114. It has been held by some American courts that the Warsaw Convention does not itself create an action for death or injuries, but only determines under what conditions and within what limits actions may be brought [1]). In that view there would be no other action than the one given by the applicable municipal law, subject to the conditions and limitations of the Convention. In the Wyman Case [2]) the court said: 'No new substantial rights were created by the Warsaw Convention and all the rules there laid down are well within the framework of the existing legal rights and remedies [...] The right to any recovery [...] must depend on some statute'. The point was elaborated by the district court of New York in the recent Komlos Case [3]) in the following words: 'The cause of action is created by the *lex loci*. The conditions which are attached thereto are created by the Warsaw Convention [...] the Warsaw Convention does not create a right of action for wrongful death...' and 'The effect of Article 17 of the Warsaw Convention seems to be this: If the decedent meets his death in the course of an "international transportation" [...], then if the place of the accident is within a nation that has

113. [6]) Cf. minutes of Mexico Session (1952), p. 132, R.C. 1952, I, pp. 122, 144 and 148.

[7]) R.C. 1952, I, pp. 149, 151 etc.

[8]) See Chapter I.

114. [1]) *Choy Adm'r* v. *P.A.A.* 1942 U.S.Av.R. 93; *Wyman and Bartlett* v. *P.A.A.* 43 N.Y.S. (2d) 420, 1943 U.S.Av.R. 1; *Komlos Adm'x* v. *Comp. Nat. Air France, Royal Indemnity Co.* v. *Same*, 1952 U.S. & C.Av.R. 310, 319 sq.

[2]) 1943 U.S.Av.R. 1, at 4 (cf. previous note).

[3]) 1952 U.S. & C.Av.R. 310, at 319 and 321.

not adhered to the Warsaw Convention and has its own Statute for wrongful death actions, the conditions and limits of the Convention [including Article 24 (2)] would nevertheless be applied in a suit for wrongful death in a forum specified as a proper forum under Article 28 of the Convention. But if the law of the place of accident does not provide for a right of action for wrongful death, the forum would apply Article 17 of the Convention, and under those circumstances it might be said that Article 17 created the right of action for wrongful death'.

The defendant in the Komlos Case had relied on the ruling in *Salamon* v. *K.L.M.* [4]) to the effect that the Warsaw Convention did create a cause of action for injury or death of a passenger 'in addition to comprehensively covering such questions as limitation of liability, the effect of contributory negligence etc....' If the holding in the Komlos Case, following the Choy and the Wyman Cases, is correct (so that the cause of action would be created by local law, and only the conditions which are attached thereto by the Warsaw Convention), then a local action for a limited amount could probably not be supplemented by the Convention.

The argument would apply especially to those countries where the limit is provided in the same statute which creates the right of action for wrongful death. This situation exists in the American States which grant only limited recovery for death. When, however, the national law bases the right of compensation for death or injuries on the general principles of liability, but fixes certain limits for these specific classes of damages, there is no question of supplementing the action granted by the national law, but only of replacing the limits which it has set [5]).

115. It is believed that no general rule can be established, but that the effect of the limits of the Convention on any limits contained in applicable national law must be determined separately for each national law, taking into account the following considerations:

(a) that in view of the similar rationale of the individual limits

114. [4]) *Salamon* v. *K.L.M. Royal Dutch Airlines* 1951 U.S.Av.R. 378.

[5]) This would seem the case with the limits provided by the Mexican Civil Code. See No. 113.

of the Rome Conventions, the national limits will have to recede sooner to these conventional limits, than to the limits of the Warsaw Convention;

(b) that where the national legislator has set the limit in the same statute from which the action itself arises, there is a stronger reason for upholding the national limit, notwithstanding any higher limit in the Convention, than where the national law bases the action on its general principles of liability and has only established limits for certain classes of damages such as death or injuries.

To the consideration under (a) the objection could be raised that especially in the situations envisaged by the Rome Conventions there is little reason to offer more protection to the victims on the surface, than they would enjoy under their local law. Though the argument seems sound in principle, it is considerably weakened by the fact that the drafters of both Conventions intended to unify not only the defences of the operator but also the protection of the persons on the surface. A proposal made at Mexico to offer the operator in addition to the defences provided by the Convention those granted by the national law of the state where the accident occurred was rejected by an overwhelming majority [1]).

From a practical point of view it is worthwhile observing that the question will not easily arise under the Warsaw Convention, since the national limits of liability will seldom be lower than those provided by Article 22 of the Convention [2]).

116. Special mention should be made of the limitation of liability with respect to handbaggage which remains in the custody of the carrier, under Article 22 (3) of the Warsaw Convention. The Convention provides a limit of liability without stating itself the principles of liability. In view of this it has been defended in one of the best commentaries on the Convention, that local law may provide a lower limit than the 5,000 gold francs limit of Article

115. [1]) Mexico Session (1951), p. 170.

[2]) The only American State which still has a lower limit in its Death Statute seems to be Colorado. The problem could also arise in connection with the Mexican limits as to injuries.

22, in which case that lower limit would apply [1]. Though there is a certain logic in holding the national legislator authorized to fix a lower limit of liability than that of the Convention, in view of the fact that he may even fully exclude the carrier's liability for handbaggage, it is believed that the general purpose of unification set by the Convention outweighs the theoretical lack of logic in setting aside a local limit of liability but upholding local exclusions of liability. A stronger argument could be built upon the rationale of including a limit concerning handbaggage in Article 22. That limit was adopted in order that the carrier would be able to calculate in advance the maximum of his risks, thus closing a gap which was left by the limitation of liability for death, wounding or delay of passengers and for loss, damage or delay of registered baggage and goods [2].

116. [1] Koffka (1937) p. 330.
[2] 3d Session CITEJA (Madrid, 1928) p. 52.

CHAPTER IV

PERSONS PROTECTED BY THE LIMITATION PROVISIONS

117. In Chapter II we have discussed against whom and with respect to what damages the limitation provisions of the air law conventions may be invoked. It now remains to be studied who may invoke the limits.

When discussing recourse claims against carriers or operators [1]) it was pointed out that besides the carrier or operator a number of persons may be held liable for damages governed by the Conventions. The question then arises whether their liability will be limited by the provisions which limit the carrier's and operator's liability. The answer to this question is not only important to the persons themselves, but will, in many cases, also affect the position of the carrier or operator, even if one accepts the view that the latter may invoke the limitation provisions with respect to recourse actions exercised against them. For often there will exist a social or economic necessity for the carrier or operator to assume the full burden of the original claim. There is a strong movement among airline pilots to require of their employers that they either indemnify them against any claims which might arise from the performance of their functions, or else take out insurance to cover their personal liability [2]). In both cases it would be the carrier who would eventually have to carry the burden of the liability of the pilots. The same is true in the event that an indemnity agreement is required by some local company taking care of the ground-handling of the carrier's aircraft [3]). Indemnity agreements are also sometimes demanded by airport authorities [4]).

117. [1]) See Nos. 86 sq.

[2]) Cf. Resolution by IFALPA of 1950, ICAO Doc. A4—WP/154.

[3]) Cf. IATA Bulletin No. 16 (Dec. 1952) pp. 75–76: A Model Liability Clause for Groundservice Agreements Between Airlines.

[4]) Cf. No. 88 (2).

It could be argued that it is up to the carrier to sign or not to sign any indemnity agreement for the benefit of third persons who might become liable in connection with the operations of the carrier's aircraft. But then one loses sight of the fact that any claims arising from the performance of services rendered on behalf of the operation of aircraft are to be considered operational costs, whoever is the person primarily liable for such claims. And obviously the operational costs eventually have to be paid by the carrier or operator, unless the community is going to pay for them[5]).

§ 1. CARRIER AND OPERATOR

A. Warsaw Convention.

118. Before going into the question as to whether persons other than the carrier or operator are protected by the limits of the Convention, and if so who, it is desirable first to determine who should be considered carrier or operator in the sense of the Conventions, to whom there can be no doubt that the limitation provisions apply. The question has to be answered for each Convention separately.

The *Warsaw Convention* does not contain any definition of who is to be considered a 'carrier'. An attempt by the Brazilian Delegate at the Warsaw Conference to insert a definition, mainly to take care of the problems arising under charter agreements failed to receive support[1]), so that one now must distil the meaning of the word from the wording and system of the Convention itself. The main choice is between the following possibilities:

(a) carrier is he who has concluded in his own name a contract for the carriage of passengers or goods.

(b) carrier is he who actually performs the carriage governed by the Convention.

There are arguments and good authorities for both solutions though it would appear that the majority of authors prefer the first one[2]). As has been pointed out in an earlier chapter, the

117. [5]) This is the case where all aviation services would be offered free of charge by the community without an indemnity agreement being required.

118. [1]) W.C. p. 97. Cf. Goedhuis (1933) p. 93.

[2]) For the first solution: Goedhuis (1933) p. 94, Koffka (1937), p. 268, Van Houtte (1940) No. 77, Riese (1949) p. 406, Shawcross and Beaumont (1951) No. 362, note (a). For the second solution: Coquoz, (1938), p. 92, Litvine (1953) No. 180. Hesitating McNair (1953) pp. 278/79.

Convention clearly presupposes the existence of some contract of carriage [3]). There can be little doubt that the drafters, when speaking of the carrier, had in mind the person who made the contract of carriage. Especially the provisions dealing with the issuance of traffic documents give evidence of that intention [4]). Article 33, which allows the 'carrier' not to enter into a contract of carriage, could also be invoked in support of this view.

But it is not difficult to find provisions where the word 'carrier' would seem to refer rather to the person actually performing the carriage. The basic Article 20 makes the carrier liable only for his own acts and those of his 'préposés'. Now the word 'préposés' in French law is generally used in the sense of servants, at least of persons who are in a subordinate position as regards their principal ('commettant') [5]). When the party who concludes the contract of carriage is not the same as the party performing it, the persons by whose negligence an accident may happen or goods may get lost, will generally not be the servants of the contracting party but those of the performing party. Performance of the carriage rather than conclusion of the contract seems to have also been in the mind of those drafting Article 1 (3) and Article 30, which both speak of 'carriage to be performed by several successive air carriers' [6]).

Though it is probably fair to say that the framers of the Convention were mainly thinking of the normal situation in which the person contracting for the carriage of passengers or goods is also to perform that carriage, which makes it dangerous to draw upon their probable intentions, the weight of arguments seems to be on the side of those who hold that the person con-

---

118. [3]) See No. 50.

[4]) Cf. Goedhuis (1933) p. 94. But Article 4 which obliges the carrier to deliver a baggage check could as well be invoked for the contrary view, since this document will generally be delivered by the performing carrier, not by the party who merely concludes the contract of carriage without performing it.

[5]) According to Article 1384 (3) Code Civil the *commettant* is liable for the consequences of the negligence or other wrongful acts of his *préposés*, which is the French equivalent of the common law *respondeat superior* rule. In view of the confusion which exists in French law between contractual and delictual liability, the rule of 1384 (3) Cod. civ. or its terminology is often applied in cases of contractual liability, though it is evident that the class of persons for whom one is liable in the performance of contracts is not the same class as to which Art. 1384 (3) refers. See also No. 196 (3).

[6]) Similarly Litvine (1953) No. 180. Cf. also Artt. 2 (1), 34 and the Additional Protocol.

tracting for the carriage, and not the mere operator as such, is the carrier in the meaning of the Convention [7]).

119. The question of who is to be considered 'carrier' thus becomes closely related with the requirement of a contract of carriage for the application of the Convention. Though it is true that there should exist some contract of carriage under which the persons or goods concerned are being carried, it is not at all necessary that that contract be concluded between the carrier and the passenger or the owner of the goods. Whenever a person carries passengers or goods by air between points indicated in Article 1 of the Convention, pursuant to a contract concluded by him for the carriage of these passengers or these goods, such person is a 'carrier' in the sense of the Convention and is protected as such by the limits of Article 22. It is irrelevant whether the person suffering damages was also a party to the contract of carriage with the carrier from whom he claims compensation. This results from Article 24:

> '(1) In the cases contemplated by Articles 18 and 19 any action for damages, however founded, can only be brought subject to the conditions and limits set out in this Convention.
> '(2) In the cases contemplated by Article 17 the provisions of the preceding paragraph shall also apply, without prejudice to the questions as to who are the persons who have the right to bring suit and what are their respective rights'.

Any actions, 'however founded', are governed by the limitation provisions of the Convention. If the words were not already sufficiently clear themselves, we have the drafting history to confirm that whether the action is founded on the contract or is brought outside the contract as an action in tort, Article 22 will

---

118. [7]) The 'Warsaw' Subcommittee of the L.C. of I.C.A.O., adopted in its Draft a provision which would make both the contracting party and the operating party liable as carrier. Article 13 (a) of this draft provided: 'when carriage is performed by an aircraft operated by a person other than the one in whose name the agreement to carry was concluded, each of such persons shall be liable as a carrier in accordance with the provisions of this Convention'. The provision was not incorporated in the Draft Protocol established by the Legal Committee in its Rio de Janeiro Session of 1953. Though the solution appears to offer the most practical approach to the problem, it seems doubtful whether it can be defended under the present convention that 'carrier' includes both the contracting and the operating party. See also Madrid Session (1952) pp. 133/134.

apply to it [1]). It is to be observed that only with respect to the cases of death or injuries to passengers (i.e. those contemplated by Article 17) does the Article contain an express proviso to the effect that the Convention does not prejudice the question as to who is entitled to bring an action. This would seem to imply that with respect to loss or damage to baggage or goods, the framers of the Convention were of the opinion that only the persons envisaged by the Convention have a right to claim compensation [2]). As to loss, damage or delay of goods, the better view would seem to be that only the consignor or the consignee has a right of action [3]). With respect to loss, damage or delay of baggage, and delay of passengers, the person contemplated as entitled to an action for damages was no doubt the passenger, though especially in case of delay the person with whom the carrier contracted – assuming him to be other than the passenger – should also be considered a good plaintiff [4]).

It may be useful to examine, in the light of the foregoing observations, the most important situations in which the status of 'carrier' with respect to certain claims could be questioned. They are all cases in which the person claiming damages has no contract of carriage with the operator of the aircraft and is suing him in tort.

120. Probably the most important group of cases is that of the charter agreements. A charterer has concluded contracts of

119. [1]) 3d Session CITEJA (Madrid 1928) p. 55. See also No. 64 (1).

[2]) The C.I.M. does not contain an analogous provision to that of Article 24. Comp. for **German** law W. Heinze in 60 B.T.I. (1952), 69 sq., criticizing the decision of the *Oberste Gerichtshof* of Cologne 2.9.1950 (published ibidem, p. 80), which held a limitation of liability provided in German railroad law not extendable to delictual liability (under § 831 B.G.B.) for acts committed by railway personnel. Heinze points to older decisions of the *Reichsgericht* to the effect that the owner of goods, who is not at the same time the shipper, cannot sue the carrier outside the contract on the basis of tortious liability (RGZ 70, 174 and RGZ 77, 317). Comp. for **French** law F. Sauvage in 5 D.M.F. (1953) 607 sq., criticizing the decisions of the Cour de Cassation, according to which the action under the bill of lading can in principle only be exercised by the person mentioned on the bill of lading.

[3]) See No. 294.

[4]) The problems arising when the passenger is not the same person as the one who contracted with the carrier has received too little attention. Cf. Cleveringa (1946) pp. 502 sq. In case of an employee travelling on business for his employer any damage for delay will generally be suffered only by the employer. See also the **French** decisions mentioned by Sauvage in 5 D.M.F. (1953) 607, at 613, which held the employers of commercial travellers entitled to claim damages in case of loss of baggage containing samples.

carriage with a number of passengers or a group of passengers [1]), or with various shippers of goods, and charters from B (operator) an aircraft for the performance of this transportation. The aircraft crashes due to negligence of B's personnel (either crew or ground personnel), and the passengers or shippers, in order to avoid the Convention, bring an action in tort against B. Whether B will be entitled to invoke Article 22 against such action will depend upon whether he can be considered a carrier within the meaning of Article 22 with respect to such persons or goods. As has been stated before, this will only be the case if he has concluded a contract of carriage with respect to these persons or goods. Any contract by which he has undertaken to carry the persons or goods from one agreed point to another will be sufficient for this purpose. The fact that an entire aircraft is reserved for such carriage does not deprive the contract of its character of a contract of carriage, nor the operator of his status of carrier within the meaning of the Convention. Nor is it essential that the persons or goods to be carried be determined at the moment the contract is concluded. Even with the normal contracts of carriage it may easily happen that a shipper contracts for the transportation of goods which he has still to buy.

Consequently it may very well occur that two different persons have the status of carrier, and are, as such, entitled to the protection of Article 22, with respect to the same passengers or goods. If a travel agent organizing a trip from New York to Paris were to issue to his clients traffic documents mentioning himself as carrier whilst chartering an aircraft with crew for the performance of that transportation, both the charterer and the operator would be carrier in the sense of the Convention, at least of Article 22, because both would have concluded a contract of carriage for the transportation of these persons between agreed points. It is not even essential that the contract concluded by the operator be for carriage between the same points as those concluded by the charterer with his customers. It may be that such a deal would be contrary to some Government regulations [2]) or to

120. [1]) See literature in No. 53 (1).
[2]) Cf. e.g. Part 207 of the Economic Regulations of the U.S. Civil Aeronautics Board.

some private agreement between airlines [3]), but that, of course, is a different matter, and in no way affects the application of the Convention.

Similarly where the charter agreement is one for the carriage of goods, the charterer will be carrier because he has concluded contracts of carriage with respect to these goods with the original shippers, and the operator will be carrier because of his contract with the charterer.

But the operator who has given his aircraft and crew in time-charter to another person has not, *by the execution of that time charter*, concluded a contract of carriage with respect to the persons or goods for whose transportation the charterer happens to use the chartered aircraft. Nothing, however, prevents the operator from concluding additional contracts of carriage by issuing separate tickets and having air waybills completed for all persons and goods carried under the time-charter agreement. The obligations which he assumes under such additional contracts are different from his general obligation under the time-charter agreement to keep an aircraft with crew during a period of time at the disposal of the charterer. Whether the issuance of separate tickets and the execution of air waybills amount to the conclusion of additional contracts of carriage, or whether they are merely to be considered as administrative formalities, will depend upon the intentions of the parties. It would seem that, as written documents drafted in the form of separate contracts, they offer prima facie evidence of the execution of additional contracts of carriage, conferring the status of carrier upon the operator.

121. The situation is not different in which the contract concluded by the operator does not comprise the entire loadcapacity of an aircraft, but is a contract for the transportation of a shipment consisting of a number of smaller shipments consolidat-

120. [3]) IATA Resolution 045, as amended in 1952, provides sub (1) (b): 'charter agreements shall be made with only one person [...] for his own use; provided that charter agreements may be made with one person on behalf of a group, whose principal aims, purposes and objectives are other than travel and where the group has sufficient affinity existing prior to the application for charter transportation to distinguish it and set it apart from the general public, but any such charter agreement shall contain a stipulation that the charterer will not permit the aircraft to be used by any person other than himself or a member of such group'.

ed by the shipper, who himself has issued in his own name separate air waybills to the original shippers. Both the operator and the consolidator are carriers with respect to the goods so carried. It is to be observed, however, that as the points of departure and destination of the consolidated shipment accepted for carriage by the operator need not be the same as those of the individual shipments accepted for carriage by the consolidator, the Convention may apply to the consolidated shipment without applying to one or all of the original shipments, and vice versa. The same is true, of course, in case of charter agreements.

122. Special mention should be made of the cases in which part of the carriage is performed by another carrier than the one who has accepted the passengers or goods for carriage. Article 30 (1) of the Convention specifically deals with these situations:

> 'In the case of carriage to be performed by various successive carriers and falling within the definition set out in the third paragraph of Article 1, each carrier who accepts passengers, baggage or goods is subjected to the rules set out in this Convention, and is deemed to be one of the contracting parties to the contract of carriage which is performed under his supervision' (french: 'sous son contrôle').

It is to be noted that Article 30 speaks of 'carriage *to be performed* by various successive carriers', not of carriage *performed* by such carriers. It therefore does not seem to deal with the situation in which the carrier, or one of the carriers, indicated as such in the ticket or air waybill, has a part of the transportation executed by another airline. Whether the contracting carrier has the right to do so will depend upon the contract of carriage [1]). Assuming that the carrier had either expressly or impliedly reserved that right, should the substitute carrier be considered only an agent of the contracting carrier, or also a carrier himself?

The answer to that question will depend upon whether the substitute carrier had concluded a contract of carriage with respect to the shipment concerned, or had only contracted to perform as his agent the contracting carrier's obligation under the original contract of carriage.

---

122. [1]) The ATA General Conditions of Carriage (1953) have expressly reserved the right for the carrier 'without notice [to] substitute alternate carriers or aircraft'. ('Passengers and Baggage': Art. 10 (2) (a), 'Goods': Art. 6 (3) (b)).

When he has issued a new air waybill to the contracting carrier, mentioning the latter as shipper, there will be no difficulty: he has assumed the obligation and status of a carrier and neither the original contracting carrier nor the original shipper can sue him otherwise than under the conditions and limitations provided by the Convention with respect to the shipment as accepted by him. If the points of origin and destination of the transportation to be performed by the substitute carrier are situated in the territories of High Contracting Parties to the Convention, his liability will, in accordance with Article 24, be governed by the Convention also as regards claims brought by the shipper or consignee of the original air waybill, irrespective of whether the carriage envisaged by the latter air waybill were also governed by the Convention. As has been pointed out before, this probably means that the original shipper, who is not the shipper under the second air waybill, has no claim at all against the substitute carrier, but can only sue the carrier with whom he has contracted.

Meanwhile, in the normal case no separate air waybill will be executed for the carriage by the substitute carrier. If the shipper's copy is amended so as to indicate the substitution, there can be little doubt – at least if the shipper received notice of the alteration [2]) –, that the substitute carrier has become one of the successive carriers by whom the carriage is to be performed, as meant in Article 30 of the Convention. But if no alteration in the air waybill is made, or if it is only made in the carrier's copy, the question becomes more difficult. It is submitted that, subject to specific provisions, express or implied, in the contract of carriage with the shipper, and subject to any contrary agreement between the contracting carrier and his substitute, the latter should be deemed in such cases to have acted as agent only for the contracting carrier, and not as independent carrier.

123. In *Rotterdamsche Bank N.V. and Banque de l'Indochine* v. *B.O.A.C. and Aden Airways* [1]) the question arose whether Aden

122. [2]) In practice the shipper's copy of the air waybill often remains with the carrier, who in executing the air waybill has acted as agent of the shipper (see Article 6 (5) of the Convention). It is believed that the air waybill offering prima facie evidence of the conclusion of the contract and the conditions of carriage (Article 11), alterations made in it as to the performing carriers will have the same evidential value.

123. [1]) (1953) 1 Lloyds List L.R. 154; 1953 U.S. & C.Av.R. 163.

Airways which operated services on behalf of B.O.A.C. between Cairo and Asmara, and between Asmara and Djibouti, should be considered 'carrier' in the sense of the Convention, while the B.O.A.C. was mentioned on the air waybill as carrier for the stretch Cairo-Djibouti. It was decided that Aden Airways should be considered carrier for two reasons: (a) because the air waybill, under the heading 'Type of Service', referred to the time-tables of the carrier, which indicated that this service was operated on behalf of B.O.A.C. by Aden Airways, a subsidiary of B.O.A.C.; and (b) because the 'Conditions of Contract' on the back of the air waybill defined 'carrier' as including all 'air carriers that carry the goods hereunder or perform any other services related to such air carriage':

> 'The actual services by which the whole carriage was to be performed are clearly set out in the air consignment note under the heading 'Type of Service'. If these services are read in conjunction with the British Overseas Airways Corporation time-table, it must have been clear to all interested parties that, while freight from Cairo to Asmara was to be paid to British Overseas Airways Corporation, this portion of the carriage was being undertaken by British Overseas Airways Corporation's subsidiary Aden Airways Dakota Services...'
> '... The definition of 'carrier' in Condition 1 strongly supports the view that the second defendants (Aden Airways) were to be considered as carriers although not mentioned in the air consignment note'. [2])

The air waybill used in this case was a K.L.M. air waybill following the prescriptions of the International Air Transport Association (I.A.T.A.). The decision, in so far as it derives an argument from the definition of carrier in the Conditions of Contract printed on the back of the document, is therefore important for all contracts of carriage concluded by members of I.A.T.A., i.e. for the large majority of carriage by scheduled airlines. But it is to be kept in mind that in this decision the contractual definition of 'carrier' is only used as an additional argument in support of an opinion which, under the circumstances of the case, could also be founded on other grounds. The main

122. [2]) (1953) U.S. & C.Av.R. 163, 167/168.

argument of the Court was the fact that the service concerned was, according to the time-table of B.O.A.C., normally operated by Aden Airways. In the majority of cases which involve incidental substitutions, that argument cannot be invoked. Though it seems questionable whether a definition of 'carrier', incorporated in the carrier's conditions of carriage for the purpose of the interpretation of these conditions, can be construed to apply also to the meaning of 'carrier' for the application of the Convention, it is believed in any case that a carrier's contractually stipulated right to substitute other carriers implies, in the absence of indications to the contrary, that the parties intended the substitute carriers to enjoy the same status of carrier as those who were already indicated in the contract of carriage. A strong argument for this view can be drawn from Article 8 of the Convention which only requires that the first carrier be indicated in the air waybill. Apparently the subsequent carriers by whom the carriage is to be performed and to whom Article 30 would apply do not have to be mentioned in the air waybill. It is to be noted that Article 3 provides that 'the name and address of the carrier *or carriers*' has to be mentioned in the ticket. The difference probably should be explained by the difference in treatment of passengers and shippers as far as successive carriage is concerned, only the latter having the right to sue the first carrier for occurrences happening with the subsequent carriers. The substitution of a carrier in the event of passenger transportation always needs the cooperation of the passenger, who of necessity receives notice of such substitution, which means that with respect to passengers the situation is always the same as that which exists in relation to carriage of goods whenever the substitution of the carrier has been brought to the knowledge of the shipper by alteration of his copy of the air waybill.

124. The above views on the meaning of the term 'carrier', where used in Article 22 of the Convention, can be thus summarized: For the purpose of the Convention the carrier is the person who has concluded a contract of carriage with respect to the transportation of the passengers or goods concerned, or who can be considered a successive carrier in the sense of Article 30. An operator who gives an aircraft with crew in time charter cannot be considered a carrier with respect to persons or goods carried by the chartered aircraft unless he has concluded additional contracts covering that carriage.

B. Rome Conventions.

125. The Rome Conventions have devoted more attention to the problem who is to be considered operator. In fact, this was one of the crucial questions in their drafting.

The Convention of 1933 contains the following definition in Article 4 (2):

> 'Operator of the aircraft means any person who has the aircraft at his disposal and who makes use thereof for his own account'.

The definition in Article 2 (2) of the Convention of 1952 is more elaborate:

> '(a) For the purpose of this Convention the term "operator" shall mean the person who was making use of the aircraft at the time the damage was caused, provided that if control of the navigation of the aircraft was retained by the person from whom the right to make use of the aircraft was derived, whether directly or indirectly, that person shall be considered the operator'.
> '(b) 'A person shall be considered to be making use of an aircraft when he is using it personally or when his servants or agents are using the aircraft in the course of their employment, whether or not within the scope of their authority'.

Both Conventions have an additional provision that the registered owner shall be presumed to be the operator subject to proof to the contrary.

It is impossible to go into all the intricate problems involved in the construction of these definitions [1]). For the purpose of this study the exact meaning of the term 'operator' in the 1952 Convention is not so important since that Convention provides in Article 9 that besides the operator, the owner, the persons upon whom liability is imposed by Articles 3 and 4, as well as the servants and agents of any of these persons cannot be held liable

125. [1]) See especially the analysis of the various possibilities by the Working Group 'Operator' of the Montreal Session (1950) of the L.C. of ICAO, Minutes and Documents, pp. 313–331.

otherwise than as expressly provided by the Convention [2]). It is believed that most borderline situations will be sufficiently taken care of by this Article, as far as the limitation provisions are concerned [3]).

126. A similar provision, however, is not contained in the 1933 Convention, which, on the other hand, is very clear in restricting the scope of the limitation provisions to the liability of the operator [1]) and does not even contain a provision like Article 24 of the Warsaw Convention to the effect that all actions can only be brought subject to the conditions and limitations of the Convention [2]). In order to determine who is protected by the limitation provisions of this Convention, it is, therefore, of even greater importance to know who is meant by 'operator', than it is under the Warsaw Convention to know who is the 'carrier'.

The basic weakness in the definition of the operator in the Convention of 1933 is that it contains three criteria which are cumulative, not alternative [3]). In order to be 'operator' one must (1) have the aircraft at one's disposal, (2) make use of it, and (3) do that for one's own account. It is not difficult to imagine situations in which no one person would fulfil these three condi-

---

125. [2]) See also Article 11 (1) limiting the liability 'in respect of all persons liable under this Convention'.

[3]) A problem *could* arise in the situation in which an independent organization of pilots provides pilots (who remain in the employment of the organization) for flying the aircraft of other people. In such a situation it was felt to be more fair to burden the user of the aircraft with the liability of the Convention than the pilots' organization (for the different solution adopted by the French Cour de Cassation as regards automobile accidents see No. 130 (4)). It seems to be especially for this reason, that Article 2 (2) (a) has been drafted in the somewhat bewildering way it reads now, conveying the impression that the *use of the aircraft* is the primary criterion, whereas in all normal situations *control of its navigation* is the determining factor. Curiously, the situation seems to have been lost sight of, when Article 9 was drafted. For that Article does not clearly cover the vicarious liability of the pilots' organization, and perhaps not even the liability of the pilots. This is especially doubtful under the French and Spanish texts which have for the English words 'servants or agents': '*préposés*', respectively '*dependientes*'.

126. [1]) Cf. Ripert at the R.C. 1953 I, 303: 'Toutes les actions en responsabilité que donne le droit commun contre les personnes autres que l'exploitant, ne nous regardent pas, et il est complètement inutile d'en parler'.

[2]) A British proposal to insert a similar provision in the Rome Convention, 1933 was withdrawn on the assurance by the Reporter (Ambrosini) that it would be superfluous: 'La Convention établit que, dès qu'il y a un dommage, il doit etre réparé d'après certaines règles' (I, 264).

[3]) Cf. Lemoine (1947) No. 953.

tions. Probably courts will be inclined to give a broad construction to the words in order to avoid the victim receiving no compensation at all [4]). The plaintiff will be wise to bring an action against all persons who possibly could be held to be operator. In that case the court has to make its choice. It is believed that in practice courts will primarily look for the person whose crew was operating the aircraft, and will find means to fit this criterion into the not too sharply phrased definition. This means that the practical result may not be too different from the solution of the Convention of 1952.

127. Besides the operator, the Rome Conventions mention some other classes of persons upon whom liability is imposed, which liability is limited in accordance with the limitation provisions. Article 5 of the 1933 Convention and Article 4 of the 1952 Convention deal with the case of unlawful use. In effect they both provide that in such cases the unlawful user and the operator (1933) or the person entitled to the navigational control (1952) shall be jointly and severally liable, unless the latter can prove 'that he has exercised due care to prevent such use'. The Convention of 1952 correctly avoids speaking of 'operator', probably because the fact of the unlawful use could be said to have taken away the quality of operator from the person who otherwise would have been operator [1]). The Convention of 1952 has added another category of persons liable under it: those from whom the right to use the aircraft was derived, provided

---

126. [4]) Cf. the Brazilian collision case reported in 1 R.B.D.A. (1951) No.1. 207 at 209 and 214. Unfortunately the point was not discussed by the court, because it was considered to have been already decided at a preliminary stage (214). Though the case did not turn upon a claim for surface damage, it is of interest for the interpretation of the Rome Convention, 1933, because Art. 129 (1) of the *Codigo do Ar* (defining the person liable for collisions) reads the same as Art. 4 (2) of the 1933 Convention.

127. [1]) It is to be observed that Article 4 only uses the criterion of 'navigational control', contrary to Article 2 (2) which has as primary criterion the use of the aircraft. The result of this departure from the principle of Article 2 seems to be that in the situations in which A has hired an aircraft from B and a crew from C, A will generally be the person liable as operator, but C, and not A will be jointly liable under Art. 4 in case of unlawful use. In the 1933 Convention the use of the word 'operator' in Article 5, meaning the person having a right to the use of the aircraft, would seem to affect the definition of operator in Article 4 (2) in the sense that 'la disposition de l'avion' should be understood to mean 'droit de disposition'. Cf. Lemoine (1947) No. 953.

the right was not given for a period of more than fourteen days [2]).

§ 2. OTHER PERSONS BURDENED WITH LIABILITY BY MUNICIPAL LAW

128. All the persons discussed so far, were persons upon whom the Warsaw or the Rome Conventions expressly have imposed liability, subject to their right to invoke the limitation provisions. We have come now to the classes of persons who cannot be held liable under the provisions of the Conventions. The problem to be examined is whether these persons might, nevertheless, invoke the protection of the limitation provisions if they could be held liable under some national law. But before we enter into a discussion of this problem, a preliminary question need be answered: should the Conventions be deemed to have set aside any absolute liabilities or legal presumptions of negligence which might be provided by national laws? The question may arise under the Warsaw and under the Rome Conventions. It does not seem to have received much attention up to now [1]). A few examples may be useful. Article 50 of the French Air Navigation Act 1924 provides that in case of lease of the aircraft the owner shall be jointly and severally liable with the lessee for any breach of 'legal obligations'. Since this Article is contained in the Part dealing with the carriage of persons or goods, it apparently refers to the lessee's liabilities arising from carriage. Would it be possible to invoke Article 50 in an action against the owner of a leased aircraft in case of carriage performed by the lessee and governed by the Warsaw Convention? Or to take another example: under Article 29 of the Czech Air Navigation Act of 1925 the person who has possession of the aircraft, the pilot, and the person from whom the right of disposition was derived, are all liable both for damages arising from transportation of passengers

---

127. [2]) The wording of the Article ('If the person who was the operator at the time the damage was caused had not the *exclusive* right to use the aircraft for a period of more than fourteen days...') raises some questions: (1) how if the aircraft is hired to a firm of two partners, neither of them having the *exclusive* right to use? (2) how if the aircraft is hired for an indefinite period and the accident happens within fourteen days?

128. [1]) It has been mentioned by Riese (1949) p. 44, and cf. Mexico Session (1951) p. 162.

and goods and for surface damages. To what extent is this liability of the pilot or of the person from whom the right of disposition was derived affected by the Warsaw and Rome Conventions if any such Convention would govern the case?

129. Three solutions seem possible: (a) the Conventions are considered to exclude any liability not specifically provided therein; (b) the Conventions are deemed to be exhaustive, setting aside any liability provided by national law, except the normal 'common law' liability for negligence or wilful misconduct; or (c) the Conventions are deemed not to affect in any way the liabilities under the national laws of persons whose liability they do not specifically regulate. It is believed that the second possibility is the better one, and most in conformity with the general purpose of the three Conventions [1]). A complete exclusion of liability of all persons other than the carrier, as far as the Warsaw Convention is concerned, or the operator and some other expressly mentioned persons, as far as the Rome Conventions are concerned, was evidently never intended [2]). For the Warsaw Convention that follows from the whole trend of the discussions before and at the Warsaw Conference and also from the work of the CITEJA on the Draft of a collision's convention where the possible liability of the non-carrying aircraft in collision cases has always been assumed as a matter of course. With respect to the Rome Convention 1933 it was unambiguously stated during the discussions at Rome [3]). As to the latest Rome Convention, the situation is even more clear because of the exhaustive enumeration in Article 9 of persons who shall have no other liability outside the Convention [4]).

The other extreme position – to the effect that the Conventions would not even affect any special liabilities arising from air carriage or surface damages which might be imposed by national

129. [1]) Cf. Riese (1949) p. 349, and Mexico Session (1951) pp. 162 sq.

[2]) Cf. Riese (1949) p. 442.

[3]) See No. 126 (1).

[4]) In maritime law a similar problem offers itself with respect to the general limitation of the shipowner's liability. Since this limitation, in French law, has been held not to protect a sea-carrier who is not the owner of the ship, French Courts had to face the problem whether to burden such persons with unlimited liability; the Cour de Cassation has adopted the view that they can not be held liable at all. See Ripert (1952) II, No. 1262.

laws on persons other than the carrier or operator – ignores the obvious purpose of the Conventions to unify the law also on the question *who* is to be held liable for the transportation or for the surface damage. Any provisions in municipal laws which specifically regulate the liability for transportation by air or for surface damages caused by aircraft certainly must be considered superseded by the Warsaw or Rome Conventions whenever the latter apply.

130. The problem becomes more difficult where the national law has a general principle of liability for injuries or damages caused by dangerous instrumentalities or by any objects, whether dangerous or not [1]). Such general principle may only lay down a presumption of negligence [2]), or it may go further than that and create a semi-absolute liability with only a limited number of defences allowed [3]). Apart from the basis of liability, it may also indicate a person to be sued in addition to the person who caused the damage with an object belonging to the former [4]). Such a

---

130. [1]) A general liability for damage caused by objects which one has in one's custody (sometimes limited to mechanical engines) exists in **France** (Art. 1384 (1) Cod. civ. as construed by the Courts), **Egypt** (Art. 178 Civil Code 1948), **Italy** (Art. 2051 Cod. Civ.), **Lebanon** (Art. 131 Code of Obligations and Contracts, 1932) and **Venezuela** (Art. 1193 Cod. Civ.). It seems also to have been accepted by a minority of the courts and the majority of the authors in **Argentine** (see A. E. de Salas, in 20 Rev. del Colegio de Abogados de Buenos Aires, 1942, 329 sq., Cammarota, *Responsabilidad extracontractual* B. A. 1946, II Nos. 420 sq., Salvat, *Tratado* VII, Nos. 2889 sq.). In some countries the principle is limited by the courts to damages caused by the defect of a thing: **Belgium, Egypt** before the 1948 Code came into force, and **Quebec.** In others the rule is limited to dangerous things such as **Hungary** (cf. P. Sebestyén in 2 Zeitschrift für osteurop. Recht (1935/36), 315), **Mexico** (Art. 1913 Cod. civ.) and **Norway** (on the Scandinavian countries generally see H. Ussing in 1 Amer. J. Compar. Law (1952) 359, 362). The scope of the rule in *Ryland* v. *Fletcher* (1868) L.R. 3 H.L. 330 probably is more limited, and does not comprise e.g. the causing of personal injuries or death (cf. *Read* v. *J. Lyons & Co. Ltd.* [1945] 1 K.B. 216, (1946) 62 T.L.R. 646).

[2]) On the rule of *res ipsa loquitur* in **English** and **American** law (especially California) see i.a. Prosser in 37 Cal. L. Rev. (1949) 183 sq. As the rule is based on common sense, it is of course also frequently applied, though without the Latin label, by civil law courts in analogous fact situations.

[3]) Thus most of the legal systems mentioned in note 1.

[4]) The liability for damages caused by things, in **French** law, is borne by the person who has the custody (*'la garde'*) of the thing. Before the decision of the *Cour de Cassation* (*Chambres réunies*) of 2.12.1941, D.C. 1942.725 (Note Ripert) it was a hotly debated point whether the *'garde'* should be considered to refer to the *right* to use, or rather to the actual use. The latter solution was finally adopted, so that the owner of a stolen car could not be held liable for accidents caused by it. A year later the criterion of use was modified into that of technical control, in a case involving a car driven by a driver whom the owner had hired from a garage. Though the owner was

rule of vicarious liability is often combined with a presumption of negligence but it need not be.

When such general rules of liability exist which either do not require negligence or which shift the burden of proof to the defendant and which impose this liability on another person than the carrier or operator as meant in the Warsaw or Rome Conventions, should they also be deemed substituted by the provisions of these Conventions? The question may be clarified by a few examples:

(a) A, who has contractually assumed the obligation to carry certain passengers between two states which are party to the Warsaw Convention, charters for that purpose an aircraft with crew from B, B retaining the full operational control. If the accident happened in France, could the next of kin of the killed passenger sue B under Article 1384 (1) of the Civil Code, as having the custody ('garde') of the aircraft with which the accident happened [5])? If A had performed the carriage with his own aircraft and crew, the question would not arise, as Article 24 certainly precludes any actions 'however founded', *against the carrier* (*A*), which are not brought 'subject to the conditions and limits set out in [the] Convention' [6]).

(b) A has his own aircraft, but in order to use it must hire a crew from B who assumes responsibility for the navigation. If damages are caused to the surface, A will be liable as operator

himself riding in the car he was not considered to have retained the '*garde*' (Cass. req. 3.11.1942. D. 1947 J. 145 with note Tunc). The Court arrived here at a different solution from that adopted by the Rome Conference of 1952 with respect to the situations in which a crew is hired from another person than the aircraft (cf. No. 125 (3)). Though formally the liability for damages caused by things (ex Art. 1384 (1) Cod. civ.) does not seem to extend the vicarious liability beyond the persons mentioned in 1384 (5) C.c., it is probably correct to say that in fact the courts will sooner accept the existence of a '*commettant-préposé*' relationship with the resulting liability of the 'commettant', where the damage is caused by a thing belonging to the 'commettant' (especially if that would be a more or less dangerous thing), than they would otherwise do. It is believed that the same may be true in other countries (thus the sole purpose of the old Florida rule holding the motorcar a 'dangerous intrumentality' was to make the owner liable for accidents).

[5]) Cf. Cass. com. 19.6.1951, D. 1951, J. 717 (see also No. 81(2)) where the next of kin of the passengers on the steamer Lamoricière were given an action ex 1384 (1) C.c. against the shipowners (French State) when the Lamoricière got lost in a storm. See the discussion of this case in Juglart, Nos. 246 sq. The same question could arise under any legal system imposing delictual liability upon the person controlling the aircraft (B) without requiring negligence, or with a shifting of the burden of proof as to negligence. Cf. Nos. 81 (2) and 131.

[6]) See No. 64 (1).

under the Rome Convention, 1952 (Article 2 (2)). But could B be held liable as 'gardien' under Article 1384 (1) of the French civil Code, supposing French law applied to the accident? [7]).

131. The question must be examined for each Convention separately. As far as the Warsaw Convention is concerned, a problem can only arise in the cases in which the operator of the aircraft has not concluded any contract of carriage with respect to the persons or goods carried. For as has been explained above, in any other case he must be considered 'carrier' for the purpose of the Convention and as such be protected by the limits of liability, whether or not the person claiming damages was himself a party to the contract of carriage concluded by him. The situation may especially arise in case of time-charters and when a carrier has part of the carriage performed by another airline acting as its agent without notice to the shipper.

It is believed that the liability provisions of the Convention must be deemed to have set aside only those principles of liability contained in national laws which purport to deal with the air carrier's liability specifically, or with a carrier's liability generally, even if such national laws would apply similar principles to other categories of persons or activities. But any *general* principles of delictual liability, such as e.g. Article 1384 (1) of the French Civil Code, are not substituted by the Convention, to the extent that they impose liability on another person than the 'carrier' whose liability is governed by the Convention. Whether a specific provision of national law must be considered to amount to a general principle, or rather to be a rule purporting to cover the same subject matter as the Convention, will depend upon the interpretation of that rule by the national courts. That this may be a difficult problem, appears from the conflicting decisions rendered by French Courts in the 'Lamoricière' Cases, concerning the liability of a sea-carrier for passengers killed in the accident of the 'Lamoricière'. The Appeal Court of Algers had held [1]) that the broad interpretation of Article 1384 (1) of the Civil Code, according to which the person who has the custody of a thing is

---

130. [7]) Cf. no. 130 (4).

131. [1]) 25.5.1949. J.C.P. 1950, II, 5729, also extensively quoted by Juglart, p. 291.

liable for the damage caused thereby unless he proves force majeure or exclusive negligence of the victim, 'was the result of a development of judgemade law originally made necessary by the power and danger of the growing use of automobiles' and not 'a fundamental private law rule on liability, generally applicable [...] to all cases, so that it should not be applied in the field of maritime law'. This view was rejected by the *Cour de Cassation* which in two decisions of 19 June 1951 held the shipowner liable in tort under Article 1384 (1) C.c. towards the dependants of killed passengers [2]).

Though Article 24 of the Convention makes it impossible to apply Article 1384 (1) C.c. to the liability of the air carrier (in the meaning of the Convention), the holding of the *Cour de Cassation* in the 'Lamoricière' Cases would seem to make Article 1384 (1) C.c. applicable against any person other than the carrier, such as the operator who has given his aircraft in time-charter without concluding contracts of carriage with respect to the passengers or goods carried in the aircraft. It is true that as a result the liability of such persons will be heavier than that of the carrier who has undertaken the carriage of the passengers and goods, but that incongruity is the consequence of the curious growth of French law, and can hardly be avoided by some interpretation of the Warsaw Convention [3]).

132. The situation with respect to the *Rome Conventions* is different, for the reason that these Conventions deal with delictual liability, so that their purpose is the same as that of the principles of delictual liability contained in national laws, at least as far as the latter are concerned with the risks and duties directly involved in the operation of aircraft.

Liabilities imposed by such laws on any persons for the operation of aircraft or for the creation of risks arising from the operation of aircraft as well as collateral liabilities created for the protection of victims against the insolvency of the persons prima-

---

[2]) D. 1951, J. 717 and J.C.P. 1951, II, 5729. Also in Droit Maritime Français, 1951, 429, with note by Ripert.

[3]) But the aircraft operator who gives his aircraft in time-charter, can make sure that he is mentioned as carrier in the tickets or air waybills issued to passengers and shippers, thereby assuming towards them the liabilities of a carrier, but also enjoying the protection attached to that status.

rily responsible, have all been set aside by the Rome Conventions, which must be considered as having unified the law in an exhaustive way with respect to all such liabilities.

This does not mean that under the Rome Conventions there may not also arise borderline cases. The case mentioned before of a user of an aircraft having hired a crew from an independent contractor for the operation of his aircraft, offers an example. To what extent are the victims of surface damages precluded from recovering from the independent contractor who provided the crew? The question is more important under the old Rome Convention than under that of 1952, since the latter has expressly provided for the liability of the agents of the operator and the owner of the aircraft (Article 9) [1]).

§ 3. SERVANTS, AGENTS AND OTHER THIRD PARTIES

133. So far we have discussed (1) which persons should be deemed included within the classes of persons upon whom the Conventions expressly impose limited liability (carrier, operator, etc.), and (2) to what extent the Conventions preclude actions against other persons based on national laws. With respect to the second question the conclusion was that the Conventions were not intended to take away all actions against any persons not mentioned by them. This makes it necessary to examine whether such other persons, if they are held liable under national law, will, nevertheless, be protected by the limitation provisions of the Conventions.

It has been said that once the possibility of actions in accordance with municipal laws against persons not contemplated by the Conventions is accepted, it would be illogical to apply the limitation provisions to such actions which do not arise under the Convention [1]). But in the closely related field of contractual limitation of liability a not less authoritative author has remarked that any other rule than that which would extend the protection of limitation of liability clauses to the servants and agents of the person whose liability was limited thereby 'would lead to absurd results' [2]).

132. 1) See No. 135.

133. 1) Riese (1949) p. 442.
2) Salmond (1945) p. 9.

It is submitted that there is nothing illogical or impossible *per se* in having certain liabilities of certain persons limited by a Convention which would not itself have created these liabilities. In the Brussels Convention of 1924, limiting the liability of shipowners, the liabilities which are limited in no way arise from the Convention itself but find their basis either in other international Conventions or in national laws. Article 22 (4) of the Warsaw Convention itself offers another example by limiting the carrier's liability with respect to hand baggage without the Convention offering any basis for that liability.

But to say that there is nothing illogical in limiting a liability which has its roots elsewhere, does not necessarily mean that the limitation provisions in the air law conventions could not actually have been intended to apply only to the liabilities imposed by the Conventions. It is only by construing the relevant provisions of each Convention individually, that an answer to the question can be given.

134. The persons who may become liable in addition to the carrier or operator respectively can be roughly divided in two broad categories, the first comprising all persons whose activities have had some connection with the carriage by air or the operation of the aircraft, the second comprising all other persons. As to the latter category there can be little doubt that the liability of these persons is not affected by the Conventions. Neither the operator of a colliding aircraft, nor the saboteur who has interfered with the engines before departure of the aircraft, nor the person whose negligence has set fire to storerooms of the airport, destroying baggage or cargo, could, with any chance of success, invoke the limitation or any other provision of the Warsaw and Rome Conventions [1]).

The first category is more important. It includes the servants and agents of the carrier or operator respectively, and ground-

134. [1]) Except that in a collision case where surface damages have been caused, both aircraft will be liable under the Rome Convention and, on the other hand protected by the limits. At the 11th Session of CITEJA (Berne 1936, Doc. 324, at pp. 80–92) the question has been extensively discussed whether in the Collisions Convention the passenger of a colliding aircraft should have any action against the operator of the other aircraft besides his action under the Warsaw Convention against the carrier. With a small majority the question was answered in the affirmative.

handling companies, airport managers, traffic control, aircraft manufacturers, repair men, etc. To the extent limitation of liability is to be founded on the consideration that any damage in excess of the limits can be better insured on the part of the person suffering damage than on the part of the aircraft, all persons connected with the operation of the aircraft should be equally protected by the limits, for the same rationale applies to all of them. The possibility of unlimited claims against any of these persons will in the long run affect the costs of operation of aircraft. Frequently the carrier or operator has to sign hold harmless agreements protecting groundhandling companies, repair services or airport managements against third party claims. The international pilot's organization (IFALPA) some time ago adopted a resolution pressing for some similar protection [2]). Since it is the direct result of such hold harmless agreements that the carrier or operator will be burdened with the claims brought against the indemnified party, the inability of the latter to invoke the legal limits of liability will mean that the carrier or operator remains menaced by the risk of unlimited liability and will have to insure himself against that risk. Thus the purpose of the limitation of his liability will be clearly defeated. This is especially true if a national law were to impose upon a carrier or operator the obligation to insure also the liability of his servants, such as was done by the Swiss legislator in Article 70 (2) of the Federal Air Navigation Act 1948, providing that the operator 'must cover by insurance the liability of the persons charged by the operator with the navigation of the aircraft or with any other services on board the aircraft, for damages caused to third parties, in the exercise of their professional activity in the service of the operator'. But even where no hold harmless agreements have been signed, or where no legal obligation to insure the liability of the servants or agents exists, unlimited claims against the persons engaged in aviation will finally result in an increase in aviation costs which, if it is not borne by the community as a whole, must be paid by aviation. The groundhandling company who has to insure against the risk of unlimited claims will charge the increased insurance premium through to his customer, the air

134. [2]) ICAO Doc. A 4–WP/154. See also Kamminga (1953) pp. 161 sq.

carrier. The same will be true in the long run for the aircraft manufacturer.

A good case, therefore, can be made *de lege ferenda* for extending the protection of the limits of liability to all persons who, economically, play a part in the carriage by air or in the operation of the aircraft. At the Rome Conference of 1952 and at the 9th (Rio de Janeiro) Session of the Legal Committee of I.C.A.O. it was partly these considerations which led to the adoption of certain provisions for the protection of the servants and agents of the operator or carrier respectively [3]).

But if one holds with Holmes that the law can be defined as 'the prophecies of what the courts will do in fact', it seems highly doubtful whether the above reasoning is sufficient to justify an interpretation of the Warsaw and Rome Conventions, as they stand at present, to the effect that their limitation provisions can be invoked by all persons connected with the carriage by air or with the operation of the aircraft. As to those persons who *are* so connected, but without being the servants or agents of the carrier or operator, there seems to be little room for hesitation, leaving aside the difficulty of establishing the exact borderline between the persons who can be considered to have acted as agents and those who cannot. To the knowledge of this author the applicability of the limitation provisions of the Warsaw or Rome Conventions to these persons has never been defended [4]).

135. This leaves us with the question of whether at least the

134. [3]) Art. 9 of the Rome Convention 1952. Cf. R.C. 1952, I, 70, and the new Art. 25A contained in the Draft Protocol established at the Rio Session (1953) of the Legal Committee of ICAO. For many of those who voted for the inclusion of these provisions, the protection of the servants or agents – especially the crew personnel – was the main motive, but in that line of thought it would have been logical also to exclude the possibility of recourse by the operator against his servants in the Rome Convention of 1952, whereas on the contrary, Article 10 of that Convention expressly has maintained any recourse action granted by national laws. On the attitude of national legislations in this respect see No. 89, especially note 2. Under the Draft Protocol to the Warsaw Convention, which does not fully take away the liability of servants and agents but only offers to them the protection of the limitation of liability provided for the carrier, no special provision as to recourse actions against the servants or agents would be necessary.

[4]) In the much criticized decision of Benvenga J. in *Wanderer* v. *Sabena* and *P.A.A.* 1949 U.S.Av.R. 25, the time limitation provisions of the Warsaw Convention have been held applicable to an action against Pan American Airways, though it is not even sure whether P.A.A. was acting as agent of Sabena. Cf. note by J. Lacombe in 12 R.G.A. (1949) 821.

servants and agents of the carrier or operator are protected by the limitation of liability. For the Rome Convention of 1952 this is not even questionable, since it expressly states in Article 9 that the servants and agents of the operator shall not be liable otherwise than expressly provided in the Convention, except when they would have acted deliberately with intent to cause damage. Since the Convention does not contain any provisions dealing with the liability of servants or agents, the result is that their liability for surface damage caused by an aircraft in flight is fully excluded unless caused intentionally.

Who are the 'servants or agents' mentioned in Article 9? The French and Spanish texts, of equal authority, have 'préposés' and 'dependientes' respectively. It is not clear who are meant by 'agents' in the English texts, assuming that they are not the same as the servants. The French 'préposés' and the Spanish 'dependientes', when used in a Convention dealing exclusively with delictual liability, surely should be limited to persons who are in a more or less subordinate position, and under the control of the operator, though they need not be bound to him by a contract of employment [1]), and though the courts are not always too difficult as to the requirement of control. The tendency with English and American courts seems to be to extend the category of persons for whom the principal can be held liable in tort beyond the circle of those who are in his service [2]), and perhaps to go a little farther than French courts. It is suggested, however, that a sensible interpretation of the Article should tend to reconcile any such differences as might exist between the legal terminologies of the three texts, by being not too liberal in construing the word 'agents' in the English text, and not too restrict-

135. [1]) For the meaning of '*préposés*' see No. 137 (2). For meaning of '*dependientes*' in Art. 1903 C. civ. and Art. 22 C. pen. of **Spain**, see i.a. the decisions of Trib. Supr. of 7.4.1881, G. 31.7.1881, T. 24, 320 (servant of independent contractor when working for defendant, not a 'dependiente' of defendant) and of 28.12.1945, R. 439 (husband whose wife was employed by railway at a levelcrossing and who during her illness took care of her work, held not to be a *dependiente* for whose negligence the railway could be held liable under Art. 22 C. pen.). The Tribunal Supremo requires a 'determinada relación de autoridad o superioridad' (18.2.1914). For the similar criterion applied to Art. 1403 (3) of the **Dutch** Civil Code see i.a. Wolfsbergen (1946) p. 260.

[2]) Cf. W. G. Friedmann in 63 Harv. L. Rev. (1949) 241, at 245: 'The traditional principle of non-liability [of the independent contractor] has been so riddled with exceptions that in modern decisions the cases where the exemption applies are far outnumbered by those in which, under one exception or another, the principal is held liable'.

ive in construing the words 'préposés' and 'dependientes' in the French and Spanish texts.

Curiously, Article 9 does not require that the servants or agents were acting within the scope of their employment. If the Article were to be taken literally, the servants or agents would be protected against liability for all their acts (except deliberate acts committed with the intent to cause damage), even when such acts would have no connection at all with their employment, with only the exception of accidents arising from the unauthorized use of their employer's aircraft (Article 4). Though the latter exception does take care of the most important cases, it seems doubtful whether the framers of the Convention had in mind such a literal interpretation.

136. The Warsaw Convention and the Rome Convention 1933 do not contain such a provision. With respect to the Warsaw Convention some authors have held that the protection of Article 22 should be extended to the 'préposés' of the carrier, for whose acts the carrier is made liable under Article 20. Thus held Lemoine in his great work on air law [1]) and more recently Gay de Montellà [2]) and Litvine [3]). Thus also, without motivation and without express reference to an agency relationship, held the single judge in the New York decision *Wanderer* v. *Sabena and Pan American Airways* [4]). But the majority of the authors hold a contrary opinion [5]). The minority view, when limited to the servants of the carrier, seems preferable, at least for the Warsaw Convention, though the arguments pro and con are fairly well in balance.

According to Article 24 of the Warsaw Convention, in the cases envisaged by Articles 17, 18 and 19, 'any action for damages, however founded, can only be brought subject to the conditions and limits provided in [the] Convention'. The Article is not restricted to actions *against the carrier*, so that, taken out of its

---

136. [1]) Traité (1946) Nos. 840–841.
[2]) Principios (1950) p. 560.
[3]) Précis, (1953), Nos. 234–235, and No. 420 for the Rome Convention, 1933.
[4]) 1949 U.S.Av.R. 25. Criticized by Shawcross and Beaumont, No. 362, footnote (a), and by Lacombe in 12 R.G.A. (1949) 821, and Abraham in 2 Z.L. (1953) 90.
[5]) Koffka (1937), p. 269, Riese (1949), p. 441, Kamminga (1953), p. 90, citing other authors.

context, it could be read to exclude any action against any third party, which undoubtedly it never was meant to do. But what the drafters did intend to do was to prevent the provisions of the Convention from being avoided by claiming outside the Convention, especially with an action in tort. When Article 24 speaks of limits, it clearly refers to the limits of Article 22, and this Article only limits the liability of the carrier. This does not mean, however, that an action for unlimited damages against any person other than the carrier could be said to be brought 'subject to the limits of the Convention', for the mere reason that these limits do not apply to such persons. It is believed that a sound interpretation, based on the spirit of Article 24 and not conflicting with its letter, leads to the conclusion that any action brought against the carrier's enterprise as such, or against members of it who can be considered part of the enterprise, are to be brought subject to the limits of Article 22. As it is practically impossible to distinguish the carrier from the community of persons whose joint activity *is* the carrier's activity, as far as the principle of the carrier's liability is concerned, so is it illogical to make such a distinction for the purpose of the limitation of liability. If the carrier's liability is to be limited, the liability of the members of the carrier's enterprise should also be limited, for any negligence of the carrier is negligence of his employees. Any other solution would defeat the purpose of Article 24, which is to prevent claimants from avoiding the provisions of the Convention by suing the enterprise outside the contract of carriage.

137. But it is more doubtful whether this reasoning may be extended to those agents of the carrier who are not his servants, such as groundhandling companies, repairmen, and similar agencies whose services are used by the carrier for the performanc of the carriage by air. Whereas it is an artifice of legal thinking to call the members of the carrier's personnel, by virtue of whose activity alone the carrier can operate, 'third parties' as between the carrier and the passenger or shipper, there is nothing artificial in calling the independent agency, which has rendered assistance to the carrier, a third party. This would mean that Article 22, when read in conjunction with Article 24, does not protect all persons for whose acts the carrier is made liable in Article 20.

For as will be discussed more lengthily in connection with the carrier's unlimited liability for the wilful misconduct of his servants and agents under Article 25, the term 'préposés' when used in regard to a contractual liability, does not only include servants, but also any other persons whose services are used in the performance of the contract [1]).

As to the criterion for distinguishing servants from other agents (independent contractors), it has been said in one of the finest studies on comparative law devoted to the *respondeat superior* rule: 'Despite the general confusion, there is, on some points at least, substantial agreement between all legal systems. The feature that is supposed to distinguish the master servant relationship in legal contemplation is the right and possibility of the master's control over the conduct of the servant' [2]). The author does not fail to add that 'reality does not correspond to the words', and that 'there are many cases where the liability of the master has remained unquestioned despite the fact that all idea of control by the master was pure fiction'.

138. There is a surprising scarcity of authorities on the general problem whether limitation of liability provisions, either legal or contractual, may be invoked by the servants and (or) agents of those whose liability is limited thereby.

Most specific in this regard is the German Air Traffic Act, 1936 as amended in 1943 which, after having restated the principles of the Warsaw Convention, provides in § 29e (2) that 'the legal provisions which impose liability upon the commander of the aircraft or upon any other person remain unaffected'. Though this provision does not directly affect the interpretation of the relevant provisions of the Warsaw Convention, it is believed that it makes an extension of Article 22 of the Convention to servants or agents of the carrier highly improbable, as far as German Courts are concerned.

---

137. [1]) The translation by the English Carriage by Air Act, 1932 into 'agents' which term has later been authentically construed to comprise both servants and agents (Sec. 54 of the Civil Aviation Act, 1949) therefore has not broadened the origianl French text of the Convention.

[2]) R. Neuner (1941), 1 sq. at 19. The criterion generally applied by the French Courts is that there should exist 'un lien de subordination et de dépendance'.

139. In *Elder, Dempster and Co.* v. *Paterson, Zochonis and Co.* etc. [1924] A.C. 522, it was held by the House of Lords that a shipowner, who was not a party to the contract of carriage, could invoke a clause in the bill of lading excluding liability for bad stowage. Here the invoked clause was held to be 'a stipulation on behalf of all the persons interested in the ship, that is to say, charterers and shipowners alike', and it was said that the owners 'took possession of the goods [...] on behalf of and as the agents of the charterers, and so can claim the same protection as their principals' [1]).

> 'When the act is done in the course of rendering the very services provided for in the bill of lading, the limitation on liability therein contained must attach, whatever the form of action and whether owner or charterer be sued. It would be absurd that the owner of the goods could get rid of the protective clauses of the bill of lading, in respect of all stowage, by suing the owners of the ship in tort' [2]).

Though the language used by the judges in this case is fairly broad, and would seem to imply that agents who perform services which are the subject of the contract generally may invoke clauses in limitation of liability invoked by their principal, it is believed, in the light of a later mentioned case, that the scope of the Elder-Dempster Case should be restricted to agency relationships such as exist between shipowners and charterers. But it is difficult to see a reason for not extending it to the relationship between the aircraft operator and the charterer, which means that the former might also rely on the exemption clauses contained in the contract made by the charterer with the shippers [3]). Whether the rule should apply in case of carriage of persons seems more doubtful, since here no bailment relationship is involved. So, when more recently an English judge was asked to apply an exemption clause to the liability of a busdriver who was sued personally by a passenger holding a free pass, the busdriver was denied that defence for the reason that the bus company, when issuing the free pass, could not be said to have

---

139. [1]) *Per* Viscount Cave at p. 533/34.
[2]) *Per* Viscount Finlay (at this point concurring with other Lords) at p. 548.
[3]) Similarly Shawcross and Beaumont (1951) No. 351.

acted as agent of its employees, even though the clause on the pass expressly excluded the liability of the company and of its servants [4]). But in a recent American case [5]) the Ohio Court of Appeals held that an agent (transport-service) was entitled to the protection of a contractual limitation of liability stipulated by his principal (a fur storage firm) in his own behalf. Again, a lower Dutch Court, in a similar situation as that of the Elder Dempster Case, arrived at the same result as the House of Lords:

'[...] it would appear unreasonable to the Court, that the cargo owner, who has agreed with the carrier/time-charterer, the K.N.S.M., on certain contractual provisions by which the liability of 'the carrier' is excluded or limited in various clauses, would, because of the fortuitous circumstance that the K.N.S.M. held the 'Rossum' in time-charter from the 'Oostzee', have more extensive claims against defendant ('Oostzee') than he has against the K.N.S.M. (carrier) [...]'.

'the abovementioned unreasonableness of the consequences of the system which would hold liability provisions only applicable as between the parties to the contract, is obvious. Therefore, one must assume, in the opinion of the Court, that whenever goods are accepted under condition that the transportation may be performed wholly or partially by third parties, or when it results from the nature of the contract, that the carriage will be performed by another person than the contracting party (as is the case when the order is given to an express agency), the contract should be deemed to contain an implied condition, that its provisions in limitation of liability also apply on behalf of subsequent carriers, or – in the case of express agencies – also on behalf of the carrier(s), even if such provisons have not been worded in general terms'. [6])

But a French Court decided in 1937 that a negligent pilot cannot, against a delictual action brought by a passenger, invoke

139. [4]) *Cosgrove* v. *Horsfall* (1945) 62 T.L.R. 140 (Appeal from Country court). Du Parcq L. J., who delivered the decision, mentioned the possibility that the company might have an action against the claimant for the breach of contract (holding its servant liable notwithstanding the liability clause), in which case it would of course have to prove its damage.

[5]) *Employer's Insurance Co.* v. *United Parcel Service of Cincinnati*, 89 Ohio App. 447/99 N.E. 2d, 794 (1950).

[6]) Rechtbank Amsterdam 7.3.1951, N.J. 1951, No. 573 (*Marine Insurance Co.* v. *N.V. Stoomvaart Mij. 'Oostzee'*).

the contractual limitation of liability of the carrier based on Articles 42 and 48 of the Act of 1924 [7]).

140. It is suggested, however, that one should apply the greatest caution in invoking cases dealing with contractual limitation of liability, as the limitation of liability provided by the Warsaw Convention is not a contractual but a legal one, the importance of which is emphasized by the special provision of Article 24. The dogmatical argument that a contractual clause has no effect except between the contracting parties, has little significance in itself with respect to the legal limitation of Article 22. Meanwhile, especially on the Continent is there a chance that courts will emphasize the contractual character of the liability under the Convention and from there draw the 'logical' – too logical – conclusion that servants or agents who themselves are no party to the contract of carriage cannot invoke the provisions of the Convention; without paying too much attention to the fact that actually the purpose of the provisions which limit the carrier's liability will be frustrated by such a logical solution.

---

139. [7]) Appel Lyon 14.1.1937, 6 R.G.D.A. (1937), 148, at 150, commented by M. Lemoine in 8 R.G.D.A. (1939) at 215 sq. But comp. Appel Paris 11.12. 1952, 7 R.F.D.A. (1935) 99 (*Jeantelot-Pilleboue* v. *C.A.M.A.T.*, *Michelson et Cie.* etc.) where the operating company 'Languedoc-Roussillon' was considered as a mere sub-contractor (the travel agency Michelson et Cie. having mentioned in the ticket its own name as 'carrier') and nevertheless apparently entitled to invoke the contractual limitation of liability permitted by the Act of 1924, provided the general conditions of the applicability of such clauses would have been complied with (which in fact was denied). See also Trib. com. de la Seine 30.7.1948, 3 R.F.D.A. (1949) 201 (*Sofimex* v. *R.U.T. and T.W.A.*) with note by Rabut. Cf. discussion of these decisions by E. Georgiadès in 7 R.F.D.A. (1953) 16, at 36 sq. For **Germany** see Koffka (1937) p. 102, to the effect that the servants of the carrier cannot invoke such clauses unless the carrier had also acted on behalf of the servants.

CHAPTER V

CALCULATION OF LIMITS

141. In the previous Chapters we have discussed the liabilities affected by the limitation of liability provisions and the persons protected thereby. This Chapter will deal with the question how the limits are to be calculated. Some of the problems which arise in this connection are special to each Convention; at least one problem, however, is common to all three. The following pages will successively deal with (1) the problems special to the Warsaw Convention, (2) those common to the Rome Conventions, and (3) the common problem of conversion into national currency. The question of how the amount of the limit is to be allocated in case of more than one claimant, will be discussed in a later Chapter.

§ 1. WARSAW CONVENTION

142. Article 22 of the Convention provides different limits for passengers, for goods and registered baggage, and for objects of which the passenger takes charge himself. It does not contain a special limit for delay as do the Berne Conventions for the railway transportation of passengers and baggage and of goods [1]. Nor does it specify, as does Article 3 of the Brussels Convention of 1924 on the limitation of the shipowner's liability [2], whether the limits must be calculated per event, per flight, or per entire carriage.

142. [1]) The International Convention of 1933, concerning the Carriage of Passengers and Baggage by Railway, (effective 1.10.1938) only limits the liability for delay as far as baggage is concerned (Art. 34). As to goods see Art. 34 of the International Convention Concerning the Carriage of Goods by Railway of the same date. Both conventions govern practically all international railway carriage on the European Continent except that to and from Russia.

[2]) International Convention for the Unification of Certain Rules Concerning the Limitation of Liability of the Owners of Seagoing Vessels, signed at Brussels August 25, 1924, and ratified by Belgium, Brazil, Danmark and Iceland, Finland, France (incl. Algers) Hungary, Monaco, Norway, Poland, Portugal, Spain and Sweden. The Convention became effective on June 2, 1931.

Whereas the first omission does not seem to create any legal problems, the second needs more careful examination. The Article provides that 'in the carriage of passengers the liability of the carrier for each passenger [3]) is limited to the sum of 125,000 francs', 'in the carriage of registered baggage and of goods, the liability of the carrier is limited to a sum of 250 francs per kilogram', and 'as regards objects of which the passenger takes charge himself the liability of the carrier is limited to 5,000 francs per passenger'. With respect to the carriage of goods the situation seems clear. The maximum liability of the carrier (outside the cases of wilful misconduct and incompleteness of documents) as far as loss, damage or delay are concerned is 250 francs per kilogram, whether one event is involved or more. When accepting goods for carriage the shipper knows that he will never receive more than 250 francs per kilogram, the carrier knows that he will never have to pay more than that sum. Thus, if in the first stage of the carriage the shipment is damaged, and in the second stage it suffers delay, the shipper or consignee will not recover more than 250 francs per kilogram for both events together. This is also true if the transportation is performed by successive carriers, and if the two events occur with different carriers. All damages which may arise from the moment the goods were received by the carrier till the moment they are delivered to the consignee – or to the shipper in case the latter instructs the carrier to send the goods back to him – will be included in the one limit of 250 francs per kilogram.

The same should probably apply to registered baggage but the situation may become complicated here if the passenger, during a nightstop, wants to take part of his baggage to his hotel. It is suggested that if the baggage was checked for a further point, the fact that the passenger temporarily takes possession of it does not affect the limit of liability, though it will affect the applicability of the Warsaw Convention to the liability of the

---

142. [3]) The French has 'envers chaque voyageur' which would seem a somewhat loose drafting, as the limitation of liability obviously does not only apply to the liability *towards* the passenger, but includes liabilities towards his next of kin and possibly towards the person (e.g. employer of the passenger) who concluded the contract of carriage (e.g. in case of delay).

The words 'envers chaque voyageur' have been inserted in 1929 (W.C. p. 193). See also No. 147 for the grounds of this insertion.

carrier during the period the baggage is not in the charge of the carrier (Article 18 (2)) [4]).

143. The problem becomes more difficult when the limitation of liability for passengers is concerned. The wording of paragraph (1) is hardly different from that of paragraph (2). Should one, therefore, conclude that the maximum of liability for all events which may cause injuries or delays from the point of departure to the point of destination (as far as the Convention applies to such events) cannot exceed the limit of 125.000 francs? This would certainly be in conformity with the correct interpretation of paragraph (2). But it would not take into account the essential difference between transportation of passengers and goods. From the moment the goods are received by the carrier till the moment they are delivered to the consignee there exists a permanent responsibility on the side of the carrier, even though, exceptionally, the Convention, may not apply continuously. The unity of the carriage is reinforced by Article 30 which makes the first and last carrier liable for the entire carriage. To put it otherwise: performance of the contract of carriage is one continuous transportation. The same is not true for the transportation of passengers. A passenger may buy a ticket providing for one or more 'stopovers', he may buy a roundtrip ticket, or a circular trip ticket, with the first and last part of the voyage separated by a half year or more. Whether he will buy one roundtrip-ticket or two separate one-way tickets may depend on such foreign matters as currency restrictions, roundtrip discounts, etc. If the carriage is performed by more than one carrier, each carrier shall be liable for his own stretch. Because of these differences it is believed that with respect to passengers the limitation of liability must be deemed to comprise all events happening on one flight. A simple nightstop would not break a flight if the passenger continues his voyage by the same aircraft. In view of the close connection between the passenger and his handbaggage [1]) a

142. [4]) This is distinct from the question how far the applicability of the Convention as to baggage follows its applicability as to the passenger. Cf. No. 49 (9).

143. [1]) Because of this connection Goedhuis (1933) p. 212 holds that the period of liability for passengers laid down in Article 17 should be deemed to apply to the limitation of liability for handbaggage. Cf. also Shawcross and Beaumont (1951) No. 417, note (c).

similar construction should be given to the limitation of liability for 'objects of which the passenger takes charge himself'.

To go one step further and have the limit of 125,000 francs apply per event seems an unwarranted departure from the text, and one which in no way would be justified by the general rationale of the limitation provisions: to enable the carrier to calculate his risks in advance of each flight.

144. We shall now discuss the problems which are special to each limit: that for passengers, that for registered baggage and goods and that for objects of which the passenger takes charge himself.

The comment on paragraph (1) dealing with *the 125,000 francs limit for passengers* can be short. Apart from the problem just discussed it does not seem to create any difficulties. Following a German proposal, a sentence was added to take care of the possibility that a court might award compensation in the form of periodical payments. In such a case, the capital value of said payments shall not exceed 125,000 francs. Apparently the capital value is to be calculated at the moment the award is given. Any subsequent changes in the interest rate will not affect the obligations of the liable carrier. But what if the national law of the court giving the award should permit the court from time to time to change the amount of periodical payments in order to adopt them to changing circumstances? If the original judgement was for a periodical payment, the capital value of which would be the equivalent of 125,000 francs, no later increase in the periodical payments would be possible, even if the capital value of the original award had fallen. But if the original award had been less than 125,000 francs, an increase would be possible. It is suggested that the moment of the original award should be taken then as the basis for calculating the capital value of the increased payments, taking into account, of course, that during the first period smaller payments were made.

145. We come now to the second paragraph of Article 22 limiting *the liability for registered baggage and goods* 'to a sum of 250 francs per kilogram' [1]). Though this is probably the most

145. [1]) The further part of the paragraph, dealing with 'declaration of value' will be discussed separately, see Nos. 274 sq.

frequently applied provision in any private air law Convention, its meaning is far from clear [2]). The paragraph can be read in three different ways:

(1) the limit should be computed on the basis of the weight of the entire baggage or of the entire shipment covered by the baggage-check or air waybill. This solution has been adopted by the Italian Codice della Navigazione [3]).

(2) the limit should be computed on the basis of the full weight of the *piece* of the baggage or the shipment from which part is lost or damaged. This solution has been adopted in the Draft Protocol established by the Legal Committee of ICAO (Rio de Janeiro, 1953).

(3) the limit should be based on the weight of the lost or damaged part of the baggage or goods only. This is the solution adopted in the Berne Conventions for railway transportation.

The importance of the question can be best explained by an example. A carrier accepts under one air waybill a shipment of 10 cases of watches, each case weighing 10 kilogram and containing 20 boxes of 4 watches. When delivered to the consignee, it appears that 1 box with 4 golden watches with a weight of 0.400 kilogram has disappeared from one case, with a total value of 4.000 Poincaré gold francs. If the first solution were accepted, the shipper or consignee could recover the full damages of 4.000 francs, since the limit for the entire shipment would be 1.000 × 250 francs or 25,000 francs. If the second solution were followed, the carrier's liability would be limited to 10 × 250 francs or 2,500 francs, or 1500 francs less than the full damages. Under the third solution, however, the maximum recovery would only be 250 francs, or

---

145. [2]) Curiously the problem has not received much attention from the numerous commentators on the Convention. Chauveau discusses it in his outstanding textbook on air law in a footnote (note (45) to No. 356, but comp. No. 366 i.f.) where he seems to take the view that in case of partial loss the limit is to be calculated on the weight of the lost baggage or goods, 'chaque kilo étant présumé avoir la même valeur'. Similarly Litvine (1953) No. 251. Cf. also Shawcross and Beaumont (1951), Nos. 389 and 417, who mention the problem without giving an opinion.

[3]) Art. 952 provides that the liability of the carrier for the carriage of good shall be limited to 300 lira per kilogram *of goods shipped*. This Article applies also to registered baggage (Art. 945). Cf. Art. 101 of the *Ley de Aviación*, 1949 of **Guatemala** (not based on the Warsaw Convention) which limits the carrier's liability for goods to '2 Quetzal per kilogram of the total weight of the goods carried'.

even 0,4 × 250 francs (= 100 francs), if one would accept prorating of the 250 francs limit for parts of kilograms [4]).

146. Nothwithstanding its great practical importance the problem does not seem to have been decided by any court; at least no recorded decision could be traced. An attempt to find judicial interpretation of similar provisions in national laws was also unsuccessful [1]).

A comparison with maritime law is of little help since the limitation of liability, following the Brussels Convention of 1924 on bills of lading, is generally expressed in an amount of money 'per package or unit' [2]). It is clear that in such system of limitation it makes no difference whether the entire package is lost or damaged or only a part, as far as the limit is concerned [3]).

---

[4]) It could be defended that Article 22, taken literally, does not provide for reduction of the 250 gold francs limit in the event of the lost or damaged goods weighing a fraction of a kilogram. But the Tribunal civil of Brussels 30.6.1950, Rev. gén. ass. resp. (1951) 4723, in a case involving a shipment weighing 26.600 kg., has calculated the limit, as a matter of course, by multiplying that figure with the limit per kilogram. Similarly Appel Paris 28.1.1953, 16 R.G.A. (1953) 180 (*Air France* v. *Nordisk Transport*) and the decision of the Amsterdam Court cited *infra* No. 149 (1). Contra Chauveau (1951) No. 356, note (45), and, for the 100 goldfrancs per kilogram limit of the Berne Convention on railway transportation: K. J. Pentinga in 55 B.T.I. (1947) 63 sq. The latter author bases his view (which is said to be in conformity with the practice of the Netherlands Railways) on a decision of the **Netherlands** Hooge Raad 20.4.1882, W. 4771, which held the 30 guilders per 50 kilogram limit for goods and the 7 guilders per kilogram limit for baggage – which limits were provided by the Railway Tariffs then in effect – not to be subject to proration in the event of parts of 50 kilograms (or of one kilogram in case of baggage) being lost or damaged. Curiously the Court invoked the alleged self-evidence of this interpretation, as far as the limit per one kilogram was concerned, as an argument for its correctness with respect to the limit per 50 kilograms.

146. [1]) A limitation of liability per kilogram in special tariffs of the **Spanish** Railways is apparently applied on the basis of the goods lost or damaged. See Resolución de la Dir. Gen. de Ferrocarriles of 18.5.1942, quoted in E. Roldán Carrillo, *Reclamaciones en los Transportes por Ferrocarril y Carretera.* Madrid, 1944, p. 484. An analogous clause in a consignment note for inland watercarriage has been twice construed by a **Netherlands** lower court, once on the basis of the third solution (Rechtbank Amsterdam 24.3.1943, N.J. 1943, No. 779) and three years later on the basis of the first solution (Same 2.1.1946, N.J. 1946, No. 772). See also A. Greebe, *Transportrecht.* 's-Gravenhage, 1944, pp. 74 sq. (in favour of third solution).

[2]) Article V (5) of the Brussels Convention on Bills of Lading of 1924. Comp. No. 36 (4).

[3]) In *The Campfire,* 1946, 156 F. (2d) 603, A.M.C. 1946, I, 644 and II, 1139, a proration clause in an air waybill was held invalid to the extent it would reduce the limit of $500 per package or unit provided in the American Carriage of Goods by Sea Act, 1936. See also Ripert (1952) II No. 2005. Proration of the £ 100 limit has been defended by G. Marais in his *Règles de la Haye.* Paris, 1926, pp. 118/119, but was later rejected by him in conformity with the majority view (see his Transports internationaux de marchandises par mer, 1949, p. 197).

But in a decision of 1947, in which the term 'unit' was construed to refer to the weight unit (Kilogram) used in the bill of lading, the French *Cour de Cassation* seems to have adopted, as a matter of course, the view that in case of partial loss the limit of liability should be calculated on the basis of the weight of the lost part of the shipment [4].

The analogy with declared value clauses would seem too weak to attach much value in this respect to Court decisions allowing or forbidding proration of the declared value in case of partial loss [5] [6].

147. Of the three possible interpretations, it is believed that the one which would base the limit on the weight of the entire baggage or shipment has least to recommend itself. Such arguments as can be based on the drafting history of the Convention, whatever their value may be, point rather to the second interpretation (weight of piece of baggage or of goods) or to the third interpretation (weight of the lost or damaged part only), unless one were to make an argument of the failure of a British proposal at the Warsaw Conference to insert in paragraph (2) the words 'for each package'. The purpose of this proposal which also comprised the insertion of the words 'towards each passenger' ('envers chaque voyageur') in paragraph (1), was to make it clear 'that the liability of the carrier applies to each particular case, and does not constitute a global liability for a total sum computed proportionately in accordance with the number of passengers and the weight of the goods and baggage carried' [1]. Whereas the

---

146. [4]) Cass. req. 28.4.1947, D. 1948, J. 505, note Ripert. The damages claimed in this case remained, however, below the limit, even when calculated on the basis of the weight of the lost part.

[5]) For France see Ripert (1952) II, No. 2005 (mentions some conflicting decisions of lower courts).

[6]) Though accepting proration of the declared value, without adopting the 'third solution' concerning Article 22, could lead to the rather curious situation that the 'Warsaw limit' computed on the full weight of the shipment would set the minimum for proration. If the declared value would be twice the Warsaw limit, the limitation of liability of the carrier would be the same (i.e. the Warsaw limit) whether 25% or 50% of the shipment would be lost, whereas in excess of a 50% loss, the limitation would increase proportionately. The question whether through a declaration of value (or a proration thereof in case of partial loss) the carrier's liability can be limited below the limit of Article 22 will be discussed in No. 278.

147. [1]) W.C. p. 193.

amendment of paragraph (1) was adopted, that concerning the limitation of liability for goods was rejected, unfortunately without the motives having been recorded.

The practical consequences of the interpretation, moreover, would be most undesirable, as it would create obstacles against such useful practices in air transportation as the pooling of baggage on one ticket, when a group of passengers are travelling together, or the consolidation of various small shipments into one larger shipment. The carrier would be impelled to avoid having more than one package shipped on one air waybill. Certainly no shipping interest would be promoted thereby. With respect to baggage, the interpretation would create even more serious difficulties. What should be the basis for calculating the limit of liability if – as not unfrequently happens – a passenger during the course of his journey had purchased an additional suitcase, and if one of the pieces of baggage checked with the carrier at the point of origin had been missing after completion of the journey? The weight of the baggage at the start of the journey or the weight after addition of the new suitcase? When the wording of the Article and its drafting history fail to give any indication, arguments based on the practical effects should weigh heavy, if they should not prevail. Therefore, it is believed that the first solution is to be rejected.

148. The arguments which militate against or in favour of the second and third solutions are more in balance. For both interpretations some, not very strong, reasons can be drawn from the history of the Article. Those in favour of the second solution can point to the Paris Draft of 1925 which had a limitation per package ('par colis') instead of on a weight basis. The change was made at the instance of IATA in order to enable the carriers to calculate in advance the extent of their risks [1]).

In view of the indubitable influence exercised by the Berne Railway Conventions [2]), the argument in favour of the third interpretation to be drawn from the analogous provisions of

---

148. [1]) Report of De Vos to the 2d Session of CITEJA 1927, p. 64 and W.C. p. 165. Cf. Goedhuis (1933) p. 208.

[2]) Especially the Berne Convention of railway transportation of goods has been a major source for the draft convention on air waybills which in 1926 was combined with the Paris 1925 draft on the liability of the air carrier.

these conventions would seem at least as strong. Article 31 of the Convention on the carriage of passengers and baggage contains a limit of 40 francs [3]) per kilogram *gross weight of baggage lost* (which is equivalent to 200 francs of the 'Poincaré gold franc' used in the Warsaw Convention) and Article 29 of the Convention on the carriage of goods has a limit of 100 francs [4]) per kilogram *gross weight of goods lost* (equivalent to 500 'Poincaré goldfrancs'). The same limits apply in case of damage to baggage or goods [5]). Whereas the railway Conventions, by adding the words 'gross weight of goods (baggage) lost' ('de poids brut manquant'), made it clear that in case of partial loss or damage only the weight of the goods lost or damaged should be taken into account in computing the limit of liability, the words were omitted from the Warsaw Convention.

A purely grammatical interpretation of the text would also be more favourable for the third (or the first) interpretation than for the second. The notion of package or 'piece' does not occur in the whole Article.

Finally there is the practical objection that the weight of the piece of baggage or of the shipment may be difficult to determine since it need not be mentioned on the baggage check or air waybill [6]). The weight of the lost or damaged part, on the other hand, is easily determined by deducting the weight of the baggage or goods at delivery from their weight as indicated on the baggage check or air waybill.

But the equity seems to be on the side of the interpretation which takes into account the weight of the entire parcel or package from which something is lost or broken. No court would be happy to award 250 francs or even 25 francs for a watch stolen from a heavy suitcase due to the negligence of the carrier, simply because the watch weighed not more than 0.10 kilogram. If the loss were

148. [3]) The Article also establishes a limit of 20 francs (or 100 Poincaré gold francs) in case the passenger cannot prove his damage.

[4]) Before the revision of 1933 the limit was 50 francs (or 200 Poincaré gold francs).

[5]) Articles 33 (baggage) and 32 (goods) of the respective Conventions.

[6]) There exists a curious difference between Article 4 (g) requiring 'the number and weight of the *packages*' to be mentioned on the baggage check, and Article 8 (i) which speaks of 'the weight, the quantity, the volume or dimensions of *the goods*', whereas Art. 8 (h) speaks of 'the number of *the packages*'. But it is suggested that the difference only stems from the fact that in Article 4 (otherwise than in Article 8) number and weight are combined in one item, which led to the use of the word 'packages', since it would be difficult to speak of 'number of baggages'. See also Nos. 259 and 269.

combined with a breaking of the suitcase, the limit for the latter damage would be substantially higher, since it would have to be based on the weight of the suitcase. It is believed, with some hesitation, that this argument of equity should prevail over the not too strong arguments of a grammatical, historical and practical nature, which can be invoked for the third interpretation [7]).

149. Before closing these remarks on the calculation of the limit for registered baggage and goods, it should be noted that the weight to be taken into account for the purpose of this provision is the *actual* weight of the baggage or goods, as evidenced – subject to proof to the contrary – by the air waybill. A fictitious weight, whether higher or lower than the actual weight, which may be agreed upon by the parties as a basis for computing the freight, or for any other reason, will be irrelevant. Any other solution would allow the carrier to have his liability limited below the limit of Article 22 (2), and would make the amount of the carrier's liability depend upon the form in which the freight rate would be established. Article 22 (2) does allow the parties to agree to an increase of the limit by a declaration of value, or otherwise, but it is clear that the introduction of a fictitious weight in excess of the actual weight for the computation of the freight to be paid, can never by itself be construed as an agreement to increase the limit of carrier's liability [1]).

150. The third paragraph of Article 22 deals with the objects of which the passenger keeps charge himself. It raises the following questions:
(1) what are the objects to which the Article refers?
(2) what is the period of applicability of the paragraph?
(3) should there be any proration in case of partial loss or damage?

---

148. [7]) The solution which bases the limit on the weight of the piece or package, rather than on the lost or damaged part, was also adopted in the Protocol established by the Legal Committee of ICAO at its 9th Session (Rio de Janeiro, 1953).

149. [1]) *Contra:* the un-published first instance decision of the district-court of Amsterdam of 7 January 1953, No. 2833/1951, in *Amstelhoeden N.V.* v. *Pan American World Airways Inc.*, with the circular reasoning that 'defendant knew this [ficticious] weight when it accepted the goods for carriage, so that it can be assumed that, by receiving freight on the basis of that weight, it has taken into account that it would also have to pay compensation on the basis of that weight for possible damage'.

The first question will be discussed in a later Chapter [1]).

As to the second question, the third paragraph of Article 22 does not indicate during which period it applies. Nor do the other paragraphs, but they refer to liabilities regulated elsewhere in the Convention, and the provisions establishing these liabilities (Article 17 and 18) do mention the period during which they apply. It is the particular characteristic of the third paragraph that it limits a liability which itself does not have its roots in the Convention, but must be based on national law. It has been suggested that Article 17 could be invoked in the event of an accident to the passenger, also as far as damage to personal objects is concerned, since this Article generally states that 'the carrier is liable for damage sustained *in the event* of the death or wounding of a passenger or other bodily injury suffered by him' [2]). It seems highly doubtful that this has ever been intended [3]). To lay down a special rule for property damage applying only if that damage is accompanied by death or injury, seems somewhat irrational. This does not mean, of course, that a court could not decide, within the framework of the national law applied by it to this liability, to apply the principle of Article 17 by way of analogy. Nor does it mean that the period of liability defined in Article 17 should not also be considered as determining the sphere of applicability of Article 22 (3). In view of the close relationship between the liability risks dealt with in Article 17 and those referred to in Article 22 (3), it seems reasonable not to extend the scope of the latter provision beyond that of Article 17 [4]).

As to the third question, whether there should be any proration of the limit of 5.000 francs in case of the loss or damage of only

---

150. [1]) See Nos. 256 and 257.

[2]) Shawcross and Beaumont, (1951) No. 417, note (c). The view, expressed by N. H. Moller, *Law of Civil Aviation*, London 1936, p. 313, that in case of an accident of a passenger the 125.000 gold francs limit of Art. 22 (1) would also apply to damage or loss of his baggage (even his registered baggage) seems untenable in view of the system and the clear intention of the liability provisons. See also § 29a (1) of the **German** Air Traffic Act 1936 (*Luftverkehrsgesetz*) as amended in 1943, which has added to the principle of Art. 17 of the Warsaw Convention the following clause: 'The same shall apply to damage caused to property which the passenger wears or carries with him'.

[3]) See the clear statement of the Reporter De Vos at the Warsaw Conference, p. 165.

[4]) Similarly Goedhuis (1933) p. 212, and (1937) p. 259.

a part of the personal objects, the answer is not difficult. The wording of the paragraph clearly excludes proration. The limit cannot even be considered as an automatically declared value, and any basis for proration (whether weight or value) would be arbitrary [5]).

§ 2. ROME CONVENTIONS

151. The limitation of liability for surface damage is laid down in Article 8 of the Convention of 1933 and Article 11 of the Convention of 1952. The general principles of limitations in the two Conventions are the same. Both have a global limit proportionate to the maximum take-off weight of the aircraft, combined with a special limit per person injured or killed (200,000 francs in the 1933 Convention, 500,000 francs in the 1952 Convention). Both have a minimum global limit (600,000 francs in the 1933 Convention, 500,000 francs in the 1952 Convention), but whereas the Convention of 1933 has a maximum limit of 2,000,000 francs, applying to all aircraft weighing 8,000 kilogram or more, the Convention of 1952 contains no such maximum. The adequateness of the limits and the problems arising from the allocation and distribution of the limits will not be discussed in this Chapter [1]), which will only deal with the difficulties which may arise in calculating the limits.

152. The Conference of 1952 clarified one point which was left somewhat obscure in the Convention of 1933: how to compute the limit if the damage is caused by two aircraft of the same operator. Article 11 of the 1952 Convention makes it clear that the limits applicable to each aircraft are to be cumulated. This was certainly also the intention in the Convention of 1933, and is not precluded by its wording.

The new Convention also amended the definition of the weight of the aircraft by making a proviso for lighter-than-air craft ('excluding the effect of lifting gas when used' in paragraph 3).

The possibility of the towing of one or more aircraft by another

150. [5]) Similarly Mazeaud III (1950) No. 2348, note (2).

151. [1]) See Chapter VIII.

aircraft does not appear to pose a serious problem as far as the computation of the limit of liability is concerned. If one of the aircraft comes down, the weight of that aircraft only is to be taken into account. If both the towing and the towed aircraft crash, the damage caused by each will be subject to the limit applicable to each. It is believed that in this case the collision articles, speaking of collision only (Article 6 of the 1933 Convention) or of collision and interference (Article 7 of the 1952 Convention), do not apply. It seems higly doubtful whether the maritime cases offer sound analogies, in view of the difference in situations and risks [1]).

153. But the real difficulties arise in respect to the special limit for persons killed or injured: (1) should this limit be applied before or after claims for death or injuries have been reduced by the global limitation per aircraft; (2) should there be for each person a cumulation of the amounts of the special limitation in case the accident is caused by more than one aircraft?

The first problem can best be clarified by an example:
An aircraft of 2,000 kilogram weight has killed two persons A and B. The damages sustained by the dependants of A amount to 500,000 francs, those suffered by the dependants of B amount to 1,000,000 francs. The accident is governed by the Rome Convention of 1952 and the global limit for the aircraft is therefore 900,000 francs. If the individual limit per person killed is applied before the global limit, this will mean that one starts by reducing the claims for B to 500,000 francs, the claims for A remaining as they are (500,000 francs). The allocation of the global limit of 900.000 francs will take place on the basis of the thus reduced claims, each amounting to 500,000 francs, so that eventually the dependants of A and the dependants of B each receive $\frac{1}{2} \times$ 900,000 francs (global limit per aircraft) or 450,000 francs, which is 90% of the full damages sustained by the former and only 45% of the full damages sustained by the latter.

If one were, however, to apply the individual limit per person killed after distribution of the global limit per aircraft, the result would be that first the global limit would be allocated, each

152. [1]) Cf. for **Dutch** law Woltman (1936) 88–90, for **England** Marsden, *Collisions at Sea*, 10th ed. London, 1953, pp. 195/196.

group of dependants receiving $\frac{900,000}{1,500,000}$ or 3/5 of their claim. The dependants of A would have allocated to them: 3/5 of 500,000 francs or 300,000 francs, and those of B: 3/5 of 1,000,000 or 600,000 francs. The latter amount would then have to be limited to 500,000 francs (limit per person killed) leaving an additional 100,000 francs for the dependants of A who would thus recover a total of 400,000 francs (instead of 450,000 francs under the other system).

We have taken the most simple example. It is clear that, in practice, the allocation would be much more complicated, especially if, apart from causing death, the aircraft would have inflicted substantial property damage. Under Article 14 (b) of the Rome Convention 1952 the death and injury claims are privileged for one half of the global limit, any unpaid part of their claims sharing proportionately with the property damage claims for the other half of the global limit. The complications can again best be illustrated by an example. If in the above given hypothetical case there had also been a property damage amounting to 750,000 francs, the two systems would work out as follows. Under the first system (applying the individual limit before allocation of the global limit) there would be two death claims cut down to 500,000 francs each, and one property damage claim of 750,000 francs.

The death claims would have a preference on half the total available amount of 900,000 francs (global limit) or 450,000 francs, or 225,000 francs for A and 225,000 francs for B. This would still leave 275,000 francs to be claimed by each on the other 450,000 francs availabe for both death and property damage claims. The total amount of claims on this undistributed 450,000 francs would amount to $2 \times 275,000 + 750,000$ francs or 1,300,000 francs. Each claim would, therefore, have to be reduced to $\frac{450,000}{1,300,000}$ or $\frac{9}{26}$, A and B each receiving, in addition to the 225,000 recovered by them, $9/26 \times 275,000$ francs or approx. 95190 francs, making an approximate total for A and B each of 320,190 francs, leaving approximately 259,620 francs for the property damage.

Under the second system (application of the individual limit only after distribution of the global limit), A will start by receiving 1/3 of the 450,000 francs available for death claims or 150,000 francs, and B twice as much, or 300,000 francs, A will remain with an unsatisfied claim of 350,000 francs and B with a claim of 700,000 francs. These remaining claims share together with the property damage claim of 750,000 francs, making a total of 350,000 + 700,000 + 750,000 francs or 1,800,000 francs, against an available amount of 450,000 francs or 25%, so that each will get only 25% of his claim, which gives A 87,500 francs, B 175,000 francs and for property damage 187,500 francs. The total amount allocated for the death of A will be 150,000 + 87,500 or 237,500 francs, and for B, 300,000 + 175,000 francs or 475,000 francs. Since both amounts are less than the special limit of 500,000 francs per person killed or injured, that limit does not come into play. Had the property damage been only 150,000 francs, there would have been available 37½% for A, B and the property damages, and B would have received 262,500 francs in addition to the 300,000 already received, which would make a total allocation of 562,500 francs. Applying the 500,000 limit for persons killed, there would remain an undistributed amount of 62,500 francs. Query: how should this amount be allocated between A and the person sustaining the property damage?

This exercise in arithmetics was necessary to explain the difficulties which will be faced by courts when applying the limits and also the different results which one obtains by applying the limits for death or injuries either before or after allocating the global limit per aircraft. From the given examples two things follow:

(1) application of the 500,000 francs limit per person *before* distribution of the global limit may result in neglecting the differences between the damages suffered in the various death cases. This will only be true when one or more of the death claims substantially exceed the individual limit of 500,000 francs (or 200,000 francs in the Convention of 1933).

(2) application of the 500,000 francs limit per person after distribution of the global limit will lead the courts into a jungle of arithmetics, and raises questions of how to allocate the undistributed amounts remaining after final application of the individual limit per person killed or injured, questions for which it is difficult to find any non-arbitrary answers.

541. Having stated the problems, it is time to examine whether the texts of the Conventions offer any guidance one way or the other. The 200,000 francs limit of the Convention of 1933 is to be found in paragraph 3 of Article 8, reading:

> 'One third of this value [i.e. of the global limit defined in paragraphs 1 and 2] shall be assigned to compensation for damages caused to property and the other two-thirds to compensation for damage caused to persons, provided that in this last case the compensation contemplated cannot exceed 200,000 francs per person injured'.

How are the words 'indemnité prévue' ('compensation contemplated') to be construed? They have been translated in the British Parliamentary Papers into 'the compensation payable' [1]), which does not seem to render accurately the french word 'prévue'. The question is important, for with the latter translation the result probably would be that the 200,000 francs limit would be applied after allocation of the global limit. But, following the translation adopted above [2]), the words could very well refer to the amount of the claim assessed by the court as being entitled to a proportionate part of the amount of the global limit, which would mean that the 200,000 francs limit had to be applied *before* the distribution of the limit per aircraft. The problem does not seem to have been appreciated either by the drafters of the Convention or by the authors commenting on it [3]).

154. [1]) British Parliamentary Papers, Misc. No. 6 (1935) Cmd. 5056. Also in Shawcross and Beaumont (1951) Nos. 1130 sq.

[2]) Which is the translation given in the U.S. Treaty Information Bulletin, No. 47, p. 27. Also in M.O. Hudson, *International Legislation*, Washington, 1937, VI, p. 335, 338.

[3]) The interpretation of the American proposal (to adopt a special limit for death and injury cases) given by the Reporter (Ambrosini) at the Rome Conference, 1933 (I, 204) rather seems to assume the special limit to be applicable before the global limit. Similarly the comment by the German Delegate Oppikofer written immediately after the Conference in 3 A.L. (1933) 211, 228, who speaks of the limits of 200.000 fr. 'within' the global limits. But Giannini, who presided at the Rome Conference, in a study also written immediately after the end of the Conference, seems to take the view that the 200.000 francs limit is to be applied after distribution of the limit per aircraft. See his *Nuovi Saggi di Diritto Aeronautico*, Milano, 1940, pp. 137 sq., at 226: after having stated that two-thirds of the limit per aircraft is destined for the personal claims, he adds 'but the compensation to be paid to each injuried person cannot exceed 200.000 francs'. The Italian legislator, when incorporating the Rome Convention into the Cod. Nav. has clearly adopted the view taken by Ambrosini and Oppikofer. Art. 968 provides: 'The claimants entitled to damages for accidents to persons [on the surface] have, *within the maximum limit of 250.000 lira per person*, a concurring claim on the two-thirds of the amount to which the total compensation by the operator is limited, etc.'.

The two provisions in the Convention of 1952 dealing with the matter are Article 11 (2) and the introductory phrase of Article 14:

> Art. 11 (2): 'The liability in respect of loss of life or personal injury shall not exceed 500,000 francs per person killed or injured'
> Article 14: 'If the total amount of the claims established exceeds the limit of liability applicable under the provisions of this Convention, the following rules shall apply, taking into account the provisions of paragraph 2 of Article 11:'

Paragraph 2 of Article 11 was adopted by the Legal Committee of ICAO at its Mexico Session, pursuant to a joint Scandinavian proposal. The proposal was explained by the Swedish Delegate as follows (as recorded in the Minutes):

> 'The second proposal was based on a provision in the Rome Convention. He gave the example of a case where the total limit was 600,000 francs and where one person was entitled to 200,000 francs and another to 1,000,000 francs. Under these circumstances the first person would have his claim reduced to 100,000 francs and the second person would get 500,000 francs. This result could not be accepted as it might be shocking to many countries. The Rome Convention provided that, where there was a risk of exceeding the limits, no person should have more than 200,000 francs for such damages, etc.' [4]).

From the example offered it would seem to follow that at least the initiators of the special limit for death or injuries had in mind that this limit would be applied *before* the global limit per aircraft. But the problem itself was not mentioned by them.

When Article 14 came up for discussion it was suggested that a reference to the new paragraph in Article 11 be inserted. Though the U.S. Delegate pointed out 'that the Drafting Committee should consider Article 10 (later to become Article 14) very carefully in order to see whether or not it was contradictory to the decision taken by the Committee in regard to the limitation of claims for compensation in respect of bodily injury' [5]), the relation between the limit per aircraft and the limit per person was not considered.

154. [4]) Mexico Session (1951), p. 129.
[5]) Mexico Session (1951), p. 180.

The wording which was adopted seems rather to suggest that application of the special limit should come after allocation of the global limit. For instead of inserting the words 'taking into account the provisions of paragraph 2 of Article 11' directly after 'the claims established', they were put at the end, so that 'the claims established', on the basis of which the distribution of the global limit is to be made, apparently should be taken to mean the claims established without yet taking into account the limits of Article 11, since otherwise the later reference to Article 11 (2) would be superfluous. On the other hand a number of Delegates at the Conference supported the individual limit for persons killed or injured for the very reason that, without an individual limit, the very large claims of some victims would practically suppress the claims of the poorer victims [6]). There can be no doubt that these delegates had in mind application of the individual limit before distribution of the global limit.

Neither the historical, nor the grammatical arguments in one way or the other, however, are of such force that they can be considered final. In that state of affairs it is believed that the typical nature of the global limit may be accepted as decisive in the sense that the distribution of the available amount per aircraft is the final thing, so that any special limits are to be applied prior to that. The limitation of the operator's liability based on the weight of the aircraft belongs to the same family as the limitation of the shipowner's liability for all debts of the shipowner arising from the venture, whether that limitation be based on the value of the ship before or after the accident, or on its tonnage, or whether it gives the shipowner the right to abandon his ship. The procedure for allocating the amount is not very different from bankruptcy proceedings. The individual claims will have to be established first before 'liquidating' the amount of liability, and that necessarily means that they must be established taking into account any special limits to the extent they are applicable. Nobody could doubt that the cargo claims against the shipowner can only be filed in the general limitation proceedings subject to the special limits established for them under the Brussels Convention on bills of ladings or analogous national laws. The

---

154. [6]) Especially the Mexican Delegate at I, 143[4]144, also I, 148.

relation between the global limit per aircraft and the special limit per person killed or injured seems sufficiently similar to ask for a similar solution.

155. The second problem arising in connection with the special limit for death or personal injuries is the question whether, in case of a collision of aircraft killing a person on the ground, the limit of 200,000 (or 500,000) francs is to be allowed for each aircraft so that the victim could recover twice the limit. As far as the global limit per aircraft is concerned, there can be no doubt that in case of collision the limits of all aircraft involved are cumulated, at least under the Convention of 1952 [1]): Article 13 (2) of this Convention provides:

> 'When the provisions of Article 7 [i.e. the collision Article] are applicable, the person who suffers damage shall be entitled to be compensated up to the aggregate of the limits applicable with respect to each of the aircraft involved, but no operator shall be liable for a sum in excess of the limit applicable to his aircraft unless his liability is unlimited under the terms of Article 12'.

The provision speaks of 'the limits applicable with respect to each of the aircraft involved'. This clearly refers to the limit of Article 11 (1), i.e. the limit per aircraft. It is believed that it does not include the limit of Article 11 (2), which is not a limit 'applicable to the aircraft', so that no cumulation of the latter limits is allowed. Though the situation in the Convention of 1933 is less clear, this is also probably the better construction of that Convention. The difficulty here is that the 200,000 francs limit is stated at the end of a paragraph dealing with the distribution of the global limit per aircraft. The problem does not seem to have been considered by the authors commenting on this Convention.

---

155. [1]) For the Convention of 1933 the situation is less clear, as Article 6, dealing with collisions, uses exactly the same wording as Article 5, dealing with the joint liability of the lawful and unlawful user ('the liability of each being subject to the conditions and limitations of this Convention'). But in the collision cases *two* aircraft are involved, and where Article 8 (limitation article) says that 'the operator shall be liable [...] up to an amount of 250 francs for each kilogram of the weight of the aircraft' (singular: 'l'aéronef'), it is clear that it refers to the aircraft operated by the operator who is held liable.

§ 3. CONVERSION INTO NATIONAL CURRENCIES

156. In all three Conventions the limits have been expressed in 'francs'. The Warsaw and the first Rome Convention contain almost identical definitions of this 'franc':

> 'The sums mentioned above [resp. given in francs in this Convention] shall be deemed to refer to the French franc consisting of 65½ milligrams gold of millesimal fineness 900. These sums may be converted into any national currency in round figures'.

When these two Conventions were drafted, the French franc actually had the goldvalue stated in the definition, after its value had been stabilised in 1928 by Poincaré. For this reason it is often referred to as the Poincaré gold franc [1]). The drafters of the Conventions wisely fixed the gold value of the unit used, whilst leaving to France the satisfaction of the French franc being taken as basis. As long as the French franc did not devaluate, calculation of the limits in France was very simple indeed, or rather no calculation was necessary. But in other countries obviously some conversion had to be made. For that reason the sentence was added that the sums 'may be converted into each national currency in round figures'. After devaluation of the franc the French Courts also became faced with the problems of conversion. These are manifold and more important than has often been realized [2]). Though the point was raised – without success – at the Mexico Session of 1951 [3]) (on the Rome Convention), and was discussed at the Session of the Warsaw Subcommittee of 1952, a number of Delegates at the Rome Conference of 1952, where the problem, for the first time, was amply studied [4]) appar-

---

156. [1]) Not to be confused with the goldfranc used in the Berne Railway Conventions (art. 56), consisting of 10/31 of one gram gold of millesimal fineness 900 (ab. 5 × the Poincaré gold franc) which is the same as the gold franc used in the Postal Conventions.

[2]) But see Sullivan in 7 J.A.L. (1936) 1 sq., 38, R. Homburg in 13 R.G.A. (1950), 229–231, J. Lacombe in 11 R.G.A. (1948), 179 sq., 207–210. Chauveau (1951), No. 354, especially note (44). Comp. with respect to analogous problems arising under the Brussels Convention of 1924 on bills of lading: Knauth (1953), pp. 283 sq., M. J. Renard in 3 D.M.F. (1951) 523 sq.

[3]) Minutes p. 281. The proposal was also made during the Session, but not supported. The published Minutes are on this point deficient.

[4]) See R.C. 1952, I, 155/58, 345/48, and II, 211.

ently were still not aware of the most unfortunate consequences of the right to convert the gold francs into 'national currencies in round figures', as laid down in the Conventions of Warsaw and of Rome (1933).

157. The two Conventions give the right to convert the gold franc into national currencies but they fail to say (1) how this conversion should be made, and (2) what moment should be taken for determining the rate of conversion.

When the national currency has a fixed gold value, there is no serious problem as to *how* conversion is to be made, since the rate of conversion obviously will be based on the relation between the gold value of the gold franc and that of the national monetary unit. This will even be the case where the official definition of the gold value of the national currency is not in conformity with economic reality. For the court or arbitrator who is to determine the rate of conversion will be bound by its national law [1]. But the problem becomes difficult whenever the local currency has no established gold value: the so-called 'floating currencies', such as are known in a number of countries, especially where there exist more than one official rate of exchange [2]. Since it was the rationale of the gold value provisions in the Conventions to avoid, as far as the limits are concerned, the effects of devaluations which would result from having the limits expressed in any local currency, generally that rate of exchange is to be preferred which is most in conformity with this rationale. But to apply a black market rate would be against the public order of the State whose currency was involved [3].

---

157. [1]) But if the court – assuming its national law would permit it to do so – were to give a judgment for damages to be paid in a foreign currency, it would not be bound by the public policy of the foreign country, the currency of which would be involved. If the country where the judgment were to be given, would have a free market both for gold and for the foreign currency concerned, the rate of conversion should be based on the relation between the marketprice for gold and that for the foreign currency.

[2]) See J. Lacombe in 9 R.G.A. (1948) 179, at 207 sq. and R. Homburg in 13 R.G.A. (1950) 229.

[3]) The question is not to be confused with the one faced by courts when they have to assess damages for loss of property in case of price control concerning such property. Establishing the limit in national currency is something entirely different from assessing damages.

158. Even if the relation between the gold value of the local currency and that of the gold franc used in the Conventions does not pose serious difficulties, there still remains the question which *date* should be chosen to determine the gold rate of the local currency. The following moments can be defended as relevant:

(1) the moment that the national legislator ratifies or adhers to the Convention or any later moment chosen by the legislator,

(2) the moment that the claim arises,

(3) the moment that judgement or an arbitral award is given,

(4) the date of payment.

159. (1) A number of national legislators have assumed the right under the conversion provisions to fix the conversion rate by statute. Thus Belgium converted in 1936 the 'Warsaw limit' of 125,000 gold francs into 250,000 Belgian francs and the 250 gold francs per kilogram into 500 Belgian francs [1]); Brazil in 1938 into 100,000 cruz. and 200 cruz. [2]); Germany in 1933 into 20,000 R.M. and 40 R.M. [3]); Italy into 160,000 lira and 300 lira [4]); Luxemburg in 1949 into 375,000 fr. and 750 fr. [5]); Switzerland in 1952 into 36,250 Sw. fr. and 72.50 Sw. fr. [6]).

If these converted amounts are applied to transportation governed by the Convention [7]), it is clear that little will be left of the intended unification with limits ranging from $272 to

---

159. [1]) Act of 7.4.1936. Similarly the Decree of 6.1.1937 for the Belgian Congo. Comp. Litvine (1953) No. 217.

[2]) *Codigo do Ar*, 1938, art. 91.

[3]) Act of 15 December 1933, R.G.Bl. 1933. II. 1040.

[4]) Artt. 943 and 952 Cod. nav. It is to be observed that the Italian legislator has slightly increased the passenger limit in relation to the limit for goods (from lira 150.00 to lira 160.000).

[5]) Art. 3 of the Act of 25.7. 1949 Memorial 1949, No. 36, also in 4 R.F.D.A. (1949) 171.

[6]) Art. 9 of the Lufttransportreglement 1952. The Scandinavian countries have converted these limits into 18, 250 and 36,50 *gold crowns*, as distinguished from their official currency, in order to prevent devaluation of the limits. This means that they simply have substituted another gold unit for the unit used in the Warsaw Convention. For the conversion of the gold crowns into the current money of these countries the same problem will arise as to the date to be taken for determining the rate of exchange, except that the choice to be made is only between the 2d, 3d and 4th possibility. The recently amended Finnish Act has in Art. 33 (2) (1) a limit per passenger of 194,500 gold marks. The author is greatly endebted to Mr. Karl Sidenbladh, who was so kind to explain to him the particularities of Scandinavian law on this point.

[7]) As to the Rome Convention, 1933, comp. the Belgian implementing Act of 11.9. 1936, Mon. belge 14.2.1937, also fixing the limits on a basis of 2 Belgian francs in one French gold franc.

$8,280, which is the actual equivalent of 125,000 gold francs. This raises two questions: (1) a question of interpretation of Article 22 (4), to-wit whether and to what extent States are allowed to fix from time to time the value of the amounts in gold francs in the local currency; (2) a question of national law, to-wit whether and to what extent a national law, enacted at the time of or after ratification of a treaty, is valid, if contrary to any of the treaty provisions.

Is the right to convert the amounts in gold francs into national currencies a right given only to the courts when fixing the extent of the liability in each case, or is it also a right given to the local legislators to fix by law the amounts of the limits in their own currency? The wording of the phrase seems to support the latter broader interpretation, for the right to make the conversion 'in round figures' would have little sense if only the right of the courts to establish the limits in each individual case had been envisaged. It is to be observed that paragraph (4) refers to the sums mentioned in the foregoing paragraphs which includes the limit of 250 francs per kilogram. It is difficult to think of any need to allow courts to state the value of 250 francs *in round figures*, subject to the necessary multiplication of the amount so fixed on the basis of the weight of the baggage or goods. Apart from that, courts are not used to establish damages *in round figures*. They would not do so anyhow for damages remaining below the limits. But it is entirely reasonable for a legislator to claim the right, when implementing the Convention and when converting its limits into the local currency, to depart slightly from the exact countervalue, in order to have round figures in its law and not complicated amounts with fractions of its monetary unit.

This interpretation is borne out by the drafting history of the Rome Convention, 1933. On a question from the Delegate of Japan whether the phrase meant 'that each contracting State may, when legislating, calculate the equivalent sum according to its national laws on the basis of the gold value of its own currency', the Reporter Ambrosini answered; 'under the Draft, the sum to be paid is fixed in an unvariable way. When each national law wants to state an equivalent of what is envisaged in Article [error for: 'paragraph'] 5 [of Article 4], I think they can do, but there should always be an equivalence between the sum paid and that which is fixed in paragraph 5 of the Draft' [9]). It is true that the final words ('but there should always be etc.') throw some doubt on the thoughts of the Reporter as to the significance of a conversion by legislation. Probably they should be understood to point to the obligation of the States to ensure that the sums to be paid are equivalent to the limits expressed in the Convention. Of course, the drafting history of the Rome Convention has only an indirect bearing on the interpretation of the Warsaw Convention, based on the similarity between the conversion clauses in both Conventions. Unfortunately the preparatory work of the Warsaw Convention does not throw any light on the issue.

In view of the wording of the provisions, it is believed that the right of the Contracting States to fix the countervalue of the limits in national currencies by way of legislation cannot be denied [10]). This does not mean, however, that the States would not have the obligation, as pointed out by the Reporter at the Rome Conference of 1933, to keep the national legislation in line with the gold value of the limits as fixed in the Conventions. But this obligation is one of public international law, only to be invoked by States. Non-compliance with it, it is suggested, does not affect the validity of a national law which would have established the equivalent in national money, if, due to subsequent devaluation, that sum were not to correspond any more with the gold value provided by the Conventions [11]). It might be different, if at the time the conversion rate was already fixed by legislation, it did not correspond with the limits of the Conventions. Whether in such a case the Convention would set aside the national law will entirely depend upon the answer to be given to the second question. This is no longer a matter of interpretation of the Warsaw Convention or the Rome Conventions 1933, but one here gets into the much debated issue of the relation between national

---

159. [9]) R.C. 1933, I, 158/159. A Netherlands proposal to change the phrase into 'they may be converted by the competent court into the currency of the State of that court' was withdrawn without motives (p. 158).

[10]) Cf. J.R. Machado in Rev. for. 124 (1949), 301 at 302.

[11]) Cf. Trib. civ. Brussels 30.6.1950, Rev. gén. ass. resp. (1951) 4723, deciding that the Act of 1936 fixing the amounts of the limits in Belgian francs prevails over the gold franc limit of the Warsaw Convention. See also Litvine, No. 217.

law and treaty, to discuss which, even summarily, would go far beyond the scope of this study. It is believed that in practice courts will in most cases try to avoid the issue by reconciling the allegedly conflicting provisions of the local law and the treaty. The necessity to do so will not easily arise if one accepts the above suggested view that there is no conflict between the national law and the Convention, provided the conversion into national currency corresponded at the time of enactment with the gold value of the limits given in the Convention.

160. It may sometimes be difficult to determine whether a national law was intended to fix a conversion pursuant to Article 22 (4) of the Warsaw Convention or Article 19 of the Rome Convention 1933. The Netherlands Air Transportation Act of 1936 offers a notable example. It was enacted 3 years after the Warsaw Convention had been ratified and it purports to deal with all air transportation, domestic and international, except that such provisions of the Warsaw Convention as differ from those of the Act of 1936 will prevail whenever the Convention applies [1]). At the time of enactment of the Act, the 12,500 guilders limit contained in its Article 30, was the countervalue of 125,000 gold francs. It could well be argued, therefore, that Article 30 (1) of the Act does not differ from, but is rather the implementation of Article 22 (1), read in conjunction with 22 (4). But the wording of Article 1 of the Act certainly does not compel such an interpretation. Under these circumstances the better construction would seem to be that the 12,500 guilders limit only applies to transportation not governed by the Warsaw Convention, now that 12,500 guilders has ceased to be the approximate equivalent of 125,000 gold francs.

161. The question of whether the Warsaw limits, as converted into local currency by the national legislator, should be deemed to present 'value debts' instead of 'money debts', so that they could be adapted by the courts to subsequent devaluations of the national currency, has been the subject of an interesting decision

---

160. [1]) Art. 1 of the Act. Cf. 'Memorie van Antwoord', Handelingen 2e Kamer 1935/36, Bijl. 201.

of the *Tribunal Civil of Brussels* of 30.6.1950 [1]). The Commercial Representative of the USSR claimed from the Sabena damage for a lost shipment of films. On the basis of the Belgian Act of 1936, which converts the 250 gold francs of Article 22 (2) into 500 Belgian francs, the liability of Sabena would have been 13,300 francs. The USSR claimed that this amount should be adapted to the devaluation of the Belgian currency of 1944, and increased by 40%. This point of view was rejected by the Court. After having stated the rule that with respect to 'money debts' ('dettes de sommes'), as distinct from' value debts', ('dettes d'indemnité ou dettes de valeur'), Article 1895 of the Civil Code forbids revaluation because of the reduced value of the national currency, and after having gone into a detailed examination of the drafting history of the Act of 1936, the Court concluded:

'... the adoption, by the Legislative Chambers, of those amendments [effecting the conversion of the gold franc limits into Belgian money] which were incorporated in Article 3 of the Belgian Act of April 1936, had the effect of setting aside any reference to the gold value of the franc and of fixing the liability of the carrier in a formal way to 500 [Belgian] francs per kilogram of registered baggage and of goods' [2]).

162. Instead of converting the limits into definite amounts of national money, the legislator can also provide the date by which the rate of exchange is to be determined. That is what the English legislator has done in Sec. 1 (5) of the Carriage by Air Act, 1932, reading:

'Any sums in francs mentioned in Article twenty-two of the

---

161. [1]) Rev. gén. ass. resp. (1951) 4723. See also Litvine (1953) No. 217.

[2]) Comp. the **Italian** decision Cass. 2.1.1950, n. 4, Giur. Ital. 1950, I, 106, also in 59 B.T.I. (1951) 16, in which the 1st Chamber of the *Corte Suprema di Cassazione*, adopting the solution already suggested by R. Niccolò (i.a. in his Note in Riv. giur. del lavoro 1949/50, II, 28), held the limitation of liability contained in the Conditions and Tariffs of the National Railways, which Conditions have force of law, to express a *value* rather than a fixed amount of money, the purchasing value of which would be indifferent. The same Court, sitting in Combined Chambers, has, however, come back from this view, in a decision of 15.5.1952, 61 B.T.I. (1953) 293. Similarly, the Court of Appeals of Napels 29.8.1950, 66 Diritto e Giurisprud. (1951) 344 with note by G. Minervini (concerning the limitation of the innkeeper's liability provided in Art. 1748 (2) Cod. civ.). It would seem that the reasoning of the 1950 decision could as wel have been followed with respect to the limits of the Cod. Nav., which also, through consecutive devaluations, have practically been reduced to zero. In this case the argument is even stronger, because these limits were clearly meant to express in Italian money the gold value established by the Warsaw Convention.

said First Schedule [i.e. the Warsaw Convention] shall, for the purposes of any action against a carrier, be converted into sterling at the rate of exchange prevailing on the date on which the amount of any damages to be paid by the carrier is ascertained by the court'.

Nothing in the Conventions prevents Contracting States from fixing the conversion rate in this manner, as long as the date which is to determine the rate of exchange does not lie before the moment the claim arises. Since the Warsaw Convention does not give guidance as to the moment at which the gold franc limits must be evaluated, the national legislators (or in the absence of national legislation: the courts) are left free to choose themselves. The moment should only not be taken previous to the date of the accident or loss, as in that case the liability could not be said to have been limited to 125,000 francs or to 250 francs per kilogram as defined in Article 22 (4). This might seem to be in contradiction with what has been said above concerning the right of the States to fix by legislation the amounts of the limits in national money, since such legislative conversion would be necessarily based on a rate of exchange prevailing at a time prior to the occurrence of the accident or loss. But that right was derived from the last phrase of paragraph (4) allowing conversion into national currency *in round figures*, and it would be difficult to invoke these words when the State had merely fixed the date for the rate of exchange to be applied.

163. We have now arrived at the problem what should be deemed the relevant moment for fixing the rate of exchange in the absence of any legislation fixing the limits in national currency or determining said moment. The choice is between the moment the claim arises, the moment judgment is given, and the moment of payment. When a devaluation takes place after an air accident has happened but before the claims arising therefrom have been settled, it becomes extremely important to know whether the limit of liability in local currency is to be determined as of the date of the accident or as of any later date. In answering this question one should keep in mind that we are not dealing here with assessing the extent of the damages suffered, but with determining the amount of *maximum liability*. The reason for having the limits in the Warsaw and Rome Conventions expressed in gold value was to avoid fluctuations in these legal limits of liability due to devaluation of the national currency in which they could otherwise have been expressed. It was not the purpose of these provisions in addition thereto to reinforce the claims, once they *would have arisen*, with a gold clause which would protect the creditor against devaluation of his claim. There can be no doubt whatsoever that any conversion into local currency by the national legislator, which would be based on the countervalue of the limits in gold francs as of the date of the accident, would be in conformity with the Convention. If the last sentence of Article 22 (4) of the Warsaw Convention means anything, it surely gives the States the right to do that much. But if that is true, the date that the claim arises should also determine the rate of exchange when the legislator has not exercised his right to convert the limits into his national currency. This would only be otherwise if the absence of legislative action on this point could be deemed to imply an intent on the part of the legislator to reinforce the limited claims arising under the Conventions by a goldclause for the protection of the creditors. It is clear that to assume such tacit intention is sheer fiction. Any legislator who would have wished to reach this result would provide that the limits have to be converted at the rate of exchange prevailing at the date of payment [1]).

164. It has been pointed out above that the English legislator has taken the date of judgment as the relevant date. The same choice has been made in the Rome Convention, 1952, Article 11 (4) of which provides:

'The sums mentioned in francs in this Article refer to a currency unit consisting of 65½ milligrams of gold of millesimal fineness 900 –. These sums may be converted into national currencies in round figures. Conversion of the sums into national curren-

163. [1]) By rendering a judgment for an amount expressed in Poincaré gold francs, the Appeal Court of Paris in its decision of 28.2.1953, 16 R. G.A. (1953) 180 (*Air France* v. *Nordisk Transport*) has in fact chosen the solution of conversion at the rate of the date of payment, without discussing the point. It is curious to note that the special Sub-Committee appointed by the Rome Conference of 1952, to revise the relative provision of the Mexico Draft, rejected the Italian proposal to take the date of payment as decisive, for the reason that 'it is usual for national courts to give their judgments for a definite amount in the national currency' (R.C. 1952, II, 212).

cies other than gold shall, in case of judicial proceedings, be made according to the gold value of such currencies at the date of the judgment, or in cases covered by Article 14, at the date of the allocation'.

Curiously the provision has retained the phrase that 'the sums may be converted into national currencies in round figures'. In view of the following sentence the right of conversion in round figures by the legislator is limited, however, to conversion into gold currencies. The wish to have this possibility in the Convention seems to have come from the Scandinavian countries, where the gold coin currencies are still being used in the national legislations which implement the international maritime and air law conventions for the expression of the legal limits of liability in national terms instead of in some foreign monetary unit such as the Poincaré gold franc [1]). Gold currencies apparently should be understood to be gold coin currencies, not gold standard currencies.

The exact meaning of the restrictive words 'in case of judicial proceedings' is not quite clear. The restriction was probably thought to be a logical consequence of the fact that the date of *judgment* was taken as the determining factor [2]). As the paragraph reads now, however, the last sentence, taken literally, does not apply to claims settled by arbitration [3]). Such a narrow interpretation would clearly be against the spirit of the Article [4]).

165. By making the date of judgment determinative of the rate of exchange, the extent of the carrier's or operator's liability will be kept uncertain as long as no final judgment on all claims has been given. A comparison with the possible influence of circumstances, occurring after the accident, on the amount of

---

164. [1]) Cf. R.C. 1952, I, 347. See also No. 159 (6) supra, and comp. Art. 4 (5) (1) of the **Swedish** Act of 1936 implementing the Brussels Convention on bills of lading.

[2]) For that reason the Draft of a revised 'Warsaw Convention', established by the 'Warsaw' Sub-Committee of the L.C. of ICAO, provided in Art. 15 (6) that conversion shall be made 'into national currencies at the rate of exchange effective on the date of judgment, *or the date when the settlement of the claim is agreed*'.

[3]) Arbitration is allowed by the last sentence of Art. 20 (1), which was added at a later stage of the Conference (I, 209 sq, 403 sq.), when the revision of Article 11 (4) had already been agreed upon (I, 155 sq.).

[4]) See also the drafting history in the previous note.

damages to be recovered in normal negligence cases, fails [1]). For the conversion of the gold franc limits into national currency is not a matter of assessing damages with a view to all facts known to the court, but a matter of determining the legal maximum of liability. In a situation of pending devaluations it will be to the advantage of claimants to delay judgment in order to have the benefit of an increase on the limit of liability, and the defendant cannot avoid the consequences thereof by tendering at an earlier date the full amount of the limit, since the date of judgment, and not the date of payment (or tender), is determinative of the extent of his liability.

Another consequence of the choice of the date of judgment would seem to be that a claimant who fails to give notice of a claim within 6 months after the accident, and who, pursuant to Article 19 of the Rome Convention, 1952, is only entitled to compensation out of the amount for which the operator remains liable 'after all claims made within that period have been met in full', might do well to wait for a devaluation of the local currency. For the resulting increase in the limit of the operator's liability may be sufficient to take care of his claim. This clearly defeats the purpose of Article 19, which is to encourage quick settlements by protecting the operator against claims filed after six months. If the claims filed within the six months period have been satisfied by one judgment, delivered after consolidation of proceedings in accordance with Article 20 (3), if necessary, it would be in conformity with the rationale of Article 11 (4) and Article 19 to consider the 'date of judgment' as used in the former Article, to refer only to the judgment in said proceedings, so that the amount of the limit in the local currency would have been definitely fixed by that judgment. This way of reasoning is to be preferred to the argument which could be made out of a rather narrow interpretation of Article 19, which provides that the claimant who has not given notice of claim within the 6 months period 'shall only be entitled to compensation out of the amount for which the operator remains liable after all claims made within that period have been met in full'. It could be argued that since

165. [1]) See on this problem i.a. G. Ferri, *Tendenze giurisprudenziali in tema di svalutazione monetaria.* Riv. ital. per le scienze giuridiche, Serie III, vol. 3 (1949), 408–426.

the timely claims were not 'met in full' the delayed claimants are not entitled to compensation, the operator being sufficiently protected by the principle of *res judicata* against additional claims from the early claimants. The argument, however, is more subtle than appealing.

Meanwhile, in the majority of cases claims are settled out of court. Due to the provision of Article 11 (4) which makes the date of judgment the determining factor, the operator who at the end of the 6 months period wants to settle all claims hitherto filed with him up to the maximum amount of his liability, has no guarantee that he may not be held liable as yet for some unknown claim when the local countervalue of the limit will be increased by a devaluation of the local currency. The result may be that the late claim will be paid in full, whereas the timely filed claims got only a pro rata part.

166. The conclusion seems inescapable that the only reasonable solution is to make the date that the claim arises the determining factor as far as the rate of conversion is concerned [1]), subject to the right of any State to give additional protection to claimants to the effect that this class of creditors may require payment on a gold value basis instead of having to accept payment on the basis of the devaluated money [2]). It is to be regretted that that solution has not been adopted at the Rome Conference of 1952.

167. Before closing this Chapter, attention should be drawn to the effect of contractual clauses dealing with this subject matter. Both the prewar and the postwar IATA Conditions of Carriage for Passengers and Baggage, as well as those for Goods, have incorporated the Warsaw limits in gold francs, the gold franc being defined as 'French francs consisting of $65^1/_2$ milligrams of gold at the standard of fineness of nine hundred thousandths' (i.e. the Poincaré franc) [1]). Thus the uniformity in limits, which the

166. [1]) The date of the accident (which is the same as the date that the claim arises) has been defended by various delegates at the Rome Conference 1952, see I, 156, 157, 158.

[2]) Protection can also be given by allowing damages for delay in payment of the compensation due. Thus Ferri, l.c. (No. 165 (1)) at p. 422. But many legal systems have fixed the liability for delay in payment of money in the form of legal interests.

167. [1]) Art. 18 (4) of the IATA General Conditions of Carriage for Passengers and Baggage (1953) limits liability for passengers to 125,000 French gold francs, and Art. 14 (3) of the IATA General Conditions of Carriage for Goods (1953) limits the liability for goods to 250 gold francs per kilogram of goods destroyed, lost, damaged or delayed. The definition of the gold franc is contained in Articles 1 of both sets of Conditions.

Warsaw Convention failed to achieve by giving the national legislators the right to convert the sums into local currencies, has to a large extent been arrived at by 'private legislation' [2]). For nothing in the Convention prevents the carriers from fixing limits in excess of the limits established in, or allowed by, the Convention. Moreover, the incorporation in the Conditions of Carriage of a limit expressed in gold francs probably works as a gold clause, giving claimants the right to demand payment of the limit – assuming the actual damages exceed the limit – on a gold value basis [3]).

It is to be observed, however, that both effects are restricted to the liabilities arising from the Conditions of Carriage. When these are less than the liabilities provided by the Convention, the provisions of the Convention will only prevail to the extent of the limits contained in the Convention. With respect to any difference between these limits and the amounts provided in the Conditions of Carriage the only basis of liability is to be found in the Conditions, not in the Convention. Thus, when the postwar Conditions of Carriage established by IATA impose the burden of proof as to negligence on the plaintiff [4]), the claimant who would not be able to prove negligence can not invoke the – supposedly more favouruable – limits contained in the Conditions of Carriage, but only those provided by the Convention as implemented by national law.

---

167. [2]) A similar unification by private agreement is offered by the Hague Rules Agreement, 1950, by which liability underwriters have accepted to adjust cargo claims at £ 200 per package under the Brussels Convention on Bills of Lading. See Knauth (1953) pp. 284 and 472 sq. and G. Marais in 3 D.M.F. (1951) 107 sq. and 159 sq.

[3]) This is not in contradiction with the above (No. 163) defended view that Article 22 (4) of the Warsaw Convention or the analogous provisions in the other Conventions, are not to be construed as including a gold clause ensuring payment on goldvalue basis to the claim creditors. There exists a clear distinction between legal limits of liability and those stipulated in contracts of carriage. The latter will generally be construed against the person limiting his liability, especially when unilaterally imposed conditions of carriage are involved (comp. No. 242). Moreover, the courts will be guided by the rule, prevailing in the great majority of countries, that in case of foreign money or gold value clauses in contracts, the rate of exchange is to be determined by the date of payment. Cf. A. Nussbaum, *Money in the Law, National and International*, Brooklyn, 1950, p. 362.

[4]) See No. 242 (2). Cf. also Art. 18 (7) (Passengers) and Art. 14 (5) (Goods) excluding carrier's liability for damage caused by property in the baggage or shipment, and 18 (8) (Passengers) excluding carrier's liability 'for damage to, or delay in the delivery of, fragile or perishable articles, money, jewelry, silverware, negotiable papers, securities or other valuables, business documents or samples, which are included in the passenger's checked baggage, whether with or without the knowledge of carrier'.

Chapter VI

WILFUL MISCONDUCT AND GROSS NEGLIGENCE: THEIR EFFECT ON LIMITATION OF LIABILITY

§ 1. INTRODUCTORY REMARKS

168. All three air law conventions [1]) which provide for a limitation of liability contain some exception to this limitation with respect to damages caused intentionally or by a wrongful conduct of similar seriousness. The scope of these exceptions in the three Conventions discussed here varies widely.

Article 25 of the Warsaw Convention reads:

'The carrier shall not be entitled to avail himself of the provisions of this Convention which exclude or limit his liability, if he has caused the damage intentionally and wrongfully or by such fault [2]) as, in accordance with the law of the Court seized of the case, is considered equivalent thereto'.
'Similarly he shall not be entitled to avail himself of the said provisions, if the damage was caused as aforesaid by one of his servants or agents acting within the scope of his employment'.

Article 14 of the Rome Convention, 1933 provides:

'The operator may not avail himself of the provisions of this Convention which limit his liability: (a) if it is proved that

168. [1]) The Convention for the Unification of Certain Rules Relating to the Assistance and Salvage of Aircraft at Sea, signed at Brussels, 1938, which was not ratified by any State, contains no exception on the limited liability of the shipowner or operator of the aircraft in case of assistance or salvage. The Draft Convention on Collisions established by CITEJA in 1936 (cf. No. 991(2)) did however, contain a similar provision (art. 4 (5)) as that of the Rome Convention, 1933.

[2]) The original French text has: 'si le dommage provient de son *dol* ou d'une *faute*' etc. These words have been inaccurately translated in the English Carriage by Air Act, 1932, as well as in the official American translation, into 'if the damage is caused by his *wilful misconduct* or by such *default*' etc.

the damage results from the gross negligence or wilful misconduct [3]) of the operator and [4]) of his servants and agents, except where the operator proves that the damage results from negligence [5]) in the pilotage, steering [6]) or navigation of the aircraft, or where his servants or agents are concerned, that he has taken the proper steps to prevent the damage: ...'

Finally Article 12 (1) of the Rome Convention, 1952 provides:

'If the person who suffers damage proves that it was caused by a deliberate act or omission of the operator, his servants or agents [7]), done with intent to cause damage, the liability of the operator shall be unlimited; provided that in the case of such act or omission of such servant or agent, it is also proved that he was acting in the course of his employment and within the scope of his authority'.

It is to be noted that each succeeding Convention has narrowed down the scope of the 'escape clause', especially as far as the wrongful acts of servants or agents are concerned, but the last Convention has also greatly limited the class of acts which bring the exception into play.

169. The problems arising under these provisions can be brought under three main headings:

(1) what kind of misconduct is required?

(2) to what extent will such misconduct by servants or agents

---

168. [3]) Though the French text has again *dol* (cf. the previous note) it is believed that this word, *since it is here combined with 'faute lourde'*, can be well translated into wilful misconduct. To the extent the notion 'wilful misconduct' comprises more than *dol*, it is covered by *faute lourde*.

[4]) The French text has '*et*', though the word '*ou*' (or) would have been more correct. The latter word has been used in the British and American government translations of the Convention (cf. No. 154 (1) and (2)).

[5]) The French text has '*faute*' which embraces both intentional and negligent acts and omissions. The British and American translations into 'negligence', therefore, are not quite exact.

[6]) The French text has '*conduite*' which has been translated in the British translation into 'handling' and in the American translation into 'operation'. The word 'handling' would seem much too broad since it also could include groundhandling, maintenance and repairs, which is certainly not included in the French word '*conduite*'. It is to be observed that the same word occurs in Article 20 (2) of the Warsaw Convention. Curiously the American Government follows here the British translation and has 'handling'. See also No. 32 (1).

[7]) The French text has *préposés* and the Spanish text *dependientes*. See on the meaning of these words Nos. 209 sq.

be treated in a like way as the carrier's or operator's own misconduct for the purpose of this exception?

(3) what is the effect of any such misconduct?

The following pages will be devoted to a discussion of these problems. As the Warsaw Convention is for all practical purposes the most important, at least at the present time, and as moreover its Article 25 has been the subject of more litigation than any other single provision of any air law convention, most attention will be given to the Warsaw Convention.

§ 2. KIND OF MISCONDUCT REQUIRED

A. Warsaw Convention.

170. Article 25 (1) of the Warsaw Convention requires 'dol' or 'une faute qui, d'après la loi du tribunal saisi, est considerée comme équivalente au dol'. This is probably the most unhappy phrase of the entire Convention [1]). It is the result and the starting point of a comedy of errors. Seldom have the dangers of conceptualistic thinking appeared so clearly as in the history of this text.

The preliminary draft which was established by the Paris Conference of 1925 did not contain any exception to the limited liability. A provision to set aside the application of the provisions which limit or exclude the carrier's liability in case of damage caused by intentional illicit acts (*actes illicites intentionelles*) was inserted by the Second Commission of the CITEJA [2]). The provision was retained in that form till the Warsaw Conference. At that Conference the U.K. Delegate Sir Alfred Dennis objected to this formula because for English speaking people it would be 'very difficult to understand these words *acte illicite intentionnel*' [3]). The difficulty he had in mind was whether the intention has to be directed toward the causing of damage. 'As to the proposed amendment concerning *faute lourde*', Sir Alfred Dennis continued,

---

170. [1]) On the history and interpretation of Article 25 see the extensive and valuable article by M. de Juglart, *Dol et faute lourde dans le transport aérien international* in Juris Classeur Périodique (1952) I, 1010, and the lucid and, as far as the conclusions are concerned, more convincing study by P. Chauveau in 6 R.F.D.A. (1952) 239 sq.

[2]) Report of De Vos to the Second Session of CITEJA, Paris 1927, Compte rendu, p. 65.

[3]) W.C. p. 40.

'this expression is not known in our laws, it is a question of degrees in negligence. We cannot translate in our language *faute lourde* in a way that it will have a legal meaning' [4]).

The Delegate of Luxemburg then explained that this formula had been chosen to avoid the French word *dol* for which there did not exist an English equivalent [5]). Sir Alfred Dennis suggested that the English words 'wilful misconduct' would cover all one wanted to say 'not only acts committed deliberately, but also acts of carelessness without any regard for the consequences' [6]).

Ripert (France) remarked that 'there would be agreement if one could find a formula sufficiently exact to avoid the [unlimited] liability of the carrier arising without a wilfully caused damage'. But he pointed out that the German proposal went further by assimilating gross negligence (*faute lourde*) to intentional acts (*dol*).

If things become very difficult in an international conference there is always the *deus ex machina* of the drafting committee, to pass them on to. But the Reporter Pittard rightly remarked that the Drafting Committee would have to know first whether or not gross negligence should be 'assimilated' to *dol*. Ripert: 'The thing is to refer the matter to the drafting committee, when it is agreed to make the assimilation, if a sufficiently precise formula can be found'. Pittard: 'We shall be prepared to assimilate gross negligence (*faute lourde*) to intentional acts, if we find a formula which will satisfy the various legal languages represented. (Signs of approval)'. Chairman: 'Then, Gentlemen, we shall refer the question to the drafting committee'. [7])

If one reads this discussion one has the impression that someone's leg was being pulled ('unintentionally'), though it is not

170. [4]) Ibidem, p. 41.

[5]) Ibidem, p. 41. The translation of the French *dol* into English is much more difficult than that of *faute lourde*. It is believed that where the word is used in relation with liability for damage it means the intentionally and wrongfully inflicting of damage. It is the same element which distinguishes the '*délits*' from the '*quasi délits*'. When speaking of liability, the notions *dol* and *faute intentionelle* are used interchangeably, see e.g. Mazeaud III (1950). No. 2522 and also I (1948) No. 674 and III (1950) No. 2543. The matter is complicated by the fact that *dol* is also used in the meaning of fraud as a factor affecting the validity of contracts (Art. 1116 C. civ.), to be invoked by a party lured into the conclusion of a contract by the fraudulent manoeuvres of the other party. Cf. Planiol-Ripert (1947) II, Nos. 218 and 713. Comp. No. 178 (1).

[6]) Ibidem, p. 40.

[7]) Ibidem, p. 42.

quite clear whose. With its terms of reference so 'defined', the Drafting Committee under Chairmanship of Giannini went to work and presented at the second reading the present formula. It was commented thus by Giannini: 'We have succeeded in finding this formula which has also satisfied our friends of Great-Britain, by which we have succeeded in adopting the expression of 'faute lourde et dol', which expression is difficult to translate into English' [8]). It is important to note that the agreed text retained the French word *dol* for which it is actually difficult to find an English equivalent, but that it replaced by an ambiguous phrase the term *faute lourde* which could easily and satisfactorily have been translated into 'gross negligence'. There can be little doubt that the real objections on the part of the British Delegation to the use of the words *faute lourde*, to which objections the Conference gave way, were not based on an hypothetical impossibility to translate these words into English, but on the view that the use of this notion would extend the scope of Article 25 in an unwarranted way. Before the vote on the Article was taken Sir Alfred Dennis explained his understanding of the text in the following words: 'I should like that it be recorded in the minutes that it followed from the explanations which have been exchanged that we have in English the expression 'wilful misconduct' to translate these words, which expression is well known and has a well defined meaning in our law' [9]).

171. On reading the minutes, one thing becomes clear – and that is about the only thing – that the discussion has been one on legal terminology, not on basic issues. The latter have been largely obscured by the smoke and dust created by a battle on legal concepts. The question which appears to have been foremost in the minds, when the formula of Article 25 was agreed upon, was not so much in what *fact situations* the provisions limiting or excluding the carrier's liability should not apply, but to what legal *terms* they should not apply.

On the one hand there was the convenient maxim of *faute lourde* being equivalent to *dol*, the sacredness of which is enhanced

170. [8]) Ibidem, p. 139.
[9]) Ibidem, p. 140.

by its latin ancestor: 'culpa lata dolo equiparatur' [1]). Of course, it is obvious that gross negligence is *not* the same thing as 'intentional wrong doing' (*dol*), What is meant by the phrase is that certain legal effects in certain situations will be the same whether the act committed amounts to gross negligence or to *dol*. The law could as well have been that the legal effects are the same whether the act committed amounts to gross negligence or to ordinary negligence. Maybe, if English law would have had a latin maxim to that effect, the *substantial* difference between the two rules would better have come to the fore. But, unfortunately English legal language prefers to put it in another way by saying that it does not know such a thing as gross negligence [2]). Again, this could not mean that English law has never to be applied to fact situations where some gross form of negligence is involved, but merely that for certain legal purposes (liability for damages) English law, as it developed in the 19th Century, does not distinguish between light and gross forms of negligence. In the same way that the 'assimilation' of *faute lourde* to *dol* actually is not at all a question of terminology, the statement that 'English law does not know gross negligence' is a manner of formulating a substantial rule of law, and one conflicting with the latin maxim.

By stating the issue in terms of conflicting concepts, the all important question whether *faute lourde* embraces categories of wrongful acts not included within the concept of 'wilful misconduct' and if so, whether or not it would be desirable to extend the sanction of unlimited liability to such acts, has been obscured. That question does not appear to have been discussed at any length. Once again, the problem was considered to be one of draftmanship only, and the difference to be one in terminology, not in views. It is important to keep that in mind, for it means that the reference to 'the law of the Court seized of the case' was not intended to be a reference to rules of substantial law but merely a reference to terminology. It was understood that by this concession to supposedly irreconcilable terminologies, the

171. [1]) Dig. 50.16.226. See also Dig. 11.6.1 § 1, Dig. 16.3.32, Dig. 17.1.29.pr., Dig. 44.7.1 § 5.

[2]) See the statement by Dennis above (No. 170 (4) and also the English Delegate at the Rome Conference, 1933, I, 319. Comp. Shawcross and Beaumont (1951), No. 364, note (b).

unity of the substantial law could be saved. If it is just a matter of words whether or not *faute lourde* is equivalent to *dol*, why not leave it to the Courts who in most cases will have to work anyhow with different languages?

But the trouble is that it is not simply a matter of words whether and when gross negligence should be treated in the same way as intentional wrongs. If a French Court does not distinguish, as far as liability is concerned, between 'clearly characterized faults or 'professional faults' on the one hand, and the intentional inflicting of damages on the other hand, and a Brazilian Court does make a distinction between these two classes of misconduct [3]), there is certainly more involved than a mere difference between the French and the Brazilian legal language!

Similarly, it is not a question of poverty of the English language that – as the English Delegate at the Rome Conference, 1933 put it – English law does not know *faute lourde*. 'Gross negligence' is probably as good an equivalent for the French *faute lourde* [4]) or a better one, as the French *faute lourde* is an equivalent of the Belgian *faute lourde*, of the Italian *colpa grave*, of the Dutch *grove schuld*, or the German *grobe Fahrlässigkeit*. The term was frequently used by English Courts in the first half of the 19th century as distinguished from ordinary negligence [5]), and it is still applied by American Courts for the purpose of invalidating exemption clauses in contracts [6]). It is true that more recently English Courts have rejected distinguishing between various degrees of negligence as far as civil liability is concerned [7]), but

---

171. [3]) Trib. de apel., Cam. civ. reunidas, Rio de Janeiro 23.9.1948, 1 R.B.D.A. (1951) No. 1, 226 at 227, confirming the court of second instance (at 221). (*Caffat Chaddoud a.o.* v. *Anglo Mexican Petroleum Co. Ltd. and Shell Mex. Argentina Comp. Ltd.*).

[4]) Cf. A. W. Knauth (1935), at 323.

[5]) See e.g. *Smith* v. *Horne* (1919) 2 Moore C.P. 18, 129 E.R. 338, *Brooke* v. *Pickwick* (1827) 4 Bing. 218, 130 E.R. 753, and numerous other decisions in 8 Engl. and Emp. Digest, pp. 41 sq. (s.v. 'Carrier' Nos. 244 sq.) including the **Australian** decision *Pettigrew* v. *Australian Steam Navigation Co. Ltd.* (1864) 1 Q.S.C.R. 113. Cf. the extensive survey of the development of the law by Blackburn J. in *Peek* v. *North Staffordshire Railway Comp.* (1863) 10 H.L.C. 473, 491 sq. Comp. *Askey* v. *Golden Wine Co. Ltd.* [1948] 2 All E.R. 35, 38, where Denning J. (as he then was) characterized plaintiff's own conduct as 'grossly negligent', when refusing him to be indemnified by defendants.

[6]) See Annotation in 175 A.L.R. 8, at 68 sq. Cf. S.N. Rittenberg in 6 J.A.L. (1935), sq. at 378.

[7]) The first clear rejection of any distinction between ordinary negligence and gross

that does not mean that the words 'gross negligence' suddenly ceased to have a meaning, only that the law was changed. If the framers of the Convention had agreed upon making gross negligence the criterion, it would not at all cause a revolution in English legal terminology, but only reintroduce a distinction which had been rejected by the Courts at an earlier stage.

172. The reason why they rejected it was that it is difficult to draw a line between the various forms of negligence. But if one sees the 1001 formulas devised by French Courts and authors to define *faute lourde* [1]), the vagueness of the borderline between the English 'gross negligence' and ordinary negligence certainly does not distinguish it from the French *faute lourde*. When the problem of unlimited liability was discussed a few years later in relation to the draft Convention on Collisions, Ripert raised the question whether' it would not be very dangerous, *in view of the fact that the criterion of 'faute lourde' is very vague*, to say that it will be sufficient for a court to decide that the error in pilotage was a *faute lourde*, in order to have the liability become unlimited' [2]).

The objections of Sir Alfred Dennis against the use of the notion *faute lourde*, therefore, actually had nothing to do with difficulties of a linguistical nature, but would have had the same value had they been raised by a French lawyer who would not have to translate them. The English Delegate was simply opposed

---

negligence, as far as the application of exemption clauses is concerned, seems to be offered by *Austin* v. *The Manchester, Sheffield and Lincolnshire Railway Comp.* (1852) 10 C.B. 454, 138 E.R. 181 and *Carr* v. *Lancashire and Yorkshire Railway Co.* (1852) 7 Ex. 707, 155 E.R. 1133 (in the latter case the jury had actually found gross negligence).

172. [1]) I.a. Mazeaud, I, (1948) No. 414 (gross negligence only a presumption of *dol*); Esmein's Note under Cass. reg. 24.10.1932, S. 1933, I, 289; Josserand's Note in D. 1933.1.49, H. Lalou, Traité pratique de responsabilité Civile, 1949. No. 415–8°. See also Voisenet, Faute Lourde, Thèse Dijon, 1934.

[2]) 9th Session of CITEJA, 1934, Doc. 244, p. 113. See also his exclamation as a member of the 3d Commission of CITEJA in 1930 (Doc. 36, p. 14): 'C'est un mot, faute lourde. Si on admet qu'un Tribunal peut condamner suivant le degré de responsabilité, cela détruit tout le système'. But comp. his explanation to the English Delegate at the Rome Conference, 1933, p. 319: 'On emploie l'expression 'faute lourde' parce que la Convention étant redigée en langue française, cette expression est très claire. C'est une faute nettement caracterisée...'. See also Esmein in Planiol-Ripert, *Traité pratique de droit civil. 2 éd.* VI, No. 403: 'la distinction de la faute légère et de la faute lourde est imprécise et ne peut guère être faite que par sentiment'.

to extending the class of cases of unlimited liability beyond the cases of wilful misconduct, which can be more clearly distinguished from negligence cases than those involving gross negligence.

173. If one then considers that the formula of Article 25 was not intended to let the national laws each establish for themselves which forms of misconduct should result in unlimited liability, but only to let them each choose the terminology most appropriate to the single uniform solution aimed at, and if one also takes into account that the English Delegation had explained to the Conference the meaning of 'wilful misconduct' and made it clear that it understood the formula of Article 25 to be fully covered by this English notion, the best interpretation of the words '*dol*, or a fault which in accordance with the law of the court seized of the case is considered equivalent to *dol*', would seem to be the definition given by Sir Alfred Dennis of the term 'wilful misconduct', i.e. 'acts committed deliberately or acts of carelessness without any regard for the consequences' [1]).

The criterion is clearly a subjective one looking to the mental attitude of the person who is accused of such act or omission. Seriousness of the consequences will not be sufficient, nor will lack of knowledge or experience, except when to undertake certain activity without a minimum of knowledge and experience would point to a 'carelessness without any regard for the consequences'.

174. Whilst this was the common ground on which agreement as to substance was reached, the labeling was left to the national laws. There can be little doubt that, at least as far as France, Italy, Germany and Switzerland are concerned, the national label for the 'fault considered equivalent to *dol* was understood to be *faute lourde*, *colpa grave*, and *grobe Fahrlässigkeit* [1]). Thus

---

173. [1]) W.C. p. 40. This is also the conclusion arrived at by P. Chauveau in his lucid comment on the decision of the Trib. Seine of 24.4.1952 (Air France accident at the Azores) in 6 R.F.D.A. (1952) 239 sq. at 250. Similarly, and with great emphasis, the 'Avocat général' Albucher in *Comp. Air France* v. *Nordisk Transport*, Appel Paris, 28.2.1953, 7 R.F.D.A. (1953) 105.

174. [1]) Though even in France the question of whether the law assimilates *faute lourde* to *dol* is a much debated point, especially in view of the fact that the courts and the legislature have in any case accepted a certain number of exceptions to said the Chairman of the Drafting Committee, which was responsible for the text of Article 25, wrote in a study on the Convention published immediately after it was signed at Warsaw, that this provision applies in cases of '*dolo o colpa grave*', 'in accordance with the principle that *fraus omnia corrumpit*', adding that the formula of Article 25 had been chosen 'with a view to the fact that English law does not know these notions' [2]). When the question of *dol* and *faute lourde* was again discussed in the Rome Conference, those who had also attended the Warsaw Conference clearly considered that Article 25 of the Warsaw Convention was intended to cover both *dol* and *faute lourde* [3]) (which is not the same as saying that they had a clear mind as to the exact

---

assimilation. The *legislature* did so in the field of *insurance* (forbidding insurance against one's own *dol* but not against one's own gross negligence) and of *workmen's compensation* (requiring *dol* or *faute inexcusable* in order for the workman to lose his right to compensation, *faute inexcusable* being construed by the Cour de Cassation to be more serious than *faute lourde*: Cass. ch. réun. 15.7.1941.D.C. 1941, 7.117). The *Cour de Cassation* has introduced a much criticized exception to the assimilation with respect to the liability of the French State *railways*, one of the arguments being that the tariffs containing the limitation of liability (which the Cour de Cassation held to apply even to cases of gross negligence of employees) had been approved by the Government. For this reason it has been argued by at least one author that in French law *faute lourde* should not be considered equivalent to *dol* as far as the limits of the Warsaw Convention are concerned (P. Rabut, *La Convention de Varsovie*, Paris, 1952, p. 30). The Cour de Cassation has also rejected assimilation in case of *indemnity agreements*: Cass. civ. 1.2.1939, G.P. 1939.1.602 and Cass. civ. 15.10.1940, G.P. 1940.2.275. Finally the *Conseil d'Etat*, in the field of government liability, has distinguished between *faute lourde* and *faute inexcusable* and has only assimilated the latter to *dol*. See Cons. d'Etat 16.6.1944, S. 1945.3.37 with note A. Mestre.

For the situation in the **Netherlands** see No. 179 (1). In **Belgium** the courts are said to reject the assimilation of gross negligence to *dol*, comp. Litvine (1953), No. 341.

As to **German** law see Riese (1949) pp. 466 and 486. Riese points to § 29e of the Air Traffic Act (*Luftverkehrsgesetz*) as amended in 1943, reproducing the principle of article 25 of the Convention for 'Non-Warsaw' traffic, which speaks of 'intention' and 'gross negligence'. Curiously the same Act might be invoked for the argument that German law does not always assimilate gross negligence to intentional wrongs, since § 29m (also added in 1943), which deals with the liability towards student pilots, only sets aside the limitation of liability in case of intentional wrongs ('*Vorsatz*'). A morc general argument could be drawn from § 276 of the Civil Code (BGB), forbidding exemption of liability for intentional acts ('*Vorsatz*') only. Koffka (1937) p. 334 comes to the same conclusion as Riese, invoking § 430 (2) HGB (Commercial Code), which makes the carrier liable for full compensation, instead of for the current market value of the goods, in case of intention or gross negligence.

As to **Swiss** law see Art. 10 of the Lufttransportreglement, 1952: 'absichtlich oder durch grobe Fahrlässigkeit' (intentionally or through gross negligence). See also Premier Congrès H. Capitant. Montreal 1939, pp. 358 and 364 for **Greece** and **Japan**.

[2]) A. Giannini, *La Convenzione di Varsavia* (Bibliotheca di diritto aeronautica XII) Roma, 1929, p. 111. Cf. Art. 789 and 1229 C. civ. and Artt. 275, 944, 952, 971 and 977 Cod. Nav. But see also Art. 1225 Cod. civ.

[3]) See i.a. Ripert in R.C. 1933, I, 223 and 319, and Giannini ibidem, I, 227.

scope of *faute lourde*), and this time the linguistical objections from the British side to these terms were overcome.

175. Notwithstanding the national label (expressly permitted by Article 25), the provision itself remains an international one, and must be construed as such, that is, with an open eye to the general purpose of unification. A country which would not generally treat intentional wrongs and gross negligence alike, should not for that reason limit the scope of Article 25 to purely intentional wrongs [1]; similarly a country where all forms of negligence except small errors [2] are, as far as liability is concerned, combined in one class with intentional wrongs, would inflate the principle of Article 25 by such national view and defeat the unification which was the main purpose of the Convention. Nor should the fact that the Conference apparently accepted the understanding of Sir Alfred Dennis as to the possibility of translating the formula of Article 25 by the English 'wilful misconduct', lead one to the view that the Article should be construed in accordance with English case law on 'wilful misconduct' [3]. The Warsaw Conven-

175. [1]) E.g. Brazil, see No. 171 (3).

[2]) Cf. G. de Valon, Clauses de non-responsabilité dans la navigation maritime et la navigation aérienne. Paris, 1940, p. 72, on the tendency of the French courts to consider *faute lourde* all acts and errors which do not have 'un caractère vraiment anodin' ('a truly innocent nature'). One French author of great authority even takes the view that a *faute lourde* should always be assumed unless the carrier can prove absence of negligence (Esmein, note in S. 1933.1.289).

[3]) On the question to what extent **English** courts will feel bound to existing precedents on the meaning of 'wilful misconduct' see Shawcross and Beaumont (1951), No. 364, where it is suggested 'with some hesitation' that 'the English Courts, in construing the Carriage by Air Act, would, in considering the meaning of "wilful misconduct", be guided by the meaning previously given by the Courts to this expression when used in contracts and other statutes, and would not look at the French text, nor consider the meaning of "dol" in the laws of other countries or in the minds of the framers of the Convention'. Most of the English cases dealing with the meaning of 'wilful misconduct' are concerned with the interpretation of this notion as used in railway tariffs. One of the leading cases in this respect is *Lewis* v. *Great Western Ry. Co.* (1877) 3 Q.B.D. 195. See other cases cited in Shawcross and Beaumont (1951), No. 364, note (e). *Query* whether these cases could not be distinguished because of the fact that they involve the interpretation of *contractual* clauses in exemption of carrier's liability, which traditionally are construed against the carrier.

Many **American** cases have dealt with the concept of 'wilful misconduct' or 'wilful negligence' or 'wilful and wanton misconduct' (or 'negligence') in the application and interpretation of the so-called 'guest-statutes', which exclude the automobile-driver's liability towards the guest passengers except in case of his wilful misconduct, etc. Other cases arose from passengers holding free passes on the railways, and from the frequently adopted rule that contributory negligence is no defence for a defendant who himself has been guilty of wilful misconduct. On the latter cases comp. W.L. Prosser, *Contributory Negligence as Defence to Violation of Statute.* 32 Minn. L. Rev. (1948) 105 sq.

tion is international law and it must be construed as such [4]), except to the extent that it refers to national law. The reference contained in Article 25 to the law of the Court seized of the case – it cannot be overemphasized – only deals with a matter of terminology. It was the unhappy solution, suggested by the Drafting Committee, for the difficulty of finding a satisfactory *wording*, but not the acknowledgment of a failure to reach agreement in substance [5]) [6]).

176. If one accepts this interpretation, it is not necessary to investigate when a country should be deemed to consider gross negligence equivalent to intentional wrongs (*dol*) [1]). The question is far from simple and leads one into theoretical debates between different schools of thought existing in most countries. Since the so-called 'equivalence' is nothing more than a way of saying that in the field of civil liability, and especially with respect to the validity of exoneration clauses, certain forms of conduct will be treated in the same way as intentional wrongs, the logical, though clearly absurd, consequence in countries which, as far as liability is concerned, do not even make a difference between ordinary negligence and wilful misconduct, would be to bring cases of mere negligence within the orbit of Article 25 [2]).

177. The above remarks on the interpretation of the words

---

175. [4]) Cf. Shawcross and Beaumont (1951), No. 98 on the interpretation of the Carriage by Air Act, 1932.

[5]) Contra Trib. civ. Seine 24.4.1952, 6 R.F.D.A. (1952) 199 sq. at 222 (*Broche-Hennessy* v. *Comp. Air France*), and less clearly *American Airlines, Inc.* v. *Ulen*, 1949 U.S.Av. R. 338, 344. Comp. M. de Juglart in J.C.P. (1952) I, 1010. The interpretation defended in the text comes very close to the one suggested by Chauveau in 6 R.F.D.A. (1952) 239 sq.

[6]) The Draft Protocol, established at the Rio Session (1953) of the L.C. of ICAO, has the following new text for Art. 25: 'the limits of liability specified in Article 22 of the Convention shall not apply if it is proved that the damage resulted from a deliberate act or omission of the carrier, his servants or agents, done with intent to cause damage; provided that, in the case of a deliberate act or omission of a servant or agent, it is also proved that he was acting in the course of his employment'. See on this text especially Rio Session (1953) I, 227 sq.

176. [1]) Riese (1949) pp. 465 sq. and 486 bases his conclusion for Germany, the Netherlands and Switzerland on such investigation.

[2]) Thus American law does not seem to make a distinction between negligence and more serious forms of misconduct as far as the possibility to exclude or limit liability towards passengers is concerned.

'dol ou faute qui, d'après la loi du Tribunal saisi, est considérée comme équivalente au dol' can be summarized as follows:

1. There was agreement that the limits and other special defences offered by the Convention should not avail to the carrier, whenever the damage had been intentionally inflicted, as well as in cases involving a conscious disregard on the part of the carrier of the consequences of his conduct, this being the notion of 'wilful misconduct' as explained by the English Delegate.
2. The Conference was unable to find a French phrase which would be easily translatable into English, the notions *dol* and *faute lourde* having been proclaimed 'unknown' in the English legal language.
3. From the fact that the untranslatable word *dol* was retained, but the easily translatable term *faute lourde* replaced [1]), it can be concluded that the rejection of the latter term by the B ritish Delegate was not really based on reasons of language difficulties, but was rather inspired by the fear that by using the notion of gross negligence the scope of Article 25 would be unduly extended.
4. It was understood that the formula of Article 25 can be rendered into English by speaking of 'wilful misconduct' which notion had been explained to comprise damage causing 'acts committed deliberately as well as acts of carelessness committed without any regard for the consequences'.

178. Before entering into a discussion of the court decisions involving Article 25, some words should be said on the curious epilogue given by the English legislator to the curious drafting history of that Article. Although there can be no doubt that the unhappy phrase ('faults which by the national court seized of the case, are considered equivalent to *dol*') had been adopted to enable the English legislator to use the notion 'wilful misconduct' which would comprise both *dol* and the somewhat mysterious

---

177. [1]) The argument raised by the Paris court in the Azores Case (see No. 184 (1)) against the thesis of Air France, that it would have been a major blunder of the Drafting Committee to retain the notion of *dol* as a criterion, since that notion was the one unknown in English law, is rather weakened by the fact that the delegates were brought under the impression that *faute lourde* was also unknown to English law.

'equivalent fault', the Carriage by Air Act, 1932 has translated *dol* by 'wilful misconduct' and has retained the phrase about the equivalent fault, the purpose of which became entirely obscure [1]). To make confusion complete the French 'faute' was translated into 'default'. It is not surprising that an English Court finds itself somewhat perplexed by the resulting text, and comes to the conclusion that the words were only inserted to take care of some oddity of foreign law [2]). Curiously, the interpretation at which English and American Courts thus have arrived is in conformity with the intention of the framers of Article 25, though that point was only reached by a fortunate combination of errors.

179. Those of the civil law countries where the Warsaw Convention has been incorporated within the national legislations, have nearly all transcribed the fault equivalent to *dol* into the national words for gross negligence; thus, the Netherlands [1]),

---

178. [1]) Except for a minor change, the official (though not binding) American translation is the same. The correctness of this translation was denied by appellant in *American Airlines Inc.* v. *Ulen*, 1949 U.S.Av.R. 338, 343, but upheld by the Court. The point raised by appellant was that 'wilful misconduct' was not a good translation for *dol* which latter term would mean 'fraud' or 'deceit'. See on the meaning of *dol* No. 170 (5).

[2]) In *Horabin* v. *BOAC* [1952] 2 All E.R. 1016, 1019 Barry J., in his instruction to the jury, said about this phrase: 'You need not trouble about the latter phrase, because in the law of this country a default or omission to do something can be just as much misconduct as the doing of something which is wrong'.

179. [1]) Art. 34 of the Air Transportation Act, 1936 (*Wet op het Luchtvervoer*, Sept. 10, 1936, Stb. 523): 'opzet of [...] grove schuld'. It is to be observed that the provisions of this Act only apply to transportation coming within the scope of the Warsaw Convention to the extent they are not in conflict with the latter (cf. No. 160 (1) supra). The use of the words '*grove schuld*' (gross negligence), therefore, cannot affect the interpretation of Article 25 of the Convention. The assimilation of gross negligence to intentional misconduct does not seem to be accepted in Dutch law as a general principle, as appears from the construction by courts and authors of Art. 1284 B.W. (where the French *dol* has been translated into '*arglist*'), corresponding with Art. 1151 of the French Civil Code (comp. e.g. Hoge Raad 18.5.1923, N.J. 1923, p. 904), which latter Article, as applied by the French courts, offers the most typical example of the assimilation in French law. But in most legal provisions dealing with limitation of liability, gross negligence ('*grove schuld*') appears in combination with intentional acts ('*opzet*') as an exception to the limitation; see Artt. 476, 527, 541 (new), 819 (new), 923 (new), 932 (new) and 944 (new) of W.v.K. See also Art. 342 (2) W.v.K.

On the meaning of '*grove schuld*' as used in Article 476 and 527 of the *Wetboek van Koophandel* (Code of Commerce), which deal with the liability of the shipowner, see Cleveringa (1946), pp. 168 sq. and the cases there cited. The meaning which this author attaches to the notion of '*opzet en grove schuld*' coincides fairly well with the

Italy[2]), Germany[3]), the Scandinavian Countries[4]), Switzerland[5]).

Brazil seems to be a notable example. When incorporating the provisions of the Warsaw Convention within the *Codigo Brasileiro do Ar* of 1938, the Brazilian legislator limited the principle of Article 25 to *'dolo'* (*dol*), and the Appeal Court (*Cameras civeis reunidas*) of Rio de Janeiro, in the important case of *A. Caffat Chaddoud et al* v. *Anglo Mexican Co.* etc. [6]) has made it clear that in Brazilian law gross negligence is not considered equivalent to *'dolo'*. It had a very strong argument in the fact that Article 83 of the same code expressly mentions *'culpa grave'* in combination with *'dolo'*. The Court (single chamber) construed *'dolo'*, however, not to be limited to the cases in which it was the defendant's actual intention to inflict damages, but to include those in which he 'foresees, realizes and, without refraining from

---

concept of 'wilful misconduct'. Similarly Losecaat-Vermeer (1939) p. 267 (on the meaning of *'grove schuld'* generally). Some courts, however, have included cases of serious negligence not involving conscious recklessness. See cases cited by Cleveringa (1946) at p. 169, and add Gerechtshof 's-Gravenhage, 12.6.1931. W. 12429, concerning Art. 342, W.v.K. In a recent decision of the Hoge Raad 12.3.1954, N.J.B. 1954, p. 257, also concerning the shipmaster's liability under Art. 342 W.v.K., the Supreme Court has defined gross negligence, for the purpose of that Article, as 'a fault bordering on intentional misconduct, as far as blameworthiness is concerned'.

[2]) Artt. 943 and 952 of the Cod. Nav. On the interpretation by Italian Courts of *'colpa grave'* see 24 Dor (1931) 45–46. See also A. de Cupis (1946) pp. 89 sq. The tendency seems to be to extend the scope of *'colpa grave'* beyond the cases of conscious recklessness.

[3]) § 29e of the Air Traffic Act (*Luftverkehrsgesetz*) 1936, as amended in 1943: *'grobe Fahrlässigkeit'*.

[4]) § 11 of the Norwegian Act of 1936 (*'grov uaktsomhet'*), § 25 of the Swedish Act of 1937 (*'grov vårdslöshet'*), and § 25 of the Danish Act of 1937 (*'grov Uagtsomhed'*).

[5]) Art. 10 *Lufttransportreglement*, 1952.

[6]) L.c. (No. 173 (3)), pp. 221 sq. and 227. Though the case did not turn upon a question of carrier's liability governed by the Warsaw Convention, but upon a question of liability in case of collision, the holdings by the Court of Appeal in Single Chamber and in United Chambers seem to have a direct bearing on the question of the air carrier's liability (actually the United Chambers expressly held that the principle of non-equivalence was only important for the liability arising from carriage). In the first instance *'dolo'* had been held to include gross negligence (l.c. p. 216). The decision of the United Chambers of the Court of Appeal was affirmed on another point by the *Supremo Tribunal Federal* 13.4.1951, Arch. Jud. 99, 204.

The analogous provision (Art. 107) of the **Guatemalan** *Ley de Aviacion Civil*, 1949, speaks of *'actos y omisiones criminales o dolosos'*. See also Art. 156 of the **Uruguayan** *Código de Legislación Aeronáutica*, 1942, Art. 79 of the **Honduras** *Ley de Aviación*, 1950 ('dolo'), and Art. 141 of the **Argentine** Draft Aeronautical Code of 1951 ('dolo'). Curiously the **Mexican** Aviation Act of 1949 (Book IV of the *Ley de Vias Generales de Comunicación*) makes a distinction between the limitation of liability for passengers (only set aside in case of *'dolo'*, Art. 343 (5)) and for handbaggage (set aside both in case of *'dolo'* and *'culpa grave'*, Art. 344), whereas it does not provide at all for unlimited liability as far as cargo and registered baggage (Art. 349), nor as far as surface damages (Art. 352 sq.) are concerned.

accomplishing the act, assumes the risk of producing the result', adding that these acts should be included not because of the assimilation of gross negligence (*culpa grave*) and *dolo*, but because they are a form of *dolo* in the broad meaning which should be given to that word [7]).

180. As has been said before, Article 25 of the Warsaw Convention may rightly claim to have given rise to more litigation than any other provision of international air law. A claim of somewhat doubtful value, if one thinks of the costs involved in litigation both to the parties and to society. For an intelligent discussion of the interpretation which the courts of various countries have given of Article 25 (1) it is useful to keep in mind two things. In the first place, it is of little sense to analyse the formulas devised by the courts as if every letter had its special significance and try to distil some very precise definition. That would be like designing a chemist's balance for weighing potatoes, or like trying to estimate the budget of the U.S.A. in dimes and cents. It is not so much that the facts upon which liability is to be based would not lend themselves to minute distinctions. But judgements or verdicts are not based on facts, but on evidence of facts, including mental facts, and that is what makes every attempt to weigh the facts (i.e. the evidence of facts) in milligrams rather futile. The point may well be illustrated by two American decisions involving one and the same aircraft accident. In one case the jury found that the carrier and his employees had taken all reasonable measures to avoid the accident, i.e. absence of negligence [1]), in the other case the jury found wilful misconduct [2]). If it is possible for courts or juries to leap over the broad river which separates absence of negligence from wilful misconduct, an attempt to indicate the borderline between wilful

---

179. [7]) L.c. (see No. 171 (3)) p. 222. The lower Court had invoked the authority of H. de Simas' commentary (1939) on the *Codigo bras. do Ar*, but that argument was refuted by the Court of Appeal by pointing to the fact that this author has only said that '*dolo*' is not limited to the cases where the defendant actually wanted to inflict damages, but includes 'dolo incidente'.

180. [1]) *Ritts* v. *American Overseas Airlines, Inc.* 1949 U.S.Av.R. 65 (accident at Stephensville, Newfoundland).

[2]) *Goepp, Adm'x* v. *American Overseas Airlines, Inc.* 1951 U.S.Av.R. 527. The verdict was set aside on appeal because of lack of evidence as to wilful misconduct and proximate cause: 1952 U.S. & C.Av.R. 486.

misconduct and negligence by delicate penstrokes seems a little pathetic.

181. The other remark to be made is concerned with the variety of fact situations to which Article 25 applies. The principle which decides whether the carrier may invoke the limits of liability of Article 22 is the same, when the carrier has failed to put a passenger's baggage on the same plane on which the passenger travels, or when a number of passengers are killed by an air crash. It is not at all clear that such entirely different cases should necessarily be treated in the same way, except perhaps to the extent that the rule purports to prevent a carrier, guilty of criminal intent, from taking advantage of the limits. But Article 25 is only carried for a very small part by that rationale. Criminal intent on the part of the carrier himself is so exceptional that the Article would have little significance if it were limited to that. It is true that the theoretical possibility of criminal intent is an easy argument gladly invoked to explain the 'obvious' necessity of inserting an exception to the rule of limited liability, but only to be forgotten at once as soon as one starts to determine the scope of the provision.

If one were to base the principle on the need for prevention it could well be argued that the rationale has an entirely different weight when aircraft accidents are concerned than in case of loss or delay of baggage or goods. For the carrier the consequences of an air accident are such that there would seem to be little need for an additional incentive to prevent such accidents by increasing his liability towards passengers and shippers. The situation is quite different as far as the groundhandling of baggage or goods is concerned. However that may be, Article 25 does not make a distinction between the various possible situations, so that any interpretation established with special regard to air accident cases should also be appropriate to govern the ordinary loss and damage claims. This does not mean that the construction of the provision could not pose special problems when applied to either of these two large classes of fact situations.

It is believed that some of the discussions on Article 25 have failed to appreciate the broad application of that principle. If, for instance, it is said that by requiring intentional misconduct one would practically require the pilot to commit suicide, it is forgotten that theft or pilferage of goods or baggage does not presuppose any suicide, and that Article 25 also applies to such irregularities, which in fact are more frequent than air accidents.

For that reason it may be useful, before entering into a discussion of the case law on Article 25, to give a survey of situations in which that Article may come into play. Such survey, of course, could never boast of anything approaching completeness. Its only purpose is to emphasize that any construction of the provision which one would adopt with a view to a certain class of fact situations should be fit to apply to a great number of entirely different situations. It is respectfully submitted that some of the discussions on the drafting (and the revision) of Article 25 – and the same applies to the drafting of the analogous provisions in the Rome Conventions – might have gained in clarity, if those engaged in these discussions had always kept in mind the richness of possibilities existing within the domain of air law.

The following list is suggested with full recognition of its arbitrariness both as to situations included or excluded and as to the way of grouping them. It is based more on practical considerations than on a strict sense of logic.

1. *Aircraft Accidents*. These may be caused by:
   a. crimes involving *mens rea*, such as crimes committed, by or on the instigation of the carrier himself, for the purpose of murdering some of the persons on board the aircraft, or for collecting insurance money, or acts of sabotage by groundpersonnel. The problem whether and when such acts are to be considered as being committed within the course of the employment will be discussed later. It does not seem helpful to include the theoretical 'suicide case' of sabotage by crew personnel.
   b. violation of statutory safety provisions relating to safety of aircraft (airworthiness certificate, necessary inspections, load maximums), adequateness and fitness of crew (licensing etc.) or flight preparation, and rules of the air. The situations envisaged here may involve reckless conduct and a voluntary taking of unnecessary risks, as well as gross stupidity or carelessness. The special problems involved in the violation of safety regulations as far

as the application of Article 25 is concerned will be discussed later [1].

c. violation of internal safety rules established by the Company.

d. dangerous conduct not involving violation of any specific rules or regulations.

It is to be observed that, apart from death or injuries to passengers, air accidents may cause losses of, or damages to baggage and goods, and delays. Delays may be caused not only to the passengers and goods carried, but also to passenger or goods which were to be carried by the crashed or stranded plane.

2. *Death of, or injuries to, passengers not caused by aircraft accidents*; including cases of:
   a. assault or indecent behaviour by personnel of the carrier;
   b. accidents during operations of embarking or disembarking caused either by defective material or by conduct of personnel. Attention should be given to special possibilities in case of embarking or disembarking from waterplanes;
   c. a rich variety of situations, such as: flying at too high an altitude either without pressurization, or with a failure of the pressurization system; bumpy flying causing passengers to fall from their seats or sickness; failure to warn passengers to use their seat belts; serving bad food; obstructions in the aircraft aisle causing passengers to fall, etc. etc.
3. *Delay in the transportation of passengers not caused by an aircraft accident.* Delays can be caused by:
   a. failure to make a reservation or a double reservation of the same seat;
   b. delayed departure of aircraft;
   c. suspension of flight;
   d. incorrect information to passenger about time of departure;
   e. omission of stop at place where passenger was to disembark;
   f. deviation or added unscheduled intermediate stops.
4. *Loss or damage of baggage or goods otherwise than through*

181. [1]) See No. 188.

aircraft accidents; which may be caused by theft or pilferage, rough handling, misdelivery, deviation resulting in confiscation by local authorities, or the throwing or destruction of goods or baggage to prevent other harm.

5. *Delay in the transportation of baggage or goods* in addition to some of the delays referred to under 3; which may be caused by:
   a. failure to make an agreed reservation, or general lack of space including 'bottlenecks';
   b. failure to put the baggage or goods on the plane;
   c. loading of baggage or goods on the wrong plane, deviations;
   d. failure to offload baggage or goods;
   e. mislaying of accompanying documents essential for regular delivery.

182. It is curious to note – though not difficult to explain – that most of the court decisions which had to construe Article 25 concerned *aircraft accidents*. As far as the author could trace only in three of the adjudicated cases involving air accidents has Article 25 been held to apply up to now, and in one of these cases that decision was reserved on appeal.

One of the cases in which Article 25 was held applicable is that of *American Airlines* v. *Ulen*. 1949 U.S.Av.R. 338. The facts were briefly as follows. Mrs. Ulen, holding a ticket for carriage from Washington D.C. to Mexico City was seriously injured when the American Airlines plane in which she was travelling crashed, shortly after take-off, close to the summit of Glade Mountain. The interrogatories answered by the defendant indicated a flight plan 'drawn up, approved, and partially executed' which violated a Civil Air Regulation forbidding flight below an altitude of 1,000 feet above the highest obstacle located within a distance of 5 miles from the center of the course to be flown [1]). Glade Mountain is 4080 feet high, and the flight plan showed that the center of the indicated course of the planes, flying at 4,000 feet would come within 1½ or, at most, 2 miles of Glade Mountain.

The lower court gave the following instruction to the jury:

182. [1]) C.A.R. 61.7401 provided: 'No scheduled air carrier aircraft shall be flown at an altitude of less than 1000 feet above the highest obstacle located within a horizontal distance of 5 miles from the center of the course intended to be flown'.

'Now, wilful misconduct is not, as I have said, merely misconduct, but wilful miscondict. So if the carrier, or its employees or agents, wilfully performed any act with the knowledge that the performance of that act was likely to result in injury to a passenger, or performed that act with reckless and wanton disregard of its probable consequences, then that would costitute wilful misconduct. [...]
'Now, the mere violation of [safety rules and regulations]... even if intentional, would not necessarily constitute wilful misconduct, but if the violation was intentional with knowledge that the violation was likely to cause injury to a passenger, then that would be wilful misconduct, and, likewise, if it was done with a wanton and reckless disregard of the consequences'. [2])

The correctness of this charge to the jury was confirmed on appeal. The Court of Appeal quoted with approval a definition of 'wilful misconduct' given by another federal court to the effect that 'wilful misconduct means a deliberate purpose not to discharge some duty necessary to safety' [3]). 'This definition squarely fits the facts in the present case. The obvious and sole purpose of Civil Air Regulation 61.7401 [...] is safety. It imposed a duty upon all scheduled carriers which appellant deliberately, knowingly, and intentionally violated'.

Though the Court based its jugdment on an interpretation of wilful misconduct according to the *lex fori*, by adopting the above refuted view that Article 25 of the Convention prescribed such application of local law, the result to which it arrived seems to be in accordance with the principle as contemplated by the framers of the Convention.

In the Ritts Case [4]) the Court held that wilful misconduct covers 'not only acts done deliberately, but also acts of carelessness without regard to the consequences'. It will be noted that this formula is about literally the same as the definition which Sir Alfred Dennis had given of the term at the Warsaw Conference [5]). 'It has been defined' the Court continues 'as that degree of neglect or conduct arising where there is a reckless indifference to the safety of human life, or an intentional failure to perform a manifest duty to the public, in the performance of which the

182. [2]) 1949 U.S.Av.R. 338, 344.
[3]) *Rowe* v. *Gatke Corp.*, 126 F. (2d) 61, 66 (1942).
[4]) 1949 U.S.Av.R. 65, 68.
[5]) See No. 170 (6).

public and the party injured had an interest'. Somewhat further in its instruction to the jury the Court explains that 'wilful misconduct is something entirely different from negligence and far beyond it, whether the negligence be culpable or gross; it involves either a deliberate intent to commit injury or intentional misconduct which is so reckless and wanton as to imply a willingness to commit injury or a complete disregard for the natural consequences of the act' [6]).

It is respectfully submitted that the Court exaggerates the difference between wilful misconduct and gross negligence. Both psychologically and practically the borderline between the two concepts is a vague one [7]). Were it not so, Courts and juries would not have such difficulty in determining whether certain acts or omissions amount to wilful misconduct. But what the Court obviously wanted to drive home to the jury was that wilful misconduct presupposes a clearly blamable state of mind.

In the Goepp Case [8]) the trial judge used language which goes even further than the previous decisions, but which did not prevent the jury from finding wilful misconduct on the basis of the same facts as those presented in the case of Ritts v. A.O.A.

> 'Wilful misconduct means the knowing, deliberate intentional performance of an act with the knowledge that the act is of such a nature that it will probably result in injury or damage, or it means the intentional performance of an act in so reckless and wanton a manner as to imply complete and callous indifference to and disregard of the probable consequences flowing from the performance of the act'.

On appeal this instruction to the jury was confirmed.

---

182. [6]) 1949 U.S.Av.R. 65, 69/70.

[7]) Cf. Prosser (1941), p. 262: 'Since recklessness often is inferred from any highly dangerous conduct, there is seldom any clear distinction between 'wanton' and 'gross negligence'. Also p. 260: 'Many courts [...] have interpreted it [gross negligence] as requiring wilful misconduct, or recklessness'. See also Note in 35 Mich. L. Rev. (1937) 804 on the similarity between 'gross negligence' as construed in Massachussets, and 'wilful misconduct' as construed in Michigan (quoted by Prosser). Also *Meek* v. *Fowler*, 3 Cal. 2d 420, 45 P. 2d 194: 'While the line between gross negligence and wilful misconduct may not always be easy to draw'. In *Crowell* v. *M.R. and R. Trucking Co.* (1946) 157 F. 2d 963, it was said that in Florida the terms 'gross negligence' and 'wilful and wanton misconduct' are considered synonymous.

[8]) 1951 U.S.Av.R. 527, 528.

183. In *Horabin v. B.O.A.C.* [1]) an English Court for the first time had to construe Article 25 of the Convention (or more accurately of the First Schedule to the Carriage by Air Act, 1932). In an elaborate and clear instruction to the jury Barry J. explained the meaning of wilful misconduct:

> 'Wilful misconduct is misconduct to which the will is a party, and it is wholly different in kind from mere negligence or carelessness, however gross that negligence or carelessness may be. The will must be a party to the misconduct and not merely a party to the conduct of which complaint is made ... To establish wilful misconduct on the part of [the] pilot, it must be shown, not only that he knowingly (and in that sense wilfully) did the wrongful act, but also that, when he did it he was aware that it was a wrongful act, i.e. that he was aware that he was committing misconduct' [2]).

The judge was careful to treat the element of 'misconduct' and the element of violation as two separate requirements. After having pointed out that in view of the grave risks involved in carriage by air, some relatively minor breach of a safety regulation may amount to misconduct, although it would not have done so under other circumstances, he further explained the element of wilfulness in the following words:

> 'In order to establish wilful misconduct the plaintiff must satisfy you that the person who did the act knew at the time that he was doing something wrong and yet did it notwithstanding or, alternatively, that he did it quite recklessly, not caring whether he was doing the right thing or the wrong thing, quite regardless of the effects of what he was doing on the safety of the aircraft and of the passengers for which and for whom he was responsible' [3]).

Later on he adds:

'What I think is the best and shortest and most complete

183. [1]) [1952] 2 All E.R. 1016, 1952 U.S. & C.Av.R. 549.

[2]) L.c. at 1019.

[3]) L.c. at 1020. Cf. A. N. Hand J. in *Pekelis Adm'x* v. *Transcontinental and Western Air, Inc.* 1951 U.S.Av.R. 1, 4/5 holding that a request from plaintiff to add to the charge to the jury that 'a deliberate purpose on the part of the carrier or one of its employees not to discharge some duty necessary to safety may constitute wilful misconduct', was properly denied 'because it failed to state that the employee must either have known that the test was necessary for safety, or his duty to make it must have been so obvious that in failing to make it his conduct would be reckless, rather than merely negligent'.

definition in English law ... one which has been used more than once in these courts, is this: To be guilty of wilful misconduct the person concerned must appreciate that he is acting wrongfully, or is wrongfully omitting to act and yet persists in so acting or omitting to act regardless of the consequences, or acts or omits to act with reckless indifference as to what the result may be' [4]).

Illustrative of the difference between wilful misconduct and the cases of gross negligence not involving wilfulness is the example he gives of two men driving motorcars and passing traffic lights after they have been changed from yellow to red:

'In both cases there are the same act, the same traffic lights, the same crossroads, and the same motor cars. In the first case the man may have been driving a little too fast. He may not have been keeping a proper look-out, and he may not have seen the lights (although he ought to have seen them) until he was too close to them and was unable to stop, and, therefore, crossed the roads when the lights were against him. He was not intending to do anything wrong, to disregard provisions of the Road Traffic Act or to endanger the lives of anyone using the road, but he was careless in not keeping a proper look-out and in going too fast, and as a result, without intending to do anything wrong, he committed an act which was clearly an act of misconduct. The second driver is in a hurry. He knows all about the lights, and he sees in plenty of time that they are changing from yellow to red, but he says to himself: Hardly any traffic comes out of this side road which I am about to cross. I will go on. I am not going to bother to stop. He does not expect an accident to happen, but he knows that he is doing something wrong. He knows that he should stop and he is able to stop, buc he does not, and he commits exactly the same act as the other driver. But in that frame of mind no jury would have very much difficulty in coming to the conclusion that he had committed an act of wilful misconduct' [5]).

184. On April 24, 1952 the *Tribunal Civil de la Seine* rendered an important and much discussed decision in the case of *Broche-Hennessy* v. *Air France* arising from the Azores Accident [1]).

183. [4]) L.c. at 1022.
[5]) L.c. at 1020. Cf. the American Restatement of the Law of Torts (Negligence), § 500.

184. [1]) J.C.P. 1952, II, 6985; G.P. 1952, 1952.1.339; D. 1952, J. 514 with note by Ripert; and 6 R.F.D.A. (1952) 199 with the extensive 'conclusions' for the gov-

After having given a careful analysis of the drafting history of Article 25, and after a detailed examination of the facts, the Court described the 'faute lourde' which French law considers 'equivalent' to 'dol' in the following words:

> 'No provision of French law defines the degree of seriousness which that fault [*faute lourde*] should present. It should not be measured by its results but evaluated on the basis of the conduct of the actor compared with a similar class – in this case carrier or flyer – placed in the same external circumstances, and having the responsibility for the personnel and the passengers, who have to rely upon him. The 'faute lourde' neither can be reduced to *culpa in concreto* neither to a professional fault, neither to a criminal offence; its field is characterized by the enormity of the misconduct betraying either incapacity or mad carelessness. It is recklessness, lack of skill, blindness approaching to conscious recklessness.
>
> '[...] Whatever are the characteristics attached to it by the authors, its assimilation to 'dol' is not based on a moral principle, as the two types of misconduct are of a different nature. But it is dictated by the necessities of a sound legal technique, as recognized by permanent tradition. It is in this case of little importance whether one wants to see in the latin maxim a simple presumption which the actor could rebut by proving his good faith [2]), or whether one feels that the realization of the probability of the result deserves the same sanction as the will to cause it – the noxiousness of the actor being the same in both cases –, or whether one simply measures the seriousness of the fault *in abstracto*.
>
> 'If one actually would consider that the assimilation ceases to be of effect as soon as the defendant has proved that he could not have the will to injure, the simple statement of fact that an entire crew, composed of audacious but experienced and perfectly balanced men, would then have brought itself by its 'dol' to an act of collective suicide, would be sufficient to rebut that presumption. Neither does the criterion of cold realization of a risk which would have been contemplated as probable and nevertheless accepted, apply to this case. For it is undeniable that the excess of confidence of some experienced pilots, sure of their material and their instruments, and

---

ernment by Substitut Mazet. The decision was discussed by P. Chauveau in 6 R.F. D.A. (1952) 239–253, by M. de Juglart in 5 Rev. trim. dr. com. (1952), 425–428 and more extensively in J.C.P. 1952 I, 1010, and by Alary in Journ. dr. int. (Clunet) 1952, pp. 866 sq.

[2]) This is the thesis defended by the brothers Mazeaud in their *Traité de responsabilité civile*, I, Nos. 414 and 675–2.

relying on visibility, was the cause of the catastrophy; such excessive confidence is the contrary of 'faute lourde' as just defined.
Finally, if 'faute lourde' were to be characterized by lack of skill, by recklessness, by conduct which the most stupid persons would not commit – (*non intelligere quod omnes intelligunt*) – it is impossible to point to such a serious error of conduct on the part of the crew'.

As courts use to do, the 'Tribunal' wisely tried to refrain as much as possible from taking sides in the debate on the character of 'faute lourde', but said that with any of the three theories mentioned by it the defendant would not have been liable of gross negligence. Nevertheless, it did reject the broader definitions of gross negligence defended by a number of authoritative authors and applied by the courts in a number of cases. In the first place, it denied that the seriousness of the fault required could be measured by its consequences, though sometimes French courts have done so [3]). Further the court denied that 'faute lourde' can be reduced to *culpa in concreto*, i.e. the failure to take as much care as the defendant would give to his own affairs [4], or to a fault of a professional character [5]), or to a criminal offence.

The decision has been criticized as running counter to the general views held by French courts and authors on the concept of 'faute lourde' [6]). The criticism would probably be justified if the interpretation of a French legal text were involved. But it has been rightly pointed out that Article 25 of the Convention should be construed as a provision of international law, not as French law [7]). The reference in Article 25 to the law of the court seized of the case, confusing though it is, was not meant –

---

104. [3]) See e.g. the lower court decisions mentioned by M. Travers, *Droit commercial international*, Vol. V, fasc. II (Paris 1933), No. 5557; but Travers quotes also decisions by the German and Austrian supreme courts and by the French Cour de Cassation to the contrary. Comp. also No. 5555.

[4]) Many of the Digest texts, which form the sources for the maxim that gross negligence is to be assimilated to *dolus*, involved cases of *culpa in concreto*. Cf. D. 16.3.32, D. 44.71.5 and see P. Jörs, *Römisches Privatrecht*, 2. Aufl. bearb. von W. Kunkel, Berlin, 1935 (Enzyklopädie der Rechts- und Staatswissenschaft, II–III), p. 180.

[5]) On this criterion especially Josserand, *La renaissance de la faute lourde sous le signe de la profession*, in D.H. 1939, p. 29 and further literature in the study of Juglart in J.C.P. 1952 I, 1010, note (21).

[6]) M. de Juglart in J.C.P. 1952 I, 1010.

[7]) Chauveau l.c. (note 1).

it may bear repetition – to leave matters of *substance* to the municipal laws.

185. In order not to draw too sweeping conclusions from the wording used in some of the above quoted decisions, it may be useful to examine separately some of the problems with which they had to deal.

If Article 25 were limited to the intentional infliction of damage, little difficulty would arise in its application [1]). But there can be no doubt that it was intended to go further than that. It has been suggested above that the definition of wilful misconduct offered by Sir Alfred Dennis in the course of the drafting of Article 25 probably offers the soundest common denominator of what the framers of the Convention had in mind when trying to find a formula which would be acceptable to the various legal systems. That definition included besides 'acts committed deliberately', 'acts of carelesness committed without any regard for the consequences'. It is true that this is still somewhat vague, but so were most probably the ideas in the minds of most of the delegates. Concrete cases do not seem to have been considered. But what the words of Sir Alfred do imply is a state of mind which may be called recklessness or at least conscious indifference for the consequences.

Both courts and authors have rightly emphasized that there is a dual requirement of 'misconduct' and 'wilfulness' [2]). But it should be kept in mind that the misconduct, or the 'breach of duty', as it has also been named, should be related to the consequences giving rise to the claim, or to put it otherwise: the misconduct must be at least an *undue risk creating conduct* [3]).

185. [1]) Except for the question arising in case of damage caused for the purpose of avoiding greater harm, and the problem of whether the intention to cause a damage, which is in no way related with the damage for which compensation is claimed, will be sufficient to bring the rule of unlimited liability into play. Both problems will be discussed in connection with the Rome Convention 1952, in Nos. 193 and 194.

[2]) See especially the Horabin Case (No. 183 (1)). Shawcross and Beaumont (1951) No. 364.

[3]) For this reason it is respectfully submitted that the definition of 'wilful misconduct' in Shawcross and Beaumont (1951), No. 364 to the effect that 'wilful misconduct' means a deliberate act or omission which the person doing or omitting – (i) knows is a breach of his duty in the circumstances; *or* (ii) knows is likely to cause damage to third parties; etc.', might better have been formulated in the cumulative, instead of in the alternative form. A breach of duty which the actor does not realize creates a risk of harm, would not be wilful misconduct. This would also seem to follow from the charge to the jury by Barry J. in the Horabin Case.

186. This brings in the difficult question what degree of probability should be required for the damage to follow from the misconduct. American Courts frequently state that the consequences should be 'probable' or 'likely' to follow: 'There must be a realization of the probability of injury from the conduct, and a disregard of the probable consequences of such conduct' [1]). In the Ulen Case the court onetime speaks of 'reckless and wanton disregard of [the] probable consequences' and another time of 'wanton and reckless disregard of the consequences' [2]). The same varying language can be found in the Ritts Case [3]). It is possible that the use of the word 'probable' or 'natural' in this connection is an inappropriate reminiscence of the 'probable and natural consequences' test often used by American Courts to exclude liability for 'remote' damages [4]). In that case it would be permissible not to attach too much importance to these words. However, in cases not dealing with the Warsaw Convention, but also construing the words 'wilful misconduct' or 'wilful negligence' – which cases have obviously been drawn upon by the Courts when construing Article 25 of the Warsaw Convention – the courts have generally emphasized the requirement that the harm complained of must have been the probable consequence of defendant's conduct, in a way that it is difficult to ignore the use of the word in the Warsaw cases.

In *Melby* v. *Anderson*, a South Dakota Court, applying a 'guest statute' which required 'wilful and wanton misconduct' on the part of the driver of an automobile in order to make him liable towards his guest passengers, construed these words as follows:

> 'Wilful and wanton misconduct (and gross negligence as it is employed in this Statute) means something more than negligence [...] to bring the conduct of the defendant within the prohibition of this Statute the jury must find as a fact that defendant intentionally did something in the operation of a motor vehicle which he should not have done [...] under such circumstances that it can be said that he consciously

186. [1]) 1949 U.S.Av.R. 338, at 344 and 345.

[2]) 1949 U.S.Av.R. 65, at 68 and 70. See also *Pekelis* v. *Transcontinental and Western Airlines Inc.* 187 F. 2d 122, 1951 U.S.Av.R. 1, 3.

[3]) 1949 U.S.Av.R. 65, at 68 and 70.

[4]) Cf. Prosser (1941) pp. 317/318 citing further literature.

realized that his conduct would *in all probability* (*as distinguished from possibly*) produce the precise result which it did produce'. (italics supplied) [5]).

Prosser even goes so far as to say that the terms wilful and wanton 'both carry the idea of reckless disregard of consequences in the face of a known risk, so great as to make it highly probable that harm will follow' [6]).

In ordinary language, to say that something will probably happen means that the chances are thought greater that that event will happen than that it will not. If somebody tells me that it will problably rain in the afternoon I am justified in concluding that the person giving me this information thinks that there is more chance of rain than that the weather will remain dry. Applying this to the statement that in order to be guilty of wilful misconduct the defendant must have thought that the damage would be the probable consequence of his conduct, one would reach the conclusion that the defendant should have evaluated the chance of the harm being caused at more than 50%. For the pilot to be guilty of misconduct, it would be necessary for him to have realized that the chance of getting out of of it safely was less than 50%! It seems unlikely that the courts or authors who have used the word 'probable' in this connection would be willing to accept such a conclusion.

The difficulty of qualifying the chance required for the occurrence of the damage is that such qualification purports to fix one and the same degree of probability, whatever the seriousness of the consequences involved. It is believed that the degree of probability required should depend upon the gravity of the harm to be feared. Realization of a 1% chance that an aircraft will crash as a result of a certain act or omission may be sufficient to make the defendant's conduct 'wilful misconduct' in the sense of Article 25, whereas realization of a 25% chance that some shipment will not arrive on time at its destination might not be sufficient to bring the case under Article 25.

186. [5]) 64 S.D. 249, 266 N.W. 135, 137. Followed in later decisions, see *Peterson* v. *Denevan* (1949) 177 F. 2d. 411. Some recent cases from other jurisdictions, also requiring probability of consequences: *Evens* v. *Texas Pac.* v. *Missouri Pac. Terminal R.R. of New Orleans* (1943) 134 F. 2d. 275, 276; *Baltimore and O.R. Co.* v. *Felgenhauer*(1948) 168 F. 2d. 12.

[6]) 32 Minn. L. Rev. (1948) 105, at 113.

There must be a 'disregard', an 'indifference' for the consequences. The less serious the consequences, the smaller the probability which should have been realized in order to evidence the cold indifference which is essential to 'wilful misconduct', if no malice is involved. When the consequences to be feared are a catastrophy such as the crash of an aircraft, the degree of probability that that catastrophy would happen as a result of the blamable act can be much lower, in order to bring to light the defendant's 'cold indifference' with respect to the consequences of his misconduct.

187. The problem of 'probability' of damage becomes still more complicated if – as is generally the case – the act or omission complained of was the result of a weighing of different risks and interests. Every pilot knows that any landing involves some risks, however small one wants to evaluate that normal risk. If the realization thereof were to withhold carriers from making landings, aviation would still be where it started: on the ground. The interest of aviation outweighs that risk. If weather conditions are not too good, the risk increases. Aviation authorities, company policies, and in the last instance, the pilot's own feelings and sense of responsibility must tell him when the risk involved outweighs the interest of the landing being made. The risk to be taken may be greater when the interest at stake in the landing being made is bigger. There may be a sick person on board the plane who has to be operated on as soon as possible, or a minister of foreign affairs going to attend some highly important and urgent meeting, or medicine which is being flown to an area where an epidemic rages. Less seriously it may also be a cargo in the timely arrival of which the pilot knows that large financial interests are involved. To say that a financial interest could never excuse the taking of an increased risk is certainly too dogmatical, as the reasoning would prevent any aviation which, as has been said before, always involves some risk, small as it may be. The only thing which can be said is that, when a financial interest is balanced against the interest of human life, the saving of the financial risk, however large it may be, can never justify a substantial increase of the risk of human life.

In order that a pilot can be blamed for wilful misconduct, he must at least have realized that the risk he was taking should not have been taken, in other words, that it was not outweighed by a risk of the same seriousness or more serious. Or in the words of Mr. Justice Barrie:

> 'The mere fact that an act was done contrary to a flight plan or to some instructions, or even to the standards of safe flying, to the knowledge of the person who did it, does not necessarily establish wilful misconduct on his part, because in the exigencies of the flight it is always possible that a pilot may consciously depart from instructions, taking the view that, in the best interests of the safety of his aircraft, it is wiser and safer for him to depart from them than to adhere to them [...] A finding on your part that the pilot acted contrary to instructions, and knew that he was so acting, does not mean that he necessarily committed wilful misconduct merely because you now think that he was wrong' [1]).

188. This brings us to another, perhaps even more thorny problem. In an early American commentary on the Convention it was said that violations of government regulations 'almost certainly' constitute wilful misconduct as used in the English and American translations of Article 25 of the Convention [1]). The argument has been pleaded in various cases but as far as this author could discover it has in its generality always been rejected by the courts [2]). If it were to be accepted, the conse-

---

187. [1]) *Horabin* v. *BOAC* [1952] 2 All E.R. 1016, 1023.

188. [1]) Sullivan in 7 J.A.L. (1936) 1, at 44. Comp. Shawcross and Beaumont (1951) No. 364: 'But if a pilot deliberately disregarded the directions of ground control [...], *or deliberately did or omitted something in breach of Regulations*, or of generally recognised standards of reasonable care [...], he would *normally* be guilty of wilful misconduct' (italics supplied). The authors are careful to add that 'this question is one of fact in each particular case'.

[2]) *Ritts* v. *American Overseas Airlines Inc.* 1949 U.S.Av.R. 65, 70; *American Airlines* v. *Ulen*, 1949 U.S.Av.R. 338, 344. See also *Horabin* v. *BOAC* [1952] All E.R. 1016, and the **Italian** Court of Appeal Milan 13.6.1941, Monitore di Tribunali 1941, 642. The **Argentine** Corte Suprema, in a case decided 9.8.1940 (19 La Ley 973), has held a violation of a traffic regulation to amount to *culpa grave* for the purpose of exempting the employer from his liability for workmen's compensation. But the Argentine decisions do not seem to agree on that point and are, of course, influenced by the circumstances, cf. note in 62 La Ley (1951) 192, at 194 and 196.

The question is connected with, but should be distinguished from, the question of whether a contractual clause exempting from liability for the consequences of negligence should be construed to cover the consequences of a breach of a statutory duty. Cf. on the latter question *Dominian Air Lines, Ltd.* v. *Strand* [1933] N.Z.L.R. 1, at 7/8 and 57 (lack of the prescribed pilot-license held not covered by clause).

quences would be that the large majority of aircraft accidents would probably involve wilful misconduct. With the increasing density of air safety and traffic regulations it is in most negligence cases possible to discover some breach of some regulation at the root of the accident [3]).

Whatever the relation between criminal statutes and tort liability is – a problem which, due to the 'split personality' of the law in Anglosaxon countries, has perhaps caused more troubles there than in the civil law systems – it is probably fair to say that generally a violation of safety regulations without some reasonable excuse creates a civil liability for the resulting consequences [4]). If the legislator has laid down his view that the smoking of cigars in aircraft creates an undue risk, a court or jury will be precluded from holding that smoking of cigars in aircraft is not creating undue risks and therefore not unreasonable [5]). If an

---

188. [3]) This was very well realized by Sullivan in 7 J.A.L. (1936) 1, at 44. Comp also W. L. Prosser's discussion of *Dart* v. *Pure Oil Co.* (Minn. 1947) 27 N.W. 2d. 555 in 32 Minn. L. Rev. (1948), 105, where plaintiff's counsel had pleaded that an action based upon intentional acts which violate a statute must be regarded as an action for an intentional or 'wilful' tort, to which contributory negligence would not be a defence. The argument was rejected by the court. 'If the contention were to be upheld, it is obvious that the consequences would be sweeping. In nearly all automobile cases, in nearly all railway cases [. . .] the action is founded upon the defendant's violation of a statute. In fact it is safe to say that today negligence actions are very much in the minority in which there is not some claim of violation of a statute, ordinance or regulation'. (Prosser, l.c. at p. 106).

[4]) But the **Dutch** Supreme Court (*Hoge Raad*) in a decision of 22.5.1953, N.J. 1954, No. 647 (*N.V. De Nederlandsche Lloyd Ongevallen* v. *N.V. West-Indische Bananen Import Compagnie*) decided that the lower court rightly could have held that defendant had not acted imprudently merely for not having driven at such a speed as to be able to stop his car at any time within visible distance of the road, as expressly prescribed in the Traffic Regulations: 'From the fact, that Van Klevens may not have driven in accordance with said Regulation, it does not necessarily follow that he drove otherwise than he should have done under the circumstances of the case' (it is to be noted that there was nothing in the circumstances of the case, that prevented him from driving in conformity with the Regulation). Similarly the same Court in 5.6.1931, N.J. 1932, p. 113 (inland water traffic regulations). Both cases involved the application of traffic regulations which probably were too generally phrased, and it is suggested that the desired result could also have been reached by a reasonable interpretation of the relevant provisions, which appears to be the approach taken by the Advocate-General in his 'conclusion' in the 1953 case. See for **U.S.A.**: Ch. Lowndes, *Civil Liability Created by Criminal Legislation*, 16 Minn. L. Rev. (1932) 361; C. Morris, *The Relation of Criminal Statutes and Tort Liability*, 46 Harv. L. Rev. (1933) 453.

[5]) The rare American cases where the court refused to accept the standard set by the legislator seem to involve outmoded statutes (such as statutes providing for a speed limit of 6 miles per hour) which by some failure of the legislator had remained on the books; they must rather be considered an act of revolt of the courts against the legislator. Cf. Prosser l.c. (note 3 above) at p. 108.

accident happens as a direct consequence of such forbidden form of smoking, the smoker will be held liable for a breach of a duty of care, i.e. he will be liable for negligence.

Can it be said, if he knowingly commits a breach of such preestablished duty of care, he is guilty of an intentional wrong if harm ensues, or at least guilty of that indifference and disregard of the consequences which would bring his conduct within the ambit of Article 25? Since it is clear that he did not want the accident to happen, there can be no question of intentional wrongdoing. As far as the possibility of conscious disregard for the consequences is concerned, it is suggested that the question of whether a conscious breach of a regulation evidences such disregard of the consequences as to make Article 25 applicable, will depend upon (1) the seriousness of the consequences which the Statute intended to prevent, (2) the degree of probability of these consequences happening as a result of a violation, and (3) the character of the interests for the sake of which the violation was committed [6]). This would seem true whether or not the rule of conduct which was violated was laid down in a government regulation.

But violation of a government regulation *may* make it more difficult for a carrier to convince the court or jury that his mind or that of his pilot was not directed at the possibility of dangers when committing the act (or omitting what should be done). It will at least be difficult for him to say that he had never thought about the possibility of the blamed conduct creating certain risks. This does not only apply, however, to government regulations but also to internal company instructions laid down in flight manuals.

Since wilful misconduct implies a mental attitude, the legal fiction that everyone is supposed to know the law, whatever its general validity in the various legal systems, can never be

188. [6]) The decision in the Dart Case (note 3 above) contains one passage, which is not mentioned by Prof. Prosser, and which could seem to lend support to those who consider that an *intentional violation* of a government regulation is necessarily wilful misconduct: 'there is no evidence of an intentional or wilful mixing of gasoline with kerosene (which was forbidden by statute) as distinguished from mere negligence on the part of the company in using reasonable care to avoid the possibility of such a mixture. It does not appear from the record that the company intentionally and wilfully sold to the grocery a mixture of gasoline and kerosene contrary to the statute'. (at p. 561). It is suggested, however, that the distinction introduced here by the court must be read with a view to the probability and the seriousness of harm involved in the specific type of conduct forbidden by the statute.

invoked in support of an allegation that the defendant has been guilty of wilful misconduct [7]). But failure to know the existing regulations *may* stem from a conscious disregard for the consequences e.g. in case a carrier deliberately had decided, because of the expenses involved, not to pass on any more to his flying personnel the newly issued Regulations. In such a case, however, not the person who unknowingly violated the statute would be guilty of wilful misconduct, but the carrier who intentionally failed to inform him about the existence of that statute.

189. In the *Horabin Case* the jury asked additional instructions on the question of 'whether misconduct can arise out of a series of acts of carelessness; and whether, if that series of acts was done on many occasions and was contrary to instructions or departed from the standard of safe flying, and if that must have been known to those who did them, that was wilful misconduct'. On this question Barry J. answered i.a.:

> 'You must look at each act and judge it in the light of all the evidence about it and all that you know about the case, and then you must pronounce an individual judgment on it in the light of your knowledge of the whole case [...] You must look at each alleged act of misconduct independently. In forming a judgment about it you are entitled to look at the evidence as a whole and to take into account all that you know as a whole and to take into account all that you know as a result of that evidence, but there must be an individual judgment on each act, and that act must in itself, in your view, amount to misconduct before any question as to wilfulness arises [...].
> 'A pilot may be guilty of a long series of errors of judgment. Each act in that series of acts may involve a departure from instructions or from the flightplan or from the accepted standards of safe flying. [...] But whether there be one act or a hundred acts, if each of them was done for the best – that is to say, if each of the acts was done in what the pilot thought was the best interests of the aircraft and passengers – then the mere fact that there is a large addition sum to be done and one act added to another does not give a total which amounts to wilful misconduct' [1]).

188. [7]) Cf. *Goepp* v. *American Overseas Airlines*, 1952 U.S. & C.Av.R. 486, 491: 'there is no proof that defendant's interpretation was conceived in bad faith, that it was arrived at with any intimation that it was incorrect'.

189. [1]) *Horabin* v. *BOAC* [1952] 2 All E.R. 1016, 1024.

To judge the meaning of this charge one should keep in mind the special fact situation involved, i.e. of an aircraft flying from airport to airport in an attempt to land but unable to do so because of weather conditions or density of traffic, and running out of fuel while trying to return to the point of departure. Under other circumstances, when there would not exist that continuous balancing of alternative risks, the instruction would have been different. It is also to be observed that the judge was careful to add: 'the number of occasions on which acts are done is, of course, of some significance in considering the state of mind of the person who does those acts'. In the same way that the violation of a statutory standard of conduct *may* justify an inference of indifference on the part of the defendant as to the possible consequences of his conduct, so *may* the fact that the defendant has frequently committed similar acts of carelessness in the performance of his duties evidence a disregard on his part for the consequences of his conduct, when one act of carelessness would not have been sufficient to warrant such an inference [2]).

190. Before finishing this discussion on the meaning of Article 25 (1) of the Warsaw Convention, it may be useful to add two remarks, self-evident as they may seem:

(1) Whatever the exact meaning of 'dol' or a fault held equivalent to 'dol' may be, there can be no doubt that the burden of proof is on the plaintiff. On this rather obvious point, at least, the courts are unanimous [1]). The law of the court seized of the case will decide what evidence will be permitted to this effect. There does not seem to exist any obstacle in the Convention against the use of evidence by inference. In fact, since the thing to be proven is largely a matter of the defendant's own state of mind or that of his employees, any evidence of wilful misconduct

---

189. [2]) Cf. Cass. req. 4.4.1933, G.P. 1933.1.83: 'la fréquence des vols dénote de la part de ses agents une incurie sans excuse' justifying the lower court's holding that defendant had committed a 'faute lourde'.

190. [1]) *Goepp* v. *American Overseas Airlines*, 1952 U.S. & C.Av.R. 486, 491 (citing earlier authorities); *Horabin* v. *BOAC* [1952] 2 All E.R. 1016, 1019; Cass. (italian) 31.7.1939, N. 3146, Riv. dir. aer. 1939, p. 407. The decision of an Italian Court of first instance which had burdened the defendant with the proof of absence of '*dolo o colpa grave*' (for the purpose of Art. 37 of the Act of 1923) seems to be unique and was reversed in due course by the Court of Appeal of Milan 13.6.1941, Monitore di Tribunali 1941, 642.

nearly always has to make use of some inferences [2]). But it would be a violation of Article 25 and of Article 22 of the Convention to apply any legal presumption which would shift the burden of proof on to the defendant [3]).

191. (2) Proof of wilful misconduct is not sufficient; there must also be evidence of sufficient causal relation between the wilful misconduct and the damages complained of. In a case of 1939, involving application of Article 37 of the old Italian Act of 1923, which required 'dolo o colpa grave' ('wilful misconduct or gross negligence') for the liability of an aircraft operator towards his guest passengers, the *Corte di Cassazione* rejected the liability of the operator, notwithstanding the fact that the aircraft did not have an airworthiness certificate and that the pilot might have been drunken, because there was no causal relation between these alleged facts and the accident [1]).

Similarly, in the Goepp Case the majority of the judges rejected unlimited liability i.a. because 'there was no evidence submitted to show that if there were any violations of air safety regulations such violations were the proximate cause of the accident' [2]). In a dissenting opinion Breitel J. pleaded for 'a liberal approach in finding proximate cause'.

---

190. [2]) Similarly F. Agró in Riv. dir. aeron. 1940, p. 69.

[3]) In its decision of 22.12.1949, 12 Transport (1950) p. 2466, the *Tribunal commercial de la Seine* held Article 25 applicable in a case where a valuable shipment of watches was lost and the carrier was unable to give any information as to the cause of the loss. The judgment was reversed on Appeal (Paris, 28.2.1953, 16 R.G.A. (1953) 180) on the argument 'qu'on ne peut du seul fait, que la Compagnie Air France se soit révélée incapable de fournir des renseignements précis sur cette perte, déduire, de sa part, un défaut de vigilance, un manque total d'organisation ou un fonctionnement défectueux de ses services de surveillance qui seraient constitutifs d'une faute lourde'.

To derive an inference of wilful misconduct or gross negligence from the fact that the carrier does not know the cause of the loss would result in shifting the burden of proof onto the carrier. Similarly for sea carriage Appel Algers 23.2.1951, 3 D.M.F. (1951) 435. Comp. Cass. civ. 12.4.1923, S. 1923.1.292. G.P. 1923.2.71 where the Court inferred existence of a *faute lourde* from the fact that a long delay could in no way be explained by the carrier. See also Esmein in S. 1933.1.289. The App. Crt. Genoa 23.11. 1925, 14 Dor (1931) 461 held it to be customary in maritime law to infer wilful misconduct or gross negligence if the carrier cannot prove the absence of a fault or the presence of only a small fault. The disappearance of a number of packages without explanation by the carrier was held to be gross negligence. Similarly decision of same court 19.7.1951, 11 Riv. dir. navig. (1951) 228. See also 24 Dor (1931) 45–46.

191. [1]) Cass. 31.7.1939. N. 3146. Riv. dir. aeron. 1939, 407.

[2]) 1952 U.S. & C.Av.R. 486, 492.

'On the matter of proximate cause it was quite reasonable for the jury to find that the pilot's sub-standard familiarity with an instrument landing on the field at Stephenville involved of necessity a relatively sub-standard familiarity with the terrain, resulting in the pilot's ignorance of the hill which, on take-off, the plane struck. This, the jury could find, was a proximate cause of the evidence. It should be obvious too that with respect to air accidents, because of the mysteries in which the fatal and more serious accidents become shrouded, a liberal approach in finding proximate cause from any kind of misconduct which may lead to multiple fatalities is socially justified, if not required. What may be required as evidence of proximate cause in a trolley car accident would not be a relevant standard in an accident involving a modern transport plane, or the jet liner now at the threshold of air transportation. The risks of air transportation are great and are assumed by the passenger; but he should have the right to rely on the carrier's adherence to officially required standards of care' [3]).

The dissenting views of Mr. Justice Breitel have been given rather extensively, because they reflect a certain line of thinking which, it is respectfully submitted, when generally followed would lead to the very destruction of what was the major purpose of the Warsaw Convention: unification of the law. In the system adopted in the Convention the carrier is liable unless *he* can prove absence of negligence or of any causal relation between some negligence and the accident. It was exactly because of 'the mysteries in which the fatal and more serious accidents become shrouded' that the framers of the Convention decided to impose the burden of proof on the carrier. They added, however, a limit on the carrier's liability, except for the exceptional cases in which it would become apparent that the accident had been caused by wilful misconduct of the carrier. The fact that the limit provided in the Convention has, in the view of many Americans, become inadequate as far as the U.S.A. is concerned should not be a reason for American Courts to change the international rules established by the Convention. It would be as wrong for a court to alleviate the burden of proof of the carrier under Article 20 (1) by a presumption in the carrier's favour, because of possible views held in the country of that court as to

---

191. [3]) Ibidem, at 493.

the social undesirability of burdening the carrier with the onus of proof.

B. Rome Conventions.

192. The Convention of 1933 abandoned the unfortunate formula of the Warsaw Convention and, at the suggestion of the British Delegate, substituted the time honoured combination of '*faute lourde ou dol*' [1]). It was understood that the term should have the same meaning as in the Warsaw Convention [2]). Since the Convention has not been ratified or adhered to by an Anglo-saxon country, it is of little use to go into the question whether under these circumstances, the words *faute lourde ou dol* should be translated by 'wilful misconduct' only, as in Article 25 of the Warsaw Convention.

The Conference of 1933 adopted, however, a most important restriction to the provision by excluding 'error ('faute') in the pilotage, steering or navigation of the aircraft'. The result is somewhat shocking in the event of a private flyer intentionally flying very low over the silverfox farm of his neighbour, knowing that great damage will result therefrom. Even in case of such malicious action the express wording of Article 14 would seem to exclude unlimited liability. Presumably the Conference, when expressly leaving out all acts or omissions in the pilotage and navigation was thinking of *faute lourde* rather than of *dol*. This is borne out by the drafting history [3]), but the text in no way reflects that intention.

The Convention of 1952 provides in Article 12 (1) that 'if the person who suffers damage proves that it was caused by a deliberate act or omission of the operator, [...] done with intent to cause damage' the liability of the operator shall be unlimited. The text is the result of long discussion. By fully omitting all conduct which is not intentional, it has avoided most of the uncertainty inherent to any formula working with terms like wilful misconduct and gross negligence. If the Convention becomes law, the rule of limited liability will only be set aside in the criminal cases.

---

192. 1) R.C. 1933, I, 228.
2) Idem, I, 319.
3) Idem, I, 231.

193. It is to be observed that Article 12 of the Convention of 1952 speaks of 'intent to cause damage', not of 'intent to cause *the* damage'. In order to explain the difficulties which might arise from the omission of the word 'the' before 'damage' [1]), it is worthwhile to examine the meaning of the formula when applied to some cases in which the omission might be invoked by counsel for the plaintiff:

(*a*) Defendant carrier, in order to kill the business of a competitor, executes a number of flights between points already served by his competitor. In the performance of one of these flights his aircraft crashes onto some buildings. The owners of the buildings claim unlimited liability, alleging that the flight was performed deliberately with the intent to cause damage to a competitor.

(*b*) Defendant, a private flyer, in order to cause damage to his neighbour's foxfarm, intends to perform a very low flight over the farm, but in the performance of the flight he hits some obstacle and crashes, causing substantial surface damage. The party who sustained these damages claims unlimited compensation because the low flying was executed with the intention of causing damages (by frightening the animals on the neighbour's fox farm).

(*c*) Defendant, a private flyer, executes some very low flights over a crowded beach for the fun of frightening the people. His aircraft crashes and kills a number of people. Plaintiffs contend that the flights were performed with the intention of causing (immaterial) damage (fright) and that, therefore, the defendant is not entitled to invoke the limits of liability.

(*d*) Defendant, after a quarrel with one of his most experienced pilots, decides to penalize that pilot by substituting a less experienced colleague for the execution of a flight which will involve extra pay for the crew. Due to the lack of experience of the substitute pilot the aircraft crashes and causes heavy surface damages. Plaintiff contends that the substitution of the less experienced pilot was an act done deliberately with the intent to

---

193. [1]) Cf. R. Golstein, in Rev. gén. ass. resp. (1953) 5090 (3). The omission occurred also in the earlier Drafts, but does not seem to have been discussed. The French text of the Article, which speaks of 'l'intention de provoquer *un* dommage' makes it abundantly clear that the omission can not be neglected as loose drafting.

cause damage to the pilot whom the defendant wanted to penalize.

There can be little doubt that in the first case (a) the claim for unlimited compensation is unfounded because of lack of sufficient causal relation between the alleged act done with intent to cause damage (i.e. the execution of the competing flight) and the damage for which compensation is claimed [2]).

The case (b) of the malicious neighbour who wants to cause actual damage by flying low over a foxfarm and frightening the animals into panic, is less easy to solve. In the case as stated it was not specified whether the surface damage caused by the crashing aircraft was sustained by the owner of the foxfarm. If it is assumed that sufficient causal relation exists between the low flying and the accident, the conclusion seems inescapable that Article 12 applies, even if it were to be a third party whose house was hit by the aircraft. It is difficult to read the provision otherwise than that it deprives any operator, who is engaged in deliberately inflicting damage upon others, from the protection of the Convention with respect to any consequences caused by such criminal activity, just as it deprives in paragraph 1 any person who has wrongfully taken possession of an aircraft from any damages caused by such criminal use of the aircraft. The only difference would seem to be that paragraph 1 requires causal relation between the malicious conduct and the damages for which compensation is claimed, whereas paragraph 2 does not.

Case (c) probably poses the most difficult problem, which is the more regrettable because it is among the cases which might most easily occur. It is believed that plaintiff's contention should be rejected, for frightening people for the fun of frightening may be a rather infantile and reprehensible hobby but it certainly is not criminal as long as no actual damages are intended. When discussing case (b) it was suggested that it was the purpose of Article 12 (2) to prevent an operator engaging in the *criminal conduct* of intentionally inflicting damages to others from benefiting from the limitation provisions of the Convention. It may

193. [2]) It is submitted that the claim could not be rejected in terms of 'duty' (i.e. by reasoning that the duty not to cause damage to the competitor, would only be owed to him) for two reasons: (1) the 'intention to cause damage' is not necessarily limited to cases where there is a duty not to cause damage, and (2) by omitting the article 'the', the relation with the harm actually inflicted has been severed; in fact, this is the very source of the difficulties.

be assumed that the Delegates at the Conference did not think of other damage-inflicting activities than those of a criminal character [3]), or at least that the damage they were thinking of was the ordinary kind of damage – when speaking of aircraft accidents – i.e. damage to property or bodily injury or death. In order to invoke Article 12 there must have been intention to cause such damage [4]). This adds another reason for rejecting plaintiff's contention in case (*a*).

Finally case (d) of the experienced pilot who is set aside by his employer for a less experienced pilot for the sole purpose of depriving the experienced pilot from the material advantages attached to flying the aircraft: It could be seriously questioned whether a sufficient causal relation exists in this case between the act which allegedly was done with intent to cause damage, and the damages for which compensation was claimed. But in any event any intention to cause damage in the sense of Article 12 must be rejected for the reason mentioned under (c).

Summarizing the comments on the four illustrative cases, it is suggested that (1) only an intention to cause bodily injury, death or property damage will be sufficient to deprive an operator from the right to invoke the limits of liability provided by the Convention, and (2) the damage for which compensation is claimed should be the proximate consequence (or whatever formula is used for defining the minimum causal relation required) of the deliberate act done with intent to cause such damage.

194. To these a third qualification must be added. When Article 12 speaks of an intention to cause damage, the intention should be directed to the causing of damage. Mere knowledge that the damage will follow as a necessary but not desired consequence of some act is not sufficient. This means e.g. that

---

193. [3]) Cf. the Australian Delegate (H. Poulton) at the Rome Conference 1952, I, 79: 'The real aim of Article 12 was to cover what, in common law countries, was a criminal act'.

[4]) Mere intention to frighten persons or animals will not be sufficient, even if it would be foreseeable that the fright could easily result into bodily injury or property damage. Cf. the situation in *Hoebee* v. *Parkman, Howe e.a.*, 1953 U.S. & C.Av.R. 235, where a student, by flying too low, caused a horse to bolt and break away and to injure plaintiff's small child. It is submitted that even if the student would have intended to frighten the horse, his liability would not be unlimited under the Rome Convention, as far as the not intended injuries to the child are concerned.

jettison of cargo or baggage in order to alleviate an aircraft in distress can never be construed as amounting to an act done with intent to cause damage. This also clearly follows from the discussions at the Conference of 1952 where it was decided that the express exception of acts and omissions 'done with the objective of avoiding greater damage' – which exception was contained in the 'Mexico Draft' submitted to the Conference – could be deleted as superfluous [1]).

§ 3. MISCONDUCT BY SERVANTS OR AGENTS

A. Warsaw Convention.

195. Article 25 (2) of the Warsaw Convention provides: 'Similarly the carrier shall not be entitled to avail himself of the said provisions if the damage is caused as aforesaid by any servant or agent of the carrier acting within the scope of his employment' [1]). Apart from the problem which will be discussed in the next paragraph, this provision raises two questions:

(1) who are the carrier's '*préposés*' (translated here as 'servants or agents') for the purpose of this Article?

(2) what is the meaning of 'agissant dans l'exercise de ses fonctions' ('acting within the scope of his employment')?

196. With respect to the first question it is necessary to consider the meaning of the same word *préposés* in Article 20 (1):

'The carrier is not liable if he proves that he and his servants and agents (*préposés*) have taken all necessary measures to avoid the damage or that it was impossible for him and [1]) them to take such measures'.

---

194. [1]) R.C. 1952, I, 84: Nunneley (USA): 'it seemed that the Conference had made it abundantly clear during its deliberations that the deletion would not result in imposing unlimited liability in the case given' (i.e. acts done with the object of avoiding greater damage). See also I, 77, 80, 83, 87, 91. Cf. Mexico Session (1951) p. 64.

195. [1]) The original French text reads: 'Ce droit lui sera également refusé si le dommage a été causé dans les mêmes conditions par un de ses préposés agissant dans l'exercice de ses fonctions'.

196. [1]) The Carriage by Air Act 1932 and the official American translation have incorrectly 'or'. The French text has *'leur'*, which refers back to the carrier ***and*** his servants or agents, mentioned earlier in the article. The change is not without importance, for it might now be argued by a carrier that once he has taken all general measures ensuring airworthiness of the aircraft, and has provided an experienced and

The most important provision in French law where the word *préposé* is used is without any doubt Artcile 1384 paragraph 5 of the *Code Civil*, which states the rule known in common law countries as *respondeat superior*. The standards applied to determine who are to be considered *préposés* for the purpose of this Article are strikingly similar to those applied at common law to determine who are to be considered 'servants' for whom the master is to be held liable, and so is the practice [2]).

Does this mean that *préposés* where used in Article 20 of the Convention should be limited to the carrier's servants? Almost certainly not [3]). The reason for distinguishing Article 1384 of the Civil Code simply is that with the Warsaw Convention we are on contractual ground and though there is sometimes a certain confusion to be found in the holdings of French courts, and a tendency to invoke Article 1384 even in contractual cases, it is now generally agreed that the liability of the parties to a contract for persons who are employed by them either as servants or agents is not to be founded on Article 1384 (5), but on the very

---

duly licensed crew, he will not be liable for an accident caused by an error of the crew since it was clearly impossible for *him* to avoid such error. The argument might especially have some appeal where the real cause of the accident was never discovered. According to what seems to be the better view, any impossibility to trace the cause of an accident is the risk of the carrier, since it was the intention of Article 20 to charge him with the burden of proof. See No. 33 (3).

[2]) See Neuner (1941) pp. 8 sq.

[3]) Lemoine (1947), No. 822: 'Tous paraissent d'accord pour [. . .] donner du terme 'préposé' une interprétation large englobant tous ceux qu'emploie le transporteur pour l'exécution du contrat'. Cf. Goedhuis (1933) p. 181, Koffka (1937) p. 323, Riese (1949) p. 454. See also the comment by De Vos (Reporter) in the 3d Session of CITEJA, 1928, Compte rendu p. 48: 'Pour le préposé il y a la question d'un mandat général, tandis que le mot 'employés' indique le simple contrat de travail. En employant le mot 'préposés', le Comité entend dire: toute personne ayant un lien avec l'employeur en vertu d'un mandat quelconque, le plus général possible, agissant au nom et pour le compte du transporteur'. It is not clear whether in this definition the 'mandat' should be related to the performance of the contract of carriage.

But Litvine (1953) No. 355, requires a master-servant relationship ('lien de subordination') in conformity with the notion of *préposés* in Art. 1384 (1) C.c. Comp. also the translation in the three **Scandinavian** Acts implementing the Convention: '*hans folk i tjenesten*' (Norwegian Act 1936, § 6); '*hans folk i deres Tjeneste*' (Danish Act 1937, § 20); '*hans folk i tjänsten*' (Swedish Act 1937, § 20). Similarly, the **Dutch** government translation of the Convention (See *Koninklijk Besluit* of 1933, Stb. No. 365) has '*ondergeschikte*' (servant), but see also the Dutch *Wet op het Luchtvervoer* (Air Transportation Act) of 1936 which, in the analogous Art. 29, has replaced '*ondergeschikten*' by '*degenen die in verband met het vervoer te werk zijn gesteld*' ('those who are charged to work in connection with the carriage'), in accordance with the terminology used in Art. 468 W.v.K. concerning the liability of the carrier in the carriage by sea (see *Memorie van Toelichting*, Handelingen Tweede Kamer 1935/1936, 201, Wetgevingsbijlagen W.P.N.R. no. 146, p. 15).

nature of the contractual obligation. The contract debtor is liable if the result contracted for has not been attained unless he is able to prove a foreign cause which cannot be imputed to him (Article 1147 Code Civil). Negligence by those persons to whom he has entrusted the performance of his obligations under the contract is not such a 'foreign cause', whether such persons were his servants or independent contractors.

The principle is based on the assumption that the contract debtor generally has to guarantee a certain result instead of having only a duty of care. The French authors often distinguish here between 'obligations de résultat' and 'obligations de moyen'[4]). The difficulty with applying this principle to the Warsaw Convention is that the system of the Convention lies somewhat between an obligation of a guaranteed result and a simple duty of care which would leave the burden of proof on the passenger or shipper. For on the one hand it does make the carrier only liable for failure to give care, but on the other hand it charges him with the proof that he 'took all necessary measures to avoid the damage'.

This somewhat hybrid character of the air carrier's liability has its effect on the meaning which should be attached to the term *préposés* in Article 20. It is submitted that this term comprises:

(1) the servants of the carrier whether or not they are engaged in the performance of the contract of carriage concerned, but applying the same limitations as to the scope of their activities, for which the carrier is to be held liable, which would apply to his delictual liability; and

(2) any persons engaged, with the authority or consent of the carrier, in the performance of the contract of carriage concerned, whether his servants or not.

Sometimes the term has been construed in a way so as to include the second category only [5]). This would mean that the carrier would be able to disclaim liability if the damages were caused by one of his servants who had nothing to do with the performance of the specific contract of carriage. To give an exam-

196. [4]) The terminology seems to go back to R. E. Demogue, *Traité des obligations*, Paris, 1925 V, No. 1237.

[5]) See authors cited *supra* note 3.

ple, suppose some administrative employee of an airline is going to move into a new office in the company's building. He finds some cases which he throws out of the room without warning anybody, and which afterwards appear to be a shipment which had been put there in order to be loaded on an early plane. It is obvious that the carrier should not be entitled to invoke Article 20 by saying that the careless officer had nothing to do with the carriage of that shipment. This would also seem true, though perhaps less apparent, when two aircraft of the same airline collide and passengers of the innocent aircraft claim damages from the carrier. It would be unfair if the carrier could reject liability by saying that the pilot of the colliding aircraft was not a *préposé* for the purpose of the contract of carriage with the passengers carried in the innocent aircraft. And it can not be argued that the passenger could claim outside the convention on a delictual basis, for Article 24 forbids such claims [6]).

197. It will not always be easy to ascertain whether a person – not a servant of the carrier – should be considered to have been engaged in the performance of the contract of carriage, and thus to fall within the second category of *préposés*.

To discuss all possible borderline cases would have little sense. There are a few classes of cases which deserve some special attention. They are all situations in which the assistance with respect to the performance of the contract of carriage is related to the aircraft or its operation. The question might arise as to whether (1) the manufacturer of the aircraft or of single parts of the aircraft, (2) repairmen, (3) people performing services in connection with departure and landing of the aircraft, and (4) traffic control people or those charged with furnishing meteorological information, are to be considered *préposés* or 'servants or agents' of the carrier.

(1) *The manufacturer of the aircraft or of parts of the aircraft.*

198. There would hardly be any question as to manufacturers not being included within the *préposés* referred to in Article 20, if it were not for the holdings in some common law jurisdictions

---

196. [6]) See No. 71.

that 'the carrier is responsible for the negligence or want of skill of every one who has been concerned in the manufacture of any portion of its apparatus' [1]). In *Nysted et al* v. *Wings et al.* a Canadian Court held that 'as the responsibility for fitness rests upon the carrier, and upon him alone, the carrier cannot be excused for any failure of his vehicle by showing that he relied upon the high reputation of the manufacturer or repairer of the machine' [2]). These decisions probably should be understood to have imposed a non-delegable duty on the carrier to provide an appropriate and reasonably safe vehicle. Non-delegable duties – that accepted notion in the field of vicarious liability for independent contractors – add an element of warranty to the pure liability for negligence, though some attempts have been made to deny that special character [3]). In *Hyman* v. *Nye* the Court, speaking through Lindley J., said that the carrier 'although not an insurer against all defects, [...] is an insurer against all defects which care and skill can guard against' [4]).

In civil law countries the problem generally would not arise in the same form since there the carrier's liability with respect to passengers is considered to result from the mere fact that the passenger does not safely arrive at the point of destination, subject only to the carrier's right to prove force majeure or exclusive fault of the victim. A defect in the vehicle would not be considered force majeure. The problem could have arisen, however, in the earlier years when the courts held the carrier's liability towards

---

198. [1]) *Curtiss* v. *The Rochester and Syracuse Railroad Co.* 18 N.Y. 534, 536, quoted in *De Vito Adm'x* v. *United Airlines* 1951 U.S.Av.R. 181, 194. In the latter case it was held i.a.: 'Insofar as concerns its duty to its passengers, however, United's reliance upon Douglas would not lessen the duty owed' (193/194).

[2]) [1942] 3 D.L.R. 336, 1942 U.S.Av.R. 120, 127. The Court gives an extensive survey of the earlier English and Canadian decisions. See also the **Irish** cases *Burns* v. *Cork and Bandon Ry.* Co. (1863) 13 I.C.L.R. 543, 15 Ir. Jur. 71, and *Ryan* v. *Clarkin*, (1935) Ir. Rep. 1, 17. In the latter case it was expressly said that the carrier was not only liable for the lack of care and skill on the part of his employees but also for the lack of care or skill of his independent contractors, including manufacturers. Both the Nysted Case and the Ryan Case rely on *Hyman* v. *Nye* (1881) 6 Q.B.D. 685, 687 where it was held to be the carrier's duty 'to supply a carriage as fit for the purpose for which it is hired as care and skill can render it', but where the question of whether the carrier is liable for the negligence of the manufacturer was not expressly dealt with. In the leading case of *Readhead* v. *The Midland Railway Comp.* (1869) L.R. 4 Q.B. 379, 393 the question was mentioned but not decided. See also No. 34.

[3]) Cf. S. Chapman, *Liability for the Negligence of Independent Contractors*, 50 L.Q.R. 71 sq. at 76/77.

[4]) L.c. see note 2.

passengers to be a delictual liability for negligence only. A study of these older decisions might reveal some interesting analogies. But it seems highly improbable, if not impossible, that the carrier's liability would ever be construed in terms of vicarious liability for the negligence of the manufacturer. In the French decisions of the last century which have dealt with the situation there is nearly always an attempt on the part of the courts to find some negligence of the carrier's employees [5]).

Of more importance in this respect is a decision by the German Reichsgericht of 1908 dealing with carriage of goods by sea. Under § 359 (2) of the Commercial Code the carrier, in order to escape liability for the consequences of a defect in the ship, has to prove that the defect could not have been discovered with the care of a careful carrier. The Court held that in the instant case the carrier had not freed himself of this burden of proof, adding however:

> 'If it would have been a hidden defect in the construction, which in view of its nature could only have been recognised by the resulting consequences, that would have exculpated the carrier; *for the wharf which sells and delivers a ship is not a performing agent* (*'Erfuellungsgehilfe'*) as meant by § 278 BGB *with respect to the contract of carriage*' (italics added) [6]).

Since § 278 BGB (Civil Code) provides for the contractual liability for the acts of servants and agents engaged in the performance of the contract, i.e. for the negligence of the persons referred to in Article 20 of the Convention, it would seem that the principle of this decision would be of direct application to the liability of the air carrier under the Warsaw Convention.

As has been pointed out above, the liability imposed by the Warsaw Convention was meant to be a negligence liability, with the burden of proof posed on the carrier. Whilst the Draft submitted to the Warsaw Conference contained a warranty as to

198. [5]) Cf. Cass. 9.7.1837, S. 1837.1.813, Lyon 22.1.1847, S. 1848.2.136. In Paris 27.11.1866, S. 1867.2.320 the Court held the carrier liable for the consequence of the breaking of a wheelband on the basis of the principle, which later on was generally to be adopted, that the carrier is liable to bring the passengers '*sain et sauf*' to their destination. But in its decision of 18.5.1872, Bull. chemins de fer, 1872, 178, the same Court absolved a carrier from liability for the consequences of the breaking of an axle which had not shown any outward signs of weakness and which had been purchased from a well known manufacturer.

[6]) R.G. 4.1.1908, RGZ 67, 300, at. p. 305.

the fitness of the aircraft, that warranty was omitted by the Conference in consideration of the decision to make the carrier liable towards passengers for the consequences of errors in pilotage or navigation [7]). Under these circumstances, and in view of the meaning of the term *préposés*, there can be little doubt that to extend the meaning of *préposés* in Article 20 of the Convention (or of 'agents' in Article 20 of the First Schedule to the Carriage by Air Act) to the manufacturer of the aircraft or of parts thereof, would be a misconstruction of that Article and would go against the intention of its drafters. Manufacturers of aircraft are not persons employed by the carrier in the performance of the contract of carriage.

(2) *Repairmen.*

199. The problem becomes more delicate when the service rendered is not the manufacture of aircraft or aircraft parts, but the repairs made. Here again the German Reichsgericht has rejected the liability of a sea carrier for the negligence of a wharf in repairing the ship with which the contract of carriage would be performed [1]). It is submitted that a distinction should be made between those repairs directly related with a flight executed in furtherance of the contract of carriage concerned, and the repairs not so related. Only the former could be said to have been made in the performance of the contract of carriage and only the people making them would be persons engaged in the performance of the contract of carriage. It is not necessary that the flight be executed for the sole purpose of performing that one contract of carriage. But it is essential that the repair be made in view of a flight by which the contract of carriage is being performed or is to be performed. This will bring within the scope of *préposés* of Article 20 the people effecting repairs at an intermediate stopping place, but also those making repairs at the point of departure, if at that time the aircraft had already been

---

198. [7]) W.C. p. 37 and preceding discussions. Article 22 (1) of the Draft (Article 20 (1) of the Convention) contained an exception to the carrier's right to exculpate himself in case of 'damages resulting from a defect in the aircraft'.

199. [1]) R.G. 27.4.1921, Hanseatische Gerichtszeitung 1921, Hauptblatt p. 205. The holding was an *obiter dictum*, to use the English terminology, but that does not affect its significance in the same way that it would in a decision of a common law jurisdiction.

determined in one way or other as the vehicle by which the contract of carriage were to be executed. This necessarily excludes any repairs made before the contract of carriage was made.

(3) *Groundhandling Agents.*

200. Those performing services in connection with departure and landing of the aircraft, other than repairs: It frequently happens that an airline has groundservices at a foreign airport where it does not have an own staff performed by the personnel of another airline. This may include services related to the landing and departure of the aircraft itself, such as the placing of wheel-chocks or the removing of rudder locks, and the preparing of the loadsheet, essential for the balance of the aircraft. But it also includes the services directly related to the passengers, baggage or goods carried. Both categories of services must be considered as being performed in the furtherance of the contracts of carriage concerned and those engaged in the performance thereof are *préposés* in the meaning of Article 20. In fact this is the class of persons envisaged by those who have pointed to the fact that *préposés* in Article 20 does not only include the carrier's servants [1]).

(4) *Traffic Control, etc.*

201. Traffic control and meteorological services pose a more difficult problem. These services are generally furnished by government agencies. Even when they are incidentally performed by a private company, that company will in most cases have been appointed for that purpose by its government. But the fact itself that these activities are carried out by governmental agencies does not necessarily mean that they are not activities in the performance of the contract of carriage for which the carrier could be held liable. Some or all of the services mentioned under (3) may also be performed by government agencies – in fact they are in a number of countries – without the carrier's liability for negligence in the performance being affected thereby.

On the other hand, however, it can be said that the typical

200. [1]) See i.a. Goedhuis (1933) p. 181. Comp. *Heyn* v. *Ocean S.S. Co.* (1927) 43 T.L.R. 358 and *Hourani* v. *Harrison* (1927) 32 Com. Cas. 305, to the effect that the servants of an independent stevedore, in off-loading a ship, must be considered servants and agents of the carrier for the purpose of Art. IV, Rule 2 (q) of the Carriage of Goods by Sea Act, 1924.

public character of these activities is evidenced by the very fact that they have so generally been drawn within the governmental sphere. In the present stage of the development of aviation the existence of these services is assumed as a natural prerequisite to flying, in the same way as the existence of traffic police, traffic-signs etc. is considered a prerequisite to road traffic. That being so, a contract of carriage by air, under normal circumstances, cannot be construed to imply an obligation of the carrier to perform these activities, either himself or through his agents. Any negligence in their performance is not negligence in the performance of the carrier's contractual obligations, and those committing the negligence are not *préposés* in the sense of Article 20. Speaking in a general way, air traffic control, radio communication and meteorological information service are not 'carrier's work' [1]). No case could be found in which negligence of the control tower or in the meteorological information had been imputed to the carrier as negligence of his agent. Where the point could have been raised, both plaintiff's counsel and the courts seem to have assumed as a matter of course that the carrier would not be liable for the negligence of these people [2]). Only in one, not very clear case, an American judge might be understood to have considered the agency entrusted with the carrying out of traffic control services as an agent of the carrier [3]). It is characteristic that in this case, which has generally been criticized for various reasons [4]), these services were performed by a private airline.

202. A few words must be added with respect to the impact of Article 30 on the question for which persons the carrier can be held liable. Article 30 deals with 'successive carriage to be per-

---

201. [1]) It seems doubtful whether the analogy of maritime law as to the shipowner's liability for errors committed by a pilot (whether compulsory or not) could be invoked in the case of errors committed by the control tower piloting an aircraft in on radar.

[2]) Cf. *Union Trust Co.* v. *Eastern Air Lines et al.* 1953 U.S.&C.Av.R. 135, 142: 'Or if the U.S. Government, acting through its agents, the men who occupy the control tower [...] failed to give the plane of the defendant Eastern Air Lines or of the defendant Bridoux proper landing instructions or clearance [...]. Then your verdict would be in favor of both of the defendants'. (In Union Trust Co. v. U.S.A. 1953 U.S. & C.Av.R. 147, dealing with the same collision case, the traffic tower was actually found guilty of negligence and the U.S.A. was held liable).

[3]) *Wanderer* v. *Sabena and Pan American Airways, Inc.* 1949 U.S.Av.R. 25. See also No. 136.

[4]) In this connection especially J. Lacombe in 12 R.G.A. (1949) 821.

formed by various successive carriers, and regarded by the parties as a single operation, whether it had been agreed upon under the form of a single contract or of a series of contracts' [1]).

The carriage must have been contemplated by the parties *to be* completed by various successive carriers. It is submitted that the exercise by the carrier who issued the ticket or air waybill, of some contractual right to have all or part of the carriage performed by other carriers [2]), would not bring the carriage under Article 30. That would not be carriage *to be* performed by various successive carriers. In such a situation the carriers who would have been substituted should be considered agents of the issuing carrier falling within the notion of *préposés* of Article 20. [3])

But when the contract was to be performed by various carriers, Article 30 (2) provides that each performing carrier shall only be liable for accidents to passengers happening on his own line, whether the transportation was covered by a series of separate contracts or by one contract concluded between the passenger and the first carrier only, even if, in the latter case, the subsequent carriers under general principles of law would be considered the agents of the first carrier. This follows from Article 30 (1) in connection with Article 1 (3). When a ticket mentions various carriers, the first carrier, therefore, can never be held liable for the subsequent carriers as he can for his *préposés*.

With respect to baggage and goods the contrary is true. Article 30 (3) creates a joint and several liability ('responsabilité solidaire') of the various carriers who were to perform the transportation, to the effect that the carrier on whose stretch the loss, damage or delay occurred will be jointly and severally liable with the first carrier towards the consignor, and with the last contemplated carrier [4]) towards the consignee. This goes

202. [1]) Art. 30 (1) in connection with Art. 1 (3).

[2]) Cf. Art. 10 (2) (a) of the IATA Conditions of Carriage for Passengers and Baggage (1954) and Art. 6 (3) (b) of those for Goods. (1953).

[3]) The District Court of Amsterdam in its unpublished decision of 7.1.1953 (no. 2833/1951) (*Amstelhoedenfabriek N.V.* v. *Pan American World Airways, Inc.*) seems to have taken a different view, but without the point having been raised as an issue.

[4]) Rather than the last actual carrier, as appears from the fact that Art. 30 (3) envisages the possibility of joint liability of the carrier on whose line the loss occurred *and* the last carrier. This seems also the conclusion to be drawn from the somewhat confusing discussion at Warsaw (W.C. pp. 87 sq.). Similarly Goedhuis (1937) pp. 289 sq.(hesitating, on account of the restrictive qualification of the consignee: 'entitled to delivery') and Koffka (1937) p. 343.

further than treating the subsequent carriers as *préposés* or 'agents' of the first carrier, because it also burdens the latter with liability for the negligence or other misconduct of employees of subsequent carriers, who could not be considered his *préposés* because of not being engaged themselves in the performance of the contract of carriage concerned [5]).

203. So far we have discussed the problem who are to be considered *préposés* or 'agents' in the sense of Article 20 (1) of the Warsaw Convention, without touching upon the question as to whether the same construction should be attached to the word where used in Article 25. The answer is not as obvious as it might appear. It could well be argued that the framers of the Convention, when drafting Article 25, had in mind the liability arising, quite independent of the contract of carriage, out of the delictual conduct of the carrier or his employees. Since in the delictual field the liability for *préposés* is generally limited to liability for servants (Art. 1384 Code Civil), the second paragraph of Article 25 could be said to refer only to the servants of the carrier. But it is felt that a much stronger indication of such intention on the part of the drafters should be required – leaving aside the question to what extent the intention is a relevant factor in construing the Convention – to set aside the strong presumption that one word, when used in two articles of the same legal instrument, both dealing with the liability of the carrier, can only have one meaning. The arguments for extending the meaning of 'préposés' in Article 20 beyond that of servants are much stronger than those which can be invoked for limiting the notion to servants, where used in Article 25 [1]).

204. We have now arrived at the second major question raised by Article 25 (2): when should the carrier's servant or

---

202. [5]) See Nos. 196 sq.

203. [1]) The English Carriage by Air Act has translated the word '*préposés*' both in Article 20 and Article 25 into 'agents' which term has been extended by s. 54 of the Civil Aviation Act (1949), to include servants. Curiously, in Article 25 (2) the phrase 'dans l'exercice de ses *fonctions*', which embraces both the activities of servants and agents, has been translated into 'within the scope of their *employment*', which terminology seems more typical for the liability of the master for his servants. Cf. Grove J. in *Stevens* v. *Woodward* (1881) 6 Q.B.D. 318, 320.

agent be considered to have acted *'within the scope of his employment'*. One preliminary observation should be made. It has been pointed out that for the purpose of Articles 20 and 25 'préposés' includes all servants of the carrier whether or not they are engaged in the performance of the contract of carriage, whereas the agents are naturally limited to those who are acting in the performance of the contract. The status of servants is independent from the contract of carriage, but the status of the agents who are not servants of the carrier only follows from their activity in relation with the contract. It is clear that this has a direct bearing on the question which acts of the agents must be considered performed 'in the exercise of their functions'. Acts of wilful misconduct, committed by an agent who is not a servant of the carrier, for which the carrier can be held responsible, will, in practice, be much rarer than such acts committed by servants of the carrier. This applies especially to intentional acts.

In discussing the question when the carrier's servants or agents must be deemed to have acted within the exercise of their functions, it is essential to keep in mind the great variety of fact situations in which this may arise, as illustrated by the list of possibilities given above. It cannot be overemphasized that Article 25 does not only deal with aircraft accidents. Similarly, it should be remembered that Article 25 is not limited to intentional acts but includes reckless disregard for the consequences to passengers or shippers. The argument that Article 25 'clearly contemplates that a servant may be guilty of wilful misconduct *within* the scope of his employment' and that, therefore, intentional wrongs committed by servants, such as thefts, should be understood to come within the scope of the provision [1]), seems to neglect the possibility of reckless misconduct for which Article 25, even with a more restricted interpretation of the phrase, would retain its importance. Indeed since most of the litigated cases involving Article 25 were concerned with alleged acts of recklessness rather than with the intentional inflicting of damages, it is difficult to say that the importance of the paragraph would be only slight, if intentional acts of servants or agents committed exclusively for their own benefit were to be considered to fall outside 'the scope of their employment'.

204. [1]) Shawcross and Beaumont (1951), No. 391 (e) in fine.

205. The difficulty of determining what acts of wilful misconduct by servants or agents should be imputed as such to the carrier, has been fully appreciated by the framers of the Convention [1]). But the minutes of the Convention fail to disclose where they felt the line should be drawn. The only indication of any intention is to be found in the requirement that the acts of the servants or agents be committed in the exercise of their functions (*'dans l'exercice de ses fonctions'*). The formula is more limited than the phrase used in Article 1384 (5) of the Civil Code: 'in the functions for which they are employed'. But it would go too far to conclude that Article 25 never applies to the misuse of their functions (*'abus de fonctions'*) by servants of the carrier, since one of the types of misconduct for which it was felt especially desirable that the principle of Article 25 (1) be extended to acts of the carrier's servants, was that of theft or pilferage by the carrier's personnel, i.e. a typical form of *'abus de fonction'* [2]). On the other hand, the wording of Article 25 (2) *does* seem to offer a strong argument against the more extreme position taken by the courts of some civil law countries in extending the master's liability to all acts of his servants in any way connected with their employment.

206. The little guidance offered by the minutes of the Warsaw Conference as to the question what acts or omissions of servants or agents should create liability of the master or principal, is the more regrettable since there exists a well known difference between the various legislations in this respect. In countries like France, Belgium, the Netherlands, Italy and Egypt, courts go much farther in accepting the master's liability for acts of his servants, than they do in England, U.S.A., Germany, Switzerland, Spain and U.S.S.R., though between the latter countries there clearly exist some important variations. It may be useful to give some sample cases illustrating the differences.

In 1915 the French *Cour de Cassation* held the master liable for injuries caused by his servant under the following circumstances:

'Plaintiff, a coach driver, was with his vehicle in the court

205. [1]) W.C. pp. 43/44.
[2]) W.C. p. 42/43.

yard of defendant to have his taximeter repaired by defendant. An employee of defendant who was carrying out the repairs interrupted his work to make fun with a comrade in the workshop. Hiding himself behind the coach he would shoot with a 'rifle-cane' which was his property. When lifting his weapon, he unintentionally shot and injured plaintiff in his eye. Defendant was held liable for this act of his employee, considering that the employee was in the place where he exercised his functions and that plaintiff had come to that place, for a purpose directly related to these functions [1])'.

At the other extreme we find decisions such as the English decision of *Stevens* v. *Woodward* [2]), in which a solicitor was not held liable when his clerk, in violation of an express instruction, had washed his hands in a lavatory in the room of his master where he was not allowed to enter, forgetting to turn off the tap.

'Grove J.: 'What is there in any way incident to his employment as a clerk? I see nothing. The case seems to me just the same as if he had gone up two or three flights of stairs and washed his hands in his master's bedroom' [3]).

206. [1]) Cass. Crim. 5.2.1915, D. 1919.1.8. See also the **Netherlands** decision of Hoge Raad 21.5.1937, N.J. 1937, 638 with note E.M.M[eyers], where the highest Court held the State liable for the injuries suffered by a private who was leaning on his rifle when a comrade, for fun and thinking that the weapon was not loaded, pulled the trigger; and the rather extreme case adjudged by the Cassation Court of **Egypt**: Cass. crim. 28.11.1946, B.O. 48, 416, Bull. législ. et jurispr. égypt. N.S. 1 (1950) 100, in which a constable, paying a visit to friends, directed his gun on one of the people present, thinking that the weapon was not loaded. The Court held that the accident was not the result of the personal visit and pointed out that the damage resulted from the fact that the constable had played with a weapon entrusted to him by the State; for these reasons the State was held liable. Though the decision was rendered under the old Code it would not have been different under the new Civil Code of 1948 which has expressly laid down that the master is not only liable for the acts committed in the exercise of his functions but also for those committed *as a result of* his functions (Art. 174).

Comp. with these decisions: *Vadyak et al.* v. *Lehigh and New England R. Co.* 318 Pa.580, 179 A. 435 (1935), in which a railway company was *not* held liable for injuries substained by a child, when its engine driver, in a spirit of mischief, released steam to frighten the child. 'It was not an act, the performance of which at that time and place was shown to be any way in furtherance of the employee's business, but was done by the engineer on his own account'. See also *Great Atlantic and Pacific Tea Co.* v. *Roch*, 160 Md. 189, 153 A. 22 (1931) (practical joke of manager of drugstore, who instead of a loaf had a dead rat, wrapped in a paper, delivered to a customer).

See also cases quoted by Neuner (1941) p. 34.

[2]) (1881) 6 Q.B.D. 318.

[3]) Ibidem, at 321. Lindley J. considered this even a 'plain case' (at 322). Perhaps the strong sense for privacy of the English people has been a factor in this decision. Both judges characterized the act of the clerk as that of a trespasser. Comp. with this case the **Dutch** decision of Rechtbank Rotterdam 18.1.1949, N.J. 1949, No. 543, in which a defendant was held liable for damage caused to plaintiff's villa in which the former's workpeople had entered without any permission, in order to eat their lunch during intermission time.

It is impossible to catch the rich variety of cases in a few simple principles. To say – as the French Courts do – that the master is liable for the servant's misuse of his functions ('abus de fonction') 'unless the wrongful act is in no way connected with the exercise of the task entrusted to the servant' [4]), certainly gives an indication that the master's liability is not excluded by the mere fact that the servant was not acting in the furtherance of his (the master's) business, but it does not say – in fact it could not – when exactly an act is to be deemed connected with the exercise of the functions and when not. After all, the formula used in England and the U.S.A. that the act should be 'incidental' to the servant's employment [5]) is not so very different. But when Professor Winfield, in discussing an American case [6]) of a train conductor kissing a female passenger against her will, finds it 'impossible to see that kissing a passenger was in any way incidental to what the conductor was employed to do' [7]), a contrary position might well be taken by some continental courts. At least the too impulsive conductor himself most probably would have disagreed with the learned author, if somebody would have cared to ask his opinion.

Formulas are elusive. It is only by seeing how they are applied that one can form an opinion about the general development of the law. It seems fair to say that there is a general tendency with the courts, at least in countries adhering to a more restrictive application of the *respondeat superior* rule, to broaden their workingsphere [8]), though this is perhaps not true as far as English law is concerned [9]). Instead of laying down general maxims, it may be preferable to mention briefly some of the typical cases which have arisen in other fields and which could easily arise in the field of aviation.

---

206. [4]) A standard formula of French Courts, see i.a. *Cass. crim. 11.5.1948*, D.H. 1948 Jur. 506, with note H. Lalou.

[5]) Cf. Winfield (1950) p. 123, Restatement Agency § 235.

[6]) *Croaker* v. *Chicago, etc. Ry.* (1875), 17 Am. Rep. 504.

[7]) Winfield (1950) p. 128, note (k). Cf. Tribunal Nice (France) 24.11.1952 D. 1953, Jur. 215, in which a barber was held liable for indecency committed by his employee when cutting the hair of a child. See also the American cases mentioned in 45 Harv. L. Rev. (1931) 342 at 348, and in Mechem (1952) § 397, note 46.

[8]) See Note in 45 Harv. L. Rev. (1931), 342 sq.

[9]) See e.g. *Mintz v. Silverton* (1920) 36 T.L.R. 399; *Warren* v. *Henleys Ltd.* [1948] 2 All E.R. 935.

207. As long as the acts are committed for the furtherance of the principal's or master's interests, the principal or master will in most cases be liable, even when the servant failed to comply with some express instruction by his master. The act must be a long way from the normal work of the servant or agent to be considered outside the course of the employment. Most of the difficulties arise in cases in which the servant's wrongful conduct was not intended to further the master's business. The acts may be criminal such as theft and pilferage, acts of sabotage and assault of passengers. They also may be reckless such as the lighting of cigarettes causing fire or explosions.

It is believed that theft or pilferage by any servant or agent of the carrier whose functions, in a general way, would be connected with the custody of baggage or goods entrusted to the carrier, should be considered to be committed within the course of the employment in the meaning of Article 25. There can be no doubt as to this interpretation being in conformity with the views prevailing in the civil law systems [1]). As has been said before, one of the reasons why it was felt desirable to extend Article 25 to wilful misconduct of servants or agents of the carrier was with a view to the possibility of thefts committed by the carrier's personnel. It is especially interesting to note that Sir Alfred Dennis, when speaking at the Warsaw Conference of the various cases which could arise in this connection, mentioned theft of baggage committed by an employee in charge of the baggage as one of the examples in which English law would have held the air carrier liable, because the act was committed by the employee in the exercise of his functions ('dans l'exercice de ses fonctions') and within the scope of his authority [2]).

---

207. [1]) See especially the well reasoned decision of the **German** *Reichsgericht* on the applicability of § 278 BGB to the theft committed by the master of a warehouse in his own time: R.G. 19.2.1921, RGZ 101, 348.

The **English** case of *Mintz* v. *Silverton* (see previous note) should probably be distinguished, as that case apparently did not involve a contract of carriage but rather a contract of hire, by which a van with driver had been hired to the plaintiff for the delivery of goods. In an almost identical situation the **German** *Reichsgericht* has arrived at the same conclusion on the same grounds and rejected the vicarious liability of the employer ex § 831 BGB (R.G. 4.12.1919, J.W. 1920, 284 (5)). In the **French** case, Appel Paris 11.5.1950, D. 1950 Jur. 438, liability of the owner of a van for thefts committed by the driver, was rejected because the latter should be considered the '*préposé*' of the company (National Railways) which hired the van with driver, rather than of the owner of the van. See also No. 211 (2).

[2]) W.C. p. 43 (translation).

The theft by a servant, however, who has nothing to do with the handling of baggage or cargo, would seem to be an act committed outside the scope of the employment, for which the carrier could not be held liable without limit. Whether the carrier could deny all liability for such an act under Article 20 – assuming that no negligence on the part of the carrier was involved – is more doubtful, as Article 20, curiously, does not contain the limiting phrase 'within the exercise of their functions' [3]).

Thefts by an employee outside the working time could only be considered as committed within the scope of his employment, if the employee had direct responsibility for the custody of the baggage and goods and misused the opportunity offered to him by this position to steal some parcels [4]).

Acts of sabotage by groundpersonnel can only be brought within the scope of their employment if these acts are directly related to the work for which the servants are employed. Especially an intentional failure to act in order to cause an accident might come under Article 25 (2), such as the airport employee who is bribed not to take away the rudder locks before departure of the aircraft. But the employee who uses his function of cleaning the aircraft to hide a time-bomb would not be acting within the exercise of his functions. The difference with the theft and pilferage cases is, that it is one of the typical responsibilities of a carrier of goods, as a bailee, to provide protection against such occurrences, whereas it cannot be said to be a typical responsibility of a carrier to protect against criminal conspiracies.

Assault of passengers or similar misconduct by the carrier's servants can only be within the exercise of the functions, if the assaulting servant had an employment which would naturally

---

207. [3]) Cf. Goedhuis (1933) pp. 182 sq. The **Swedish, Danish** and **Norwegian** Acts of 1936 and 1937 use the same formula for Art. 20 and 25 (see also No. 196 (3)). It is to be observed that Art. IV, sec. 2 (q) of the Carriage of Goods by Sea Act, 1924 (Schedule), which allows the sea carrier to disclaim liability for damages 'arising without the actual fault or privity of the carrier, or without the fault or neglect of the servants or agents of the carrier', does not contain the limiting phrase either. According to Winfield (1950) p. 129, this means that the sea carrier is liable for all faults or neglect of his agents or servants whether it occurs in the course of employment or not. The conclusion seems to go a little too far, since obviously some limitation must be accepted in any case. Winfield refers to *Brown and Co.* v. *Harrison* (1927) 96 L.J.K.B. 1025, but that case did not turn upon the question of whether the acts of the servants of the stevedore had been committed within the course of the agent's employment.

[4]) Cf. R.G. 19.2.1921, RGZ 101, 348.

bring him into contact with the passengers. As far as agents are concerned, they should have been engaged in work concerning the passengers themselves, since only thereby could they be considered 'agents'. But even if this condition is fulfilled, it seems highly doubtful whether such abnormal acts by servants or agents should be considered as having been committed within the course of employment unless they were done for the furtherance of the carrier's interests. In the U.S.A. the carrier's liability for assaults by servants, not coming within the latter category, does not seem to have been based on principles of agency but on a special duty on the part of the carrier to protect passengers against such behaviour by his servants [5]). The carrier's liability, in that case, is not a vicarious liability for the wilful misconduct of his servant's to which Article 25 (2) could be applied, but direct liability for a non-wilful breach of his own duty to protect the passengers against such misconduct.

208. To the extent that Article 25 also applies to reckless conduct, the problems are less serious, which can arise in respect to the question whether the acts were committed in the exercise of the servant's or agent's functions. The borderline cases are to be found in the area of those activities which themselves are not performed in the furtherance of the carrier's business. It is believed that the criterion should be whether the carrier, in the performance of the work for which his servants or agents are employed, had a special duty of care with respect to the interests invaded by the servant's or agent's act or omission. It is interesting to apply this criterion to the much litigated point whether the causing of a fire or explosion by the lighting of a cigarette is an act for which the employer can be held vicariously liable [1]). When a salesman made a business call on his employer on the premises of a customer and started a fire by lighting a cigarette and throwing the unextinguished match away, the employer was not held liable [2]). Indeed, it cannot be said that as far as the performance of the employer's work was concerned (the

---

207. [5]) Mechem (1952) § 402.

208. [1]) See 'cigarette-cases' cited by Neuner (1941) p. 34, note (107). See also Mechem (1952) §§ 375/377.

[2]) *Kelly* v. *Louisiana Oil Refining Co.* (1933) 167 Tenn. 101, 66 S.W.2d 997.

making of a business call) the employer owed a special duty of care with respect to the premises where the call was made. Similarly an employer, generally, should not be liable for the fire started by a bus driver by throwing away a match in a neighbouring field [3]). But when the performance of the employer's business creates a fire or explosion hazard, there is a special duty of care for the employer with respect to all interests menaced by that hazard, and he would be liable for the negligence or recklessness of his servant in lighting a cigarette or tossing away an unextinguished match while doing that work for his master. The Courts generally seem to have arrived at the same conclusion, be it with slightly different reasoning [4]). It has been said that in these cases the lighting of a cigarette during performance of the work was a negligent way of performing it [5]). But it would be difficult to apply this reasoning e.g. in the case of a stewardess who would negligently throw away a match in the airplane after having lighted a cigarette for herself. To say that smoking a cigarette and throwing away the match is a negligent way of serving the passengers with refreshments etc. would seem a little farfetched. Yet it is felt that such an act should be deemed committed 'in the exercise of her functions' [6]). The special duty of care for the carrier towards passengers and goods carried, as well as the duty of care created by the hazards of aviation, make the throwing away of a lighted match in an aircraft during working time a breach of that duty, whether it is committed by the carrier or by his servants. The same would apply to the freightclerk whilst doing his work in the neighbourhood of cargo.

---

208. [3]) Mechem (1952) § 376.

[4]) *Century Insurance Co.* v. *N. Ireland Road Transport Board* [1942] A.C.509, following *Jefferson* v. *Derbyshire Farmers* [1921] 2 K.B. 281. In both cases the defendant's servant was handling petrol. In *Williams* v. *Jones* (1865) 3 H. & C. 602 the master's liability for a servant, who was smoking while making a signboard and who set plaintiff's shed in which he was working on fire, was rejected. The case has been distinguished from the earlier mentioned cases because here the smoking could not be said to have been a negligent way of performing the work. Stoljar in 12 Mod. L. Rev. 44, at 53. Contra Winfield (1950), p. 124.

[5]) See cases in previous note. Adde Mechem (1952) § 376 and Restatement Agency § 235, comment.

[6]) Cf. *Tomlinson* v. *Sharpe* 226 N.C. 177, 37 S.E. 2d 498 (1942), where it was emphasized that the tortious act was not committed on premises, nor by the use of any instrumentality, over which the defendant had any control.

B. Rome Conventions.

209. Article 14 (a) of the Rome Convention 1933 makes the operator unlimitedly liable for the gross negligence or wilful misconduct of his servants, unless he proves *'that he has taken all proper measures to prevent the damage'* [1]. Article 12 of the Rome Convention 1952 makes the operator unlimitedly liable for the deliberate acts or omissions of his servants or agents, if the *plaintiff* proves that the servant or agent 'was acting in the course of his employment and within the scope of his authority'. Following the same system as under Article 25 (2) of the Warsaw Convention, we shall first discuss who are the persons whose misconduct can deprive the operator of his right to invoke the limits of liability.

The only binding text of the Convention of 1933 speaks of '*préposés*', whereas the three equally authentic texts of the Convention of 1952 speak of 'servants or agents', '*préposés*' and '*dependientes*' respectively.

210. Three preliminary observations must be made. In the first place, it is to be kept in mind that the Rome Conventions do not deal with contractual liability but only with delictual liability. In the second place, attention should be given to the fact that, whilst the Warsaw Convention founded the liability of the carrier on negligence, be it with a shifting of the burden of proof, the Rome Conventions provide for absolute liability with hardly any defences left to the operator. Finally, it is to be kept in mind that in the field of delictual liability governed by the Rome Conventions, the variety of fact situations to which the sanction of unlimited liability may become applicable is much more limited. Apart from liability for damages caused by the throwing of goods, the only cases which, in practice, could arise appear to be acts of sabotage by groundpersonnel and the cases of liability for noise or low flying. The practical interest of discussing theoretical cases of pilots who would deliberately make their aircrafts crash seems slight.

211. The first observation is of special importance in construing

209. [1]) A similar formula was used in Article 9 of the Taormina and Montreal Drafts (both of 1950) of the Rome Convention.

the words '*préposés*' and '*dependientes*'. In the field of delictual liability it seems difficult to attach other meanings to these terms than the meaning given to them in the context of Article 1384 of the French Civil Code – or Article 1903 of the Spanish Civil Code and Article 22 of the Spanish Penal Code – that is of 'servants' [1]). At least for the Convention of 1933 it is, therefore, believed that gross negligence or wilful misconduct of a servant of an independent contractor who would not have become a servant of the operator [2]) could not deprive the operator of his right to invoke the limitations of liability.

With respect to the Convention of 1952 the situation is less clear because the English text which has the same authenticity as the French and Spanish texts speaks of 'servants or agents', where the latter speak of *préposés* and *dependientes* respectively. It is to be observed that the same difference in terminology occurs in Article 9 where the liability of servants and agents (respectively *préposés* or *dependientes*) is excluded except in case of deliberate acts done with intent to cause damage. In the discussion of that provision it has been suggested that the conflict between the three equally valid texts can only be reconciled by some compromise in the sense that courts basing themselves upon the English text should not be too easy in accepting an agency relationship in the absence of a master-servant relationship, whilst courts bound by the French or Spanish texts should not be too conservative in accepting an agent of the operator as a *préposé* or a *dependiente* of the operator. The rather vague borderlines which limit the scope of the three notions in the respective legal systems make such compromise not too difficult. In any case there does not seem to exist a valid ground for attaching a different meaning to the words, as used in Article 9, from the meaning to be adopted for Article 12.

212. Where the Convention of 1933 gives the operator the

---

211. [1]) Comp. No. 137 (2).

[2]) Where a person, who is on the payroll of A, is charged by A to perform certain work for B, the wellknown question arises whether such a person must be considered the servant of A or that of B, for the purpose of determining whether A or B should be held vicariously liable for his acts. It has been said that 'the techniques employed by the various [legal] systems [with respect to this problem] are so similar that the comparison cannot be useful' (Neuner (1941) at p. 1).

right to exculpate himself in order to escape unlimited liability for the acts of his servants, it is not sufficient to determine the borderline between the persons having sufficient ties with the operator to be called his servants on the one hand, and the persons for whom the operator cannot be held responsible, on the other hand. But the line should also be drawn at the top level between the persons whose acts must be considered as acts of the operator himself, and persons who are to be considered his servants. That problem is well known in maritime law where many national laws as well as the Brussels Convention for the Limitation of the Liability of Shipowners (1924) provide that the shipowner is not allowed to invoke the limitation of liability with respect to claims arising from his 'actual fault or privity', or 'with his privity or knowledge'. There has sometimes been a natural tendency with the courts to extend the class of persons whose acts must be considered acts of the shipowner himself [1]). It seems not impossible that a similar tendency would have developed with respect to the Rome Convention 1933 if that Convention had been more widely adopted. The problem does not arise under the Convention of 1952, since its added requirement that the servant 'was acting in the course of his employment and within the scope of his authority' embodies the same criterion which decides whether such acts, if committed on a higher level, are to be considered the acts of the operator himself.

213. We now come to the scope of the acts of the servants for which the unlimited liability can be imposed. Here the two Rome Conventions are wide apart. That of 1933 does not contain any limitation, thus it could be argued that even acts committed entirely outside the course of the employment may lead to unlimited liability. It is well to point out in this connection that actually Article 14 (a) of the Convention of 1933 is not founded

---

212. [1]) Cf. Knauth (1935) at 326. See also the **Belgian** decision applying the Brussels Convention: Cass. 4.12.1947, Rev. gén. ass. resp. (1950), No. 4621, where the failure of a local agent to check on the seaworthiness of the ship prior to her departure was held a personal fault of the shipowner, to which the limits of liability did not apply. As formulated *per* Haldane L.C. in *Lennard's Co.* v. *Asiatic Co.* [1915] A.C. 713 the 'fault or privity' must be that of the persons who are 'really the directing mind and will of the corporation, the very *ego* and centre of the personality of the corporation', but in practice the courts do not always seem to apply this criterion.

on the principle of vicarious liability for the acts committed by one's servants, but that it creates an unlimited liability for the presumed negligence of the operator himself, a presumption which may be rebutted. This is not the place to discuss what reason there can be to impose unlimited liability in one case of ordinary negligence whereas generally the Convention requires gross negligence [1]). But even when taking into account this general possibility for the operator to exculpate himself for the misconduct of his servants, it would go beyond the clear purpose of the Article to burden the operator with acts committed by people who happened to be on his payroll, when there would not exist any real connection between those acts and the employment. In such cases it should be held that for the purpose of this provision the persons can not be considered 'préposés' of the operator.

214. Article 12 of the Convention of 1952 requires that the servant or agent was acting 'in the course of his employment and within the scope of his authority' [1]). This text is the result of prolonged discussions of the Legal Committee of ICAO and of the Diplomatic Conference [2]). All the way through, there was a conflict of two basic views, which separated the Committee and the Conference in two groups with almost equal voting strength. On the one hand there were those who felt that the principle of vicarious liability of the master for the acts of his servants should be applied to the cases of unlimited liability arising from criminal acts, subject to some mitigating exceptions. This group had most of its support from the Delegates with Latin background. One of the reasons brought forward in defence of this view was that, without the operator's unlimited liability for the intentional acts of his servants, there would be very few cases, if any, of unlimited liability of the operator [3]). On the other side there was the group – including the Anglosaxon, Scandinavian and Nether-

213. [1]) See No. 46.

214. [1]) French: 'au cours de l'exercice de leurs fonctions et dans les limites de leurs attributions'. Spanish: 'en el ejercicio de sus funciones y dentro de los limites de sus atribuciones'. The same distinction has been made in Art. 2 (2) (b).

[2]) See especially Mexico Session (1951) pp. 52 sq., R.C. 1952, I 76 sq. and 471 sq.

[3]) On the weakness of this argument see No. 46.

lands Delegates – of those who felt that, in view of the rationale of the unlimited liability, that exception should not, by application of the *respondeat superior* rule, be extended beyond the cases of personal blameworthiness.

The final text was adopted with the smallest possible majority, following a proposal by the American Delegate which had instead of 'within the scope of his authority' the words: 'within the scope of his *express* authority' [4]):

> 'The phrase 'within the scope of his express authority' was intended to encompass the area in which the servant or agent had authority by reason of the authority conferred on him by the operator, to take action. The phrase, 'the scope of his express authority' was somewhat broader than the phrase used in the Mexico City text [5]). The language here dealt with a situation in which it was within the scope of the express authority of the agent to act in the fashion contemplated and it was not a question of express direction by the operator that the agent take such actions'. [6]).

Though from the discussion on the American proposal it would seem that not all delegates had exactly the same understanding of its meaning [7]), and though it could be questioned whether the words 'within the scope of the authority' add much to the 'course of the employment' in English legal terminology [8]), there can be no doubt that its adoption was considered by all a victory for those who rejected the application of the principle of vicarious liability to the sanction of unlimited liability for the intentional causing of damage. The deletion of the word 'express' before 'authority', was made, because 'authority did not need to be qualified', and because 'the limits of the authority of an operator were not generally determined in writing or otherwise in express words' [9]). There can be little doubt that the double

214. [4]) R.C. 1952, I, 471.

[5]) The Mexico City text had: 'unless, in the case of an act or omission of the servants or agents concerned, the operator proves that it was done without his express authority'.

[6]) Nunneley in R.C. 1952, I, 473.

[7]) Comp. Ambrosini, who supported the American proposal, R.C. 1952, I, 475.

[8]) The 'scope of authority' formula has been omitted in the text of a new Article 25 contained in the Draft Protocol to the Warsaw Convention, established at the Rio Session (1953) of the L.C. of ICAO. See the text at No. 175 (6).

[9]) R.C. 1952, I, 475 and 476.

requirement expressed by the words 'in the course of his employment and within the scope of his authority' was meant to cut off as much as possible the malicious activities pursued by servants or agents for their own account. The intentional act or omission must fall within the very field of the activities entrusted to the servant or agent. This is made perhaps even more clear in the French and Spanish texts: 'dans les limites de leurs attributions', and 'dentro de los limites de sus atribuciones'. Whilst the deliberate failure of a servant to take away the rudder locks before departure of the aircraft in accordance with his instructions might still be considered an omission 'in the course of his employment and within the scope of his authority', the act of sabotage of a freight clerk, who would mix water or some other material with the fuel, certainly would fall outside the scope of his authority.

215. It is to be observed that the only additional proof required is that the servant was acting in the course of his employment etc., not that his act or omission, *also as far as it was deliberate and with the intent to cause damage*, was done or made in the course of his employment. This means that if an operator would have instructed his servant to commit a certain act without knowing that it could cause damage – due to his ignorance of certain facts or circumstances – he could become liable without limit, if his servant, aware of the consequences, would misuse his authority by deliberately performing that act with the intent to cause damage [1]). Though the Convention of 1952 has considerably narrowed the scope of the operator's unlimited liability for his servants' misconduct, it cannot be said, therefore, that it has completely ruled out his unlimited liability whenever he would not be guilty himself of criminal intent.

§ 4. EFFECT OF THE CARRIER'S OR OPERATOR'S WILFUL MISCONDUCT

A. Warsaw Convention.

216. Article 25 of the Warsaw Convention provides that the carrier *shall not be entitled to avail himself of the provisions of this*

215. [1]) See Nunneley in R.C. 1952, I, 477.

Convention which exclude or limit his liability, if the damage is caused by his wilful misconduct or that of his servants or agents. Only one of the two problems raised by the italicized words has so far received due attention from most of the commentators, namely the problem which are the provisions that exclude or limit the carrier's liability. Since this study is only devoted to a discussion of the limitation of liability to fixed amounts, and since there can be no doubt that they have been envisaged in the first place with 'the provisions which limit the carrier's liability', we shall not deal with this problem here [1]).

The other question raised by the phrase is of direct interest to the problem of limitation of liability. Article 25 does not say that the carrier's liability in case of wilful misconduct shall be unlimited, but only that the provisions *of the Convention* which limit the liability can not be invoked by the carrier [2]). The same formula is used in Articles 3, 4 and 9 which contain the sanction on the non-compliance with the requirements as to the issuance of tickets, baggage checks and air waybills. It will be discussed also in that connection [3]).

If the carrier is precluded from invoking the provisions *of the Convention* which limit his liability, does that mean that he also has lost the right to invoke any such provisions contained in the applicable national law or in the contract of carriage? It is believed that a distinction should be made between limitation provisions in national laws and contractual limitation clauses [4]). One of the main purposes of the Convention was to put an end to the great diversity of municipal law, with all the intricate problems arising therefrom, by establishing a set of uniform rules of law. That purpose would be greatly defeated if it were left to the national legislator to set aside the sanction of Articles 3, 4, 9, and 25. For that reason the view, defended by some authors [5]), that in case of wilful misconduct the Convention ceases to be applicable and is replaced by the normally applicable national law, should be rejected.

216. [1]) See No. 69 (5).
[2]) Similarly H. Müller (1932) p. 106. Müller seems to be the only commentator on the Warsaw Convention who has paid attention to the restriction contained in the phrase 'dispositions de la présente Convention'.
[3]) See Nos. 224 sq.
[4]) The distinction is neglected by Müller (1932) p. 106.
[5]) M. Maschino, in 14 Droit aérien (1930) 4 sq. at 12, Gay de Montellà (1950) p. 561.

But the same reasoning does not apply to conditions of contract limiting the carrier's liability. The Convention has not ruled out the freedom of the parties to agree on special terms. It does contain some specific provisions limiting that freedom. Article 23 forbids a carrier to contract out of his liability as provided by the Convention, or to limit that liability *below the limits established by the Convention.* Article 32 forbids a carrier to avoid the Convention by contractual choice of law or choice of jurisdiction. For the rest Article 33 provides that nothing in the Convention prevents a carrier from making regulations which do not conflict with its provisions.

It is difficult to see how any of these provisions could be said to forbid or invalidate a clause in the contract of carriage which would limit the carrier's liability to the amounts mentioned in Article 22 (or in excess thereof) [6]).

217. Yet it is believed that, different from Articles 3 (2), 4(4) and 9, Article 25 must be deemed also to set aside any contractual limits of liability. The other view would neglect the legal climate in which Article 25 was born. That was chiefly the climate of civil law, and in civil law countries the rule that limits of liability can not be invoked by someone guilty of *dol* or of a fault so serious that it should be considered equivalent to *dol,* has been developed mainly in respect of contractual liability clauses. It is this old principle which the framers of the Convention had in mind when drafting the Convention. If they have failed to mention contractual limits of liability in Article 25, it can only have been because they considered the invalidity of such clauses in cases of *dol* or 'faults equivalent thereto' to be a matter of course. As the rule of non-applicability of limits of liability, which was laid down in Article 25, was most generally known by its application to contract clauses, it would go against the spirit – if not against the letter – of the Article, to hold contractual limits of liability not affected by it. The same cannot be said of the sanctions of Articles 3 (2), 4(4) and 9. These provisions were adopted at the instigation of the English Delegate, in substitution of the penal sanctions, which those who had drafted the requirements as to traffic documents had originally in mind.

216. [6]) Comp. No. 226.

218. Even if one would not accept this interpretation, and would hold contractual limits of liability unaffected by Article 25, that would not bring the carrier very far. For the validity of such clauses will be determined by the applicable national law, just as the validity of any other contractual clauses dealing with subject matters left open by the Convention will be subject to applicable national law. Since there exists a general aversion to the limitation of liability in case of wilful misconduct, the carrier, in most cases to which Article 25 applies, would have no success in invoking the clause in his contract limiting his liability to the amounts of Article 22. But in a case of wilful misconduct of his servants or agents it might be that a national law would allow him to limit his liability [1]). Even then, however, the contract will often be of little avail to him, if he is sued in tort by a dependant of a killed passenger with whom there would be no privity of contract [2]).

B. Rome Conventions.

219. The problem has little importance as far as the Rome Conventions are concerned. It is true that the Convention of 1933 uses the same formula as Article 25 of the Warsaw Convention, by providing that 'the operator may not avail himself of the provisions of this Convention which limit his liability'. But since nothing in this Convention generally forbids people to agree between themselves on terms which would differ from the provisions of the Convention [1]), the possibility of contractual limitation of liability is only one of the aspects of the freedom of contract left intact by the Convention. The limitation of liability could even be below the limits provided in the Convention.

---

218. [1]) This is the case in the **Netherlands** H.R. 26.3.1920, N.J. 1920, 476, W. 10592; Gerechtshof 's-Gravenhage 17.2.1936, N.J. 1936, No. 433 ('Ooievaar'); H.R. 3.6.1938, N.J. 1938, No. 920 ('B.O.V.A.G. Clause'), see also Losecaat-Vermeer (1939) p. 268. It seems also to be the case in **England**: *Carr* v. *Lancashire and Yorkshire Railway Co.* 7 Ex. 707, 155 E.R.1133 (1852), and *Shaw* v. *Great Western Railway Co.* [1894] 1 Q.B. 373. It is to be observed that some national laws which generally would not forbid limitation of liability for the wilful misconduct of servants or agents, have special provisions with respect to air transportation – along the lines of the Warsaw Convention – which do forbid a contractual limitation of liability. See e.g. § 49f of the **German** Luftverkehrsgesetz, as amended in 1943, and Art. 948 and 953 of the **Italian** Cod. Nav.

[2]) See No. 248.

219. [1]) See Nos. 79 sq.

220. The Rome Convention of 1952 simply says that 'the liability of the operator shall be unlimited'. This wording raises an entirely different problem from that discussed in connection with Article 25 of the Warsaw Convention. Could it be said that by imposing unlimited liability upon the operator the latter would not only be deprived from the protection of Article 11, but also precluded from invoking the second sentence of Article 1 (1) which states that 'there shall be no right to compensation if the damage is not a direct consequence of the incident giving rise thereto'? Courts are often inclined to be more easily satisfied about the sufficiency of the causal relation existing between certain act and the damage for which compensation is claimed, if the act was committed intentionally, than if only negligence is involved [1]). It is believed that this should not lead one to hold that Article 12 has also set aside the limitation contained in Article 1 (1). In practice, the term 'direct consequence' leaves enough latitude to attach a certain interest to the character of the fault involved, distasteful as that may be to the sense of logic of some authors. But where the Convention provides for joint liability, and one of the persons liable would be held guilty of an intentional act as meant in Article 12, the same court could not hold that person liable for certain consequences if it would have qualified these consequences 'indirect' with respect to the liability of the other person who was not guilty of any intentional act.

220. [1]) Cf. **American** Restatement of the Law of Torts, §§ 279–280, Prosser (1941) pp. 39/40.Also already Pothier, Traité des Obligations, No. 168.

CHAPTER VII

SPECIAL CASES OF UNLIMITED LIABILITY

221. In the preceding Chapter we have discussed the unlimited liability resulting from wilful misconduct or similar faults. The present Chapter will be devoted to some other cases in which the limits of liability cannot be invoked by the carrier or operator. The following cases of unlimited liability will be examined:

(1) the case in which the air carrier is precluded from invoking the limits of the Warsaw Convention because of the absence of a ticket, baggage check or air waybill, or because he carries baggage or goods under a baggage check or air waybill which does not contain a certain number of particulars prescribed by the Convention.

(2) the case in which the air carrier cannot invoke the limit of Article 22 (2) of the Warsaw Convention because of a declaration of value made by the shipper.

(3) the case in which the operator cannot invoke the limits of the Rome Convention, 1952, because he has wrongfully taken the aircraft and makes use of it without the consent of the person entitled to its use [1]).

§ 1. UNLIMITED LIABILITY AS A SANCTION FOR NON-COMPLIANCE WITH REQUIREMENTS CONCERNING TRAFFIC DOCUMENTS (WARSAW CONVENTION)

A. Contractual Clauses Unaffected.

222. Article 3 (2) of the Warsaw Convention provides:

'The absence, irregularity or loss of the passenger ticket does not affect the existence or the validity of the contract of

221. [1]) The case in which the operator cannot invoke the limits of the Rome Convention, 1933, because he has not furnished one of the securities prescribed by that Convention (Art. 14 sub b), will not be discussed, as that provision is too closely related with the insurance problems raised by the Convention of 1933, a study of which would go beyond the scope of the present study.

carriage, which shall none the less be subject to the rules of this Convention. Nevertheless, if the carrier accepts a passenger without a passenger ticket having been delivered he shall not be entitled to avail himself of those provisions of this Convention which exclude or limit his liability'.

Similar provisions exist with respect to the delivery of a baggage check and the issuance of an air waybill, with the one important difference that the sanction is not only imposed for carriage without a baggage check or air waybill, but also in case of incompleteness of such documents. This makes it necessary to discuss the requirements for tickets, baggage checks and air waybill separately.

223. But before entering into an examination of the special questions of interpretation of the three Articles, something should be said about the history of the severe sanctions imposed by Articles 3 (2), 4 (4) and 9, as well as about the problem raised in the same way by all three provisions as to the effect of the sanction on limitations of liability provided outside the Convention.

The Draft Convention on the carrier's liability established by the First Conference on International Private Air Law of Paris 1925, did not contain any sanctions on the requirements as to the traffic documents. That was an invention of the CITEJA when working on a separate Convention on Air Waybills, in accordance with its instructions from the Paris Conference of 1925, by which it was created. At that time the signing of the Brussels bills of lading convention of 1924 was fresh in the minds of all those engaged in the codification of private air law, and it seemed logical, therefore, also to have a convention on air waybills. It was also logical that such a Convention should contain certain prescriptions as to the particulars to be contained in air waybills, though the Brussels Convention was not very elaborate on that point; but the Rapporteur de Vos was more inspired by the Berne Convention on railroad transportation (CIM) than by the Brussels Convention.

Once a number of form requirements had been inserted in the Draft, the question arose what should be the sanction in case of non-compliance with these requirements. That problem does not seem to have worried the framers of the Brussels Convention as much, nor the national legislators when laying down prescriptions as to the contents of maritime bills of lading. It could be asked why the normal sanction in case of non-compliance with a private law obligation, to-wit liability for the resulting damages, would not be sufficient. But it was realized that only in a very few cases would the omission of certain particulars from the traffic documents result in actual damages. That being the case, it seems curious that the drafters did not seem to have asked themselves, for whose protection the form requirements were inserted. If in practice no actual harm follows from non-compliance with these prescriptions, why then attach so much importance to their being complied with?

The other possible sanction would have been a criminal sanction to be provided by national laws. It was this possibility which the drafters originally had in mind but the idea was relinquished at the instance of the British Delegate who explained that a penal sanction would be unacceptable under English law. In view of the fact that Section 320 of the Merchant Shipping Act, 1894 does contain a penal sanction for the transportation of passengers on emigrant ships without a ticket in the approved form having been signed by the carrier, the pertinence of this declaration might be questioned. But in any case, the Second Commission of the CITEJA was so impressed by this difficulty in English law, that they accepted the suggestion of Sir Alfred Dennis to deprive the carrier of certain advantages offered to him by the liability convention, in case he should carry goods without an air waybill in the approved form having been issued.

When it was decided to combine the draft of 1925 on the carrier's liability with the CITEJA draft on air waybills, it was a matter of legal harmony to add some provisions on the form of tickets and baggage checks and to include similar sanctions for them. Thanks to the intervention of the Greek Delegate Youpis – who all the time had been fighting in vain against the sanction of unlimited liability – the sanction, as far as tickets are concerned, was limited to the failure to deliver a ticket [1]). A tribute

223. [1]) W.C. p. 101. At the 3d Session of CITEJA (1928) p. 25, the Greek proposal had been rejected, as the sanction was felt to be an essential provision of the Convention.

should be paid to this Delegate who seems to have been the only one taking part in the drafting of the Convention with an open eye for the odd and undesirable consequences of a sanction, which has no relation at all to the seriousness of the fault committed, nor to the interest protected.

224. Similar to Article 25, Articles 3, 4 and 9 all provide that 'the carrier shall not be entitled to avail himself of those provisions of the Convention which exclude or limit his liability'. It has been suggested that this would bring the carrier back under the sway of national laws [1]). This view has rightly been rejected [2]). Articles 3, 4 and 5 (2) expressly state that, notwithstanding the absence, irregularity or loss of the documents, 'the contract of carriage shall none the less be subject to the rules of the Convention'. In the course of the discussions on these provisions Ripert characterized the sanction as 'très énergique', since 'the provisions of the Convention will be applicable to [the carrier] to the extent they are unfavourable to him, and since he will not be able to invoke the exemptions contained in the Convention' [3]). Articles 17, 18 and 19 of the Convention therefore remain applicable. But Articles 20 and 22 cannot be invoked by the carrier [4]).

225. Is it possible for the carrier to invoke provisions not contained in the Convention, but in some applicable national law or in the contract of carriage, which exclude or limit his liability? Articles 3, 4 and 9 only forbid the carrier to avail himself of 'those provisions *of this Convention* which exclude or limit his liability'.

The authors who have dealt with this problem [1]) generally

---

224. [1]) M. Maschino in 14 Droit Aérien (1930), 4, at 12. Hesitating A.N. Sack in 4 A.L.R. (1933), 345 at 369.

[2]) Goedhuis (1937) pp. 155/156, Koffka (1937), p. 280, Lemoine (1946) No. 834.

[3]) CITEJA, 2d Session (1927), p.26. It is submitted that there is nothing contradictory in providing on the one hand that the provisions of the Convention will remain generally applicable but that certain of its provisions cannot be invoked. Cf. Litvine (1953), Nos. 362 and 363, who suggests that 'absence' of a ticket should be understood to refer to the impossibility, in which the carrier might find himself, of producing the ticket as the document of contract.

[4]) On the question of whether Articles 21, 26, 28 and 29 are also affected by the sanction see No. 69 (6).

225. [1]) A.N. Sack in 4 A.L.R. (1933) 345, at 396, Koffka (1937), p. 280, Goedhuis (1937) pp. 155/156, H. Müller (1932) p. 108. Comp. Chauveau (1951) No. 232.

have failed to make a distinction between provisions in national laws and contractual exemption or limitation clauses. It is submitted that such a distinction imposes itself. The question of whether the Convention has set aside national laws dealing with the same subject matter is entirely different from the question to what extent it has outruled contractual liability provisions. As far as limits of liability or other defences for the carrier, provided by *national legislation*, are concerned, it would be contrary to the main purpose of the Convention, to-wit unification of the law, to hold such provisions of local law applicable to the liability created by Articles 17, 18 and 19 of the Convention. If such provisions would be applicable in the cases of Articles 3 (2), 4 (4), 9 and 25, why should they not also remain applicable in all other cases governed by the Convention?

But the situation is entirely different when we consider the contractual exemption or limitation clauses. There is nothing inconsistent or illogical in not holding all provisions of the Convention to be of a mandatory character. Though it is true that there exists nowaday a general tendency to restrict the freedom of contract, it certainly cannot be said that the Convention would lose its sense, if it were considered possible to set aside by contract some of its liability provisions. If this were the case, all non-mandatory law would be meaningless.

226. Whether Articles 17, 18 and 19, which make the carrier liable, are of a mandatory character is a question which can only be decided by an interpretation of those provisions in the Convention which expressly deal with the validity of contractual exemption and limitation of liability clauses. These are Articles 23 and 33 [1]):

> 'Article 23: 'Any provision tending to relieve (exonerate) the carrier of liability or to fix a lower limit than that which is laid down in this Convention shall be null and void, but the nullity of any such provision does not involve the nullity of the whole contract, which shall remain subject to the provisions of this Convention'.
> Article 33: 'nothing contained in this Convention shall prevent the carrier either from refusing to enter into any contract of

226. 1) Article 32 only deals with contractual clauses providing a choice of applicable law, or a choice of jurisdiction. Cf. Koffka, (1937) p. 346.

carriage, or from making regulations which do not conflict with the provisions of this Convention'.

Article 23 only nullifies contractual provisions which *relieve* the carrier of liability and those which fix a *lower limit* than those provided by the Convention. A contractual limitation of liability at the same amount as fixed in Article 22, or in excess thereof, is therefore not affected by Article 23. For it cannot be said that such a clause would still be a provision which 'relieves' the carrier of liability. If that were the case it would have been completely superfluous also to mention provisions which fix a lower limit than that which is laid down in the Convention. Article 23 clearly distinguishes between such contractual clauses which purport to raise a complete bar against claims from passengers or shippers, and those which only limit the amount of such claims. Such a distinction was and is well known in French law – and French law has largely determined the climate of the Warsaw Convention – in which Article 103 of the Code of Commerce, forbidding carriers to exclude their liability, is construed by the courts to permit limitation of liability [2]). It would have been much easier simply to say that 'any provisions tending to exclude or to limit the carrier's liability established by the Convention will be null and void' [3]). But Article 23 does not do that, and there would have to be some very strong arguments if one were to ignore the clear wording of this provision. Such an argument has not been brought forward by those authors who hold a contractual limitation of liability at the amount of the Warsaw limits or in excess thereof as a provision 'relieving' the carrier of liability [4]).

227. No such argument can be drawn from the drafting history of Articles 3, 4 and 9. When the Rapporteur De Vos introduced for the first time the sanction of what is now Article 9

226. [2]) The relevant paragraphs of this Article were added with the so-called 'Loi Rabier' of 17.3.1905. The validity of limitation-of-liability clauses was upheld i.a. by Cass. civ. 12.7.1923, S. 1925.1.84 and Cass. civ. 14.4.1924, D.H. 1924, 393, S. 1926.1.195. Cf. Planiol-Ripert (1947) II, Nos. 794 sq. esp. 797.

[3]) Cf. the revised texts of Aitt. 3, 4 and 9 proposed in theDraft Protocol established by the L.C. of ICAO at its Rio Session (1935) using the phrase: 'he shall not be entitled to avail himself of *any provisions* which limit his liability'. The new wording was chosen to prevent the carrier from invoking contractual limitation of liability provisions permitted by the Convention. See Rio Session (1953) I, 291.

[4]) Koffka (1937), p. 330, Riese (1949), p. 468.

at the full session of the CITEJA, he offered the following explanation:

> 'It was felt impossible by certain delegates, especially the British Delegation, to introduce the obligation of an air waybill for all carriage. Said Delegation considers it very difficult to get the introduction of an adequate penal sanction, which would correspond with that obligation, adopted by its legislation. The British experts have made the observation that without imposing the principle of such obligation the practical result nevertheless would be the same. For them it would be possible to arrive at the same result in the following way: (1). the carriers should be impelled to serve themselves of an air waybill whenever they conclude a contract for international carriage, without making it, however, illegal for them to dispense with it [... The British Delegation proposes] that the Convention provides, that when a contract of carriage is concluded without an air waybill containing the essential particulars having been established, the carrier shall loose the advantages conferred upon him by Articles 5, 6 and 7 of the preliminary draft of the Convention on liability [i.e. Articles 20 and 22 of the present Convention], without the other provisions of that preliminary draft being however affected thereby and that such a contract, as far as the subject matters dealt with in the quoted articles are concerned, shall be governed by common law' [1]).

If anything, this might be an argument for those who hold that the national laws apply generally in these situations, but in no way is there any indication of an intention to impose unlimited liability as a mandatory rule.

228. It has been said above that limitation provisions in national laws cannot be invoked in the situations in which Articles 3 (2), 4 (4) or 9 can be applied, not because that would be contrary to the provisions of these Articles, but because it would be contrary to the purpose and spirit of the Convention to draw upon national laws for defences not given by the Convention. Does this mean that national laws can not be applied to the question of validity of the contractual limitation of liability clauses which are not affected by Article 23 of the Convention? The answer to that question depends upon whether Article 23

227. [1]) CITEJA, 2d Session, p. 25 (translation).

should be understood as purporting to deal exhaustively with the validity of contractual liability clauses. It is believed that it does not, and that its only purpose is to nullify certain clauses, not to establish the validity of all other clauses. For the validity of such other clauses one, therefore, must look to the national law applicable, just as the validity of the contractual 'regulations which do not conflict with the provisions of this Convention', referred to in Article 33, is to be determined by the applicable national law. Article 24, which is of primary importance in determining the relationship between the Convention and national laws, merely provides that actions for damages, however founded, can only be brought subject to the conditions and limits set out in the Convention. It would be absurd to say, of course, that a contractual clause limiting the carrier's liability in one of the cases in which the Convention itself has excluded application of its own limitation provisions, must be considered one of 'the conditions or limits set out in the Convention', subject to which actions for damages can only be brought.

229. By way of summary it can be said that what seems to be the majority view – i.e. that Articles 3 (2), 4 (4) and 9 of the Convention impose an unlimited and absolute liability on the carrier which cannot be set aside by contract – has its source in two basic misconceptions:

(1) that said articles would by themselves impose unlimited liability, whereas the only thing they do is deprive the carrier of the protection of those provisions *of the Convention* which exclude or limit his liability;

(2) that the entire liability system of the Convention would be mandatory law, whereas Articles 23 and 33 only nullify certain well defined clauses, and leave the freedom of contract with respect to any other clauses unaffected.

B. Choice of Law As to Validity of Contractual Clauses.

230. If it is true that the validity of the contractual limitation of liability clauses which are not in conflict with Article 23, depends upon the provisions of national law, the question arises which is the national law applicable. This raises one of the nicest problems of conflict of laws. The choice is between at least six possibilities: the law chosen by the parties, the law of the place where the contract was made, the law of the place where the accident, damage or loss occurred, the law of the place of destination, the national law of the aircraft, and of course the law of the forum, that stepchild of the authors cherished by the courts [1]). As usual, most of the court decisions on this question are yielded by the inexhaustible source of conflict of law cases in the U.S.A. [2]). The American courts seem divided. Next to decisions which hold the *lex loci delicti* applicable, arguing that the cause of action is also created by that law, there are also decisions which apply the law of the contract. Perhaps the trend is in the latter direction [3]). This solution also seems to be favoured by Canadian courts [4]).

But the Dutch Supreme Court, with unflinching logic, applied Siamese law to the question of whether an exemption clause could be invoked against an action of the dependants of an air passenger killed at Bangkok at the start of his trip from Bangkok to Amsterdam [5]). The Court of Appeal had held [6]) that the validity of the exoneration clause should be tested both by Dutch law, as the law of the contract [7]), and by Siamese law, being the *lex loci delicti*:

---

230. [1]) Cf. on this question the Note on *Limitation of Carrier's Liability and the Conflict of Laws*, 54 Harv. L. Rev. (1941) 663; M. Hancock, *Torts in the Conflict of Laws*. Ann Arbor, 1942, pp. 200 sq.; C.W. Dubbink, *Onrechtmatige daad in het internationael privaatrecht*, 's-Gravenhage, 1947, pp. 125/126.

[2]) See the digest of decisions in the Annotations in 57 A.L.R. (1928) 175, (influence of public policy), 72 A.L.R. (1931) 250, and 30 A.L.R. 2d (1953) 1398 (carriage of passengers only) and literature mentioned in preceding note.

[3]) *Conklin* v. *Canadian-Colonial Airways Inc.* (1935) 194 N.E. 692, 266 N.Y. 244, 1935 U.S.Av.R. 97. See also Restatement–Conflict of Laws, § 338, and 30 A.L.R. 2d (1953) 1398. It is believed that in practice the rule finds only general application in the carriage of goods, see 72 A.L.R. 250.

[4]) *Canadian Pacific Railway Co.* v. *Parent*, (1914) 24 Queb. K.B. 193, (1915) 51 Can. L. Rev. 234, [1917] A.C. 195, also extensively quoted by Hancock, l.c. (note 1), pp. 201/202.

[5]) Hoge Raad, 18.3.1938, N.J. 1939, No. 69, annot. by E.M.M[eyers] (Accident of the '*Ooievaar*'). Criticized by C.L.K. van Gorcum in Rechtsgeleerd Magazijn Themis 1939, 152 sq. at 155.

[6]) Gerechtshof 's-Gravenhage, 17.2.1936, N.J. 1936, No. 433. See also the second decision of the same court in this case of 1.2.1937, N.J. 1937, No. 549, and the lower court decision of 28.2.1935, N.J. 1936, No. 164.

[7]) Though the contract was concluded in Bangkok, the Appeal Court, affirming the lower Court's decision on this point, held Dutch law applicable to it, because the flight involved was not an incidental flight operated by a Dutch company, but an intermediate stretch on a scheduled service regularly operated between the Netherlands and the Netherlands East-Indies. The nationality of the passenger does not seem to have received any consideration.

'...even though the claim, based on tort, is governed by Siamese law, the question of whether a clause of a contract governed by Dutch law can be invoked against such a claim, nevertheless should be answered with reference to Dutch law to the extent that its validity should be examined on the basis of that law, as the clause could never be a defence against the claim if it would be ineffective under Dutch law.'

The view was rejected by the Supreme Court which held the question of the validity of the exemption clause entirely governed by the *lex loci delicti*.

French courts are said to favour the law of the contract [8]). But it is believed that this statement, in its generality, is only correct as far as carriage of goods is concerned, where the claim is rarely based on delictual liability. Special mention should be made of Article 10 of the Italian *Codice della Navigazione* which declares the national law of the aircraft applicable to contracts of carriage, which rule will possibly be extended to the validity of contractual liability clauses.

231. It is to be observed that the question of validity of liability clauses has a number of aspects, which explains the rich variety of views as to the choice of the applicable law. First, there is the question of whether there has been the 'meeting of the minds' necessary for a binding contract. This is the problem posed in the 'ticket cases'. How far and under what circumstances can a printed clause on a ticket or air waybill be held a contract binding upon the party who has accepted that document? That being decided, the question arises as to what is the exact meaning of the clause. In the pure logic of international private law these are both questions concerning the conclusion of the contract and should therefore be governed by the law of the place where the contract is made [1]). Assuming that the clause is construed to mean

230. [3]) See H. Batiffol, *Traité élémentaire de droit international privé*, Paris, 1949, No. 623, and his *Conflicts de lois en matière de contrats*, Paris, 1938, No. 505.

231. [1]) In the highly interesting **Italian** decision of the Corte di Appello di Trieste (acting as *Corte di Cassazione*) of 31.5.1952, 18 Riv. del dir. d. navig. (1952) 188 (*Comp. di Assecurazione di Torino* v. *Sidarma*) it was decided that in the case of a bill of lading issued in Brazil for carriage by an Italian ship from Brazil to Italy, the question whether a clause (choice of jurisdiction) would be binding upon a shipper, if not specifically signed by him, is governed by Italian law (Art. 1341, Cod. civ.) in conformity with Art. 10 of the Cod. d. Nav. ('Contracts of [...] carriage are governed by the national law of the ship or aircraft, unless otherwise agreed'), and not by Brazilian that all liabilities are excluded or limited thereby, the law of the contract may hold such a stipulation null and void as against public policy or the *bonos mores*, which again would seem a matter on which the *lex contractus* may rule. But if it does not do so, the *lex loci delicti* may hold its principles of delictual liability to be of a mandatory character, not to be set aside by private contracts. As a matter of logic, the *lex loci delicti* should be applied to that problem.

We have entered the famous battleground of 'characterization' or 'qualification' in the conflict of laws, and no better example could probably be offered of the dangers attached to posing these problems always in simple terms of qualification. If an English Court will go far in accepting the validity of clauses excluding one's liability in tort [2]), but will be very difficult in construing such clauses as being intended to exclude liability for negligence [3]), the result may be the same (as well as the motifs in the back of the judges' mind) [4]), as when a French Court shows less imagination in construing the 'probable intention' of the parties, but holds the clause simply null and void as against public policy. In the English construction the defendant's defence based on the exemption clause fails as a matter of *contract*, in the French construction his plea is rejected because of the mandatory character of *delictual* liability.

---

law as *lex loci actus* (in conformity with Art. 26 of the '*Legge Preliminari*' to the Cod. civ.). The annotator Dati criticizes this decision, as in his opinion the *lex loci actus* should prevail (argument *a contrario* ex Art. 5 Cod. Nav.).

[2]) See especially Bramwell L. J. in the leading case of *Lewis* v. *The Great W. R. Comp.* (1877) 3 Q.B.D. 195 at 204, and the Privy Council decision (Canada) in *Ludditt* v. *Ginger Coote Airways Ltd.* [1947] A.C. 233, 1947 U.S.Av.R. 1. On exemption clauses generally see the special chapter in the second edition of Charlesworth (1947) pp. 602 sq. and Shawcross and Beaumont (1951) Nos. 350 sq.

[3]) See e.g. (though not binding in England) the Privy Council decision (Canada) in *Canada Steamship Lines Ltd.* v. *Regem* [1952] 1 All E.R. 305, in which a liability clause in a lease contract, to the effect 'that the lessee shall not have any claim or demand against the lessor for detriment, damage or injury of any nature [... and] that the lessee shall at all times indemnify and save harmless the lessor from and against all claims [...] in any manner based upon, occasioned by or attributable to the execution of these presents, or any action taken or thing done or maintained by virtue hereof, etc.', was held not to apply to damage caused by the negligence of the lessor. See also the Scottish case *Mc Kay* v. *Scottish Airways Ltd.*, 1948 U.S.Av.R. 79, and cases cited by Shawcross and Beaumont (1951) No. 353 sub (b) and (e).

[4]) Comp. Annotation in 175 A.L.R. 8, at 18: 'By construing every exemption clause which does not expressly refer to negligence, as not intended to include negligence, the courts have succeeded in emasculating liability exemption conditions generally and by this device have found a convenient subterfuge for practically invalidating stipulations limiting liability for negligence'.

Another example is offered by the characterization of the action brought by dependants of a killed passenger. In order to give these persons the advantage of the shifting of the burden of proof, connected in French law with contractual liability, French Courts invented the fiction of an implied stipulation by each passenger on behalf of his dependants for a right to compensation in case of his death. More recently it was found that the same result can better be reached by allowing the dependants a delictual action under Article 1384 (1) of the Civil Code, which also burdens the carrier with the onus of proving force majeure [5]). In the older construction the action was clearly a contractual one, and as such governed by the law of the contract, whereas in the later construction the action was a delictual one, and conflict-of-laws logic would apply the *lex loci delicti* to it.

These illustrations, both taken from the problems arising from the carriage of persons or goods, may suffice to prove that the labels 'contract' and 'tort' or 'delict' are legal devices adapted to the structure and the particularities of each legal system, and that the reason why preference is given to the one or the other has sometimes little to do with the arguments invoked for the choice between the *lex loci contractus* or the *lex loci delicti*.

In addition to the problems of qualification, the impact of the public policy of the lex fori is to be mentioned. In the field of exemption clauses the court's public concepts will often play a decisive part, especially as far as liability for death or injuries to passengers is concerned [6]). Since public policy is a conveniently elastic concept, it may happen that a court holds a more severe view of it, when the victim is a citizen of its own state and the carrier a foreign company, than in the reverse situation.

Summarizing these observations on the applicable law, it can be said, with respect to the carriage of passengers, that exemption or limitation of liability clauses run a good chance of being held invalid by the courts, if either the law of the contract, or the *lex loci delicti* or the *lex fori* do not accept such clauses. If the law of the forum coincides with one of the other possible laws, the chance of the clause being held null and void is greatly enhanced. The same applies to the carriage of goods or baggage,

231. [5]) See No. 81 (2).
[6]) See American cases in 57 A.L.R. (1928) 175.

except that here the *lex loci delicti* will generally not be invoked, and that, moreover, the public policy of the forum will play a less preponderant role. There is also a chance that the courts will attach more attention to a contractual choice of law in an air waybill than in a passenger ticket, because of the tradition in maritime law as to bills of lading, and because of the more commercial atmosphere in which these transactions are performed.

C. Municipal Laws As To Validity of Contractual Clauses.

232. In view of the considerable lack of clarity and certainty as to the choice of law, it is perhaps more important to consider how the various legal systems generally deal with liability clauses contained in contracts of carriage. The following observations will be limited to what seem to be some general trends in modern legislations, and to the major variations.

Though closely related in fact, three questions should be distinguished: (1) whether the passenger or shipper must be deemed to have agreed to the relevant clause; (2) whether, assuming such agreement, the clause is not invalid as being contrary to the public policy of the applicable law or of the lex fori; and (3) whether the party against whom the clause is invoked is bound by it, in case he is not the passenger or shipper himself.

It is believed that a failure to distinguish between the first two questions has often lead to the pronouncement of too general statements as to the invalidity of clauses by which one of the parties wants to contract out of its liability [1]). When two big companies, after ample consideration by their legal staffs of all matters involved, would arrive at a certain agreement as to the way the risks of damages, whether caused by negligence or otherwise, should be distributed between themselves, it is clear that courts would not easily upset such an agreement in favour of the company which would claim damages in violation of the agreed

---

232. [1]) But in the new **Egyptian** Civil Code of 1948 the Court's powers to hold onerous clauses invalid has been expressly limited to 'contracts concluded by adherence'. See Art. 149: 'When the contract is made by adherence, the judge may, if the contract contains onerous clauses, modify such clauses or hold the adhering party not bound by them, in conformity with the rules of equity. Any agreement to the contrary will be null and void'.

terms [2]). But when an exemption clause printed on a ticket is invoked against a passenger, because of the legal fiction that the passenger, in accepting the ticket, agreed to all terms which the carrier unilaterally had printed thereon – though everyone knows that in practice the passenger would not read these conditions, and anyhow would not have any other choice but to accept them – the courts naturally and rightly will feel a certain responsibility as to the reasonableness of such conditions of contract, as a counterpart of their accepting the legal fiction which alone makes such conditions a part of the contract.

It has been rightly pointed out that inequality of bargaining power between the carrier on the one hand and the passenger or shipper on the other hand need not be a 'disparity in economic power'. In fact, it is of little interest whether the passenger or shipper happens to be a millionaire. The inequality is rather manifested here 'in the very fact that one party takes time and employs expert advice to draw up the form of the paper that passes in the transaction while the other party has no real opportunity to scrutinize' [3]).

233. The question of whether the passenger or shipper must be deemed to have agreed to the limitation of liability contained or referred to in the ticket or air waybill, has again two different

---

232. [2]) Comp. *Philippine Air Lines Inc.* v. *Texas Engineering and Manufacturing Co. Inc.* 1950 U.S.Av.R. 401 (U.S. Crt. App.), involving a hold harmless agreement between Eastern Air Transport Co. and Texas Co. covering the risks connected with test-flights. One of the parties tried to avoid the hold harmless agreement by the argument that one cannot escape by contract one's liability for negligence. Said the Court: 'We recognize the applicability of the doctrine in cases involving negligence of common carriers, public utilities, etc.'. After having stressed that here the contract was one between private corporations, the Court continued: 'The language used was the result of arms length bargaining between the parties. [. . .] That one should save the other harmless from simple negligence is no more against public policy in this instance than an indemnity clause in an insurance policy would be'. Cf. Annotation in 175 A.L.R. 8, at 16 and the note in 37 Col. L.R. 248, at 262.

It is suggested that the decisions of the French Cour de Cassation involving hold harmless agreements between the National Railways and companies receiving permission to have a side track connected with the railways network ('contrats d'embranchement'), which agreements were upheld by the Cour de Cassation even in the case of gross negligence, can also be explained by the same consideration, though the argument offered was rather that these were cases of one party holding the other harmless from third party claims and not simple exemption clauses by which the injured party would lose his claim. Cf. Cass. civ. 15.10.1940, S. 1941.1.60.

[3]) See the excellent Note on *Contract Clauses in Fine Print* in 63 Harv. L. Rev. (1950) 494, at 503.

aspects:' (1) whether sufficient notice was given of the invoked stipulation, and (2) the interpretation of such a clause. The two questions are not entirely unconnected, for a passenger will generally not be deemed to have received sufficient notice of a clause on a ticket, if the scope of the clause would be abnormally large, such as is not to be expected on a ticket [1]); in such a case it may also be said that for the same reasons the clause must be construed in a restrictive way.

234. Before examining the question of sufficient notice as a condition for the binding effect of printed clauses, a preliminary observation must be made concerning the possibility that the binding effect be refused because of the status of the party against whom it is invoked. If a minor of age, or a married woman whose national law does not allow her to bind herself by contract without approval of her husband, or an insane person, had bought a ticket or shipped a package, the construction in terms of contract, generally followed in respect to standard clauses printed on tickets or air waybills, leads to the rejection of the binding effect of such clauses, whenever the party receiving the ticket or air waybill is unable to bind himself by contract. The point illustrates the artificiality of the whole construction: what sensible reason could there be to hold an adult passenger injured in an accident, bound to the limitation of liability provisions, which everyone knows he never really saw, whereas the 18 years boy injured in the same accident could ignore such clauses in his ticket? The question does not seem to have often been raised. Perhaps everyone feels instinctively the utter futility of distinguishing on this point between various passengers or shippers because of their age or similar circumstances. But once invoked, there is a good chance that courts would feel bound to follow the line of logic, especially if that would allow them to escape an exemption clause which they generally do not look upon with much favour [1]).

---

233. [1]) Comp. *Crooks* v. *Allan* (1879) 5 Q.B.D. 38, at 40, *per* Lush J.: 'If a shipowner wishes to introduce into his bill of lading so novel a clause, as one exempting him from general average contribution [..] he ought not only to make it clear in words, but also to make it conspicuous by inserting it in such type and such part of the document that a person of ordinary capacity and care could not fail to see it'. For **Germany** see H. Joerges (1933) p. 60 (quoting i.a. R.G. 103, 84 sq.).

234. [1]) Cf. Appel Bordeaux 20.1.1947, 2 R.F.D.A. (1947), 321 with note Lemoine,

235. Generally it can be said that passengers and shippers have received sufficient notice of, and must therefore be deemed to have agreed to, liability clauses imposed by carriers, if such clauses were printed on the ticket or air waybill delivered to the passenger or shipper [1]). But the generality of this statement is subject to a number of restrictions and exceptions.

236. (1) In some countries mere publication, or filing with the appropriate authorities, of the Conditions of Carriage is considered sufficient to bind passengers and shippers. A typical example is offered by the legislation of the U.S.A.: Section 403 of the Civil Aeronautics Acts, 1938 requires every air carrier to

---

in which the Court held that an exemption clause could in no event be invoked against a minor of age carried as a guest on a flight made by a member of an aviation club. The point was also raised in the Italian decision *Greco* v. *Sisal*, Cass. Civ. I, 14. 4.1950, n. 983, Giur. compl. d. C.S. Cass., Serie II, vol. 30, 1951, 1, No. 7. In this case the Court held a minor of age bound to the General Conditions of a football-pool, because of the fact that they had been approved by the Government, and that the participants in the pool were necessarily anonymous. The point of the binding effect of standard clauses on minors and insane persons is extensively commented upon by Giordano in his note under the decision.

235. [1]) For **England** i.a.: *Parker* v. *S.E.Ry* (1877) 2 C.P.D. at 422, *Acton* v. *Castle Mail Co.* (1895) 1 Com. Cas. 135, and decisions mentioned by Shawcross and Beaumont (1951) No. 350 note (b) and Charlesworth, (1947) p. 605. See also J. G. Gazdik, *Uniform Air Transport Documents and Conditions of Contract*, in 19 J.A.L.C. (1952) 184, at 190 sq. (English and U.S.A. law).

For **France**: Cass. civ. 9.3.1942 D.P. 1942.2.62, R.G.D.A. 1946, p. 91 (*Soc. Transports Aériens* v. *Kunzewa*) overruling earlier decisions of lower courts to the effect that clause must be signed by passenger. But comp. Cass. civ. 16.1.1924, D.P. 1924.1. 17, providing that bill of lading must have been signed by shipper in order that the exemption clause printed on it may be invoked against him. See also note by R. Roger under Appel Paris 3.5.1949, D. 1950, Jur. 282.

For the **Netherlands** see Gerechtshof Leeuwarden 8.3.1950, N.J. 1950, No. 725 ('*Lemmerboot*') in which the reference on the ticket is not even held essential in view of the well known custom of carriers of establishing General Conditions of Carriage. Similarly Rechtbank Assen 4.11.1919, W. 10554 (carriage of goods).

For **Germany** see Joerges (1933) p. 59: Whenever, in view of the character of the business, the existence of Standard Conditions should be assumed, as in the case of transportation business, it is sufficient if the General Conditions have been published in such a way that it is actually possible for the public to take notice of them. See R.G. 103, 84; 112, 253; and 122, 75. Comp. R.G. 117, 112.

For the **U.S.A.** see note in 63 Harv. L. Rev. (1950), 494 at 500 sq.: Printed clauses on train tickets and baggage checks 'which the layman generally does not think of as embodying the contract between carrier and customer' have frequently been held not to bind the passenger, though there are also contrary decisions. Under federal legislation (49 U.S.C. § 319, 1946) the passenger is bound to clauses on his baggage check. Binding force of printed clauses on bills of lading is generally accepted, cf. the Uniform Bills of Lading Act, adopted by some 27 States. Also with respect to boat-tickets, passengers are generally held bound to clauses printed thereon, at least when they are printed on a sufficiently conspicuous place.

'file with the Authority [i.e. the Civil Aeronautics Board], and print, and keep open to public inspection, tariffs showing all rates, fares and charges for air transportation between points served by it, [...] and showing to the extent required by regulations of the Authority, all classifications, rules, regulations, practices and services in connection with such air transportation'. The Civil Aeronautics Act follows here the pattern of the Interstate Commerce Act. As with respect to the latter Act, the courts have held that 'with respect to [...] matter, required by the Civil Aeronautics Act of 1938 [...] or by regulations promulgated by the Civil Aeronautics Board pursuant to said act, the tariff regulations do as a matter of law control the carrier and the passenger or shipper, and this without any actual notice or knowledge other than the constructive notice, afforded by the filing of such tariffs so required' [1]).

Without special legislation Netherlands courts have held that a passenger taking passage on a steamship line must be deemed to have submitted himself to the General Conditions of Carriage which normally govern the transportation by such carriers, if the carrier by filing its conditions of carriage with the court [2]) has enabled the public to take cognizance of them [3]). The binding

236. [1]) *Shortley* v. *North Western Airlines* (D.C. Columbia) 1952 U.S. & C. Av.R. 233, 236. See Markham and Blair, *The Effects of Tariff Provisions Filed under the Civil Aeronautics Act, 1938*, 15 J.A.L.C. (1948) 251 and the partial refutation by R. G. King, Jr. in 16 J.A.L.C. (1949) 174. See also on the effect of the Interstate Commerce Act the Note in 98 Univ. Penns. L. Rev. (1949) 93. In the Shortley Case the passenger was held not bound by a time limit on notice of claim, contained in the tariff but not printed on the ticket, since such a provision was not required by the Act or by the Economic Regulations of the C.A.B. to be filed with the C.A.B. See other decisions in No. 239 (2). In a recent amendment to Part 221 of its Economic Regulations (Jan. 25, 1954, Regul. No. ER-195), the C.A.B. has expressly provided that 'No provision of the Board's Regulations issued under this Part or elsewhere shall be construed to require on and after March 2, 1954, the filing of any tariff rules stating any limitation on, or condition relating to, the carrier's liability for personal injury or death'. This author was unable to find any provision in the Economic Regulations which would require the filing of tariff rules relating to the carrier's liability for baggage and goods.

[2]) Though Standard Conditions are frequently filed with the Clerk of the District Court, there is little legal basis for such action. The only provision which seems to have a direct bearing on the registering of Standard Conditions is Art. 1917 of the Civil Code, providing i.a. that registration of a deed or document is full evidence that such deed or document existed at the date of registration. See also Art. 18 (1) of the Act of 1843, as amended (*Tarief van Justitie-kosten en Salarissen in Burgerlijke Zaken*).

[3]) Gerechtshof (Court of Appeal) Leeuwarden 8.3.1950, N.J. 1950, No. 725 ('*Lemmerboot*'): 'as the said Conditions had been filed in 1924 with the Clerk of the district

effect of published conditions of carriage in sea and inland water transportation on scheduled services is expressly provided in Articles 517 f, 533 e, 586 and 924 of the Commercial Code (*Wetboek van Koophandel*) [4].

Recent decisions of the German *Reichsgericht* and *Bundesgerichtshof* have also construed the applicability of General Conditions in terms of a voluntary submission by the shipper or passenger, thereby dropping the fiction of an agreement. But it is not clear whether some reference in the ticket or air wayblil is not still required [5].

237. (2) Sometimes and in some countries printed clauses are only held binding upon the other party if they were signed by that party. The most notable example is offered by Article 1341 (2) of the Italian Civil Code of 1942:

> 'In any event the conditions which establish, in favour of the party by whom they have been drawn up, limitations of liability [...], have no effect, if they have not been specifically approved in writing [by the other party]'.

It seems doubtful whether a mere signing of the entire contract would be sufficient to cover the requirement of this provision and whether the passenger's or shipper's signature should not be especially written under the relevant clause [1].

---

court of Rotterdam, so that everybody could have taken cognizance of their contents, and as it is commonly known that steamshiplines, such as this, usually perform the transportation under certain Conditions (especially as far as their liability is concerned) A. should also be deemed, when concluding the subject contract of carriage with defendant, impliedly to have submitted himself to said Conditions'. The decision was delivered before the Act of 1939 (Stb. 201), dealing with the transportation on inland-waters and replacing Title 13 of Book II of the Commercial Code, became effective. Article 924 (2) in connection with Art. 856 (2) of the new Title 13 provides that the conditions of carriage and tariffs published and made available by the carrier are applicable to the transportation, unless different terms have been agreed upon in writing and signed by both parties. Similar provisions existed already for sea-carriage on scheduled lines (Artt. 517f and 533e W.v.K.).

In **Belgium** the courts seem to require a more formal agreement by shipper or passenger with the applicability of General Conditions; their publication in the 'Moniteur' was held insufficient by the Court of Appeal of Brussels 23.11.1946, Transport 1952, p. 6568.

236. [4] See previous note. For inland-water transportation of persons the binding effect of published conditions of carriage is not limited to carriage by scheduled services (Art. 924).

[5] See decisions in No. 239 (4).

237. [1] Much has already been published on Art. 1341 C.c. See i.a. V.S. Scialoja in 72 Foro ital. (1949) fasc. V–VI.

The French Court de Cassation has regularly held that a bill of lading must be signed by the shipper in order that the carrier may invoke the clauses printed thereon [2]).

238. (3) In order to become a part of the contract of carriage, it has often been held that the conditions should have been brought to the notice of the passenger or shipper before or at the time the contract was made [1]). But when the person contracting with the carrier is another than the passenger, the latter is bound by the clauses on the ticket in accepting it, even though such acceptance takes place after the contract was made [2]). In accepting the ticket the passenger must be deemed to become himself a party to the contract on the terms expressed in the ticket. It is suggested that this is even true when the original contract was concluded by the passenger himself, unless at the moment of concluding the contract the passenger was made to believe that different conditions would apply. As was said by

---

237. [2]) Ripert (1952) II, No. 145 bis. See also decision cited in 235 (1).

In the **South-African** decision *C.S.A.R.* v. *McLaren* (1903) Transvaal L. Rep. 1903, 727, a passenger was allowed to prove that he could not reasonably be assumed to have read the conditions on a ticket not signed by him, which decision is to be compared with *Bhikagee* v. *South Aviation Pty. Ltd.* 4 S.Afr.L.Rev. (1949) 105, where the passenger was precluded from proving that he could not read the invoked clauses (since he did not understand the language), on the ground that he had signed the ticket.

See also *Ludditt* v. *Ginger Coote Airways* 1947 A.C. 233, [1947] U.S.Av.R. 1 (passenger who signed ticket precluded from proving that he had no notice of conditions printed thereon).

Art. 45 of the General Aviation Act, 1941 of **China** provides i.a. that liability clauses in tickets or air waybills are only binding, if approved by the Minister of Communications, and signed by the passenger or shipper.

In a **Czechoslovakian** decision of a civil tribunal at Prague, cited by E. Balogh in 3.R.G.D.A. (1934) 70 (also in 2 Z.L. 56) the mere delivery of a ticket bearing an exemption clause was held not sufficient for the passenger to be bound thereby.

238. [1]) For **England** see Charlesworth (1947) pp. 609 sq. For **Germany** the decision of the Reichsgericht in R.G.E. 66, 39. For **Italy** see Art. 1341 (1) Cod. civ., providing that 'the general conditions of contract established in advance by one of the contracting parties are binding upon the other party, if *at the moment the contract was made* the latter had notice of them or should have known them by the exercise of ordinary diligence'.

The holding of the **French** Cour de Cassation of 9.3.1942, D.P. 1942. 2.62 R.G.D.A. 1946, p. 91 that 'the fact of having embarked in the airplane necessarily implies the tacit acceptance by the passenger of the conditions of carriage of which she had received notice by the previous delivery of the ticket', would seem to imply that the moment *when* the ticket was delivered is not essential provided it is delivered before embarkation. But see also Appel Paris 23.7.1937, 6 R.G.D.A. (1937) 444, and decisions mentioned by Chauveau (1951) No. 408.

[2]) Shawcross and Beaumont (1951) No. 351, especially note (f).

the French Cour de Cassation, 'the fact of having embarked on the airplane necessarily implies the tacit acceptance by the passenger of the conditions of carriage of which she had received notice by the previous delivery of the ticket' [3]).

239. (4) Conditions on tickets or air waybills, whenever required, should be in readable print, and, according to English decisions, they should be printed on the face of the ticket, or at least bear some clear indication on the face of the ticket referring to the place where they are to be found [1]). Whether a reference to the carrier's General Conditions of Carriage, available for inspection at the carrier's offices, will always be held sufficient notice to bind the passenger or the shipper, will vary from country to country. An American Federal court has held that a clause on a ticket reading: 'the time limits for giving notice of claims and the institution of suit are set forth in Carrier's tariffs', was insufficient notice of the applicable time limit so that the carrier was precluded from taking advantage of the provision [2]). The requirement of Article 1341 of the Italian Civil Code that a number of clauses contained in standard conditions must be specifically signed by the party to whom the document is issued, seems to exclude incorporation by mere reference in the ticket or air waybill of the carrier's Conditions of Carriage, at least as far as those clauses are concerned which Article 1341 expressly requires to be signed. Though there are some older decisions of the German *Reichsgericht* which require more than a mere reference to the Conditions of Carriage [3]), the German Supreme Court's attitude since its important decision of 1941 [4]) now seems well

238. [3]) See supra note 1. Similarly Mazeaud, III (1950) No. 2557.

239. [1]) See Charlesworth (1947) pp. 605/606.

[2]) *Shortley* v. *North Western Airlines* 1952 U.S. & C.Av.R. 233. See also *Glenn* v. *Cia. Cubana de Aviación et al.* 1952 U.S.&C.Av.R. 182, 185 and *Thomas* v. *American Airlines* 1952 U.S.& C.Av.R. 240, and the decision of the C.A.B. in *Continental Charters, Inc., complaint of M. Battista et al.* Docket nr. 5573, 1952 U.S. & C.Av.R. 472 sq. See also No. 236 (1).

[3]) RGZ 103, 84 (1921), RGZ 109, 304 (1922), RGZ 117, 102 (1927), the first two cases dealing with freightforwarders, the last one with an airline ticket. In R.G. 14.1. 1931, J. W. 1931, 1958, at 1959, the Court held that a mere reference in a ticket does not suffice for the customer to be bound by the Conditions, if the ticket does not contain informations where the Conditions are available for inspection.

[4]) R.G. 31.1.1941, Deutsches Recht 1941, 1210 (insurance policy): 'Generally spoken, the conclusion of contracts, which are made with reference to very extensive

established in the sense that the passenger or shipper who enters into a contract with a public carrier must be assumed to subject himself to the latter's Conditions of Carriage without the fiction of an actual agreement as to the contents of these Conditions being maintained. A mere reference to Conditions of Carriage will be sufficient for the passenger or shipper being bound thereby, and probably such reference is not even necessary whenever the kind of business is such that the customers could reasonably expect the existence of standard conditions.

240. (5) When the passenger or shipper has not been able to read the language used on the ticket or air waybill there is a chance that the courts will not hold him bound to the conditions expressed in that language, at least if the language is a different one from the language spoken at the place where the contract is made [1]). But a South African court rejected the plea of a passenger that he did not understand the language of the ticket, in a case in which the ticket had been signed by the passenger [2]). For international carriers the language question offers a thorny problem. It can hardly be expected of them that they have separate forms of tickets or air waybills printed for every country where they are selling transportation, in view of the complicated character of the traffic documents in use in air transportation. Since the English language has become the most commonly used language in international aviation, it seems reasonable that a foreign carrier should be allowed to use that language in his traffic documents, and a passenger or shipper who does business with such a carrier and accepts his document should not afterwards complain of not having been able to read the conditions on it.

General Conditions, can hardly be considered to constitute an agreement to all clauses which form the contents of the contract, but rather a submission to an in advance prepared system of legal rules, and it is of little relevance what specific knowledge the person voluntarily adhering to that system of rules had of its contents'. See also RGZ 170, 42 and RGZ 171, 46. The submission theory has been reaffirmed by the *Bundesgerichtshof* in some recent cases: BGH 19.1.1951: 1, 86, and 5.10.1951: 3, 203 and seems now firmly established in Germany. See also BGH 24.9.1952: 7, 191.

240. [1]) Cf. the **Czechoslovakian** decisions of 1925 and 1927 mentioned by Juglart, No. 224, at p. 256.

[2]) *Bhikagee* v. *South Av. Pty. Ltd.*, 4 S. Afr. L. Rev. (1949) 105.

241. At this point it may be worthwile to consider for a moment how the preceding observations affect the problem under discussion, i.e. the significance of limitation of liability provisions in the Conditions of Carriage of air carriers, when the latter are precluded from invoking the limits of liability established by the Convention. Since the sanction of unlimited liability under the Convention for death or wounding of passengers is only imposed in case of failure to deliver a ticket, and not in case of omission of one of the prescribed particulars, a contractual limitation of liability can only be invoked in two situations:

(1) when the contract is governed by a legal system which holds the carrier's Conditions of Carriage applicable without an express reference in the ticket being required, such as in the Netherlands, and perhaps in Germany [1]).

(2) when, due to the special circumstances of the situation, the shipper or passenger must be deemed to know about the applicability of the Conditions of Carriage because of earlier contracts of carriage concluded with the carrier [2]), or because he had received notice by previous correspondence [3]).

With respect to baggage and goods the situation is somewhat different, for the sanction may apply even when a baggage check or air waybill has been made out, if only the document does not contain all required particulars. If the baggage check or air waybill has only a reference to the carrier's conditions of carriage and does not reproduce the limitation of liability provisions, the question arises whether such reference is sufficient. And if the limitation of liability is expressly provided on the document [4]), the applicable law may require that the document, or even the specific clause, be signed by the passenger or shipper in order to be binding upon him.

---

241. [1]) See decisions in No. 236 (3) (Netherlands) and No. 239 (4) (Germany).

[2]) Cf. Gerechtshof 's-Gravenhage 18.12.1924, W. 11307, aff'd by Hooge Raad 26.6.1925, N.J. 1925, 977 (towing conditions) and Rechtbank Assen 4.11.1919, W. 10554. Contrary thereto, the **French** decisions mentioned in note by R. Roger under Appel Paris 3.5.1949, D. 1950 Jur. 282, and the **Belgian** appeal decision Brussels 23.11.1946. Transport 1952, p. 6568.

[3]) **German** Reichsgericht in RGZ 13, 75.

[4]) Which is the case with the passenger ticket and baggage check and air waybill, as uniformly established by IATA: clause 4 (b) of the Conditions of Contract on the IATA ticket and the identical clause on the IATA air waybill.

242. Assuming that sufficient notice has been given of the contractual clause limiting the carrier's liability to an amount equal to or in excess of the Warsaw limits, there may be a question as to the interpretation of the clause. Though there exists in the whole field of liability clauses a general parallelity of trends in the various legal systems, the similarity in the rules on the *interpretation* of such clauses is especially striking. Probably without exception the Courts all over the world will construe liability clauses, contained in conditions of carriage, against the person by whom the conditions were drafted [1]). But there is a difference in the extent to which they will go in restricting the effect and scope of such clauses. Especially English Courts go very far in denying any effect to liability clauses with respect to damages caused by the negligence of the person invoking the clause, unless liability for negligence was specifically mentioned therein or unless the clause would have no effect at all if it were not also applied to damage caused by negligence. But expressions such as 'in any circumstances' or 'any injury whatsoever' are generally held sufficient to include cases of negligence. Especially in view of the fact that the IATA Conditions of Carriage contain a complete disclaimer of liability for any consequences not arising from the negligence or wilful fault of the carrier [2]), the additional provision that 'in any event liability of carrier for death, injury or delay of a passenger shall not exceed 125, 000 French gold francs, or its equivalent', or that 'in the absence of (a) declaration [of value] by shipper, liability of carrier shall not exceed 250 French gold francs or their equivalent per kilogram of

---

242. [1]) See **English** cases mentioned in no. 231 (3). For **U.S.A.** see Annotation in 17 A.L.R. 8, 18 sq. and Note in 37 Col.L.Rev. (1937) 248, 251. For **Germany** i.a. R.G.Z. 117, 102 (1927). But **Dutch** Courts appear to be less inclined to sacrifice the obvious intention of a clause to the aims of restrictive interpretation, comp. Hooge Raad 26.3.1920, W. 10592 (Postal Tariffs), Gerechtshof 's-Gravenhage 18.12.1924, W. 11307, aff'd by Hooge Raad 26.6.1925, N.J. 1925, 977 (towing conditions) and Rechtbank Arnhem 27.5.1937, reversed (on another point) by Hooge Raad 3.6.1938, N.J. 1938, No. 920 ('BOVAG clause' relating to liability of motorcar-repairshop).

[2]) Art. 18 (1) of the new IATA Conditions of Carriage for Passengers and Baggage (1953) (identical with Art. 16 (3) (a) of the IATA Conditions of 1949) provides that 'Carrier is not liable for any death, injury, delay, loss or claim of whatsoever nature [...] arising out of or in connection with carriage or other services performed by Carrier incidental thereto, unless such damage is proved to have been caused by the negligence or wilful fault of Carrier and there has been no contributory negligence of the passenger'. A similar provision is contained in Art. 14 (1) of the new Conditions for Cargo (Art. 11 (3) (a) of the 1949 Conditions). The same clauses are printed on the IATA tickets and air waybills.

cargo destroyed, lost, damaged or delayed' [3]), is most probably sufficient to cover cases of negligence and wilful fault.

243. The English deviation cases, deserve special mention as an example of restrictive construction of liability clauses. The rule has been stated by Shawcross and Beaumont in the following way:

> 'the carrier cannot claim the benefit of any special contract covering the carriage, and so cannot rely on any provisions contained in it which exclude or limit his liability; unless a contrary intention is clearly shown, such a special contract will be construed as applicable only to the performance by the carrier of the actual service contracted for, and not to the performance of some other journey or service voluntarily substituted by him' [1]).

Scrutton L. J. in *Gibaud* v. *G. E. Railway* used a more general formula:

> 'the principle is well known [...] that if you undertake to do a thing in a certain way, or to keep a thing in a certain place, with certain conditions protecting it, and have broken the contract by not doing the thing contracted for in the way contracted for, or not keeping the article in the place in which you have contracted to keep it, you cannot rely on the conditions which were only intended to protect you if you carried out the contract in the way in which you had contracted to do it' [2]).

An American federal court rejected plaintiff's contention – as being based on an 'archaic theory' – that the liability clauses of a tariff filed with the C.A.B. could not be invoked by the carrier in case of baggage having wrongly been carried beyond the point of destination [3]).

---

242. [3]) Art. 18 (4) of the new IATA Conditions for Passengers (Art. 16 (3) c of the 1949 Conditions), and Art. 14 (3) of the new Conditions for Cargo (Art. 11 (3) c of the 1949 Conditions). These clauses are also printed on the IATA ticket and air waybill.

243. [1]) Shawcross and Beaumont (1951) No. 354; Charlesworth (1947), p. 615. See also supra No. 61 on the effect of deviation on the applicability of the Warsaw Convention.

[2]) [1921] 2 K.B. 416, 435. Quoted with approval in *L. & N.W. Railway Co.* v. *Neilson* [1922] 2 A.C. 263.

[3]) *Lichten* v. *Eastern Airlines, Inc.* 1949 U.S.Av.R. 80, 88. See also the Note in 39 Harv.L.Rev. (1926) 647 on the effect of deviation on carrier's limitation of liability, where it is said to be 'well settled that a deviating carrier loses the benefit of a contract limiting its liability as insurer'.

Civil law countries do not seem to have an equivalent of the English deviation rule, though in extreme cases they might come to the same result by a restrictive interpretation of the liability clause or by considering the deviation to amount to intentional misconduct or gross negligence, which would not be affected by any contractual limitation or exemption of liability [4]).

244. Assuming that sufficient notice of the contractual limitation of liability was given to the other party, and that the clause is found to be clear as to its application to all forms of liability for negligence, gross negligence and delictual liability, there still remains the question of whether it is permissbile under the applicable law for the carrier to limit his liability by contract. In view of the enormous literature on that question and the vast mass of court decisions, the following observations should be considered only as a short summary of what seem to be the general trends in a number of countries. A distinction will be made between (1) liability for death or wounding of passengers, (2) liability for delay of passengers, and (3) liability for loss, damage or delay of goods or baggage.

245. *Accidents to passengers.* As far as the carrier would be liable for accidents not caused by his negligence or that of his servants or agents, such liability can generally be limited by contract. Since in American and English law the carrier's liability for passengers is based on negligence, the question can only arise in civil law countries. In the Netherlands, Belgium, Switzerland and Germany there can be little doubt that any liability of the carrier not arising from his negligence can in any case be limited. Probably this is also true for France, since the minimum effect generally attached by the courts to liability clauses is that of imposing on the plaintiff's shoulders the onus of proving negligence. Only if it were held that the quasi-absolute liability ex Article 1384 (1) of the Civil Code is also mandatory law which cannot be excluded or limited by contract, would it be possible for a passenger to avoid the limitation of liability clause without

---

243. [4]) In the IATA Conditions of Carriage for Goods (1953) the carriers have reserved the right to deviate from the route stated on the air waybill (Art. 6 (3) (a)).

proving the carrier's negligence [1]). But in the famous *Lamoricière Case* where the Cour de Cassation seems for the first time to have held Article 1384 (1) applicable in the case of carriage of passengers, the non-applicability of the contractual limitation of liability was not based on the mandatory character of the provision of this Article, but on the fact that the next of kin, suing in their own name, were not a party to the contract invoked by the carrier. As to Italian law, Article 948 of the *Codice della Navigazione* forbids the air carrier to modify the legal provisions as to his liability and as to the limits of compensation in the carriage of persons. As the *Codice della Navigazione* does not contain the sanction of unlimited liability in case of non-delivery of a ticket, Article 948 seems not to affect the carrier's right to limit his liability in these situations provided the limit is not below the one laid down in the *Codice* (i.e. 160,000 lira or $ 278 per passenger). Nor do the general provisions of Articles 1228 and 1229 Cod. civ. in any way restrict the right to limit one's liability outside the cases of negligence. In Argentine a carrier who offers his services to the public is not allowed to limit or exclude his liability, which seems also to apply to his liability outside negligence [2]).

The possibility of an air carrier, under local law, limiting his liability outside negligence, is of special importance in view of the fact that the effect of the sanction of Article 3 – and the same applies to Articles 4 and 9 – is to deprive the carrier not only of the protection of Article 22 of the Convention, but also of the general defence offered in Article 20 (1) that he has taken all necessary measures to avoid the damage. In other words, the sanction for non-compliance with the form requirements makes the liability of the carrier under the Convention an absolute one, without even allowing him the defence of Acts of God or the foreign enemy. Provided the carrier has limited his liability to the Warsaw limits or in excess thereof, such contractual limitation of liability would, under most legal systems, be valid; thus the extreme consequences of the sanction could be softened. It must be kept in mind, however, that in the absence of a ticket – and

---

245. [1]) Thus Trib. civ. Bordeaux 29.6.1953, 7 R.F.D.A. (1953) 381, D. 1954 Jur. 83, note G. Ripert (*Vizioz* v. *Air France*).

[2]) Art. 204 (2) of the Cod. Comercio; see also Art. 162 of the same Code.

only then does the sanction apply – it will often be hard to prove a contract in limitation of liability.

246. As soon as we arrive at the carrier's liability for his *negligence* towards passengers, the obstacles of national legislations against contractual limitation of that liability become more general. In England and Scotland such clauses are held valid [1]) and the same is probably true for the Netherlands [2]). In Germany the *Reichsgericht* used to deny validity to liability clauses under Article 138 of the Civil Code, as being *contra bonos mores*, 'when the holder of an actual monopoly position misuses his position by imposing out of egoistic motifs unreasonable sacrifices on the general public, especially if he makes the other party to the contract renounce any protective rights which are given to the latter by law' [3]). In the quoted case the contractual clauses were upheld because they were in conformity with the liability provisions of the Warsaw Convention. It is not impossible therefore, that a contractual limitation invoked to limit the unlimited liability provided by the Convention would be rejected by German courts as against the *bonos mores*.

In Switzerland the carrier who operates his business on the basis of a government permit or concession, as is usually the case, is allowed to exclude or limit his liability for negligence, but the court may hold such exemption or limitation void as far as the carrier's personal negligence is concerned. Limitation of liability for gross negligence is always ineffective [4]).

---

246. [1]) See *Ludditt* v. *Ginger Coote Airways Ltd.* [1947] A.C. 233, 1947 U.S.Av.R. 1, and for **Scotland** *McKay* v. *Scottish Airways Ltd.* 1948 U.S.Av.R. 76.

[2]) See decision in the Ooievaar Case supra (No. 230 (5)), in which the exemption was held valid even in the case of gross negligence of employees. The decision of the Hoge Raad of 22.12.1950, N.J. 1951, No. 222 ('*Lemmerboot*') also seems to imply that a carrier can exclude or limit his liability for negligence towards his passengers, but this decision only dealt with the effect of such clause on the rights of dependants claiming outside the contract.

[3]) RGZ 161, 76; 9 A.L. (1939) 172, at 176. § 29f of the *Luftverkehrsgesetz* of 1936, as amended in 1943, forbids contractual limitation of the air carrier's liability provided by §§ 29a to 29e (included) of the Act, i.e. a liability along the lines of the Warsaw Convention limited to R.M. 20,000 per passenger. A limitation of the liability under the Warsaw Convention in excess of that amount does not seem, therefore, to be affected by § 29f.

[4]) Art. 100 (1) and (2) and Art. 101 (2) and (3) of the Code of Obligations. For the carrier who is not operating on the basis of a permit or concession, limitation of liability is only ineffective as far as his own intentional acts or gross negligence are concerned.

In France it seems doubtful whether the courts allow a carrier to limit his liability for death or injuries to passengers caused by his negligence. The only effect such clauses probably have is that of burdening the plaintiff with the onus of proof of negligence [5]). The situation is complicated by the Air Navigation Act of 1924 which permits an air carrier to exclude his liability for the consequences of the 'risks of the air' and for the acts of the crew on board the aircraft [6]), but not for his personal negligence [7]). A limitation of liability for negligent acts of the crew, therefore, seems to be allowed under French law. Article 42 in connection with Article 48 of the Act requires that the carrier exclude his liability *by an express clause*. Does this mean that the exemption or limitation clause has to make specific mention of the risks of the air and the acts of the crew? Probably not, for the Cour de Cassation has held that an exemption clause which is partially invalid, remains effective to the extent the exemption of liability intended by it is permitted [8]). It is to be observed that Article 42 requires an express clause but does not say that that clause should be contained in a ticket. The passenger may have accepted it in another document.

In the U.S.A. contractual limitation of the carrier's liability

---

246. [5]) See generally G. de Valon, *Les clauses de non-responsabilité dans la navigation maritime et la navigation aérienne.* Paris, 1940. According to Mazeaud the courts would hold limitation of liability clauses also effective in case of proven negligence, but he fails to quote any decisions.

[6]) Art. 42 speaks of 'faults committed by any person employed on board the aircraft in the navigation of the aircraft'. It does not, therefore, comprise acts committed by a steward(ess). The provision is generally construed, moreover, to be limited to acts of navigation committed by the persons indicated, though literally taken the liability for any acts committed by these persons could be excluded. Cf. Lemoine (1947) No. 728, Juglart (1952) No. 227 in fine.

[7]) Art. 42 (1) of the Act provides: 'Le transporteur peut, par une clause expresse, s'exonérer de la responsabilité qui lui incombe à raison des risques de l'air et des fautes commises par toute personne employée à bord dans la conduite de l'appareil, qu'il s'agisse des voyageurs ou des marchandises.' Art. 43 provides: 'Est nulle aussi toute clause ayant pour objet d'exonérer le transporteur de la responsabilité, tant de son fait, que de celui de ses préposés, relativement au chargement, à la conservation et à la livraison des marchandises. Est nulle aussi toute clause ayant pour objet d'exonérer le transporteur de la responsabilité de ses fautes personnelles.' Art. 42 and 43 are contained in the Chapter on carriage of goods, but Art. 48 permits a carrier to exclude his liability towards passengers in the conditions set out in Art. 42. Though it does not refer to Art. 43, there can be no doubt that the same restrictions apply to the carriage of passengers (Juglart (1952), No. 236). See on the interpretation of these articles Lemoine (1947) Nos. 718 sq. and Juglart (1952) Nos. 226 sq.

[8]) Cass. civ. 12.5.1930 and 11.2.1931. D. 1932.1.5 with note Ripert. Comp. Chauveau (1951) No. 403, holding the general disclaimer clause of the IATA conditions valid as far as risks of the air and errors in navigation of the aircraft are concerned.

towards his passenger is generally held void as far as his negligence is concerned [9]. In a few jurisdictions, especially in the State of New York, such clauses seem to be valid if the passenger is offered the opportunity, against payment of a higher fare, to be carried without limitation of the carrier's liability [10]. Moreover, a number, if not the majority, of jurisdictions allows a carrier to contract out of his liability for negligence in case of free carriage [11].

From the above survey it will be clear that at least as far as his liability towards passengers is concerned, the carrier does not enjoy the same protection as is offered to him by Article 22 of the Convention, if he has to rely on a similar limitation of liability in his contract of carriage. In a number of countries such a contractual clause will be held void.

247. With respect to goods and baggage, the carrier is more generally allowed to limit his liability even for negligence. Apart from the countries mentioned above, which give him such a right even in connection with accidents to passengers, the right to limit his liability for baggage and goods is also given the carrier in France and the U.S.A., to mention only the most notable examples. In France the *Loi Rabier*, which in 1905 made it impossible for carriers to contract out of their liability, has always been construed to allow them to limit their liability as long as such limitation would not be so low as virtually to amount to a complete exemption [1]. It would appear difficult for a French court to hold the Warsaw limit a practical exclusion of liability, since France has itself signed and ratified the Warsaw Convention. If the limitation of liability is in the form of a declaration of value made by the shipper or passenger prior to the transportation, the Cour de Cassation refuses even to examine whether the declared value was not so far below the real value,

---

246. [9] See S. N. Rittenberg, *Limitation of Airline Passenger Liability*, 6 J.A.L. (1935) 365 sq. and Williston (1936) IV, § 1109.

[10] *Conklin* v. *Canadian Colonial Airways* 1935 U.S.Av.R. 97, where the validity was rejected because the passenger was only offered a choice between various limits of liability.

[11] See note 9 above.

247. [1] Cass. civ. 12.7.1923. S. 1925.1.84 and other decisions in Planiol-Ripert (1947) II, Nos. 794 and 797.

that the effect was a practically complete exoneration for the carrier [2]).

In the U.S.A. too, a carrier of goods or baggage can in practice limit his liability for negligence, by offering a choice of rates to the shipper or passenger, so that the customer has the possibility of having his property carried at a higher limit of liability by paying a higher freight rate [3]). Whereas this device does not seem to have met with favour, except in New York, as far as accidents to passengers are concerned, it has been generally adopted for the carriage of property. Declaration of valuable goods, to enable the carrier to take certain safeguards and to claim a higher rate and to make him safe against unforeseeable high claims, is a principle which has its roots in the early days of transportation [4]). Since the customer profits by the cheaper rate, he should not at the same time have the advantage of the higher liability of the carrier attached to the higher rate. This consideration, and the unforeseeability of damages in case of loss of abnormally valuable goods, have made the choice of rates on the basis of the applicable limits of liability a feature common to transportation of goods in many countries. It is not surprising, therefore, that the U.S.A. is not the only country where the choice of rates device is offered as an escape from the general bar on contractual limitation of liability [5]).

247. [2]) Cass. civ. 19.3.1952, D. 1952 J. 401. Comp. critical note by Mazeaud in 51 Rev. trim. droit civil (1952) 380. In this case a limitation of liability by a bus company to 140 francs per piece of baggage, unless a higher value would be declared by the passenger, was upheld by the Court, reversing the contrary decision of the 'Tribunal'. See also Cass. com. 8.5.1950, G.P. 1950.2.77, mentioned by Hémard in his note in 4 Rev. trim. droit com. (1951) 349. In Cass. civ. 7.5.1945, G.P. 1945.2.29 the Court had rejected a limitation of liability to 3600 fr. (the claim being for 5400 fr.), notwithstanding a choice of rates having been offered, because such a limit was said to render the compensation 'illusory'! This decision seems difficult to reconcile with that of 1952.

[3]) See i.a. Note in 37 Col.L.Rev. 248 with further literature and decisions. Williston (1936) IV, § 1110. Outside transportation the option device is also used by the private telegraph companies in the U.S.A., cf. Annotation in 175 A.L.R. 8, at 17.

[4]) See e.g. the *Arrêt du Conseil sur le Service des Messageries* of 7.8.1775, in Recueil Général des Anciennes Lois Françaises, vol. XXIII 219, at 223: 'Ceux qui ne feront point sur le registre du préposé la déclaration du contenue dans les valises, coffres, malles et autres fermant à clef, ne pourront demander, pour la valeur des choses qui seront dans lesdites valises ou coffres non déclarés, plus que la somme de cent cinquante livres, lorsqu'elles seront perdues, etc.' Comp. Artt. 96 and 469 W.v.K. (**Dutch**), § 429 (2) HGB (**German**), and 46 U.S. Code, sec. 181 (also in Knauth (1953) p. 425) for undeclared valuables.

[5]) See for **Spain** F. M. Sànchez Gamborino, *Modificación convencional de la responsabilidad del porteador en el contrato de transporte terrestre*, 189 Rev. gen. legisl. y

Though it is probably fair to say that the majority of legal systems does allow a carrier to limit his liability in one way or another with respect to baggage and goods, that does not mean that there are no countries which forbid such limitation [6]) [7]).

248. We now have come to the third reason why it may be preferable for a carrier to be protected by the limits of the Warsaw Convention instead of having to rely on his conditions of contract. By virtue of Article 24, the carrier who is entitled to invoke the limits of Article 22 may do so against any action, however founded, and by whomever brought. The same does not apply if he can only rely on the limitation of liability contained in his contract of carriage. Assuming that the clause itself is

---

jurisprud. (1951) 707, at 712. In **Brazil** Art. 12 of the *Decreto legislativo* No. 2.681 of 7.12.1912 (*Lei das Estradas de Ferro*) forbids railway companies to limit their liability unless the possibility of carriage at unlimited liability is offered, and an appropriate reduction is granted. In **Mexico** the Supreme Court has construed Art. 69 of the *Ley de Vías Generales de Comunicación* (on surface transportation), to mean that the carrier must accept unlimited liability under the normal rate quoted to the public, but may offer a reduction on that rate as a consideration for the limitation of his liability. See the decisions of 20.6.1951, Seman. Jud. (1951) 108 (2), 1908, and of 11.1. 1952, Seman. Jud. (1952) 111 (1), 231. But the special provision of Art. 349 (4) of the Act, in the Chapter on Aviation, provides generally that in case the goods are carried with an agreed declared value, the liability of the carrier shall be limited to that value.

See also Art. 34 of the C.I.M. and the commentary of Nánássy (1946) at pp. 589 sq.

247. [6]) See e.g. Art. 81 of the **Venezuelan** *Ley de Aviación Civil*. For **Argentine** see Art. 204 (2) Cod. Com.

[7]) The limitation of liability contained in the IATA Conditions of Carriage for Goods (1953) is phrased as follows: 'the charges for carriage having been based upon the value declared by the shipper, it is agreed that any liability shall in no event exceed the shipper's declared value for carriage stated on the face of the air waybill and in the absence of such declaration by shipper liability of carrier shall not exceed 250 gold francs, or their equivalent per kilogram of goods destroyed, lost, damaged or delayed' (Art. 14 (3)). The provision as to baggage in the IATA Conditions of Carriage for Passengers and Baggage (1953) reads as follows: 'the passenger having been offered a choice of rates according to value, any liability of Carrier in respect of baggage and other personal property is limited to its declared value (or its actual value if less) which shall not exceed \$ 100 (U.S. currency) or its equivalent per passenger, unless a higher valuation is declared in advance etc.' (Art. 18 (5)). The somewhat complicate wording was clearly chosen to satisfy the requirements of American law. It is to be observed that the Conditions for Goods are based on the Warsaw Convention, whereas those for Passengers and Baggage contain a limit, which is not calculated on the weight of the baggage, as in the Convention, but is a fixed maximum of \$ 100 per passenger, in accordance with carriers' practices prevailing in North America. In case the lost or damaged baggage weighs more than 6 kilograms, the \$ 100 limit will be less than the applicable Warsaw limit and will be void in accordance with Article 23 of the Convention. It seems questionable whether such a clause could be given effect as far as the liability in excess of the Warsaw limit is concerned resulting from non-compliance with the form requirements concerning the baggage check.

held valid and duly agreed upon, it will only bind such persons as are or become party to the contract, or those who derive their rights from such persons.

This point is especially important whenever the carrier wants to limit his liability with respect to the death of a passenger. A number of legal systems consider the dependants, who sue in their own name for the loss of support and the grief suffered as a consequence of the death, not bound to a contract in limitation of liability entered upon by the deceased. Thus do the courts of various civil law countries [1]), and also the English case of *Nunan* v. *Southern Railway Co* [2]). But U.S.A. courts in the rare cases of

---

248. [1]) **Netherlands**: Hoge Raad 22.12.1950, N.J. 1951, No. 222 ('Lemmerboot'), affirming Gerechtshof Leeuwarden 8.3.1950, N.J. 1950, No. 725, which decision dealt with a case of inland water carriage. It has been argued (Cleveringa (1946) p. 503) in connection with Art. 522 (3) W.v.K., dealing with carriage of persons by sea, that the action given by that Article to the limitatively enumerated dependants of a killed passenger, must be considered to be based on the contract of carriage, and that therefore any valid clauses of the contract may be invoked against these dependants. A similar reasoning could be defended with respect to Art. 24 (2) of the Air Transportation Act of 1936, which also enumerates the dependants who may recover in case of the death of a passenger, and which Act is also applicable to 'Warsaw' traffic. It is believed, however, that neither Art. 522 (3) W.v.K., nor Art. 24 (2) of the Act of 1936 were meant to deprive the dependants of the right to sue the carrier outside the contract (ex Art. 1406 B.W.) by proving his negligence.

For **France** see decisions in Mazeaud, III (1950) No. 2556, and see also Trib. civ. Bordeaux 29.6.1953, 16 R.G.A. (1953) 277 with note Juglart. For **Quebec** see decision quoted by W.C.J. Meredith in 26 Can. B.Rev. (1948) 95, at 108. In **Belgium** the question seems to be controversial, but an exemption clause was held binding by the lower court of Brussels in a case where the claimants, being heirs of the deceased, had succeeded into his rights and obligations: Brussels Trib. 6.5.1950, Pas. 1950, III, 96; 4 R.F.D.A. (1950) 411, 418; 1950 U.S.Av.R. 367 (*Pauwels* v. *Sabena*). For **Italy** comp. Cass. civ. 27.7.1939, Respons. civile e previd. 1940, p. 35, in which a settlement by the deceased was held no bar against action by his dependants.

[2]) [1924] 1 K.B. 223. When the carrier has fully excluded his liability, however, so as to bar any claim from the passenger himself, if the latter would have survived, the next of kin, whose only rights must be derived from the Fatal Accidents (Lord Campbell) Act, 1846, will also be barred from recovering damages by virtue of the provisions of that Act. Meanwhile it is subject to doubt whether the rule of the Nunan Case applies to actions brought by dependants of a passenger pursuant to para. (1) of the Second Schedule of the Carriage by Air Act, 1932. This Schedule contains 'Provisions as to Liability of Carrier in the Event of the Death of a Passenger' (Heading), and provides in para. (1) that 'the liability shall be enforceable for the benefit of such of the members of the passenger's family as sustained damage by reason of his death'. Whether or not one wants to consider the action of dependants under the Carriage by Air Act as a contractual one, it would appear that the liability of the carrier towards them was not meant to be different from the liability towards the passenger if he would have survived the accident. There is no wording in the Carriage by Air Act – such as the wording of the Lord Campbell's Act, relied upon by the Court in the Nunan Case – to support a distinction between exemption of liability and limitation of liability clauses. Clearly, if the parties would have agreed to a higher limit of liability than the Warsaw limit (vide Art. 22 (1)), such agreement could be invoked by the depend-

free transportation, in which exemption of liability is allowed, appear to have held the next of kin bound by the contract of the killed passenger [3]). A similar rule applies in Scotland [4]). In Germany the same result is reached by a liberal interpretation of § 846 of the Civil Code [5]).

With respect to goods the question of whether the person claiming damages will be considered a party to the contract and, as such, bound by its terms, will arise less frequently, but from time to time the carrier may see himself barred by the court from invoking the contractual limitation of liability because of lack of privity with the person claiming compensation. Generally, the consignee will be held bound to the contract [6]). This has been expressly laid down in Article 13 (3) of the Warsaw Convention, giving to the consignee 'the rights which flow from the contract of carriage'. But the situation becomes less clear and certain, when the owner of the goods, who is neither shipper nor consignee, sues the carrier in tort for loss or damage caused by the latter's negligence [7]). If the owner has charged the shipper to forward the goods, he will generally be bound by the contract

ants in an action under the Second Schedule. That being so, the carrier should also be allowed to invoke a limitation of liability clause, permitted by the Convention, in an action brought by dependants.

[3]) *North Pacific Ry. Comp.* v. *Adams* 192 U.S. 440 (1904), *Francis* v. *South Pacific Comp.* 333 U.S. 445 (1948). See also 25 C.J.S. 1145. These cases did not involve a limitation of liability but a complete exemption so that it is not quite clear whether there would be room for the English rule, but the way the decisions are formulated would rather indicate that the binding effect was based on the general character of the action by dependants, not on some express wording of the applicable Death Statutes. This is at least true for the Adams Case.

[4]) See *McKay and Craigie* v. *Scottish Airways Ltd.* 1948 U.S.Av.R. 76. Comp. the interesting case of *Horn* v. *North Brit. Ry. Comp.* (1878) S.R. 1055. It is to be observed that the action which Scottish law gives to the dependants of a killed person is not based on a Statute, such as is the case in England, but on general principles of the law, so that in Scotland there would not seem to be room for the artificial distinction between complete exemption clauses and limitation clauses, which the English court felt bound to make because of the wording of the Lord Campbell's Act. See *M'Namara* v. *Laird Line Ltd.* (1924) (not reported) quoted in 12 Encyclopedia of the Laws of Scotland, p. 503.

[5]) RGZ 65, 317, and 117, 162. § 846 of the Civil Code provides that contributory negligence of the deceased may be invoked in an action brought by the dependants.

[6]) Contra the Trib. com. Brussels 7.10.1949, as related in Transport 1952, p. 6568.

[7]) Cf. for the **Netherlands** (maritime law) Cleveringa (1946) pp. 156 sq. and A. C. van Empel in *Rechtskundige Opstellen aangeboden aan R.P. Cleveringa*, Zwolle, 1952, pp. 83 sq., and Rechtbank Amsterdam 7.3.1951, N.J. 1951, No. 573. For **England** see Shawcross and Beaumont (1951) No. 351, and *Elder Dempster and Co.* v. *Paterson Zochonis and Co.* [1924] A. C. 522. Foı **Germany** see Joerges (1933), p. 49, and W. Heinze in 60 B.T.I. (1952) 69 sq.

clauses accepted by the shipper, provided, at least, that such clauses are not unusual. In Anglosaxon countries the owner probably should be considered an undisclosed principal in such cases. In civil law countries the construction of the undisclosed principal does not appear to exist in the form known to the common law, and courts and authors must find other ways of avoiding the situation that the owner can ignore a contract made by a carrier who may not even have known that he was not dealing with the owner [8]). Since the courts often do not look too favourably on limitation of liability clauses imposed by carriers, they may be inclined to invoke the holy principle that contracts cannot bind third parties. In such a situation the carrier will keenly feel the lack of the protection offered by Article 24 of the Convention.

249. It was necessary to discuss in some detail the problems arising when the carrier has to base his defence on the limitation provisions of the contract of carriage instead of on those of the

---

248. [8]) See especially Cleveringa (1946), pp. 160 sq.

The carrier may try to avoid the unlimited liability arising from the independent claims from persons who are not a party to the contract of carriage and therefore not bound by its terms, by inserting in his Conditions of Carriage a clause imposing an obligation on the passenger or shipper to hold the carrier harmless from third party claims with respect to death or injuries to the passenger, or loss or damage to the goods. The courts are generally more inclined to accept the validity of hold harmless agreements than of exemption of liability clauses, but the reason of this attitude probably has to be sought in the kind of contracts in which hold harmless clauses most frequently occur (i.e. contracts between parties with equal bargaining power), rather than in the fact that with hold harmless clauses the injured party does not lose his claim as he does in case of exemption clauses. See on the validity of hold harmless clauses for the **U.S.A.** the Restatement of the Law of Contracts II § 572 and the Annotation in 175 A.L.R. 8, at 20 sq. (also stressing the factor of the equal bargaining power). For **French** law H. Lalou, *Traité pratique de responsabilité civile, 4e éd.* 1949, Nos 507, 515 and 515 bis (mentioning the decisions referred to in No. 232 (2)). On the possibility for the carrier to protect himself against unlimited third party claims for the loss or damages of goods carried by a hold harmless clause in his Conditions of Carriage see also Williams (1951) pp. 120 sq., 427 sq. and 444 sq., and Cleveringa (1946) p. 161 note 3.

In maritime law the validity of the so-called 'both to blame collision clause' in bills of lading has been rejected by the U.S. Supreme Court: *U.S.* v. *Atlantic Mutual Insurance Co.* 1952 A.M.C. 659. This clause has the purpose to protect the carrier against the unlimited recourse claim by which the shipowner of a colliding ship may try to receive contribution for damages paid (outside the scope of application of the Maritime Collisions Convention of 1910) to the shippers of goods carried on the carrier's ship. It was devised by shipowners after the U.S. Supreme Court had decided in *The Chattahoochee* (1899) 173 U.S. 540, that the limitations of liability of the Harter Act cannot be invoked against the recourse claims from the shipowners of colliding vessels. See Knauth (1953) pp. 210 sq. Comp. Nos. 94 (1) and 95 (2) above.

Convention. As will be clear from this discussion, it would be an error to think that one would completely emasculate the sanctions of Articles 3, 4 and 9 by holding that they do not affect the carrier's right to invoke contractual limitation of liability clauses. There always remains the important result that the binding effect of printed carrier's clauses, especially in international transportation, can be objected to for many reasons, whereas the validity of Article 22 of the Convention (in connection with Article 24), in the cases to which it applies and provided no wilful misconduct is proven, is not subject to any such objections.

D. Requirements to which Sanction is Attached.

250. So far we have discussed the significance and effect of the sanction provided in Articles 3, 4 and 9. It remains to be considered in which cases the sanction is imposed.

Tickets. According to Article 3 the sanction applies 'if the carrier accepts a passenger without a passenger ticket having been delivered'. The phrase requires some comment. *'If the carrier accepts a passenger'*. At what moment does the carrier 'accept a passenger'? At the moment the contract of carriage is concluded? That may be a long time before the transportation is supposed to commence, e.g. at the time the carrier confirms through the telephone or otherwise that the passengers can be carried on a certain flight in accordance with the request of the passenger. It is to be observed that the same wording is used in Article 4 and 9 speaking of baggage and goods. The acceptance of baggage and goods clearly does not have to coincide with the moment the contract of carriage is concluded. That is especially manifest with regard to baggage, where the contract of carriage is generally concluded at the moment the carrier agrees to carry the passenger, at least as far as the baggage is concerned, for which no extra charge has to be paid. It is believed that by analogy with baggage and goods, passengers should be deemed accepted by the carrier at the moment the latter takes the passenger under his care. This view finds support in the situation of successive carriage, in which case the second carrier certainly cannot be said to have accepted the carrier at the moment the contract of carriage was concluded with the first carrier.

What if the carrier issues the ticket sometime after he has 'accepted' the passenger? Will his original failure be remedied by the later issuance? Probably not with respect to liabilities which arose before issuance. As to the transportation after the late issuance of the ticket, there is more room for doubt. It is believed that the better view would be to allow the carrier at any time to issue the ticket before the passenger embarks on the plane. The point does not seem to have received much attention from the authors.

251. *'Without a passenger ticket'*. It has been contended by one early commentator on the Convention that the ticket should comply with all requirements enumerated in the first paragraph of the Article [1]). That view has rightly been rejected quasi-unanimously by the authors as well as by the Courts which had to deal with the point [2]). Both the wording of Article 3 (2), when compared with that of Articles 4 (4) and 9, and the history of the provision make it abundantly clear that the framers of the Convention meant to impose the sanction with respect to the ticket only in case of a complete failure to deliver a ticket, and did not want to attach the sanction to the omission of the prescribed particulars. This raises the question of which condition should be fulfilled for a slip of paper to become a ticket, the delivery of which will be sufficient for the purpose of Article 3 (2). It is believed that any document will do which shows itself to be 'a ticket' for the transportation concerned. A letter by which a carrier merely confirms a booking probably would not be sufficient, unless the letter were to contain an express statement that it should be considered a ticket [3]).

252. The provision speaks of *a* passenger ticket. Does this mean that for every passenger a separate ticket has to be issued? It is believed that it does not. The provision of paragraph 2 was added to give substance to the obligation imposed by paragraph 1 of Article 3. Nothing in the latter paragraph indicates that the

251. [1]) Y. J. Blanc-Dannery, *Convention de Varsovie etc.* Paris, 1933, p. 28.
[2]) *Grey* v. *American Airlines Inc.* 1950 U.S.Av.R. 296, Trib. Brussels 6.5.1950, Pas. 1950, III, 96; 4 R.F.D.A. (1950) 411; 1950 U.S.Av.R. 367 (*Pauwels* v. *Sabena*).
[3]) According to Koffka (1937) p. 280, any document which, in an unambiguous way, gives a right to transportation would be sufficient, apparently also a letter.

carrier has to issue for every passenger a separate ticket. It says generally that 'in the carriage of passengers the carrier must deliver a passenger ticket'. This leaves it entirely for the carrier to issue one ticket for a group of passengers as long as delivery of such a group ticket to one person of the group can be considered delivery to all members of the group, which presupposes that the person receiving the ticket can be said to have acted on behalf of the others. Another condition to be set on such group ticket is that it should indicate in one way or other that it is meant as ticket for the transportation of all persons concerned. The point does not arise whenever a separate ticket is delivered to each passenger, since the mere fact of delivery to the passenger then is sufficient indication that it is intended to cover *his* transportation. Article 3 wisely does not require the name of the passenger to be mentioned on the ticket, though at present it is customary to have the name filled in [1]). There is no reason, however, why in the future air carriers might not decide to introduce the simple nameless ticket used in railway transportation.

253. *'Being delivered'*. Though the Article does not say so, delivery of the ticket obviously should be made to the passenger or to somebody whom the carrier may suppose to be authorized to collect the ticket on behalf of the passenger. The person who has concluded the contract of carriage with the carrier generally must be considered a person whom the carrier may suppose to be authorized to collect the ticket. The passenger who has agreed to be carried under the contract concluded by another person, cannot afterwards deny the authority of such other person to act as his agent in taking delivery of the ticket, unless he has clearly expressed himself to the contrary [1]).

---

252. [1]) At the 8th (Madrid) Session of the L.C. of ICAO (1951) the idea of requiring also the name of the passenger to be mentioned on the ticket was unanimously rejected (Minutes, pp. 100/101).

253. [1]) Cf. *Ross* v. *Pan American Airways Inc.* 1949 U.S.Av.R. 168, 174/175: 'The Convention itself does not say, nor does appellant argue, that the language of Article 3 make physical delivery of the ticket into the passenger's own hand a requisite for the limitation of liability [...]. There is, of course, no affirmative showing here of any specific instruction from appellant to Abraham accrediting him to act for her in respect to this particular kind of ticket or any ticket [...]. Whether or not all this added up, as a matter of law, to a sufficient showing of authority in Abraham, it can hardly be disputed that, when a ticket bearing appellant's name and all particu-

254. With respect to the *baggage check,* Article 4 (4) provides that 'if the carrier accepts baggage without a baggage check having been delivered, or if the baggage check does not contain the particulars set out at (d), (f) and (h) above, the carrier shall not be entitled to avail himself of those provisions of the Convention which exclude or limit his liability'. Other than with the passenger ticket, the sanction is here imposed not only for the failure to issue a baggage check, but also for the omission therein of certain particulars:

(1) the number of the passenger ticket,
(2) the number and weight of the packages,
(3) a statement that the carriage is subject to the rules relating to liability established by the Convention.

255. Though the provision speaks of baggage without restriction, there can be no doubt that it only applies to baggage for which the carrier is obliged under para. (1) to deliver a baggage check, i.e. 'baggage, other than small personal objects of which the passenger takes charge himself'. It is believed that the essential criterion for determining whether a baggage check has to be issued must be sought in the words 'of which the passenger takes charge himself'. For all such objects, irrespective of their size and nature, no baggage check has to be delivered [1]) as clearly appears from the prescription of para. (3) under (e), that the baggage check should contain a statement that delivery of the baggage will be made to the bearer of the baggage check. Such a statement would be impossible for objects which remain in the charge of the passenger. It is to be observed that Article 22 (3) speaks generally of 'objects of which the passenger takes charge himself', without limitation to small personal objects.

The distinction is of the greatest importance for the following reasons:

---

lars as to the intended route as well as a reference to the Warsaw Convention limitation, was laid in front of appellant on the table at the airport, she, by thereafter boarding the plane as a traveller on that ticket, impliedly, if not expressly, ratified and adopted what had been done by the Army, and later by Abraham, in taking out that ticket in her name'. In this case U.S.O. Camp Shows Inc., through its officer Abraham, had organized a trip to Lisbon for Miss Froman, who was going to entertain soldiers during the war.

255. [1]) Thus also Koffka (1937) p. 282.

(*a*) for objects which remain with the passenger no baggage check has to be issued, and the sanction of para. (4) will not be applicable.

(*b*) to such objects the liability provisions of Article 18, 19 and 20 do not apply, but instead the rules of the national law applicable to the contract.

(*c*) to such objects a different limit of liability applies, i.e. 5,000 gold francs per passenger instead of 250 gold francs per kilogram.

256. It follows that three different systems of liability are provided in the Convention with respect to the property of the passenger:

(1) with respect to baggage for which a baggage check has been delivered the carrier is liable up to a limit of 250 gold francs per kilogram, unless he proves that he has taken all necessary measures to avoid the damage, or that the damage was due to negligence in the navigation (Artt. 18, 20 and 22);

(2) with respect to baggage for which a baggage check should have been delivered but has not been, the carrier is liable without limit and without any defences being offered to him, except for a contractual limitation of liability at or above the Warsaw limit;

(3) with respect to property of which the passenger takes charge himself, the carrier's liability is not laid down in the Convention and must be based on national law and/or the contract of carriage, subject to a conventional limit of 5,000 gold francs per passenger.

257. *'If the carrier accepts baggage'*. If follows from the wording and system of Article 4 that only acceptance of baggage with a view to the carriage and before the baggage is brought into the plane, has been contemplated. For according to paragraph (2) the baggage check should contain the place of departure and the weight of the packages, and absence of the baggage check is said not to 'affect the existence or the validity of the contract of carriage'. It can hardly be expected of the carrier to weigh any baggage which the passenger keeps with himself until he has entered the plane. This answers the problem as to what are the objects which the passenger himself brings aboard the aircraft, and which are there taken from him by the steward or stewardess in order to be rendered to the passenger before he leaves the aircraft. Such objects are not accepted by the carrier *for carriage*, but only for storage for the time that the passenger is in the plane. The acceptance of the goods is viewed by neither of the parties as an agreement to carry. The situation is not different from that of the passenger checking his coat on board of an oceansteamer; and who would ever consider such act as the conclusion of a contract of carriage? In case the carrier does not deliver, with respect to such objects, a baggage check containing the three particulars mentioned above, the sanction of Article 4 (4) will not apply. Whether the carrier's liability for such objects will also not be governed by Articles 18 and 20 during the period that they are in his custody, seems more doubtful. There are good reasons to apply these provisions at least by way of analogy.

258. The baggage check must contain in the first place *'the number of the passenger ticket.'* Curiously Article 3 does not prescribe that the passenger ticket should be numbered. Query: what if the passenger ticket does not bear a number?

The requirement poses a practical problem which has been solved by the airlines using the IATA ticket in such a way that the baggage check has been combined together with the ticket into one document, so that the number of the ticket automatically accompanies the baggage check. There is nothing in the Convention to forbid such solution.

259. The second compulsory requirement is *'the number and the weight of the packages'*. Must the baggage check mention the weight of each individual package, or is it sufficient for the total weight to be filled in? The latter solution is certainly preferable. Just as 'the number' necessarily refers to the total baggage, so does 'the weight'. The reason why Article 4 speaks of packages instead of baggage in connection with the weight – differing from Article 8 sub (i), which speaks of 'la marchandise' (the goods) – must be sought in the fact that in Article 4 number and weight are combined in one phrase. It was impossible, of course, to speak of the number of baggage.

260. Finally the baggage check must contain *'a statement* *that the carriage is subject to the rules relating to liability established by this Convention'*. This requirement raises the difficulty that the same airline may perform both carriage which is governed by the Convention, and carriage which is not. It would be impracticable to require from a carrier to use different types of tickets for the two categories of carriage, if it were only for the many uncertainties and difficulties involved in determining whether certain carriage is governed by the Convention, difficulties which are causing headaches to the legal experts who have made a study of the Convention. How could one then expect passage-employees to solve such problems on the spot?

It would be possible, of course, to have the rules of liability of the Convention also apply to 'non-Warsaw' traffic. The difficulty with that solution, however, is that the clause might easily be held effective only as far as the rules of the Convention are favourable to the passenger, not as they are favourable to the carrier by limiting his liability. In order to avoid that consequence, the IATA airlines have drafted a formula to the effect that the rules of liability of the Convention shall apply if the transportation is 'international carriage' as defined by Article 1 of the Convention [1]). Whether the transportation is international, the passenger – who anyhow should be an expert in the Warsaw Convention – can easily determine with his knowledge of the places of departure and destination and the agreed stopping places, assuming that he knows by heart the countries which have ratified the Convention. Preposterous as these assumptions are, they are not much more unrealistic than the idea that by telling a passenger in a printed clause that the rules of liability of the Convention will apply to his carriage, he would have any clear ideas about his legal rights. With this requirement we are in the fairyland of legal thinking, where fairy passengers will thoroughly study all the fine print on their tickets before embarking on the plane, and, when seeing the Warsaw clause, will decide that they should protect themselves by insurance, in view of the provisions of Article 22. It has been said that the IATA formula is an evasion of the Convention and that it is meaningless, because it merely states that the Convention applies when it applies. This is not

260. 1) McNair (1953) p. 193 (29) believes, however, that the Convention requires a positive and unqualified statement.

correct, for it was one of the purposes of the discussed clause to make the courts of 'non-Warsaw Countries' apply the Convention when they would be seized of actions arising from 'Warsaw-carriage', and this purpose is fully served by the formula of the IATA documents.

The question has been raised whether, assuming such a court would feel bound by the contractual choice of law implied in the clause, it would also have to apply the sanctions of Articles 4 (4) and 9, or whether the latter provisions are not included in the 'rules relating to liability established by the Convention' [2]. The former view would seem preferable.

261. Would it be possible for a passenger who had accepted a baggage check in a language which he could not read, to allege non-compliance with Article 4 of the Convention on the ground that he had not received sufficient notice of the statement that the carriage was subject to the liability provisions of the Convention? Almost certainly not, unless it could be said that the language used was chosen in order to hide the clause from the passenger. The requirements of Article 4 (2) are mere form requirements, and there is nothing in the Article saying that the passenger should have received actual notice of the prescribed particulars. But it has been held that a statement that the carriage is subject to conditions of contract based on the rules of liability of the Convention is insufficient [1].

262. With respect to the *carriage of goods* Article 9 provides that 'if the carrier accepts goods without an air consignment note having been made out, or if the air consignment note does not contain all the particulars set out in Article 8 (a) to (i) inclusive, and (q) the carrier shall not be entitled to avail himself of the provisions of this Convention which exclude or limit his liability'.

The sanction applies *'if the carrier accepts goods'*. With respect to the analogous provision concerning the acceptance of a passen-

260. [2] H. Müller (1932) p. 88.

261. [1] *Westminster Bank, Ltd.* v. *Imperial Airways Ltd.* [1936] 2 All E.R. 890, 1936 U.S.Av.R. 39, and comp. *Philippson* v. *Imperial Airways Ltd.* [1939] A.C. 332, [1939] 1 All E.R. 761, 1939 U.S.Av.R. 63.

ger for carriage, it has been suggested that as long as the carrier issued the ticket before embarkation of the passenger, the requirement of Article 3 should be considered sufficiently satisfied with respect to any liabilities arising after delivery of the ticket. The problem is more complicated as far as the carriage of goods is concerned, for three reasons:

(i) the period of liability for goods under the Convention starts from the moment the goods arrive at the airport and are brought under the custody of the carrier, whereas with respect to passengers the period of liability starts with 'the operations of embarking'.

(ii) the air waybill must be made out by the shipper when offering the goods for carriage, and not by the carrier, as is the case for the passenger ticket and baggage check.

(iii) the requirements as to the contents of the air waybill are most elaborate, whereas no mandatory requirements are provided for the contents of the tickets, those for the baggage check being limited to only four particulars. If one looks at the impressive list of particulars which, according to Article 8, should be mentioned on the air waybill, it is clear that in practice it will often be impossible to have the air waybill made out at the moment of acceptance of the goods. In these cases the carrier generally will offer a simple receipt containing only part of the information necessary, and will make out the air waybill at a later date, just as shipping companies often accept goods from shippers against a mate's receipt, the bill of lading being issued later.

Article 6 (5) provides that 'if, at the request of the consignor, the carrier makes out the air waybill, he shall be deemed, subject to proof to the contrary, to have done so on behalf of the shipper'. A shipper who delivers his goods to a carrier without the accompanying air waybill should probably be deemed to have impliedly requested the carrier to establish the air waybill on his behalf. Such a procedure is certainly not against the spirit of the Convention even if it would appear to be against its letter. It is suggested, therefore, that as long as the air waybill has been made out before commencement of the actual carriage by air, the carrier will be protected by the limits and other defences of the Convention with respect to any liabilities arising after issuance of the air waybill. But a contrary view could be defended on the basis of a literal interpretation of the text.

In any case, the second carrier who would take over the goods after an air waybill had been made out, could not be penalized under Article 9 for the fact that the first carrier had accepted the goods without an air waybill having been established. That follows clearly from the wording of Article 9 and 30 (1) [1]).

263. *'Without an air waybill having been made out'*: when can it be said that an air waybill has been made out in accordance with Article 9? Article 5 (1) provides that 'every carrier of goods has the right to require the consignor to make out and hand over to him a document called an 'air waybill', and Article 6 (1) says that 'the air waybill shall be made out by the consignor in three original parts and be handed over with the goods', and that one part shall be signed by the consignor, one part, which is to accompany the goods, by both consignor and carrier, and one part destined for the consignee by the carrier only. From the wording of Article 5 (1) it follows that in the terminology of the framers of the Convention the making out of an air waybill does not presuppose the signature of the carrier, since the air waybill is made out by the consignor alone and only thereafter signed by the carrier. But it is believed that even the signature of the shipper (which, according to Article 6 (4), may be printed or stamped) is not so essential that without it no air waybill could be said to have been made out. The exceptional sanction of Article 9 must be construed in a restrictive way, and where it does mention a number of particulars which should be contained in the air waybill, but does not speak of the signature of shipper and carrier, the absence of the latter will not deprive the carrier from the benefits of the Convention, no more than would the fact that the air waybill had been made out in fewer than three copies [1]).

264. The particulars which have to be mentioned on the air waybill, if the carrier wants to avoid the sanction of Article 9,

---

262. [1]) McNair (1953) p. 191 (hesitating).

263. [1]) Chauveau (1951) No. 233, Litvine (1953) Nos. 257–258.

are as many as 17 (or 19), to-wit: (1) the place and (2) date of execution, (3) the place of departure and (4) of destination, (5) the contemplated stopping places, (6) the name and (7) the address of the consignor, (8) the name and (9) address of the first carrier, (10) the name and (11) address of the consignee, if the case so requires, (12) the nature of the goods, (13) the number of the packages, (14) the method of packing and (15) the particular marks or numbers upon them, (16) the weight, (16 or 17) the quantity, and (16 or 18) the volume or dimensions of the goods, and (17 or 19) a statement that the carriage is subject to the rules relating to liability established by the Convention. Some of the items required need comment.

265. With respect to the *stopping places*, it is to be noted that only the 'arrêts *prévus*', or the *contemplated* stopping places have to be mentioned. The words have been somewhat loosely translated in the English Carriage by Air Act 1932 into 'agreed stopping places'. For the purpose of this particular phrase, however, the difference does not seem to be too important, since the stopping places must have been in the contemplation of both parties, and it is believed that that must have been mutually realized. It will be up to the shipper or consignee who wants to invoke Article 9, to prove that some place had been contemplated (or in England agreed) as a stopping place. It has been held that the 'agreed' stopping place may be incorporated into the air waybill by a printed reference to the carrier's time table [1]).

266. The '*first carrier*', whose name and address must be mentioned on the air waybill, is the carrier who according to the contract of carriage, is to perform the first part of the transportation. That may be another than the airline whose air waybill is issued. When the Article requires the address of the carrier, any indication from which one can find without difficulty where the carrier has his offices will suffice. This also applies to the requirement as to the address of the shipper and consignee.

267. *The name and address of the consignee* has only to be

---

265. [1]) *Kraus* v. *K.L.M.* 1949 U.S.Av.R. 306.

mentioned 'if the case so requires'. The phrase was added in order not to prevent the issuance of air waybills to the order of the shipper [1]). Up to now this possibility does not seem to have been used by the airlines [2]).

268. *The number of the packages, the method of packing, the particular marks or the numbers on the packages.* The text is not clear as to whether it is sufficient to have only one of these particulars mentioned, or whether the only choice is between the two last mentioned particulars. The latter solution seems preferable, as the other two items are so entirely different from each other and from the last two items, that it would not make sense to say that the information as to the number of packages could be replaced e.g. by the method of packing. The text of the English Carriage by Air Act and the American Government translation have clarified the point by inserting the word 'and' after the words 'method of packing'.

269. The same problem arises with respect to *'the weight, the quantity, the volume or the dimensions of the goods'*, but with this distinction that here all four particulars are of a similar nature, so that there is nothing illogical in providing that it will suffice to fill in only one of the four [1]). Meanwhile, the English text has made the enumeration cumulative also here, by inserting the word 'and' before 'the volume and dimensions', so that at least in England and those countries which have adopted the same text for their legislation [2]), the volume or dimensions of a

---

267. [1]) CITEJA, 3d. Session (Madrid 1928) Minutes, pp. 68–69, W.C. p. 105. On the question of negotiability of the air waybill see F. Legrez in 3 R.F.D.A. (1949) 353 sq., A. Schweickhardt in 5 R.F.D.A. (1951) 19 sq., the author's report in Rio Session (1953) II, 51 sq. esp. at 59, C. da Rocha Guimarães in 1 R.B.D.A. (1951) No. 2, 46, J. T. Sneed in 65 Harv. L. Rev. (1952) 1392, Juglart (1952) No. 250, and McNair (1953) p. 195.

[2]) The IATA air waybill bears the express statement 'not negotiable'.

269. [1]) Litvine (1953), Nos. 371–372.

[2]) India (1934), Australia (1935), Ireland (1936), Canada (1939), New Zealand (1940), Ceylon (1950) and Union of South-Africa (1946, not yet effective). See Shawcross and Beaumont (1951) No. 113. The Belgian delegate to the CITEJA has also taken the view, when commenting on a question submitted by I.A.T.A., that the enumeration in Art 8 (i) is cumulative, rather than alternative, See *Réunion de la 2e Commission*, Stockholm 1932, CITEJA, Doc. 176, p. 56.

shipment probably must be mentioned in addition to the number of packages and the quantity.

The practical result of this interpretation is most unfortunate, as it compels shippers and carriers to much extra work which serves no practical purpose at all. Outside the British Commonwealth the accumulative interpretation does not appear to have been accepted [3]. It is to be observed that it does not only make the 'volume or dimensions' a mandatory requirement, but also the 'quantity' of the goods. Obviously, in a number of cases it is impossible to speak of the quantity of a shipment. What is the quantity of a suitcase containing personal belongings, shipped under an air waybill? And how to describe in any exact way the volume or dimensions of e.g. a bicycle? Certainly, it should be sufficient if either the weight, or the quantity, or the volume, or the dimensions of the goods are mentioned on the air waybill.

In any case it will be sufficient to mention the weight, quantity etc. of the total shipment, without it being necessary to give these particulars for each individual package contained in the shipment. The French text is even clearer on that point than the text of the Carriage by Air Act 1932, by speaking of *'la marchandise'* [4].

270. As to the statement that *the carriage is governed by the rules of liability established by the Convention,* the problems arising in connection with this item have already been discussed in connection with the baggage check [1].

271. A general remark as to the particulars to be filled in under Article 8 must be added. Does the sanction of Article 9 apply if one or more of the required particulars have been mentioned, but incorrectly? It is believed that it does not [1].

---

269. [3] The **U.S.A.** Government translation has made the same distinction between items (h) and (i) as suggested in the text. Also the **German** Government translation in Reichsgesetzblatt 1933, II, p. 1039, and the **Swedish** Act of 1937. But comp. Art. 958 (d) of the **Italian** Cod. Nav. which requires i.a. the quantity, the number, the weight *and* the dimensions of the goods to be mentioned.

[4] See also No. 148 (6).

270. [1] See No. 260. For a discussion of the analogous 'clause paramount' in the Carriage of Goods by Sea Acts of Anglosaxon countries, see Knauth (1953), pp. 156 sq.

271. [1] Koffka (1937), p. 293.

This follows from Article 10, as far as the particulars relating to the goods are concerned. But it is clear that also for other particulars, such as the address of the shipper or consignee, it would be unreasonable to penalize the carrier for errors committed therein. Only if the carrier were knowingly to fill in the wrong information on any of the points listed by Article 8, could it possibly be said that he had accepted the goods without the air waybill containing all the prescribed particulars.

272. It has been argued that the carrier, who is held deprived of his right to invoke the limits and other defences of the Convention because of incompleteness of the air waybill, has a right of recourse for the resulting increase of his liability against the shipper whose duty it is to make out an air waybill complying with article 8 [1]). Article 10 provides that 'the consignor is responsible for the correctness of the particulars and statements relating to the goods which he inserts in the air waybill', and that 'the consignor will be liable for all damage suffered by the carrier or any other person by reason of the irregularity, incorrectness or incompleteness of the said particulars and statements'. This Article was already contained in the first Drafts of the Convention on Air Waybills – which was later to be combined with the Draft Liability Convention established by the Paris Conference of 1925 – before it was decided to adopt the sanction of Article 9. It is probable that the author of the draft, the Belgian Rapporteur De Vos, when proposing the principle of what later became Article 10, was inspired by the analogous provisions of the C.I.M. and the Brussels Convention on Bills of Lading of 1924 [2]). Clearly, the increased liability of the carrier imposed by Article 9 was never considered as a possible 'damage' in the sense of Article 10 for which the shipper should bear the liability. The damages referred to in Article 10 are for example customs-fines imposed because of incorrect description of the goods, or damages caused by the goods to aircraft or property of the carrier or of other cargo owners, due to the fact that the carrier was not informed about the true nature of the goods. To assume that Article 10

272. [1]) Goedhuis (1933), p. 129.
[2]) Art. 7 of the C.I.M. and Art. III (5) of the Brussels Convention. Cf. Goedhuis (1937), p. 174.

makes the shipper liable towards the carrier for the increased liability towards the shipper which Article 9 imposes on the carrier would make nonsense of the Convention. Any interpretation which avoids such an absurd result, is to be preferred.

One such interpretation would be to say that Article 10 refers to the incompleteness, irregularity or inexactness of each individual statement regarding the goods, whereas Article 9 envisages the total absence of one or more of the prescribed particulars [3]). It is submitted that a better distinction between the two Articles is that Article 10 deals with a different kind of damage than Article 9. If the shipper were to fail to give any information as to the nature of a shipment of explosives, as required in Article 8 (g), and if damage were to be caused by these goods to the aircraft or to other shipments, the shipper would be liable towards the carrier for such damages or for the third party claims resulting therefrom. But if the shipment were to get lost or delayed, the carrier would be liable towards the shipper for such loss or delay without being entitled to invoke the limits or other defences of the Convention. Only in case the loss of the goods was caused by their own nature, without the nature being mentioned by the shipper on the air waybill, would there be room for doubt as to whether Article 9 or Article 10 should prevail. In such an event, however, there would also be a case of contributory negligence of the shipper, and Article 9 probably has not taken away the defence of contributory negligence of the shipper [4]).

273. According to Article 6 (5), 'if, at the request of the consignor, the carrier makes out the air waybill, he shall be deemed, subject to proof to the contrary, to have done so on behalf of the consignor'. In practice, the air waybill is often, if not in most cases, made out by the carrier acting as agent of the shipper. The shipper will be liable towards third parties, including subsequent carriers and owners of other cargo, for omissions or errors committed by the carrier who issues the air waybill on his behalf, but he will have a right of recourse against the latter, based on the agency relationship. The carrier's liability towards

272. [3]) Cf. Koffka (1937), p. 293 and 295, Coquoz (1938), p. 114, Lemoine (1947) No. 590, Litvine (1953), No. 263.
[4]) See No. 69 (6).

the shipper for such claims or damages is not a liability under the Convention; consequently it is not governed by the provisions of Articles 18 sq. of the Convention. Any limitation of liability or exemption provided in the carrier's Conditions of Carriage – provided their applicability had been extended to such services incidental to the transportation [1]) – would not be affected by Article 23 of the Convention, which only restricts the carrier's right to exclude or limit his liability *under the Convention.*

§ 2. DECLARATION OF VALUE (WARSAW CONVENTION)

274. Article 22 (2) of the Warsaw Convention provides:

> 'In the carriage of registered baggage and goods, the liability of the carrier is limited to a sum of 250 francs per kilogram, unless the consignor has made, at the time when the package was handed over to the carrier, a special declaration of the value at delivery and has paid a supplementary sum if the case so requires. In that case the carrier will be liable to pay a sum not exceeding the declared sum, unless he proves that that sum is greater that the actual value to the consignor at delivery'.

It is to be observed that 'the special declaration of the value at delivery' ('déclaration spéciale d'intérêt à la livraison') has been dealt with by the framers of the Convention as a unilateral act of the shipper, as a result of which the 250 gold francs limit of the Convention is substituted by another conventional limit. It is not a contractual limitation of liability, agreed upon by the parties, to set aside the Conventional limit. As has been pointed out before, contractual clauses in limitation of liability are not ruled out altogether by the Convention, but only to the extent they would tend to limit the carrier's liability below the limits fixed by the Convention (Article 23) [1]). The increased limit resulting from a declaration of value must be considered a 'limit fixed by the Convention', no less than the 250 gold francs limit, so

---

273. [1]) The IATA General Conditions of Carriage (1953) are applicable 'to all carriage of passengers and baggage [resp. cargo], *including all services* incidental thereto' (Art. 2 (1).

274. [1]) See No. 226.

that the carrier cannot in his contract try to limit his liability below the special value at delivery, declared by the shipper. The fact that the declaration of value of Article 22 (2) is a unilateral act, not a contract clause, is also important because of the consequence, that the approval by the carrier is not required for the 250 gold francs limit to be substituted by the limit of the declared value [2]).

275. The concept of the declaration of value of Article 22 has at least two different sources, and perhaps three, which have influenced its character. In the first place, there is the idea that a shipper or passenger should inform a carrier about the nature of valuable articles in order that he can take special measures for their safe carriage and can adapt the price of transportation to the increased risks involved. Closely related with this aspect is the possibility that the failure of a shipper to state the exceptional value of a shipment may amount to contributory negligence [1]). The construction in terms of contributory negligence comes close to that according to which damages arising from the unexpected value of baggage or goods are said to be unforeseeable by the carrier, the carrier being held entitled to rely on the value declared by the shipper or passenger. That construction is especially followed in France [2]). Both sources may have been of influence in determining the unilateral nature of the declaration of value in Article 22.

Though it is true that the declaration of value of Article 22 is a unilateral action, not a bilateral contract clause, the rule that parties can in advance agree on the amount of damages to be paid in case of a breach of contract probably was also at the back of the minds of those who inserted the provision in the Convention. In fact, the unilateral character of the declaration of value was

---

274. [2]) Though it is true that nothing in the Convention obliges a carrier to accept goods for carriage (Art. 33), once he has accepted a shipment with a declared value he cannot by a clause in his contract set aside the effect of such declaration provided by the Convention. The difference does not seem to have been fully realized by Litvine (1953) No. 376. Comp. also Shawcross and Beaumont (1951) No. 389 note (b): 'The declaration must be intended and understood as a contract that the carrier is responsible for the higher amount'.

275. [1]) See Nos. 106 sq.
[2]) Comp. No. 106.

apparently not clear to the framers of the Convention, as appears of the Minutes of the Paris and Warsaw Conferences [3]). This source of inspiration may have been of special influences in determining the nature of the value to be declared, to-wit a value at delivery for the shipper, instead of the actual value of the goods, which would have been more in line with the idea that the carrier should be informed in advance about goods having a more than average value. Finally the choice of rate principle – so important in the American transportation law, but also well known outside the U.S.A. [4]) – may have lent some of its colour to the provision of Article 22 (2). There can be no doubt that the analogous provisions of the Brussels Convention on bills of lading and of the Berne Convention on railroad transportation [5]) have also been a source for the drafting of the declared value provision of the Warsaw Convention. Especially the wording of the Brussels Convention reveals some striking similarities [6]).

276. Article 22 requires a special declaration of the value at delivery made by the shipper at the time that the package was handed over to the carrier. It is not a condition that the declaration be made in the air waybill [1]). True, according to Article 8 (m) 'the amount of the value declared in accordance with Article 22 (2)' must be mentioned on the air waybill, but that only means that the first carrier may demand that in case of declaration of value by the shipper the declared value be inserted in the air waybill, and probably also that a second carrier, who has carried the goods without knowing of the declaration of value, will not be bound thereby.

The Brussels Convention differs on this point by making an insertion of the declared value a condition for its effectiveness.

---

275. [3]) See Pittard at Paris Conference of 1925 (ed. 1936) p. 64, and De Vos at W.C. p. 165.

[4]) See No. 247 (4) and (5).

[5]) Art. 35 C.I.M. and Art. 4 (5) of the Brussels Convention. Cf. Goedhuis (1937) p. 260 and 263 sq. for the differences with the C.I.M.

[6]) The Brussels Convention has: 'unless the ***nature and value*** ef such goods have been declared ***before shipment*** and ***inserted in the bill of lading***. This declaration ***if embodied in the bill of lading*** shall be prima facie evidence, but shall not be binding or conclusive on the carrier.' (the differences are italicized).

276. [1]) Similarly Koffka (1937) p. 329. Contra Chauveau (1951) No. 361.

277. The declaration must be made at the moment the goods are delivered to the carrier [1]). This does not mean that a declaration of value made at a later date is necessarily without effect, but in order to be binding upon the carrier such a later declaration should have been agreed to by him, which agreement will be implied from the fact that he allowed the declaration to be inserted in his part of the air waybill. Though the paragraph has been drafted in a way to make the qualification of the declared value as a value *at delivery* a condition for the application of Article 22 (2) thereto, it is believed that any declaration of value made for the apparent purpose of determining the liability of the carrier will be sufficient. That excludes declaration of value made for customs purposes only [2]).

278. What is the effect of a declaration of value below the 250 gold francs limit? The wording of Article 22 (2) does not exclude such a declaration, but the framers of the Convention seem to have envisaged only declared values in excess of the established limit [1]). This is also the interpretation attached by most authors to the analogous provisions of the Brussels Convention on bills of lading [2]). On the other hand, it could well be argued that there is nothing unreasonable in holding a shipper, who wants to profit from a lower rate corresponding with the low value declared by him, precluded from invoking the higher Warsaw limit. It is to be observed in this connection that a declaration of value does not only affect the limit of the carrier's liability but also creates prima facie evidence of the damage involved for the shipper in the loss of the goods. The provision of Article 10 which makes the shipper responsible for the correctness

---

277. [1]) Comp. Brussels Convention (See No. 275 (6)): 'before shipment'.
[2]) See the *obiter dictum* of Lewis J. in *Westminster Bank* v. *Imperial Airways Ltd.* [1936] 2 All E.R. 890, at 898, 1936 U.S.Av.R. 39, at 53, and *Mayers* v. *K.L.M.* 1951 U.S.Av.R. 428.

278. [1]) See citations in no. 275 (3). See also Planiol-Ripert-Esmein, *Traité pratique* VI, no. 407 (note 4) with respect to the words 'à moins que la valeur ait été déclarée' in the limitation provision of Art. 41 of the Act of 1924: 'Il semble que cela exclut une clause limitative fixant un chiffre inférieur.' The **Italian** Cod. Nav., Art. 952, speaks expressly of 'the *higher* amount corresponding with the actual value'.
[2]) S. D. Cole, *Carriage of Goods by Sea Act, 1924, 4th ed.* London, 1937, pp. 85–87, Scrutton (1948) p. 463, Knauth (1953) p. 270, Gramm, *Das neue deutsche Seefrachtrecht.* Berlin, 1938, p. 179. *Contra*: H. Wüstendörfer, *Neuzeitliches Seehandelsrecht.* Hamburg, 1947, p. 275.

of the particulars and statements – the original text uses here the word 'déclarations' – relating to the goods which he inserts in the air waybill, and which makes him liable for all damage suffered by the carrier or any other person by reason of the incorrectness of such declaration, could also be invoked as an argument for holding the shipper precluded from contending that the actual value would be in excess of the value declared. This argument would have some force especially if the carrier were to have his liability insured up to the declared value, so that any excess liability would have to be paid by him.

279. The declaration has to be made 'against payment of an additional charge, if the case so requires' ('moyennant le paiement d'une taxe supplémentaire éventuelle'). It is believed that this phrase only gives a right to the carrier to ask for an additional charge in case of declaration of value by the shipper. It certainly does not require that such additional charge is paid at the moment the goods are delivered to the carrier, as all freight charges will frequently be paid by consignee. But even if by error no additional charge would have been added to the air waybill, the declaration of value at delivery would remain effective, provided it was really meant to be such a declaration, and subject to the carrier's right to ask for payment of the additional charge [1]). The fact that no additional charge was paid by the shipper – in case of a prepaid shipment – *may* be an indication, however, that the declaration was not intended to be a declaration of value at delivery [2]).

280. The effect of a declaration of value at delivery is threefold: (1) the 250 gold francs limit on the carrier's liability is replaced

279. [1]) *Contra* Chauveau (1951), No. 361. Comp. Mayne on *Damages, 11th ed.* 1946, p. 346 on declaration of value under the English Railway and Canal Traffic Act, 1854, quoting *Behrens* v. *G. N. Ry.* (1861) 7 H. & N. 950, 31 L.J. Ex. 299, to the effect that the failure of the carrier to collect a supplemental charge does not deprive the shipper from the right to invoke his declaration of value.

[2]) Comp. decisions in No. 277 (2). Conversely not every payment of a surcharge based on the nature of the goods will be sufficient to give a declaration of value the effect of a declaration as meant in Article 22 (2). This will not be the case if the surcharge is not paid and collected in view of the increased liability intended by the declaration, but for other reasons e.g. because of the fact that valuable cargo can bear a higher freight. See the *obiter dictum* in the Westminster Case and Litvine (1953) No. 378.

by the amount of the value declared, (2) the declaration of value offers prima facie evidence of the actual value for the shipper at delivery, and (3) the carrier can not allege any damage claimed by the shipper or consignee to be too remote in accordance with the principles of applicable law, as long as the damage does not exceed the amount of the declared value [1]. These three aspects of the declaration of value need some further comments.

281. The substitution of the 250 gold francs limit by the declared value does not pose any special problems as long as the entire shipment gets lost or suffers damage or delay. But what happens in case of partial loss, damage or delay? The difficulties in applying the 250 gold francs limit per kilogram to these situations have been discussed above [1], and the conclusion reached was that only the weight of the package concerned – but always the whole weight of the package – is to be taken as a basis for calculating the limit of liability. Does a similar conclusion have to be adopted in the case of declaration of value, meaning that the declared value should be prorated in case of partial loss or damage? It is submitted that nothing prevents a shipper from declaring a value at delivery per kilogram, in which case the maximum liability of the carrier for partial loss or damage will be the number of kilograms of the part lost or damaged times the declared value per kilogram. The same result can be reached by inserting a declared value for the entire shipment coupled with a proration clause [2]. It is believed that such a clause is not in conflict with Article 23 of the Convention. That could be said still less of a declaration of value specifying the value of each package. But in the absence of a proration clause and of a declaration of value per kilogram, the maximum liability for partial loss probably is the same as for the entire loss of the shipment or the part of the shipment to which a declaration of value would apply [3].

280. [1]) Comp. Koffka (1937), p. 329.

281. [1]) See Nos. 145 sq.

[2]) The present IATA Conditions (Goods) do not contain a clear proration clause for the cases of declaration of value.

[3]) G. Marais, *Régles de la Haye*, Paris, 1926, pp. 118/119, held that Art. 4 (5) of the Brussels Convention allows proportional reduction of the declared value in case of partial loss or damage, but in a later study the author has adopted the more generally accepted view; see his *Transports internationaux de marchandises par mer*, 1949. p. 197.

282. The second effect of the declaration of value is that of relieving the shipper or consignee from the burden of proving that he has actually suffered damages to the amount of the declared value. The phrasing of the Article on this point is rather ambiguous. In the first part of the sentence it is said that 'the carrier will be liable to pay a sum *not exceeding* ('jusqu' à concurrence de') the declared sum', which would appear to make the declaration of value a mere substitution for the *maximum* of liability, but the second part of the sentence clearly is based on the principle that prima facie the declaration of value does not only fix a maximum of liability but also a minimum. Taken literally, the limitation provided by the first part could not be invoked by the carrier if he proves that the declared value exceeds the actual value, which makes nonsense of the sentence. The Draft established by the Paris Conference of 1925 was better worded on this point, squarely stating that 'the carrier will be liable to pay *the declared value* unless etc.'.

It is not clear what prompted the drafters of the Convention to insert the words 'jusqu' à concurrence de' [1]), which have been translated in the English and American texts as 'not exceeding'; perhaps the possibility of damage, delay or partial loss. For the provision, by the general way it has been phrased - so as to apply to all cases of damages for which the carrier may be liable – poses a curious problem as to whether the presumption of damages to the amount of the declared value also applies in cases other than those of total loss. It is submitted that it does not, as the alternative solution leads to obviously unacceptable and unintended results, especially in case of delay. In the cases where the presumption of damage does apply, however, it cannot be set aside by contract, as that would be contrary to Article 23 [2]).

283. The third effect of the declaration of value was said to be that any damages suffered by the shipper or consignee [1]),

282. [1]) Art. 7 (2). The words 'jusqu' à la concurrence de' have been added only at the Warsaw Conference, without the reason for this addition having been recorded.

[2]) The provision of Art. 14 (3) of the IATA Conditions of 1953 (Goods) that 'all claims shall be subject to proof of value', as far as it tends to impose the burden of proof on the claimant, would seem to be ineffective for declared value shipments.

283. [1]) Though Art. 22 only speaks of 'the actual value *for the consignor* at delivery', it is submitted that any special value for the consignee should also be taken into account. This follows from the spirit, if not from the letter, of Art. 13 (3).

whether they are the proximate consequences of the occurrence or not and whether they are foreseeable or not, must be paid by the carrier. The carrier must pay the actual value for the shipper at delivery, which may be more than the market value of the goods at destination, e.g. when the shipper would have to pay a penalty to the consignee in case of non-arrival of the goods, or when the shipper would have been able to make an exceptionally high price for the goods. But it is believed that the term 'actual value' ('intéret réel') excludes damages of a non-economical nature [2]).

284. A final observation has to be made with respect to the effect of the carrier's wilful misconduct (or of the omission of some required particulars in the air waybill) on the declaration of value by the shipper. As far as the declared value is to be considered a Conventional substitute for the 250 gold francs limit – not a contractual limitation of liability – wilful misconduct of the carrier or his servants would seem to result in the carrier being precluded, pursuant to Article 25, from invoking the increased limit fixed by the declaration of value [1]). As to the proof of damage in excess of the declared value, the onus will naturally lie on the claimant [2]). Under certain circumstances a declaration of value by the shipper below the actual value may amount to contributory negligence [3]), and since that defence is probably not taken away from the carrier by Articles 9 and 25 [4]), it may reduce or even exclude the liability of the carrier in accordance with the principles of the applicable national law. This may especially be the case if the carrier's unlimited liability

---

283. [2]) Similarly Koffka (1937) p. 327. *Contra* Goedhuis (1937) pp. 262/263, and Van Houtte (1940) No. 64.

284. [1]) *Contra* Goedhuis (1937) p. 264 on the ground that 'the declaration of value at delivery entails the *extension* of the liability of the carrier, *not a limitation*' so that it would not be affected by Art. 25.

[2]) But the **Italian** decision Cass. civ. I, 31.3.1952, no. 876, involving a railroad case, held the shipper in any event precluded from proving a higher value of the good than the one declared by him. The Brussels Convention takes away all liability of the carrier if the nature or the value of the goods has been knowingly misstated by the shipper in the bill of lading. It is a matter of controverse whether this sanction also applies in case of a declaration below the actual value: *Pro*: G. Van Bladel, *Connaissements et règles de la Haye*, Bruxelles, 1929, pp. 223/224; *contra*: Marais, *Règles de la Haye*, Paris, 1926, pp. 120/121.

[3]) See No. 108.

[4]) See No. 69 (6).

is not based on his wilful misconduct but on some irregularity in the air waybill. When wilful misconduct is involved, a plea of contributory negligence will generally fail, either because the contributory negligence of the shipper will be deemed 'absorbed' by the more serious misconduct of the carrier (continental law), or because of the fact that the carrier had 'the last clear chance' to avoid the damage (common law). Of course, the fact of a wrong impression having been created as to the real (high) value of the goods, may characterize as simple negligence an act or omission of the carrier which otherwise would have amounted to wilful misconduct.

§ 3. WRONGFUL TAKING OF AIRCRAFT (ROME CONVENTION, 1952)

285. Article 12 (2) of the Rome Convention, 1952 provides: 'If a person wrongfully takes and makes use of an aircraft without the consent of the person entitled to use it, his liability shall be unlimited'. It was felt that the unlawful user, the 'Schwarzflieger' as he is called in Germany, should not benefit from the limits of liability. In earlier drafts the circle of persons thus deprived of the protection of the limitation of liability was much broader, but at the Mexico Session an English proposal restricted the circle to its present scope [1]). It has been argued with much ground that to the man on the surface whose property is damaged it makes little difference whether the aircraft was being used by someone entitled to its use or not, and that the penalty to be imposed on such unlawful use should better be left to criminal law, but proposals to that effect were twice rejected by a large majority [2]). According to Article 2, the user of the aircraft is the person liable as operator. According to Article 2 (2) (b) he shall be considered to be making use of (the) aircraft when he is using it personally or when his servants or agents are using the aircraft in the course of their employment, whether or not within the scope of their authority. The person who entrusts the use of the aircraft to another for a period of not

285. [1]) Art. 9 (2) of the Taormina Draft. See Mexico Session (1951) p. 178, and the long discussion at Rome, I, 94 sq. and 107 sq. on a French proposal to extend the scope of the provision to any *mala fide* unlawful users.

[2]) Mexico Session (1951) 180, R.C. 1952, I, 99 and 108.

more than fourteen days is jointly and severally liable with the latter (Article 3). There can be no doubt that the thief and the 'joyrider' will be liable under the Convention as operator for the damages they cause with the aircraft. According to Article 12 (2) their liability will be unlimited. As has been discussed with respect to the first paragraph of Article 12, unlimited liability does not mean that the person liable cannot deny his liability under Article 1 (1) as far as indirect consequences are concerned.

It was the clearly expressed intention of the drafters that mere unlawful use would not be sufficient. There should also be wrongful taking. The lessee who would continue to fly an aircraft after expiry date of the lease does not fall within the scope of Article 12, irrespective of his good faith. Similarly a servant of the owner, who as a pilot would always have access to the aircraft, could not be held guilty of wrongful taking if it could be proven that he would have flown without the consent of his master. The answer becomes more doubtful if the pilot would have taken the aircraft in his own time outside the course of his employment. All will depend upon the circumstances of the case. But from the discussion at the Rome Conference it is clear that Article 12 (2) was only meant to prevent a person guilty of criminal conduct in using the aircraft from benefiting from the limits of the Convention.

286. It is to be observed that, where the applicable national law – which generally will be the *lex loci delicti* – would impose vicarious liability on a person for the 'joyflying' committed by another, the latter's unlimited liability under the Convention might be held to result into unlimited liability for the person vicariously liable. Thus the owner of a hangar or of a repair place for private aircraft might be held liable for a joyflight undertaken by one of his employees with the aircraft of a customer. If there had been wrongful taking by that employee, the employer might be held liable without limitation for damages caused by the aircraft in countries which are liberal in assuming sufficient connection between the act of an employee and the course of his employment [1].

---

286. [1]) See No. 206.

Chapter VIII

DISTRIBUTION OF LIMIT IN CASE OF PLURALITY OF CLAIMANTS

§ 1. INTRODUCTORY REMARKS

287. Under both the Warsaw and the Rome Conventions the problem can arise as to what part of the limited amount of the carrier's or operator's liability should be awarded to each of the various claimants whose claims result from an occurrence to which one limit applies. The question has received more attention in connection with the Rome Conventions, not so much because it will more frequently arise, but rather because, with the limit per aircraft, the possibility of more than one person suffering damages and claiming compensation, without any relationship existing between such persons, is more obvious in the event of surface damage. In view of the greater frequency of claims under the Warsaw Convention, and of claims which exceed the limits, the problem with respect to that Convention is perhaps of greater practical interest.

The two major aspects of the question are:

(1) how is the amount of the limit to be distributed among the various people entitled to compensation?

(2) how can it be avoided that the limit will be exceeded, if various claimants are going to sue the carrier or operator before different courts, perhaps even in different countries?

The Warsaw Convention does not contain an answer to either of these questions, the two Rome Conventions deal with both.

288. Before discussing these two questions, a preliminary observation must be made, which in fact is closely connected with the two problems stated above. Should the available amount of the limit be distributed over the existing claim rights, or only over the claims actually lodged against the carrier or operator to the extent they are justified? Under the first alternative the carrier or operator could invoke the concurring rights of any other persons, even if they were not to exercise their right, in reduction of the claims brought by the plaintiffs. Under the second alternative, only such rights as are actually exercised can be taken into account for the distribution of the available amount.

Article 9 of the Rome Convention, 1933 provides that 'the right' of each person suffering damage shall be reduced proportionately [1]), which is in conformity with the first solution. The Rome Convention of 1952 speaks in Article 14 of 'the claims established'. The French and Spanish texts have, 'indemnités fixées' and 'indemnizaciones fijadas' respectively, which does not seem to be exactly the same as '*claims* established'. All the way through this Article the English text speaks of 'claims' and the French and Spanish texts of 'indemnités or 'indemnizaciones' [2]). Whereas the English text offers an argument for the second solution, according to which only actual claims have to be taken into account, that argument fails as far as the equally binding French and Spanish texts are concerned: under the first alternative the court would also have to establish the indemnities to which the non-claiming parties are entitled.

Meanwhile, the problem is not too important for the Rome Conventions, in view of the rule that persons claiming after six months will only be 'entitled to compensation out of the amount for which the operator remains liable after all claims made within that period have been met in full' [3]). Such a provision does not occur, however, in the Warsaw Convention, and it is not clear whether the carrier may invoke the rights to compensation of

---

288. [1]) The authentic French text has: 'il y a lieu de procéder à la réduction proportionnelle *du droit* de chacun' etc. The English Government translation has rendered this into: '*the compensation due to each* of such persons shall be reduced etc.'

[2]) Except that, without any apparent reason, at the end of the first sentence of para. (b) the word 'claims' has been translated into French 'dommages' and Spanish' 'creditos'. Comp. Art. 19 where 'claim' has first been rendered into 'demande en réparation' and 'reclamación', and later on in the Article into 'demandes' and 'demandas'.

[3]) Art. 19 of the Convention of 1952, and Art. 10 (2) of the Convention of 1933.

dependants of a killed passenger who have not, or have not yet, themselves claimed, in order to reduce the part of the claiming parties. The Second Schedule of the English Carriage by Air Act, 1932 provides in paragraph (4) that 'the Court [...] may at any stage of the proceedings make any such order as appears to the Court to be just and equitable in view of [...] any *proceedings which have been, or are likely to be, commenced* outside the United Kingdom in respect of the death of the passenger in question' (italics added). This does not necessarily mean, however, that *for the purpose of determining the share* of the persons claiming damages, the Court could not take into account the rights of other persons outside England, unless such persons had commenced, or would be likely to commence, proceedings against the carrier. The quoted paragraph only states a rule of proceedings and does not say anything with respect to matters of substance such as the apportionment of the available amount [4]).

289. Two different points of view are possible: One can consider the moment or moments that the various claims arise, and hold that the amount of damages to which each person is entitled will be determined at that moment; in that view it would make no difference to the right of each claimant, whether or not the other claimants are going to exercise their rights. According to the other view, the only thing which the carrier or operator can demand is not to be obliged to pay more than the limit of his liability. It is believed that courts will avoid the extreme consequences of either points of view. If it is clear that one of the potential claimants is not going to exercise his right at all, the other claimants will probably be allowed to profit from such abstention, unless it was clearly intended to be for the benefit of the carrier or operator. But if one of the claimants reaches a settlement with the carrier on the basis of a moderately calculated claim, the other claimants who, though having suffered the same damages, would be less moderate in their claims, should not be allowed to invoke the relation between their claim and that of the person

---

288. [4]) Para. (3), which speaks of division 'between the persons *entitled*', especially when read in conjunction with para. (2), offers an indication that it is not essential for all persons to have lodged a claim in order to be taken into account for determining the shares attributable to the various claimants.

with whom the carrier had settled, in order to receive a greater share of the amount of the carrier's maximum liability. It will be up to the court to determine what would be a fair share to each of the persons having suffered damages, irrespective of the claims lodged by them.

§ 2. DISTRIBUTION OF AMOUNT OF LIMIT AMONGST VARIOUS CLAIMANTS

290. In deciding who the persons entitled to damages are and what the respective shares they may claim, it is immaterial where such persons are living and where they might start legal proceedings. Such a decision therefore will require a choice of the applicable law: If there were to exist a complete harmony in the choice of law rules of the various countries, and if the different courts could be trusted always to apply the rules of the applicable national law in the same manner, the carrier or operator would be safe from the risk that his total liability – arising from judgments delivered by different courts – could exceed the amount of the limit. Actually, of course, no such harmony in choice of law rules and in the manner courts apply the various rules of national laws, does exist. The result may be that one court, on the basis of its own choice of law rules, arrives at a different distribution than the court of another country where the carrier is sued by another claimant, with the result that the sum of the amounts awarded by both courts will be more (or less) than the limit. In order to avoid such a situation, the courts, to the extent their rules of procedure allow them, should try to cooperate as much as possible by staying the proceedings, in case an earlier action has been started in a different court.

291. Who are the various persons entitled to compensation?

In the case of death of passengers or of persons on the surface, claims may be brought by the following persons: the estate or the heirs claiming as such, dependants who used to be, or were entitled to be supported by the deceased, or who suffered grief because of his death, if the applicable law allows recovery of such damage [1]). Most laws appear to refuse an action to insurers who,

291. [1]) Comp. No. 112.

because of the accidental death of the killed passenger, have to pay the amount insured, but in the case of workmen's compensation the insurance carrier is often, if not generally, given some action against the person liable, whether by way of subrogation or otherwise. As a rule no action is given to the employer because of the loss of his employee, but in some cases certain employers are allowed to claim compensation for the pension they must start paying at an earlier date than if no accident had occurred.

292. In case a passenger or a person on the ground suffers non-fatal injuries, the circle of persons entitled to claim compensation is generally more limited. In the Netherlands only the person injured will have an action [1]). At common law the husband is given an action for loss of consortium in case of a non-fatal accident to his wife [2]), and the employer has a right of action for the loss of services of his injured employee [3]). French courts, though not inclined to limit the circle of persons who may claim damages in case of fatal accidents, have only in recent years, and in exceptional circumstances, awarded damages for the grief suffered because of serious non-fatal injuries to another person than the one claiming damages [4]).

293. In case of loss of or damage to baggage, the person entitled to claim damages, besides the passenger, is the party who concluded the contract of carriage with the carrier, if the contract was not concluded by the passenger himself, and the owner of the goods contained in the baggage, but the latter cannot claim as such under the contract of carriage, and must therefore prove the carrier's negligence [1]). Though Article 24 does not

292 [1]) Art. 1407 B.W., as construed by the Hoge Raad 2.4.1936, N.J. 1936 No. 752.

[2]) *Hyde* v. *Scyssor*. 1620, Cro. Jac. 538. See for American law Prosser (1941) pp. 938 sq.

[3]) See Prosser (1941), p. 991.

[4]) Cass. civ. 22.10.1946, D. 1947, 59. The *Chambre des Requêtes* in its decision of 22.12.1942, D. 1945, 99, had rejected such action. See also Ripert in D. 1948, Chron. 1.

293. [1]) Unless the passenger can be considered to have acted as the agent of the owner in having his baggage registered by the carrier. Comp. the French decisions mentioned in No. 119 (4) with respect to baggage of commercial travelers. See also *Marshall* v. *York, Newcastle* and *Berwick Ry. Co.* (1851) 21 L.J. (C.P.) 34, for the question of whether a passenger, whose ticket was bought by his employer, can claim damages for loss of his baggage.

provide with respect to baggage and goods – as it does with respect to passengers – that the indication ot the persons entitled to claim is not affected by the Convention, this does not seem to be sufficient ground for holding all persons other than the passenger – and the contract-party who is not himself the passenger – barred from claiming compensation for loss of baggage. The Convention does not contain any indication who is entitled to claim [2]), so that that point must be deemed governed by national law, subject to the conditions and limits set by the Convention.

294. As to loss of or damage to goods carried, it is not quite clear whether only the shipper and the consignee or even only one of them can bring a claim against the carrier. The Convention contains some express provisions with respect to the right to claim, so that it could be argued that with respect to goods only the person or persons indicated in the Convention can bring an action against the carrier. With respect to goods the argument *a contrario* which can be derived from the second paragraph of Article 24 in support of this view, therefore, has more value than when invoked in respect of baggage.

Unfortunately, the Convention fails to establish a clear and complete system as to the person or persons entitled to claim with respect to goods. Article 12 (4), which provides that the right of the shipper ceases at the moment that of the consignee begins in accordance with Article 13, speaks of the shipper's right of disposition over goods *in transitu*, but it does not deal with his right to claim in case of loss, damage or delay. According to Article 13 (3), 'if the carrier admits the loss of the goods, or if the goods have not arrived at the expiration of seven days after the date on which they ought to have arrived, the consignee is entitled to put into force against the carrier the rights which flow from the contract of carriage'. This provision does not say a word on the rights of the shipper [1]). Article 14 provides that 'the consignor and the consignee can enforce all the rights given

---

293. [2]) Though Art. 30 (3) of the Convention starts to speak both of baggage and goods, it goes on by only mentioning the shipper and consignee as entitled to claim damages. The English legislator has corrected that obvious omission by adding 'the passenger'. See also No. 119.

294. [1]) Nor does it speak of the case of damage to goods.

them by Article 12 and 13 respectively, each in his own name, whether he is acting in his own interest or in the interest of another'. Finally, Article 30 (3) provides, for the case of successive carriage, that the consignor will have a right of action against the first carrier, and the consignee who is entitled to delivery will have a right of action against the last carrier, and that each may, moreover, take action against the carrier who performed the carriage during which the loss, damage or delay took place. During the discussion at Warsaw on this provision the Swiss Delegate Pittard expressed the view that there are never two persons entitled to claim at the same time. The shipper would have the right to claim as long as the goods were not delivered. When the consignee has taken delivery, he has the right to claim, and the shipper does not have it any more. This system was said to be also the system of the continental 'droit commun' [2]).

This view was not contradicted by any of the other Delegates. It was in conformity with the principles adopted in the Berne Convention on railroad transportation, which was of great influence in the drafting of Articles 12 and those following [3]). The conclusion seems justified that the Warsaw Convention does not permit the consignor and consignee to claim at the same time, but that it attaches this right to the right of disposition, as far as the consignor is concerned, and to the right to take delivery as far the consignee is concerned [4]). If one adopts this view, a question of apportioning the amount of the limit between various claimants will not arise under the Convention with respect to the carrier's liability for goods. The only possibility of concurrent claims against one carrier would be that of a recourse claim by a person against whom the shipper or consignee would also have brought an action.

295. As to the global limitation of liability under the Rome Conventions, the possibility of concurring claimants is obvious and it is of little sense to enumerate the various cumulations of claims which may arise.

---

294. [2]) W.C., pp. 87/88.

[3]) Art. 41. Comp. Goedhuis (1937) p. 182.

[4]) Comp. No. 119. See also W.C., pp. 79 sq. (the only case of plurality of claimants envisaged by the delegates was that of death of passengers).

296. As a general principle, the available amounts of the limits of liability will be distributed pro rata among the claimants. The Rome Conventions contain express provisions to that effect [1]), but there can be no doubt that the same rule applies to the limits of the Warsaw Convention. A major exception to this rule is, however, provided by the Rome Convention of 1952: 'If the claims are both in respect of loss of life or personal injury and in respect of damage to property, one half of the total sum distributable shall be appropriated preferentially to meet claims in respect of loss of life and personal injury and, if insufficient, shall be distributed proportionately between the claims concerned. The remainder of the total sum distributable shall be distributed proportionately among the claims in respect of damage to property and the portion not already covered of the claims in respect of loss of life and personal injury' [2]).

297. A second exception is offered by the provision contained in both Rome Conventions (Articles 10 and 19 respectively) to the effect that claims, which have not been reported to the operator within six months after the date of the accident, will be satisfied only after all claims brought within that period have been met. This preference comes even before the preference of personal accident claims over property damage claims under the Convention of 1952. If more than one claimant should fail to give notice within the 6 months period, the preference of personal accidents claims laid down in Article 14 of the Convention of 1952 would remain applicable to the apportionment of the undistributed part of the limit, in such a way that these claims

---

296. [1]) Art. 9 (1933) and 14 (1952) respectively.

[2]) Art. 14 (b).

Art. 8 (3) of the Convention of 1933 is based on a different principle, by providing that one third of the limit shall be appropriated to compensation for property damage, and two thirds to compensation for death or personal injuries. Comp. Art. 7 of the Brussels Convention of 1924 for the limitation of the liability of shipowners, which appropriates an amount of £ 8 per ton exclusively for death or injury claims, the unsatisfied parts of these claims sharing together with all other claims in the additional limit based on the value of the ship (with a maximum of £ 7 per ton). A similar system is followed in the **English** Merchant Shipping Act, 1894, Sec. 503. The system adopted by the **American** legislator (U.S. Code, Sec. 46, par. 183, as amended in 1935 and 1936), is somewhat different in that it first distributes the general limit amongst all claims, including death and injury claims; thereafter, an additional amount of $ 60 per ton of the ship is distributed amongst the latter claims, to the extent they were not satisfied under the first distribution. Comp. Robinson (1939) § 123.

would be first satisfied out of the remainder, until the amounts awarded on all personal accident claims (including both the timely notified claims and the claims of which notice was given after six months) would total half the amount of the available limit per aircraft. But the amounts to be paid for one person killed or injured should never exceed the 200,000 or 500,000 francs limit per person. If a dependant of a killed person would bring a claim after the 6 months period together with some late property damage claims from other claimants – a large portion of the available limit per person having been awarded already under the first distribution to other relatives of the victim – it is believed that he will only be entitled to share in the undistributed part of the global limit per aircraft on the basis of the amount of the difference between the limit per person and the amounts already paid in the first distribution, not on the basis of that part of the limit per person to which he would have been entitled if he had brought his claim in time, and still less on the basis of his full claim.

298. Apart from the preferential treatment of certain claims expressly provided by the Rome Conventions, it is possible that the national law which determines who may claim and how much gives a preference to one of these claims over the other. Only with respect to the distribution of the global limit per aircraft would such preferential treatment seem forbidden by the express provisions of the Rome Conventions which require reduction of the claims 'in proportion of their amounts'. But the Warsaw Convention does not contain such a requirement, nor do the Rome Conventions as far as the limit per person killed or injured is concerned. Nothing, therefore, would seem to prevent a national legislator from deciding that, in the distribution of the limit per passenger or person on the surface, certain claims will have a preference over others, in the same way that the national legislators are left free to establish which persons will have a claim at all, and for what amounts. Whether the legislator has intended to give a preferential treatment to certain claims, may not always be easy to determine [1]).

---

298. [1]) The question should be distinguished, of course, from that of establishing the succession in which various dependants may claim damages. If a certain dependant

299. The question of recourse claims concurring with original claims needs some special attention. To the extent that such actions are purely delictual, in the form of contribution between joint tortfeasors, the problem is probably not different from those arising in any case of concurring claims. But in the majority of situations the recourse actions will have some contractual foundation. Thus the recourse action of an employee or agent often, if not generally, will have to be based on the contract of employment or agency [1]); recourse actions from ground handling companies, airport authorities or aircraft manufacturers often arise from some indemnity agreement in existence between such agencies and the carrier or operator. In an earlier Chapter the question was discussed whether contractual recourse actions fall within the scope of the limitation provisions of the Conventions. With respect to the Warsaw Convention the conclusion was that they do [2]), whereas Article 25 of the Rome Convention 1952 probably takes them out of the sphere of the Convention [3]). An intermediary situation exists under the Rome Convention 1933, which, pursuant to Article 22, would appear not to apply to recourse actions based on contracts of carriage or of employment with the person against whom recourse is taken [4]).

But it has also been pointed out that nothing prevents the parties to a contract from setting aside the limits of liability which otherwise would apply to claims arising out of the contract, including recourse claims. It will be a matter of interpretation of the contract concerned whether the parties should be deemed to have intended to do so. In case of express indemnity or hold harmless agreements such intention generally may be inferred.

Supposing a contractual recourse claim arises which was intended by the parties not to be limited by the limits of the Convention, should such recourse claim be taken into account in determining the shares to be apportioned to the other claimants? In fact, the problem is not limited to recourse claims, though, as

---

is said to have a right to claim before certain other dependant, there is not a situation of concurring claims, since the one claim suppresses the other.

299. [1]) See Nos. 89 and 90.
[2]) See No. 92.
[3]) See No. 100.
[4]) See No. 100.

far as the Warsaw Convention is concerned, it will especially arise with such claims. But under the Rome Convention, 1933 it is quite possible that two airlines could agree to hold each other harmless from damages inflicted to each other's property, which agreement might comprise surface damage caused by aircraft in flight.

It is believed that contractual recourse claims (or under the Rome Convention 1933, any contractual claim) should only be taken into consideration in determining the amounts to be received by the other claimants, whenever a claim would also have existed without a contract. Otherwise it would be possible for the carrier or operator to reduce the compensation available for his potential victims by agreeing to heavy contractual liabilities. But if his liability would also exist without a contract there would be no reason to attach a further effect to the contract than that of setting aside the limitation of the carrier's or operator's liability *towards the other party to the contract*. Such a contract certainly is never meant to deprive a party from his share in the amount to which the carrier's or operator's liability is limited by the Conventions.

§ 3. APPLICATION OF LIMITS IN CASE OF CLAIMS BEING BROUGHT BEFORE MORE THAN ONE COURT

300. We have now arrived at the second question: How can it be avoided that the limit be exceeded, if various claimants are going to sue the carrier or operator before different courts? The danger that a carrier or operator may be held liable towards various claimants by different courts to an amount in excess of the limits provided by the Convention has not only been appreciated in relation to the Rome Conventions, though it is more obvious there, and has received more attention. The Draft of a combined Convention on carrier's liability and on air waybills submitted to the third Session of CITEJA at Madrid (1928) contained a provision which read (in French): 'In case of death all actions must be brought before the first court regularly seized of the matter, and the judgment rendered shall be binding in all Contracting States'. The English Delegate was opposed to such a general rule concerning the binding effect of judgments, and only the first half of the provision was retained. At the Warsaw Conference the problem again was the subject of extensive discussions. The German Delegate correctly pointed out that, by taking away the second half of the provision concerning the binding effect of judgments, one would seriously weaken the position of the claimants, who would be compelled to go to the court first seized of the case without any guarantee that a judgment by that court could be executed in the country where the carrier would have assets. The result of the discussion was that, following a suggestion of Ripert, the entire provision was deleted. Ripert made the observation that in practice the cases of dependants of a killed passenger bringing actions in different countries would be rare, and that it would be dangerous to adopt general rules in order to cover these exceptional situations [1]). It is a fact that the absence of rules as to the distribution of the maximum amount of the carrier's liability amongst various claimants has caused less difficulties than one might have expected.

301. The risk of different claimants bringing several actions before different courts with respect to one accident is probably greater under the Rome Conventions than under the Warsaw Convention, in view of the fact that under the system of global limitation of liability of the Rome Conventions no relationship has to exist between the different people suffering damages. Yet, even with respect to the Rome Conventions, it may be doubted whether the importance of the problem has not been exaggerated, for nearly always the victims will be domiciled in the country where the accident occurs and will prefer to bring their action there. In practice, the danger of various claims being brought before courts of various countries may even be smaller in the case of surface damage than in the case of killed passengers. Persons travelling by air are often people with international ties, and the probability of their leaving behind dependants domiciled in different countries would seem greater than the chance that John Smith, killed in his garden by a falling aircraft, will turn out to have relatives in foreign countries supported by him.

---

300. [1]) W.C., pp. 81 and 83/84.

However that may be, the difficulties arising from plurality of claimants have received more attention in connection with the Rome Conventions, especially that of 1952, than in connection with the Warsaw Convention. At the Conference of 1933 the Netherlands Delegation submitted a proposal to deal with that problem [1]). But the elaborate provisions proposed were not adopted by the Conference for the reason that they were thought to be of a procedural nature and that, therefore, they would fall outside the scope of the Convention [2]). Similar objections had been raised already at Warsaw against the proposals brought forward at that Conference.

But when, after the Second World War, a new Convention on surface damage became a subject of discussion, the necessity of express provisions to avoid that the operator would have to pay more than the limit of his liability in the event of more than one claim being adjudicated, appears to have been foremost in the minds of those who took part in the framing of the new Convention: perhaps too much so. When reading the discussions of the Mexico Session (1951) of the Legal Committee of ICAO, and of the Diplomatic Conference of 1952, one cannot help feeling that the practical importance of the problem has been exaggerated by a number of Delegates. It has been rightly pointed out that in the large majority of cases the limitation of the operator's liability on the basis of the weight of his aircraft will not come into play [3]).

302. Though most often claims will be settled and not adjudicated, the only legal problem to solve is that arising when more than one judgment is rendered for claims to which one and the same limit applies. The judgments may be separated in time only, being rendered by one and the same court. They may also be rendered by different courts, and by courts of different countries.

With respect to the possibility of subsequent judgments, the two Rome Conventions contain an incomplete solution, providing that claims which have been notified to the operator within

---

301. [1]) R.C. 1933, II pp. 92/93.
[2]) R.C. 1933, I, pp. 164 sq.
[3]) R.C. 1952, I, p. 194.

six months of the accident shall be met before claims which are reported afterwards. The solution is incomplete only in so far as it does not protect the operator in the situation where two or more claims are brought successively after the six month's period. To be absolutely safe, the operator should wait till the two years period of the Convention of 1933, or the three years period of the Convention of 1952, have elapsed, to the detriment of the victims.

303. But even if one of the claims has been brought within the 6 months period and the others thereafter, there is nothing which safeguards the operator against the court holding the compensation awarded to the first claimant to exceed the amount of damages to which he was entitled. True, Article 10 of the Convention of 1933 provides that the claimants after six months 'shall only be able to exercise their rights against the amount which has not been distributed', and Article 19 of the Convention of 1952 speaks of 'the amount for which the operator remains liable after all claims made within that period have been met in full'. These provisions could be taken literally to mean that any payment of claims brought within the six months period, irrespective of whether and to what extent claimants were legally entitled to the compensation received, could be invoked against later claimants. But that can hardly be the meaning of the quoted phrases, because it would be an invitation to collusion. With such interpretation even a settlement between the operator and the early claimant would be sufficient, since it is difficult to read into the provisions the requirement that the amount of compensation must have been fixed by court or jury.

304. With respect to the possibility of different courts being seized of claims falling under one limit of liability, the Convention of 1952 contains some elaborate provisions. If the different courts are all situated in the country where the accident occurred, Article 20 (3) provides that 'each Contracting State shall so far as possible ensure that all actions arising from a single incident [. . .] are consolidated for disposal in a single proceeding before the same court'. According to paragraph 2, 'each Contracting State shall take all necessary measures to ensure that the defendant and all other parties interested are notified of any proceedings concerning them and have a fair and adequate opportunity to defend their interests'.

305. But the most serious problem does not arise if actions are brought before different courts of one country, but if the courts of different countries are seized of claims to which one limit of liability applies. The Convention of 1952 has solved that problem by simply forbidding claimants to sue the operator in an other country than the country where the damage occurred. That is going very far in protecting the operator. Whilst otherwise the victim would normally be allowed to elect the court of a country where the defendant would have sufficient assets, that right is taken away from him by the Convention of 1952. Under Article 16 of the Convention of 1933 the claimant has the choice between the courts of the defendant's ordinary place of residence, and the court of the place where the damage was caused.

The necessary consequence of the single forum solution adopted in 1952 is to grant executory effect to the judgment of the court of the *locus delicti* in all other Contracting States. As has been discussed above, this was the reason why the Warsaw Conference finally decided to refrain from dealing with the whole problem. Execution of foreign judgments is a subject so beset with difficulties that an attempt to adopt the principle in an international convention, and one which is open to all countries which want to adhere to it [1]), seriously endangers its wide ratification. It may be questioned whether the importance of protecting the operator against the possibility of the total amount of claims brought before different courts exceeding the limit of his liability, warrants the inclusion in the Convention of provisions concerning the execution of foreign judgments. A less stringent rule – which certainly leaves more loopholes – such as the one contained in Article 11 of the Convention of 1933, offered perhaps a more prudent approach to the problem. That Article provides: 'If several injured parties take proceedings under the provisions of the preceding Articles and of Article 16 before courts situated in

---

305. [1]) This difference with the Berne Railroad Conventions (see Art. 59), which do provide for the execution of foreign judgments rendered in one of the Contracting States (Art. 55), has been emphasized at various occasions. See i.a. W.C., p. 80.

different countries, the defendant may, before each of such courts, give evidence of the total amount of the claims and liabilities, in order to avoid that the limits of his liability be exceeded'.

306. Once the single forum solution is adopted, and the consequence accepted that judgments delivered by that jurisdiction should be executed in the other countries, it must be determined, which exceptions should be allowed to the Contracting States with respect to their obligation to execute the foreign judgment of the *forum loci delicti*. By keeping these exceptions restricted to certain formal requirements, one would make the Convention inacceptable for a large number of countries. In view of the varying standards of justice, many countries would find it difficult to bind themselves in advance to execute the judgment delivered anywhere in the world by any country deciding to adhere to the Convention. But if one inserts a broad escape clause permitting the countries to refuse execution if the foreign judgment is found to be against their public policy, the victims of aircraft accidents are exposed to refusal of execution in the country where the operator has executable assets, after having been forbidden to sue the operator directly in that country.

The Conference of 1952 has chosen the last alternative. But the claimant who finds his request for an exequatur rejected in the country where he seeks execution, is given the opportunity to bring a new suit in that country. Though this takes away the extreme hardship for the victim of not being allowed to sue the operator in the latter's country, it still means that, in addition to the proceedings before the courts in his own country, he will have to go through the proceedings necessary for getting exequatur and through a full scale law suit in the country where the operator has assets.

307. It would seem that the interests of the victims have been somewhat sacrificed to those of the operators, and this even in the majority of cases where no actual interest of the operator is involved, i.e. in the cases where there is no real danger that the limits of his liability will be exceeded by the total amount of claims. An attempt to restrict the effect of the single forum solution to the situations where such possibility would actually exist was rejected on the ground that one never can say with certainty that no claims will be brought in excess of the limits [1]). Theoretically that may be true, practically it certainly is not. But some of the Delegates at the Rome Conference of 1952 have been fascinated so much by theoretical possibilities, that they have neglected the normal situations to which the Convention will be applied.

308. The preceding observations on the system adopted in the Convention of 1952 have been of a general nature. It is time now to give a more detailed comment on the elaborate provisions of Article 20.

As has been said before, paragraph 1 states the single forum principle by providing that actions may only be brought before the courts of the Contracting States where the damage occurred. The freak situation of damage occurring in more than one state can better be left to the ingeniousness of the annotators when such case would arise. The paragraph contains an important exception in that it allows one or more claimants to agree with one or more defendants to having the claim decided by the court of another Contracting State. The exception was first rejected by a solid majority who held it to be a violation of the sacred single forum principle [1]). In a later stage there was one of these curious changes of mood, such as sometimes occur at international conferences, and the exception was adopted [2]). This time the opponents, or at least a sufficient number of them, felt satisfied by the restriction, that 'no such proceeding [in an other Contracting State] shall have the effect of prejudicing in any way the rights of persons who bring actions in the State where the damage occurred'. This restriction does not mean that any payment made as a consequence of such proceedings should be ignored by the courts of the State where the damage occurred, but only that these courts are not bound by decisions of courts in other Contracting States to which parties, by common agreement, would have submitted their case. It is believed that

307. [1]) R.C. 1952, I, p. 178.

308. [1]) R.C. 1952, I, p. 195.
[2]) R.C. 1952, I, p. 485.

even without these express words the courts of the *locus delicti* would not be bound by such foreign decisions, since there is nothing in the Convention which binds them even to decisions rendered by other courts of the place where the damage occurred. It is true that according to paragraph 3 the states must *so far as possible* ensure that actions arising from a single incident are consolidated in a single proceeding before the same court. But that will not always be possible, e.g. if a new claim is lodged after an earlier claim had already been finally disposed of.

309. The second 'exception', to the effect that 'the parties may also agree to submit disputes to arbitration in any Contracting State', actually is not an exception at all. The addition of this rather meaningless sentence is the final result of a more ambitious proposal by the Brazilian Delegation, which would have obliged the Contracting States to ensure execution, in accordance with the provisions of their national laws, of arbitral awards given in any Contracting State [1]). As there is nothing in the Convention which prevents parties from submitting their disputes to arbitration – they are even free to settle their disputes without arbitration – the sentence must probably be considered as the meaningless remnant of the projected but not adopted provision on arbitration. Certainly no special significance should be attached to the limitation to 'arbitration *in any Contracting State*' [2]).

310. Paragraphs 4 to 12 (inclusive) of Article 20 deal with the execution in other Contracting States of judgments rendered in the country where the damage occurred. According to Paragraph 4, the Contracting State where the operator (the text speaks more accurately of 'the judgment debtor') has his residence or principal place of business, or, if the assets available in that State and in the State where the judgment was pronounced are insufficient, any other Contracting State where the operator has assets, must grant execution of any final judgment rendered in the Contracting State where the damage occurred.

311. Execution may only be refused in any one of the following cases:

---

309. [1]) See R.C. 1952, II, pp. 153 and 217, and I, pp. 210 sq. and 404 sq.
[2]) R.C. 1952, II, p. 217.

(1) when the judgment was given by default and the defendant did not acquire knowledge of the proceedings in sufficient time to act upon it;

(2) when defendant was not given a fair and adequate opportunity to defend his interests;

(3) when the judgment is in respect of a cause of action which had already, as between the same parties, formed the subject of a judgment or an arbitral award which, under the law of the State where execution is sought, is recognized as final and conclusive;

(4) when the judgment has been obtained by fraud of any of the parties;

(5) when the right to enforce the judgment is not vested in the person by whom the application for execution is made;

(6) when the judgment is contrary to the public policy of the State in which execution is requested. (Paragraphs 5 and 7)

The exeptions under (4) and (6) open broad possibilities to escape the necessity of enforcing a foreign judgment which, in the country where execution is sought, would be considered injust. But – as it was said before – without such escape clauses the Convention would have been inacceptable to a large number of countries. It is to be observed that it is sufficient if the judgment itself is considered contrary to the public policy, which appears to go one step further than to require that *its enforcement* in the State where execution is sought would be contrary to the public policy of that State.

312. Though this 'exception' is not mentioned (no doubt because it was considered too obvious), execution may also be refused if the judgment debt has been satisfied. Difficulties might arise in this connection when the defendant invokes compensation or a final settlement including i.a. the judgment debt. Also in case of a binding agreement of the creditors, according to which the judgment creditor would only receive part of the award, it could be doubted whether execution can be refused with respect to the unsatisfied part of the claim.

313. But a more notable omission in the list of exeptions is that of the judgment being in excess of the applicable limit.

Only with respect to claims brought within the six months period of Article 19, paragraph 9 of Article 20 provides that execution *shall* not be granted if the aggregate of such judgments exceeds the applicable limit of liability. This provision does not deal with claims brought after the six months period, nor does it cover at all the situation where a judgment has been rendered on only one claim in excess of the applicable limit.

The analogous provision of the Mexico Draft (paragraph 8 of Article 20) provided generally that 'the court applied to [...] shall not be obliged to execute *judgments* exceeding in aggregate the relevant limit until they have been reduced in accordance with Article 14 by the courts of the State where the actions were brought'. The Drafting Committee at the Rome Conference, apparently without any instruction from the Conference on that point [1]), changed 'judgments' into 'such judgments' [2]), thereby referring to the judgments on actions filed within the time limit of Article 19, mentioned earlier in the paragraph. For the third reading the Drafting Committee then split the paragraph into three subparagraphs, and, accepting the full consequence of the imprudently added word 'such', limited the scope of the last subparagraph expressly to 'the case of actions brought in the State where the damage occurred by those persons who have complied with the time limit referred to in Article 19'. This text was adopted without further discussion by a tired Conference [3]).

The result of this unfortunate drafting episode seems to be that execution of judgments in excess of the limits of liability on claims filed after the six months period can only be refused on the ground that such judgments would be against the public policy of the State where execution is asked. But if the municipal law of that State would itself impose unlimited liability on operators of aircraft, the validity of that argument could be denied with good reason. Fortunately the Courts, sometimes, have their reasons, which Reason does not know about.

314. According to the last words of paragraph 9, the Courts

313. [1]) R.C. 1952, I. pp. 252/253.
[2]) R.C. 1952, II. p. 233.
[3]) R.C. 1952, I, p. 540.

must refuse execution 'until such judgments [rendered in the State where the damage occurred] have been reduced in accordance with Article 14'. According to the Mexico Draft the scaling down should be left to the State where the actions were brought. The relevant words were omitted at the instance of the Australian Delegate because 'nowhere in the Convention was an obligation cast on the court of the country where the damage was caused to scale down the claims'. He suggested that a provision to that effect be added to one of the earlier paragraphs of the Article [1]). The suggestion was referred to the Drafting Committee which, for unknown reasons, failed to take action on it. The (unintended?) result appears to be, that now the Court applied to for execution may also itself reduce the judgment amounts in accordance with Article 14, which may be a more practical solution.

315. According to the first subparagraph of Article 20 (9) 'the court to which application for execution is made shall refuse execution of any judgment rendered by a court of a State other than that in which the damage occurred until all the judgments rendered in that State have been satisfied' [1]). The provision was added to take care of the possibility opened in paragraph 1, of some claimants and defendants agreeing to have their case decided by a court of an other country than the one where the damage occurred [2]). It does not cover the not improbable situation that the court elected by the parties would be situated in the country in which other claimants would try to obtain execution of the judgments rendered in the State of the accident. It is believed that also in such a case the judgment rendered outside the country where the damage occurred can not be invoked as a reason to refuse execution of judgments rendered *in* that country

314. [1]) R.C. 1952, I, p. 252.

315. [1]) The French and Spanish texts have for the English word 'satisfied': 'exécutés' and 'ejecutadas' respectively.
The English text seems more correct. The paragraph starts with the introductory words 'Notwithstanding the provisions of paragraph 4 of this Article'. As para. 4 deals with judgments rendered in the country where the damage occurred and para. 9 with judgments rendered in other countries, the phrase is superfluous and meaningless.
[2]) R.C. 1952, I, pp. 488/489.

except if refusal can be based on one of the exceptions of paragraphs 5 (especially sub c) or 7 (public policy).

316. States which would have bound themselves by bilateral or multilateral treaties with other states to execute the judgments of these other States, may find themselves put in a difficult position by ratifying the Convention of 1952, if such other State or States would not become a Party to the Convention. If a person having suffered surface damage would secure a judgment against the operator in one of these latter states, and would ask its execution in the State which would have ratified the Convention, this State might be bound under the bilateral treaty to execute the judgment, whereas, under Article 20 of the Convention, it would have to refuse execution.

317. Paragraph 10 deals with the execution of judgments as far as legal costs are concerned. 'Payment of costs recoverable under the judgment shall also be enforceable'. But 'the court applied to for execution may, on the application of the judgment debtor, limit the amount of such costs to a sum equal to 10% of the amount for which the judgment is rendered enforceable'. This probably means only that the Convention imposes an obligation on the Contracting States to execute judgments as to legal costs up to 10% of the main amount of the judgment. For legal costs in excess thereof no obligation to grant execution exists, provided the judgment debtor has demanded that execution be refused. Nothing in the Convention prevents the claimant from having the judgment executed in the country where it was rendered for the legal costs in excess of 10%.

The question of the applicability of the limits of liability to legal costs has been discussed in No. 102.

ANNEX I

WARSAW CONVENTION

Original text

CONVENTION POUR L'UNIFICATION DE CERTAINES RÈGLES RELATIVES AU TRANSPORT AÉRIEN INTERNATIONAL

Signée à Varsovie le 12 octobre 1929

[Les Hautes Parties Contractantes ...]

Ayant reconnu l'utilité de régler d'une manière uniforme les conditions du transport aérien international en ce qui concerne les documents utilisés pour ce transport et la responsabilité du transporteur;

A cet effet ont nommé leurs Plénipotentiaires respectifs, lesquels, dûment autorisés, ont conclu et signé la Convention suivante:

CHAPITRE I

OBJET – DÉFINITIONS

ARTICLE 1ER

(1) La présente Convention s'applique à tout transport internatio-

English translation [1])

CONVENTION FOR THE UNIFICATION OF CERTAIN RULES RELATING TO INTERNATIONAL CARRIAGE BY AIR.

Signed at Warsaw, October 12, 1929

[The High Contracting Parties...]

Having recognized the advantage of regulating in a uniform manner the conditions of international carriage by air in respect of the documents to be used for such carriage and of the liability of the carrier, have nominated to this end their respective Plenipotentiaries, who, being thereto duly authorized, have concluded and signed the following Convention: –

CHAPTER I

SCOPE – DEFINITIONS

ARTICLE 1

(1) This Convention applies to all international carriage of persons,

[1] This Translation is based on the text of the First Schedule of the British Carriage by Air Act, 1932, subject to some changes, indicated in the footnotes, on points where the text of the British Act appears to have departed somewhat from a literal translation in order to make the text run more smoothly, or in order to clarify or correct apparent or assumed errors in the French text. Apart from some very minor differences, the wordings used in the Carriage by Air Act (abbreviated CAA) have been indicated in the footnotes.

nal de personnes, bagages ou marchandises, effectué par aéronef contre rémunération. Elle s'applique également aux transports gratuits effectués par aéronef par une entreprise de transports aériens.

(2) Est qualifié 'transport international', au sens de la présente Convention, tout transport dans lequel, d'après les stipulations des parties, le point de départ et le point de destination, qu'il y ait ou non interruption de transport ou transbordement, sont situés soit sur le territoire de deux Hautes Parties Contractantes, soit sur le territoire d'une seule Haute Partie Contractante, si une escale est prévue dans un territoire soumis à la souveraineté, à la suzeraineté, au mandat ou à l'autorité d'une autre Puissance même non Contractante. Le transport sans une telle escale entre les territoires soumis à la souveraineté, à la suzeraineté, au mandat ou à l'autorité de la même Haute Partie Contractante n'est pas considéré comme international au sens de la présente Convention.

(3) Le transport à exécuter par plusieurs transporteurs par air successifs est censé constituer pour l'application de cette Convention un transport unique lorsqu'il a été envisagé par les parties comme une seule opération, qu'il ait été conclu sous la forme d'un seul contrat ou d'une série de contrats et il ne perd pas son caractère international par le fait qu'un seul contrat ou une série de contrats doivent être exécutés intégralement dans un territoire soumis à la souveraineté, à la suzeraineté, au mandat ou à l'autorité d'une même Haute Partie Contractante.

luggage or goods performed by aircraft for reward. It applies equally to gratuitous carriage by aircraft performed by an air transport undertaking.

(2) For the purposes of this Convention the expression 'international carriage' means any carriage in which, according to the stipulations [1]) made by the parties, the place of departure and the place of destination, whether or not there be a break in the carriage or a transhipment, are situated either within the territories of two High Contracting Parties, or within the territory of a single High Contracting Party, if a stopping place has been contemplated [2]) within a territory subject to the sovereignty, suzerainty, mandate or authority of another Power, even though that Power is not a party to this Convention. A carriage without such a stopping place [3]) between territories subject to the sovereignty, suzerainty, mandate or authority of the same High Contracting Party is not deemed to be international for the purposes of this Convention.

(3) A carriage to be performed by several successive air carriers is deemed, for the purpose of this Convention, to be one single [4]) carriage, if it has been regarded by the parties as a single operation, whether it had been agreed upon under the form of a single contract or of a series of contracts, and it does not lose its international character merely because one contract or a series of contracts is to be performed entirely within a territory subject to the sovereignty, suzerainty, mandate or authority of the same High Contracting Party.

[1]) CAA: '*contract*'.
[2]) CAA: '*if there is an agreed* stopping place'. Comp. No. 49 (3).
[3]) CAA: 'an *agreed* stopping place'.
[4]) CAA: '*undivided*'.

ARTICLE 2

(1) La Convention s'applique aux transport effectués par l'Etat ou les autres personnes juridiques de droit public, dans les conditions prévues à l'article 1er.

(2) Sont exceptés de l'application de la présente Convention les transports effectués sous l'empire de conventions postales internationales.

CHAPITRE II

Titre de transport

SECTION 1. – BILLET DE PASSAGE

ARTICLE 3

(1) Dans le transport de voyageurs, le transporteur est tenu de délivrer un billet de passage qui doit contenir les mentions suivantes:

a) le lieu et la date de l'émission;

b) les points de départ et de destination;

c) les arrêts prévus, sous réserve de la faculté pour le transporteur de stipuler qu'il pourra les modifier en cas de nécessité et sans que cette modification puisse faire perdre au transport son caractère international;

d) le nom et l'adresse du ou des transporteurs;

e) l'indication que le transport est soumis au régime de la responsabilité établi par la présente Convention.

(2) L'absence, l'irrégularité ou la perte du billet n'affecte ni l'existence, ni la validité du contrat de transport, qui n'en sera pas moins soumis aux règles de la présente Convention. Toutefois si le transporteur accepte le voyageur

ARTICLE 2

(1) This Convention applies to carriage performed by the State or by other legal entities of public law [1]) provided it falls within the conditions laid down in Article 1.

(2) This Convention does not apply to carriage performed under the terms of any international postal Convention.

CHAPTER II

Documents of Carriage

SECTION 1. – PASSENGER TICKET

ARTICLE 3

(1) In the carriage of passengers the carrier must deliver a passenger ticket which shall contain the following particulars: –

(*a*) the place and date of issue;

(*b*) the places of departure and of destination;

(*c*) the stopping places as contemplated [2]), provided that the carrier may reserve the right to alter the stopping places in case of necessity, and that if he exercises that right, the alteration shall not have the effect of depriving the carriage of its international character;

(*d*) the name and address of the carrier or carriers;

(*e*) the indication [3]) that the carriage is subject to the system of [4]) liability established by this Convention.

(2) The absence, irregularity or loss of the passenger ticket does not affect the existence or the validity of the contract of carriage, which shall none the less be subject to the rules of this Convention. Nevertheless, if the carrier accepts

[1]) CAA: 'by *legally constituted* public *bodies*'.
[2]) CAA: '*agreed* stopping places'.
[3]) CAA: '*a statement*'.
[4]) CAA: '*rules relating to*'.

sans qu'il ait été délivré un billet de passage, il n'aura pas le droit de se prévaloir des dispositions de cette Convention qui excluent ou limitent sa responsabilité.

SECTION 2. – BULLETIN DE BAGAGES

ARTICLE 4

(1) Dans le transport de bagages, autres que les menus objets personnels dont le voyageur conserve la garde, le transporteur est tenu de délivrer un bulletin de bagages.

(2) Le bulletin de bagages est établi en deux exemplaires, l'un pour le voyageur, l'autre pour le transporteur.

(3) Il doit contenir les mentions suivantes:

a) le lieu et la date de l'émission;
b) les points de départ et de destination;
c) le nom et l'adresse du ou des transporteurs;
d) le numéro du billet de passage;
e) l'indication que la livraison des bagages est faite au porteur du bulletin;
f) le nombre et le poids des colis;
g) le montant de la valeur déclarée conformément à l'article 22, alinéa 2;
h) l'indication que le transport est soumis au régime de la responsabilité établi par la présente Convention.

(4) l'absence, l'irrégularité ou la perte du bulletin n'affecte ni l'existence, ni la validité du contrat de transport qui n'en sera pas moins soumis aux règles de la présente Convention. Toutefois si le transporteur accepte les bagages

the [1]) passenger without a passenger ticket having been delivered he shall not be entitled to avail himself of those provisions of this Convention which exclude or limit his liability.

SECTION 2. – LUGGAGE TICKET

ARTICLE 4

(1) In the carriage of luggage, other than small personal objects of which the passenger takes charge himself, the carrier must deliver a luggage ticket.

(2) The luggage ticket shall be made out in duplicate, one part for the passenger and the other part for the carrier.

(3) The luggage ticket shall contain the following particulars: –

(a) the place and date of issue;
(b) the places [2]) of departure and of destination;
(c) the name and address of the carrier or carriers;
(d) the number of the passenger ticket;
(e) the indication [3]) that delivery of the luggage will be made to the bearer of the luggage ticket;
(f) the number and weight of the packages;
(g) the amount of the value declared in accordance with Article 22 (2);
(h) the indication [4]) that the carriage is subject to the system of [5]) liability established by this Convention.

(4) The absence, irregularity or loss of the luggage ticket does not affect the existence or the validity of the contract of carriage, which shall none the less be subject to the rules of this Convention. Nevertheless, if the carrier accepts

[1]) CAA: '*a* passenger'.
[2]) CAA: '*place*'.
[3]) CAA: '*a statement*'.
[4]) CAA: '*a statement*'.
[5]) CAA: '*rules relating to*'.

sans qu'il ait été délivré un bulletin ou si le bulletin ne contient pas les mentions indiquées sous les lettres *d*), *f*), *h*), le transporteur n'aura pas le droit de se prévaloir des dispositions de cette Convention qui excluent ou limitent sa responsabilité.

SECTION 3. – LETTRE DE TRANSPORT AÉRIEN

ARTICLE 5

(1) Tout transporteur de marchandises a le droit de demander à l'expéditeur l'établissement et la remise d'un titre appelé 'lettre de transport aérien'; tout expéditeur a le droit de demander au transporteur l'acceptation de ce document.

(2) Toutefois, l'absence, l'irrégularité ou la perte de ce titre n'affecte ni l'existence, ni la validité du contrat de transport qui n'en sera pas moins soumis aux règles de la présente Convention, sous réserve des dispositions de l'article 9.

ARTICLE 6

(1) La lettre de transport aérien est établie par l'expéditeur en trois exemplaires originaux et remise avec la marchandise.

(2) Le premier exemplaire porte la mention 'pour le transporteur'; il est signé par l'expéditeur. Le deuxième exemplaire porte la mention 'pour le destinataire'; il est signé par l'expéditeur et le transporteur et il accompagne la marchandise. Le troisième exemplaire est signé par le transporteur et remis par lui à l'expéditeur après acceptation de la marchandise.

(3) La signature du transporteur doit être apposée dès l'acceptation de la marchandise.

(4) La signature du transporteur peut être remplacée par un timbre; celle de l'expéditeur peut être imprimée ou remplacée par un timbre.

luggage without a luggage ticket having been delivered, or if the luggage ticket does not contain the particulars set out at *d*), *f*) and *h*) above, the carrier shall not be entitled to avail himself of those provisions of the Convention which exclude or limit his liability.

SECTION 3. – AIR CONSIGNMENT NOTE

ARTICLE 5

(1) Every carrier of goods has the right to require the consignor to make out and hand over to him a document called an 'air consignment note'; every consignor has the right to require the carrier to accept this document.

(2) Nevertheless, the absence, irregularity or loss of this document does not affect the existence or the validity of the contract of carriage which shall, subject to the provisions of Article 9, be none the less governed by the rules of this Convention.

ARTICLE 6

(1) The air consignment note shall be made out by the consignor in three original parts and be handed over with the goods.

(2) The first part shall be marked 'for the carrier', and shall be signed by the consignor. The second part shall be marked 'for the consignee'; it shall be signed by the consignor and by the carrier and shall accompany the goods. The third part shall be signed by the carrier and handed by him to the consignor after the goods have been accepted.

(3) The carrier shall sign on acceptance of the goods.

(4) The signature of the carrier may be stamped; that of the consignor may be printed or stamped.

(5) Si, à la demande de l'expéditeur, le transporteur établit la lettre de transport aérien, il est considéré, jusqu'à preuve contraire, comme agissant pour le compte de l'expéditeur.

(5) If, at the request of the consignor, the carrier makes out the air consignment note, he shall be deemed, subject to proof to the contrary, to have done so on behalf of the consignor.

ARTICLE 7

Le transporteur de marchandises a le droit de demander à l'expéditeur l'établissement de lettres de transport aérien différentes lorsqu'il y a plusieurs colis.

ARTICLE 7

The carrier of goods has the right to require the consignor to make out separate consignment notes when there is more than one package.

ARTICLE 8

La lettre de transport aérien doit contenir les mentions suivantes:

a) le lieu où le document a été créé et la date à laquelle il a été établi;
b) les points de départ et de destination;
c) les arrêts prévus, sous réserve de la faculté, pour le transporteur, de stipuler qu'il pourra les modifier en cas de nécessité et sans que cette modification puisse faire perdre au transport son caractère international;
d) le nom et l'adresse de l'expéditeur;
e) le nom et l'adresse du premier transporteur;
f) le nom et l'adresse du destinataire, s'il y a lieu;
g) la nature de la marchandise;
h) le nombre, le mode d'emballage, les marques particulières ou les numéros des colis;
i) le poids, la quantité, le volume ou les dimensions de la marchandise;

ARTICLE 8

The air consignment note shall contain the following particulars: –

(*a*) the place and date of its exetion;
(*b*) the places [1]) of departure and of destination;
(*c*) the stopping places, as contemplated, [2]) provided that the carrier may reserve the right to alter the stopping places in case of necessity, and that if he exercises that right the alteration shall not have the effect of depriving the carriage of its international character;
(*d*) the name and address of the consignor;
(*e*) the name and address of the first carrier;
(*f*) the name and address of the consignee, if the case so requires;
(*g*) the nature of the goods;
(*h*) the number of the packages, the method of packing, [3]) the particular marks or numbers upon them;
(*i*) the weight, the quantity, the volume or the dimensions [4]) of the goods;

[1]) CAA: '*place*'.
[2]) CAA: '*agreed* stopping places'. Comp. No. 265.
[3]) CAA: '*and*'. See No. 268.
[4]) CAA: '*and* the volume or dimensions. See No. 269.'

j) l'état apparent de la marchandise et de l'emballage;

k) le prix du transport s'il est stipulé, la date et le lieu de paiement et la personne qui doit payer;

l) si l'envoi est fait contre remboursement, le prix des marchandises et, éventuellement, le montant des frais;

m) le montant de la valeur déclarée conformément à l'article 22, alinéa 2;

n) le nombre d'exemplaires de la lettre de transport aérien;

o) les documents transmis au transporteur pour accompagner la lettre de transport aérien;

p) le délai de transport et l'indication sommaire de la voie à suivre (via) s'ils ont été stipulés;

q) l'indication que le transport est soumis au régime de la responsabilité établi par la présente Convention.

ARTICLE 9

Si le transporteur accepte des marchandises sans qu'il ait été établi une lettre de transport aérien, ou si celle-ci ne contient pas toutes les mentions indiquées par l'article 8 *a*) à *i*) inclusivement et *q*), le transporteur n'aura pas le droit de se prévaloir des dispositions de cette Convention qui excluent ou limitent sa responsabilité.

ARTICLR 10

(1) L'expéditeur est responsable de l'exactitude des indications et déclarations concernant la marchandise qu'il inscrit dans la lettre de transport aérien.

(*j*) the apparent condition of the goods and of the packing;

(*k*) the freight, if it has been agreed upon, the date and place of payment, and the person who is to pay it;

(*l*) if the goods are sent for payment on delivery, the price of the goods, and, if the case so requires, the amount of the expenses incurred;

(*m*) the amount of the value declared in accordance with Article 22 (2);

(*n*) the number of parts of the air consignment note;

(*o*) the documents handed to the carrier to accompany the air consignment note;

(*p*) the time fixed for the completion of the carriage and a brief note of the route to be followed, (*via*) [1]) if these matters have been agreed upon;

(*q*) the indication [2]) that the carriage is subject to the system of [3]) liability established by this Convention.

ARTICLE 9

If the carrier accepts goods without an air consignment note having been made out, or if the air consignment note does not contain all the particulars set out in Article 8 (*a*) to (*i*) inclusive and (*q*), the carrier shall not be entitled to avail himself of the provisions of this Convention which exclude or limit his liability.

ARTICLE 10

(1) The consignor is responsible for the correctness of the indications and declarations [4]) relating to the goods which he inserts in the air consignment note.

[1]) CAA has omitted '(*via*)'.
[2]) CAA: '*a statement*'.
[3]) CAA: '*rules relating to*'.
[4]) CAA: '*particulars* and *statements*'.

(2) Il supportera la responsabilité de tout dommage subi par le transporteur ou toute autre personne à raison de ses indications et déclarations irrégulières, inexactes ou incomplètes.

ARTICLE 11

(1) La lettre de transport aérien fait foi, jusqu'à preuve contraire, de la conclusion du contrat, de la réception de la marchandise et des conditions du transport.

(2) Les énonciations de la lettre de transport aérien, relatives au poids, aux dimensions et à l'emballage de la marchandise ainsi qu'au nombre des colis, font foi jusqu'à preuve contraire; celles relatives à la quantité, au volume et à l'état de la marchandise ne font preuve contre le transporteur qu'autant que la vérification en a été faite par lui en présence de l'expéditeur, et constatée sur la lettre de transport aérien, ou qu'il s'agit d'énonciations relatives à l'état apparent de la marchandise.

ARTICLE 12

(1) L'expéditeur a le droit, sous la condition d'exécuter toutes les obligations résultant du contrat de transport, de disposer de la marchandise, soit en la retirant à l'aérodrome de départ ou de destination, soit en l'arrêtant en cours de route lors d'un atterrissage, soit en la faisant délivrer au lieu de destination ou en cours de route à une personne autre que le destinataire indiqué sur la lettre de transport aérien, soit en demandant son retour à l'aérodrome de départ, pour autant que l'exercice de ce droit ne porte préjudice ni au

(2) The consignor will be liable for all damage suffered by the carrier or any other person by reason of the irregularity, incorrectness or incompletenes of his indications and declarations [1]).

ARTICLE 11

(1) The air consignment note is *prima facie* evidence of the conclusion of the contract, of the receipt of the goods and of the conditions of carriage.

(2) The statements in the air consignment note relating to the weight, dimensions and packing of the goods, as well as those relating to the number of packages, are *prima facie* evidence of the facts stated; those relating to the quantity, the volume and the condition of the goods do not constitute evidence against the carrier except so far as they have been checked by him in the presence of the consignor and are stated in the air consignment note to have been checked, or so far as they relate to the apparent condition of the goods [2]).

ARTICLE 12

(1) Subject to his liability to carry out all his obligations under the contract of carriage, the consignor has the right to dispose of the goods by withdrawing them at the aerodrome of departure or destination, or by stopping them in the course of the journey on any landing, or by calling for them to be delivered at the place of destination or in the course of the journey to a person other than the consignee named in the air consignment note, or by requiring

[1]) CAA: '*the said 'particulars* and *statements*'.

[2]) CAA: 'except so far as they both have been, and are stated in the air consignmentnote to have been, checked by him in the presence of the consignor, or relate to the apparent condition of the goods'.

transporteur, ni aux autres expéditeurs et avec l'obligation de rembourser les frais qui en résultent.

(2) Dans le cas où l'exécution des ordres de l'expéditeur est impossible, le transporteur doit l'en aviser immédiatement.

(3) Si le transporteur se conforme aux ordres de disposition de l'expéditeur, sans exiger la production de l'exemplaire de la lettre de transport aérien délivré à celui-ci, il sera responsable, sauf son recours contre l'expéditeur, du préjudice qui pourrait être causé par ce fait à celui qui est régulièrement en possession de la lettre de transport aérien.

(4) Le droit de l'expéditeur cesse au moment où celui du destinataire commence, conformément à l'article 13 ci-dessous. Toutefois, si le destinataire refuse la lettre de transport ou la marchandise, ou s'il ne peut être atteint, l'expéditeur reprend son droit de disposition.

ARTICLE 13

(1) Sauf dans les cas indiqués à l'article précédent, le destinataire a le droit, dès l'arrivée de la marchandise au point de destination, de demander au transporteur de lui remettre la lettre de transport aérien et de lui livrer la marchandise contre le paiement du montant des créances et contre l'exécution des conditions de transport indiquées dans la lettre de transport aérien.

(2) Sauf stipulation contraire, le transporteur doit aviser le

them to be returned to the aerodrome of departure, provided that he shall [1]) not exercise this right of disposition in such a way as to prejudice the carrier or other consignors and that he shall repay any expenses resulting therefrom [2]).

(2) If it is impossible to carry out the orders of the consignor the carrier must so inform him forthwith.

(3) If the carrier obeys the orders of the consignor for the disposition of the goods without requiring the production of the part of the air consignment note delivered to the latter, he will be liable, without prejudice to his right of recovery from the consignor, for any damage which may be caused thereby to the person who is lawfully in possession of that part of the air consignment note.

(4) The right conferred on the consignor ceases at the moment when that of the consignee begins in accordance with Article 13. Nevertheless, if the consignee declines to accept the consignment note or the goods, or if he cannot be communicated with, the consignor resumes his right of disposition.

ARTICLE 13

(1) Except in the cases [3]) set out in the preceding article, the consignee is entitled, on arrival of the goods at the place of destination, to require the carrier to hand over to him the air consignment note and to deliver the goods to him, on payment of the charges due and on complying with the conditions of carriage set out in the air consignment note.

(2) Unless it is otherwise agreed, it is the duty of the carrier to give

[1]) CAA: '*He must*'.
[2]) CAA: '*occasioned* by *the exercise* of *this right*'.
[3]) CAA: *circumstances*'.

destinataire dès l'arrivée de la marchandise.

(3) Si la perte de la marchandise est reconnue par le transporteur ou si, à l'expiration d'un délai de sept jours après qu'elle aurait dû arriver, la marchandise n'est pas arrivée, le destinataire est autorisé à faire valoir vis-à-vis du transporteur les droits résultant du contrat de transport.

ARTICLE 14

L'expéditeur et le destinataire peuvent faire valoir tous les droits qui leur sont respectivement conférés par les articles 12 et 13, chacun en son propre nom, qu'il agisse dans son intérêt ou dans l'intérêt d'autrui, à condition d'exécuter les obligations qui le contrat impose.

ARTICLE 15

(1) Les articles 12, 13 et 14 ne portent aucun préjudice ni aux rapports de l'expéditeur et du destinataire entre eux, ni aux rapports des tiers dont les droits proviennent, soit de l'expéditeur, soit du destinataire.

(2) Toute clause dérogeant aux stipulations des articles 12, 13 et 14 doit être inscrite dans la lettre de transport aérien.

ARTICLE 16

(1) L'expéditeur est tenu de fournir les renseignements et de joindre à la lettre de transport aérien les documents qui, avant la remise de la marchandise au destinataire, sont nécessaire à l'accomplissement des formalités de douane, d'octroi ou de police. L'expéditeur

notice to the consignee as soon as the goods arrive.

(3) If the carrier admits the loss of the goods, or if the goods have not arrived at the expiration of seven days after the date on which they ought to have arrived, the consignee is entitled to exercise [1]) against the carrier the rights which flow from the contract of carriage.

ARTICLE 14

The consignor and the consignee can enforce all the rights given them by Articles 12 and 13 respectively, each in his own name, whether he is acting in his own interest or in the interest of another, provided that he carries out the obligations imposed by the contract.

ARTICLE 15

(1) Articles 12, 13 and 14 do not affect either the relations of the consignor or the consignee with each other or the relations of third parties whose rights are derived either from the consignor or from the consignee.

(2) Any clause deviating from the provisions of Articles 12, 13 and 14 must be written in the air consignment note [2]).

ARTICLE 16

(1) The consignor must furnish such information and attach to the air consignment note such documents as are necessary, before the goods are delivered to the consignee, to meet the formalities of customs, octroi or police [3]). The consignor is liable to the carrier

[1]) CAA: '*put into force*'.

[2]) CAA: '*The provinsions* of Articles 12, 13 and 14 *can only be varied by express provision* in the air consignment note'. Comp. No. 70 (1).

[3]) CAA: 'as are necessary to meet the formalities of customs, octroi or police before the goods can be delivered to the consignee'.

est responsable envers le transporteur de tous dommages qui pourraient résulter de l'absence, de l'insuffisance ou de l'irrégularité de ces renseignements et pièces, sauf le cas de faute de la part du transporteur ou de ses préposés.

(2) Le transporteur n'est pas tenu d'examiner si ces renseignements et documents sont exacts ou suffisants.

for any damage occasioned by the absence, insufficiency or irregularity of any such information or documents, except in case of fault on the part of of the carrier or his agents [1]).

(2) The carrier is under no obligation to enquire into the correctness or sufficiency of such information or documents.

CHAPITRE III

RESPONSABILITÉ DU TRANSPORTEUR

ARTICLE 17

Le transporteur est responsable du dommage survenu en cas de mort, de blessure ou de toute autre lésion corporelle subie par un voyageur lorsque l'accident qui a causé le dommage s'est produit à bord de l'aéronef ou au cours de toutes opérations d'embarquement et de débarquement.

ARTICLE 18

(1) Le transporteur est responsable du dommage survenu en cas de destruction, perte ou avarie de bagages enregistrés ou de marchandises lorsque l'événement qui a causé le dommage s'est produit pendant le transport aérien.

(2) Le transport aérien, au sens de l'alinéa précédent, comprend la période pendant laquelle les bagages ou marchandises se trouvent sous la garde du transporteur, que ce soit dans un aérodrome ou à bord d'un aéronef ou dans un lieu quelconque en cas d'atterrissage en dehors d'un aérodrome.

(3) La période du transport aérien ne couvre aucun transport terrestre, maritime ou fluvial effectué en dehors d'un aérodrome. Toutefois lorsqu'un tel transport

CHAPTER III

LIABILITY OF THE CARRIER

ARTICLE 17

The carrier is liable for damage sustained in the event of the death or wounding of a passenger or any other bodily injury suffered by a passenger, if the accident which caused the damage so sustained took place on board the aircraft or in the course of any of the operations of embarking or disembarking.

ARTICLE 18

(1) The carrier is liable for damage sustained in the event of the destruction or loss of, or of damage to, any registered luggage or any goods, if the occurrence which caused the damage took place during the carriage by air.

(2) The carriage by air within the meaning of the preceding paragraph comprises the period during which the luggage or goods are in charge of the carrier, whether in an aerodrome or on board an aircraft, or, in the case of a landing outside an aerodrome, in any place whatsoever.

(3) The period of the carriage by air does not extend to any carriage by land, by sea or by river performed outside an aerodrome. If, however, such a carriage

[1]) CAA: '*unless the damage is due to the* fault *of* the carrier or his agents'.

est effectué dans l'exécution du contrat de transport aérien en vue du chargement, de la livraison ou du transbordement, tout dommage est présumé, sauf preuve contraire, résulter d'un événement survenu pendant le transport aérien.

ARTICLE 19

Le transporteur est responsable du dommage résultant d'un retard dans le transport aérien de voyageurs, bagages ou marchandises.

ARTICLE 20

(1) Le transporteur n'est pas responsable s'il prouve que lui et ses préposés ont pris toutes les mesures nécessaires pour éviter le dommage ou qu'il leur était impossible de les prendre.

(2) Dans les transports de marchandises et de bagages, le transporteur n'est par responsable, s'il prouve que le dommage provient d'une faute de pilotage, de conduite de l'aéronef ou de navigation, et que, à tous autres égards, lui et ses préposés ont pris toutes les mesures nécessaires pour éviter le dommage.

ARTICLE 21

Dans le cas où le transporteur fait la preuve que la faute de la personne lésée a causé le dommage ou y a contribué, le tribunal pourra, conformément aux dispositions de sa propre loi, écarter ou atténuer la responsabilité du transporteur.

ARTICLE 22

(1) Dans le transport des personnes, la responsabilité du transporteur envers chaque voyageur

takes place in the performance of a contract for carriage by air, for the purpose of loading, delivery or transhipment, any damage is presumed, subject to proof to the contrary, to have been the result of an occurrence [1]) which took place during the carriage by air.

ARTICLE 19

The carrier is liable for damage occasioned by delay in the carriage by air of passengers, luggage or goods.

ARTICLE 20

(1) The carrier is not liable if he proves that he and his agents have taken all necessary measures to avoid the damage or that it was impossible for him and [2]) them to take such measures.

(2) In the carriage of goods and luggage the carrier is not liable if he proves that the damage was occasioned by negligent pilotage or negligence in the steering [3]) of the aircraft or in navigation and that, in all other respects, he and his agents have taken all necessary measures to avoid the damage.

ARTICLE 21

If the carrier proves that the damages was caused by or contributed to by the negligence of the person suffering damage [4]), the Court may, in accordance with the provisions of its own law, exonerate the carrier wholly or partly from his liability.

ARTICLE 22

(1) In the carriage of passengers the liability of the carrier toward [5]) each passenger is limited to the

---

[1]) CAA: *'event'*.
[2]) CAA: *'or'*. See No. 196 (1).
[3]) CAA: *'handling'*. See No. 32 (1).
[4]) CAA: *'injured* person'.
[5]) CAA: *'for'*.

est limitée à la somme de cent vingt-cinq mille francs. Dans le cas où, d'après la loi du tribunal saisi, l'indemnité peut être fixée sous forme de rente, le capital de la rente ne peut dépasser cette limite. Toutefois par une convention spéciale avec le transporteur, le voyageur pourra fixer une limite de responsabilité plus élevée.

(2) Dans le transport de bagages enregistrés et de marchandises, la responsabilité du transporteur est limitée à la somme de deux cent cinquante francs par kilogramme, sauf déclaration spéciale d'intérêt à la livraison faite par l'expéditeur au moment de la remise du colis au transporteur et moyennant le paiement d'une taxe supplémentaire éventuelle. Dans ce cas, le transporteur sera tenu de payer jusqu'à concurrence de la somme déclarée, à moins qu'il ne prouve qu'elle est supérieure à l'intérêt réel de l'expéditeur à la livraison.

(3) En ce qui concerne les objets dont le voyageur conserve la garde, la responsabilité du transporteur est limitée à cinq mille francs par voyageur.

(4) Les sommes indiquées ci-dessus sont considérées comme se rapportant au franc français constitué par soixante-cinq et demi milligrammes d'or au titre de neuf cents millièmes de fin. Elles pourront être converties dans chaque monnaie nationale en chiffres ronds.

ARTICLE 23

Toute clause tendant à exonérer le transporteur de sa responsabilité ou à établir une limite inférieure à celle qui est fixée dans la présente Convention est nulle et de nul effet,

sum of 125,000 francs. Where, in accordance with the law of the Court seized of the case, damages may be awarded in the form of periodical payments, the equivalent capital value of the said payments shall not exceed 125,000 francs. Nevertheless, by a special contract with the carrier, the passenger may establish a higher limit of liability [1]).

(2) In the carriage of registered luggage and of goods, the liability of the carrier is limited to a sum of 250 francs per kilogram, unless the consignor has made, at the time when the package was handed over to the carrier, a special declaration of the value at delivery and has paid a supplementary sum if the case so requires. In that case the carrier will be liable to pay a sum not exceeding the declared sum, unless he proves that that sum is greater than the actual value to the consignor at delivery.

(3) As regards objects of which the passenger takes charge himself the liability of the carrier is limited to 5,000 francs per passenger.

(4) The sums mentioned above shall be deemed to refer to the French franc consisting of $65\frac{1}{2}$ milligrams gold of millesimal fineness 900. These sums may be converted into any national currency in round figures.

ARTICLE 23

Any provision tending to relieve the carrier of his liability or to establish a lower limit than that fixed [2]) in this Convention shall be null and void, but the nullity

[1]) CAA: 'by special contract the carrier and the passenger may agree to a higher limit of liability'.

[2]) CAA: 'to relieve the carrier of liability or to fix a lower limit than that which is laid down'.

mais la nullité de cette clause n'entraîne pas la nullité du contrat qui reste soumis aux dispositions de la présente Convention.

of any such provision does not involve the nullity of the contract, which shall remain subject to the provisions of this Convention.

ARTICLE 24

(1) Dans les cas prévus aux articles 18 et 19 toute action en responsabilité, à quelque titre que ce soit, ne peut être exercée que dans les conditions et limites prévues par la présente Convention.

(2) Dans les cas prévus à l'article 17, s'appliquent également les dispositions de l'alinéa précédent, sans préjudice de la détermination des personnes qui ont le droit d'agir et de leurs droits respectifs.

ARTICLE 24

(1) In the cases covered by Articles 18 and 19 any action for damages, however founded, can only be brought subject to the conditions and limits set out in this Convention.

(2) In the cases covered by Article 17 the provisions of the preceding paragraph also apply, without prejudice to the question as to who are the persons who have the right to bring suit and what are their respective rights.

ARTICLE 25

(1) Le transporteur n'aura pas le droit de se prévaloir des dispositions de la présente Convention qui excluent ou limitent sa responsabilité, si le dommage provient de son dol ou d'une faute qui, d'après la loi du tribunal saisi, est considérée comme équivalente au dol.

(2) Ce droit lui sera également refusé si le dommage a été causé dans les mêmes conditions par un de ses préposés agissant dans l'exercice de ses fonctions.

ARTICLE 25

(1) The carrier shall not be entitled to avail himself of the provisions of this Convention which exclude or limit his liability, if the damage is caused by his wilful misconduct [literally: his intentional misconduct or such fault on his part as, in accordance with the law of the Court seized of the case, is considered to be equivalent to intentional misconduct] [1]).

(2) Similarly the carrier shall not be entitled to avail himself of the said provisions, if the damage is caused as aforesaid by any agent of the carrier acting within the scope of his employment.

ARTICLE 26

(1) La réception des bagages et marchandises sans protestation par le destinataire constituera présomption, sauf preuve contraire, que les marchandises ont été livrées en bon état et conformément au titre de transport.

(2) En cas d'avarie le destinatai-

ARTICLE 26

(1) Receipt by the person entitled to delivery [literally: the consignee] of luggage or goods without complaint is *prima facie* evidence that the same have been delivered in good condition and in accordance with the document of carriage.

(2) In the case of damage, the

1) CAA: 'by his *wilful* misconduct or by such *default* [...] equivalent to *wilful* misconduct'. See No. 178.

re doit adresser au transporteur une protestation immédiatement après la découverte de l'avarie et, au plus tard, dans un délai de trois jours pour les bagages et de sept jours pour les marchandises à dater de leur réception. En cas de retard, la protestation devra être faite au plus tard dans les quatorze jours à dater du jour où le bagage ou la marchandise auront été mis à sa disposition.

(3) Toute protestation doit être faite par réserve inscrite sur le titre de transport ou par un autre écrit expédié dans le délai prévu pour cette protestation.

(4) A défaut de protestation dans les délais prévus, toutes actions contre le transporteur sont irrecevables, sauf le cas de fraude de celui-ci.

Article 27

En cas de décès du débiteur, l'action en responsabilité, dans les limites prévues par la présente Convention, s'exerce contre ses ayants droit.

Article 28

(1) L'action en responsabilité devra être portée, au choix du demandeur, dans le territoire d'une des Hautes Parties Contractantes, soit devant le tribunal du domicile du transporteur, du siège principal de son exploitation ou du lieu où il possède un établissement par le soin duquel le contrat a été conclu, soit devant le tribunal du lieu de destination.

(2) La procédure sera réglée par la loi du tribunal saisi.

person entitled to delivery must complain to the carrier forthwith after the discovery of the damage, and, at the latest, within three days from the date of receipt in the case of luggage and seven days from the date of receipt in the case of goods. In the case of delay the complaint must be made at the latest within fourteen days from the date on which the luggage or goods have been placed at his disposal.

(3) Every complaint must be made by written reservation on [1]) the document of carriage or by separate notice in writing despatched within the time provided for such complaint [2]).

(4) Failing complaint within the times aforesaid, no action shall lie against the carrier, save in the case of fraud on his part.

Article 27

In the case of the death of the person liable, an action for damages lies in accordance with the terms of this Convention against his estate [3]).

Article 28

(1) An action for damages must be brought, at the option of the plaintiff, in the territory of one of the High Contracting Parties, either before the Court having jurisdiction where the carrier has his domicile [4]) or has his principal place of business, or has an establishment by which the contract has been made, or before the Court having jurisdiction at the place of destination.

(2) Questions of procedure shall be governed by the law of the Court seized of the case.

[1]) CAA: '*in writing upon*'.
[2]) CAA: 'the *times aforesaid*'.
[3]) CAA:) '*those legally representing* his estate'.
[4]) CAA: '*is ordinarily resident*.

ARTICLE 29

(1) L'action en responsabilité doit être intentée, sous peine de déchéance, dans le délai de deux ans à compter de l'arrivée à destination ou du jour où l'aéronef aurait dû arriver, ou de l'arrêt du transport.

(2) Le mode du calcul du délai est déterminé par la loi du tribunal saisi.

ARTICLE 30

(1) Dans les cas de transport régis par la définition du troisième alinéa de l'article ler, à exécuter par divers transporteurs successifs, chaque transporteur acceptant des voyageurs, des bagages ou des marchandises est soumis aux règles établies par cette Convention, et est censé être une des parties contractantes du contrat de transport, pour autant que ce contrat ait trait à la partie du transport effectuée sous son contrôle.

(2) Au cas d'un tel transport, le voyageur ou ses ayants droit ne pourront recourir que contre le transporteur ayant effectué le transport au cours duquel l'accident ou le retard s'est produit, sauf dans le cas où, par stipulation expresse, le premier transporteur aura assuré la responsabilité pour tout le voyage.

(3) S'il s'agit de bagages ou de marchandises, l'expéditeur aura recours contre le premier transporteur et le destinataire qui a le droit à la délivrance contre le dernier, et l'un et l'autre pourront, en outre, agir contre le transporteur ayant effectué le transport au cours

ARTICLE 29

(1) The right to damages shall be extinguished if an action is not brought within two years, reckoned from the date of arrival at the destination, or from the date on which the aircraft ought to have arrived, or from the date on which the carriage stopped.

(2) The method of calculating the period of limitation shall be determined by the law of the Court seized of the case.

ARTICLE 30

(1) In the case of carriage to be performed by various successive carriers and falling within the definition set out in the third paragraph of Article 1, each carrier who accepts passengers, luggage or goods is subjected to the rules set out in this Convention, and is deemed to be one of the contracting parties to the contract of carriage in so far as the contract deals with that part of the carriage which is performed under his supervision.

(2) In the case of carriage of this nature, the passenger or his estate [1]) can take action only against the carrier who performed the carriage during which the accident or the delay occurred save in the case where, by express agreement, the first carrier has assumed [2]) liability for the whole journey.

(3) As regards luggage or goods, the [passenger or] consignor will have a right of action against the first carrier, and the [passenger or] consignee who is entitled to delivery will have a right of action against the last carrier, and further, each may take action against the carrier

---

1) CAA: '*representative*'.

2) The French text has '*assuré*'. The earlier drafts had '*assumé*' which at a certain stage, perhaps by mistake, was altered into *assuré*. See CITEJA 3e Session (Madrid, 1928) pp. 60, 68 and 127.

duquel la destruction, la perte, l'avarie ou le retard se sont produits. Ces transporteurs seront solidairement responsables envers l'expéditeur et le destinataire.

CHAPITRE IV

DISPOSITIONS RELATIVES AUX TRANSPORTS COMBINÉS

ARTICLE 31

(1) Dans le cas de transports combinés effectués en partie par air et en partie par tout autre moyen de transport, les stipulations de la présente Convention ne s'appliquent qu'au transport aérien et si celui-ci répond aux conditions de l'article 1er.

(2) Rien dans la présente Convention n'empêche les parties, dans le cas de transports combinés, d'insérer dans le titre de transport aérien des conditions relatives à d'autres modes de transport, à condition que les stipulations de la présente Convention soient respectées en ce qui concerne le transport par air.

CHAPITRE V

DISPOSITIONS GÉNÉRALES ET FINALES

ARTICLE 32

Sont nulles toutes clauses du contrat de transport et toutes conventions particulières antérieures au dommage par lesquelles les parties dérogeraient aux règles de la présente Convention soit par une détermination de la loi applicable, soit par une modification des règles de compétence. Toutefois, dans le transport des marchan-

who performed the carriage during which the destruction, loss, damage or delay took place. These carriers will be jointly and severally liable [to the passenger or] to the consignor and the [1]) consignee.

CHAPTER IV

PROVISIONS RELATING TO COMBINED CARRIAGE

ARTICLE 31

(1) In the case of combined carriage performed partly by air and partly by any other mode of carriage, the provisions of this Convention apply only to the carriage by air, provided that the carriage by air falls within the terms of Article 1.

(2) Nothing in this Convention shall prevent the parties in the case of combined carriage from inserting in the document of air carriage conditions relating to other modes of carriage, provided that the provisions of this Convention are observed as regards the carriage by air.

CHAPTER V

GENERAL AND FINAL PROVISIONS

ARTICLE 32

Any clause contained in the contract of carriage and all special agreements entered into before the damage occurred by which the parties purport to depart from [2]) the rules laid down by this Convention, whether by deciding the law to be applied, or by altering the rules as to jurisdiction, shall be null and void. Nevertheless for the

[1]) CAA: has correctly added the words between brackets ('*passenger or*'), but has incorrectly changed 'the consignor and the consignee' into 'the consignor *or* consignee'.

[2]) CAA: '*infringe*'.

dises, les clauses d'arbitrage sont admises, dans les limites de la présente Convention, lorsque l'arbitrage doit s'effectuer dans les lieux de compétence des tribunaux prévus à l'article 28, alinéa 1.

carriage of goods arbitration clauses are allowed, subject to this Convention, if the arbitration is to take place within the jurisdictions [1]) referred to in the first paragraph of Article 28.

ARTICLE 33

Rien dans la présente Convention ne peut empêcher un transporteur de refuser la conclusion d'un contrat de transport ou de formuler des règlements qui ne sont pas en contradiction avec les dispositions de la présente Convention.

ARTICLE 33

Nothing contained in this Convention shall prevent the carrier either from refusing to enter into any contract of carriage, or from making regulations which do not conflict with the provisions of this Convention.

ARTICLE 34

La présente Convention n'est applicable ni aux transports aériens internationaux exécutés à titre de premiers essais par des entreprises de navigation aérienne en vue de l'établissement de lignes régulières de navigation aérienne, ni aux transports effectués dans des circonstances extraordinaires en dehors de toute opération normale de l'exploitation aérienne.

ARTICLE 34

This Convention does not apply to international carriage by air performed by way of experimental trial by air navigation undertakings with the view to the establishment of a regular line of air navigation, nor does it apply to carriage performed in extraordinary circumstances outside the normal scope of air commerce [2]).

ARTICLE 35

Lorsque dans la présente Convention il est question de jours, il s'agit de jours courants et non de jours ouvrables.

ARTICLE 35

The expression 'days' when used in this Convention means current days not working days.

ARTICLE 36 [3])

The Convention is drawn up in French in a single copy which shall remain deposited in the archives of the Ministry for Foreign Affairs of Poland and of which one duly certified copy shall be sent by the Polish Government to the Government of each of the High Contracting Parties.

ARTICLE 37

(1) This Convention shall be ratified. The instruments of ratification shall be deposited in the archives of the Ministry for Foreign Affairs of Poland, which will notify the deposit to the Government of each of the High Contracting Parties.

---

[1]) CAA: '*one of* the jurisdictions'.
[2]) CAA: 'an air *carrier's business*'. Comp. Nos. 49 (1) and 57.
[3]) Articles 36 to 41, being of less legal interest, are given in the English translation only.

(2) As soon as this Convention shall have been ratified by five of the High Contracting Parties it shall come into force as between them on the ninetieth day after the deposit of the fifth ratification. Thereafter it shall come into force between the High Contracting Parties who shall have ratified and the High Contracting Party who deposits his instrument of ratification on the ninetieth day after the deposit.

(3) It shall be the duty of the Government of the Republic of Poland to notify to the Government of each of the High Contracting Parties the date on which this Convention comes into force as well as the date of the deposit of each ratification.

ARTICLE 38

(1) This Convention shall, after it has come into force, remain open for accession by any State.

(2) The accession shall be effected by a notification addressed to the Government of the Republic of Poland, which will inform the Government of each of the High Contracting Parties thereof.

(3) The accession shall take effect as from the ninetieth day after the notification made to the Government of the Republic of Poland.

ARTICLE 39

(1) Any one of the High Contracting Parties may denounce this Convention by a notification addressed to the Government of the Republic of Poland, which will at once inform the Government of each of the High Contracting Parties.

(2) Denunciation shall take effect six months after the notification of denunciation, and shall operate only as regards the party who shall have proceeded to denunciation.

ARTICLE 40

(1) Any High Contracting Party may, at the time of signature or of deposit of ratification or of accession declare that the acceptance which he gives to this Convention does not apply to all or any of his colonies, protectorates, territories under mandate, or any other territory subject to his sovereignty or his authority, or any territory under his suzerainty.

(2) Accordingly any High Contracting Party may subsequently accede separately in the name of all or any of his colonies, protectorates, territories under mandate or any other territory subject to his sovereignty or to his authority or any territory under his suzerainty which has been thus excluded by his original declaration.

(3) Any High Contracting Party may denounce this Convention, in accordance with its provisions, separately or for all or any of his colonies, protectorates, territories under mandate or any other territory subject to his sovereignty or to his authority, or anyother territory under his suzerainty.

ARTICLE 41

Any High Contracting Party shall be entitled not earlier than two years after the coming into force of this Convention to call for the assembling of a new international Conference in order to consider any improvements which may be made in this Convention. To this end he will communicate with the Government of the French Republic which will take the necessary measures to make preparations for such Conference.

This Convention done at Warsaw on the 12th October, 1929, shall remain open for signature until the 31st January, 1930.

(Here follow the signatures on behalf of the following countries: –

Germany, Austria, Brazil, Denmark, France, Great Britain and Northern Ireland, the Commonwealth of Australia, the Union of South Africa, Italy, Luxembourg, Poland, Switzerland and Yugoslavia).

ADDITIONAL PROTOCOL

(With reference to Article 2)

The High Contracting Parties reserve to themselves the right to declare at the time of ratification or of accession that the first paragraph of Article 2 of this Convention shall not apply to international carriage by air performed directly by the State, its colonies, protectorates or mandated territories or by any other territory under its sovereignty, suzerainty, or authority.

The following States have SIGNED the Convention: Australia, Austria, Brazil, Denmark, France, Germany, Great Britain and Northern Ireland, Italy, Luxembourg, Poland, Switzerland, Union of South Africa, and Yugoslavia.

The following States have RATIFIED or ADHERED to the Convention (as of January 1, 1954):

AFRICA

BELGIUM (all territories subject to the sovereignty or authority of –)

BRITISH COLONIES etc.: Basutoland, Bechuanaland (Protectorate), Gambia (Colony and Protectorate), Gold Coast (Colony, Ashanti, Northern Territories, Togoland under British Trusteeship), Kenya (Colony and Protectorate), Mauritius, Nigeria (Colony, Protectorate, Cameroons under British Trusteeship), Northern Rhodesia, Nyasaland Protectorate, St. Helena and Ascension, Seychelles, Sierra Leone (Colony and Protectorate), Somaliland (Protectorate), Southern Rhodesia, Swaziland, Tanganyika, Uganda (Protectorate), Zanzibar (Protectorate).

ETHIOPIA

FRANCE (all terrotories whose external relations are under French authority).

ITALY (all terrotories under Italian administration).

LIBERIA

SPANISH MOROCCO

AMERICA

ARGENTINA

BRAZIL

BRITISH COLONIES etc.: Bahamas, Barbados, Bermuda, British Guiana, British Honduras, Jamaica (including Turks and Caicos and Caymen Islands), Leeuward Islands, Trinidad and Tobago, Windward Islands.

CANADA

MEXICO

NETHERLANDS ANTILLES AND SURINAM

UNITED STATES

ANNEX I

Asia and Australia

Australia, including Nauru, New Guinea, Norfolk Island, Papua.

British Colonies etc.: Aden, Brunei, Federation of Malaya, Malacca, Penang, Johore, Kedah, Kelantan, Negri Sembilan, Pahang, Perak, Perlis, Selangor and Trenggany, Fiji, Hong Kong, North Borneo, Sarawak, Singapore, Western Pacific (British Solomon Islands Protectorate, Gilbert and Ellice Islands Colony and Tonga).

Burma

Ceylon

France (all territories whose external relations are under French authority and the Associated States: Cambodia, Laos and Viet-Nam).

India

Indonesia

Israel

Japan

Netherlands New Guinea

New Zealand (including Cook Islands, Tokelau Islands and Western Samoa).

Pakistan

Philippines

Union of Soviet Socialist Republics

United States (all territories subject to the sovereignty or authority of the United States).

Europe

Belgium

Bulgaria

Czechoslovakia

Denmark and Faroe Islands

Finland

France

Germany

Great-Britain (including Channel Islands and Isle of Man, Cyprus, Falkland Islands and Dependencies, Gibraltar, Malta).

Greece

Hungary

Iceland

Ireland

Italy

Liechtenstein

Luxembourg

Netherlands

Norway (including all territories subject to the sovereignty or authority of Norway).

Poland

Portugal

Rumania

Spain

Sweden

Switzerland

Union of Soviet Socialist Republics

Yugoslavia

ANNEX II

CONVENTION

ON DAMAGE CAUSED BY FOREIGN AIRCRAFT TO THIRD PARTIES ON THE SURFACE

Signed at Rome, 7 October 1952

THE STATES SIGNATORY to this Convention

MOVED by a desire to ensure adequate compensation for persons who suffer damage caused on the surface by foreign aircraft, while limiting in a reasonable manner the extent of the liabilities incurred for such damage in order not to hinder the development of international civil air transport, and also

CONVINCED of the need for unifying to the greatest extent possible, through an international convention, the rules applying in the various countries of the world to the liabilities incurred for such damage,

HAVE APPOINTED to such effect the undersigned Plenipotentiaries who, duly authorised, HAVE AGREED AS FOLLOWS:

CHAPTER I

PRINCIPLES OF LIABILITY

ARTICLE 1

1. Any person who suffers damage on the surface shall, upon proof only that the damage was caused by an aircraft in flight or by any person or thing falling therefrom, be entitled to compensation as provided by this Convention. Nevertheless there shall be no right to compensation if the damage is not a direct consequence of the incident giving rise thereto, or if the damage results from the mere fact of passage of the aircraft through the airspace in conformity with existing air traffic regulations.
2. For the purpose of this Convention, an aircraft is considered to be in flight from the moment when power is applied for the purpose of actual takeoff until the moment when the landing run ends. In the case of an aircraft lighter than air, the expression 'in flight' relates to the period from the moment when it becomes detached from the surface until it becomes again attached thereto.

ANNEX II

Article 2

1. The liability for compensation contemplated by Article 1 of this Convention shall attach to the operator of the aircraft.

2. (*a*) For the purposes of this Convention the term 'operator' shall mean the person who was making use of the aircraft at the time the damage was caused, provided that if control of the navigation of the aircraft was retained by the person from whom the right to make use of the aircraft was derived, whether directly or indirectly, that person shall be considered the operator.

(*b*) A person shall be considered to be making use of an aircraft when he is using it personally or when his servants or agents are using the aircraft in the course of their employment, whether or not within the scope of their authority.

3. The registered owner of the aircraft shall be presumed to be the operator and shall be liable as such unless, in the proceedings for the determination of his liability, he proves that some other person was the operator and, in so far as legal procedures permit, takes appropriate measures to make that other person a party in the proceedings.

Article 3

If the person who was the operator at the time the damage was caused had not the exclusive right to use the aircraft for a period of more than fourteen days, dating from the moment when the right to use commenced, the person from whom such right was derived shall be liable jointly and severally with the operator, each of them being bound under the provisions and within the limits of liability of this Convention.

Article 4

If a person makes use of an aircraft without the consent of the person entitled to its navigational control, the latter, unless he proves that he has exercised due care to prevent such use, shall be jointly and severally liable with the unlawful user for damage giving a right to compensation under Article 1, each of them being bound under the provisions and within the limits of liability of this Convention.

Article 5

Any person who would otherwise be liable under the provisions of this Convention shall not be liable if the damage is the direct consequence of armed conflict or civil disturbance, or if such person has been deprived of the use of the aircraft by act of public authority.

Article 6

1. Any person who would otherwise be liable under the provisions of this Convention shall not be liable for damage if he proves that the damage was caused solely through the negligence or other wrongful act or omission of the person who suffers the damage or of the latter's servants or agents. If the person liable proves that the damage was contributed to by the negligence or other wrongful act or omission of the person who suffers the damage, or of his servants or agents, the compensation shall be reduced to the extent to which such negligence or wrongful act or omission con-

tributed to the damage. Nevertheless there shall be no such exoneration or reduction if, in the case of the negligence or other wrongful act or omission of a servant or agent, the person who suffers the damage proves that his servant or agent was acting outside the scope of his authority.

2. When an action is brought by one person to recover damages arising from the death or injury of another person, the negligence or other wrongful act or omission of such other person, or of his servants or agents, shall also have the effect provided in the preceding paragraph.

ARTICLE 7

When two or more aircraft have collided or interfered with each other in flight and damage for which a right to compensation as contemplated in Article 1 results, or when two or more aircraft have jointly caused such damage, each of the aircraft concerned shall be considered to have caused the damage and the operator of each aircraft shall be liable, each of them being bound under the provisions and within the limits of liability of this Convention.

ARTICLE 8

The persons referred to in paragraph 3 of Article 2 and in Articles 3 and 4 shall be entitled to all defences which are available to an operator under the provisions of this Convention.

ARTICLE 9

Neither the operator, the owner, any person liable under Article 3 or Article 4, nor their respective servants or agents, shall be liable for damage on the surface caused by an aircraft in flight or any person or thing falling therefrom otherwise than as expressly provided in this Convention. This rule shall not apply to any such person who is guilty of a deliberate act or omission done with intent to cause damage.

ARTICLE 10

Nothing in this Convention shall prejudice the question whether a person liable for damage in accordance with its provisions has a right of recourse against any other person.

CHAPTER II

EXTENT OF LIABILITY

ARTICLE 11

1. Subject to the provisions of Article 12, the liability for damage giving a right to compensation under Article 1, for each aircraft and incident, in respect of all persons liable under this Convention, shall not exceed:

(*a*) 500 000 francs for aircraft weighing 1000 kilogrammes or less;

(*b*) 500 000 francs plus 400 francs per kilogramme over 1000 kilogrammes for aircraft weighing more than 1000 but not exceeding 6000 kilogrammes;

(*c*) 2 500 000 francs plus 250 francs per kilogramme over 6000 kilogrammes for aircraft weighing more than 6000 but not exceeding 20 000 kilogrammes;

(*d*) 6 000 000 francs plus 150 francs per kilogramme over 20 000 kilogrammes for aircraft weighing more than 20 000 but not exceeding 50 000 kilogrammes;

(*e*) 10 500 000 francs plus 100 francs per kilogramme over 50 000 kilogrammes for aircraft weighing more than 50 000 kilogrammes.

2. The liability in respect of loss of life or personal injury shall not exceed 500 000 francs per person killed or injured.

3. 'Weight' means the maximum weight of the aircraft authorised by the certificate of airworthiness for takeoff, excluding the effect of lifting gas when used.

4. The sums mentioned in francs in this Article refer to a currency unit consisting of 65½ milligrammes of gold of millesimal fineness 900. These sums may be converted into national currencies in round figures. Conversion of the sums into national currencies other than gold shall, in case of judicial proceedings, be made according to the gold value of such currencies at the date of the judgment, or, in cases covered by Article 14, at the date of the allocation.

Article 12

1. If the person who suffers damage proves that it was caused by a deliberate act or omission of the operator, his servants or agents, done with intent to cause damage, the liability of the operator shall be unlimited; provided that in the case of such act or omission of such servant or agent, it is also proved that he was acting in the course of his employment and within the scope of his authority.

2. If a person wrongfully takes and makes use of an aircraft without the consent of the person entitled to use it, his liability shall be unlimited.

Article 13

1. Whenever, under the provisions of Article 3 or Article 4, two or more persons are liable for damage, or a registered owner who was not the operator is made liable as such as provided in paragraph 3 of Article 2, the persons who suffer damage shall not be entitled to total compensation greater than the highest indemnity which may be awarded under the provisions of this Convention against any one of the persons liable.

2. When the provisions of Article 7 are applicable, the person who suffers the damage shall be entitled to be compensated up to the aggregate of the limits applicable with respect to each of the aircraft involved, but no operator shall be liable for a sum in excess of the limit applicable to his aircraft unless his liability is unlimited under the terms of Article 12.

Article 14

If the total amount of the claims established exceeds the limit of liability applicable under the provisions of this Convention, the following rules shall apply, taking into account the provisions of paragraph 2 of Article 11:

(*a*) If the claims are exclusively in respect of loss of life or personal injury or exclusively in respect of damage to property, such claims shall be reduced in proportion to their respective amounts.

(*b*) If the claims are both in respect of loss of life or personal injury and in respect of damage to property, one half of the total sum distributable shall be appropriated preferentially to meet claims in respect of loss of life and personal injury and, if insufficient, shall be distributed proportionately between the claims concerned. The remainder of the total sum distributable shall be distributed proportionately among the claims in respect of damage to property and the portion not already covered of the claims in respect of loss of life and personal injury.

CHAPTER III

Article 15

SECURITY FOR OPERATOR'S LIABILITY

1. Any Contracting State may require that the operator of an aircraft registered in another Contracting State shall be insured in respect of his liability for damage sustained in its territory for which a right to compensation exists under Article 1 by means of insurance up to the limits applicable according to the provisions of Article 11.

2. (*a*) The insurance shall be accepted as satisfactory if it conforms to the provisions of this Convention and has been effected by an insurer authorised to effect such insurance under the laws of the State where the aircraft is registered or of the State where the insurer has his residence or principal place of business, and whose financial responsibility has been verified by either of those States.

(*b*) If insurance has been required by any State under paragraph 1 of this Article, and a final judgment in that State is not satisfied by payment in the currency of that State, any Contracting State may refuse to accept the insurer as financially responsible until such payment, if demanded, has been made.

3. Notwithstanding the last preceding paragraph the State overflown may refuse to accept as satisfactory insurance effected by an insurer who is not authorised for that purpose in a Contracting State.

4. Instead of insurance, any of the following securities shall be deemed satisfactory if the security conforms to Article 17:

(*a*) a cash deposit on a depository maintained by the Contracting State where the aircraft is registered or with a bank authorised to act as a depository by that State;

(*b*) a guarantee given by a bank authorised to do so by the Contracting State where the aircraft is registered, and whose financial responsibility has been verified by that State;

(*c*) a guarantee given by the Contracting State where the aircraft is registered, if that State undertakes that it will not claim immunity from suit in respect of that guarantee.

5. Subject to paragraph 6 of this Article, the State overflown may also require that the aircraft shall carry a certificate issued by the insurer certifying that insurance has been effected in accordance with the provisions of this Convention, and specifying the person or persons whose liability is secured thereby, together with a certificate or endorsement issued by the appropriate authority in the State where the aircraft is registered or in the State where the insurer has his residence or principal place of business certifying the financial responsibility of the insurer. If other security is furnished in accordance with the provisions of paragraph 4 of this Article,

a certificate to that effect shall be issued by the appropriate authority in the State where the aircraft is registered.

6. The certificate referred to in paragraph 5 of this Article need not be carried in the aircraft if a certified copy has been filed with the appropriate authority designated by the State overflown or, if the International Civil Aviation Organization agrees, with that Organization, which shall furnish a copy of the certificate to each contracting State.

7. (*a*) Where the State overflown has reasonable grounds for doubting the financial responsibility of the insurer, or of the bank which issues a guarantee under paragraph 4 of this Article, that State may request additional evidence of financial responsibility, and if any question arises as to the adequacy of that evidence the dispute affecting the States concerned shall, at the request of one of those States, be submitted to an arbitral tribunal which shall be either the Council of the International Civil Aviation Organization or a person or body mutually agreed by the parties.

(*b*) Until this tribunal has given its decision the insurance or guarantee shall be considered provisionally valid by the State overflown.

8. Any requirements imposed in accordance with this Article shall be notified to the Secretary General of the International Civil Aviation Organization who shall inform each Contracting State thereof.

9. For the purpose of this Article, the term 'insurer' includes a group of insurers, and for the purpose of paragraph 5 of this Article, the phrase 'appropriate authority in a State' includes the appropriate authority in the highest political subdivision thereof which regulates the conduct of business by the insurer.

Article 16

1. The insurer or other person providing security required under Article 15 for the liability of the operator may, in addition to the defences available to the operator, and the defence of forgery, set up only the following defences against claims based on the application of this Convention:

(*a*) that the damage occurred after the security ceased to be effective. However, if the security expires during a flight, it shall be continued in force until the next landing specified in the flight plan, but no longer than twentyfour hours; and if the security ceases to be effective for any reason other than the expiration of its term, or a change of operator, it shall be continued until fifteen days after notification to the appropriate authority of the State which certifies the financial responsibility of the insurer or the guarantor that the security has ceased to be effective, or until effective withdrawal of the certificate of the insurer or the certificate of guarantee if such a certificate has been required under paragraph 5 of Article 15, whichever is the earlier;

(*b*) that the damage occurred outside the territorial limits provided for by the security, unless flight outside of such limits was caused by *force majeure*, assistance justified by the circumstances, or an error in piloting, operation or navigation.

2. The State which has issued or endorsed a certificate pursuant to paragraph 5 of Article 15 shall notify the termination or cessation, otherwise than by the expiration of its term, of the insurance or other security to the interested contracting States as soon as possible.

3. Where a certificate of insurance or other security is required under paragraph 5 of Article 15 and the operator is changed during the period of the validity of the security, the security shall apply to the liability under this Convention of the new operator, unless he is already covered by other insurance or security or is an unlawful user, but not beyond fifteen days from the time when the insurer or guarantor notifies the appropriate authority of the State where the certificate was issued that the security has become ineffective or until the effective withdrawal of the certificate of the insurer if such a certificate has been required under paragraph 5 of Article 15, whichever is the shorter period.

4. The continuation in force of the security under the provisions of paragraph 1 of this Article shall apply only for the benefit of the person suffering damage.

5. Without prejudice to any right of direct action which he may have under the law governing the contract of insurance or guarantee, the person suffering damage may bring a direct action against the insurer or guarantor only in the following cases:

(*a*) where the security is continued in force under the provisions of paragraph 1 (*a*) and (*b*) of this Article;

(*b*) the bankruptcy of the operator.

6. Excepting the defences specified in paragraph 1 of this Article, the insurer or other person providing security may not, with respect to direct actions brought by the person suffering damage based upon application of this Convention, avail himself of any grounds of nullity or any right of retroactive cancellation.

7. The provisions of this Article shall not prejudice the question whether the insurer or guarantor has a right of recourse against any other person.

ARTICLE 17

1. If security is furnished in accordance with paragraph 4 of Article 15, it shall be specifically and preferentially assigned to payment of claims under the provisions of this Convention.

2. The security shall be deemed sufficient if, in the case of an operator of one aircraft, it is for an amount equal to the limit applicable according to the provisions of Article 11, and in the case of an operator of several aircraft, if it is for an amount not less than the aggregate of the limits of liability applicable to the two aircraft subject to the highest limits.

3. As soon as notice of a claim has been given to the operator, the amount of the security shall be increased up to a total sum equivalent to the aggregate of:

(*a*) the amount of the security then required by paragraph 2 of this Article, and

(*b*) the amount of the claim not exceeding the applicable limit of liability.

This increased security shall be maintained until every claim has been disposed of.

ARTICLE 18

Any sums due to an operator from an insurer shall be exempt from seizure and execution by creditors of the operator until claims of third parties under this Convention have been satisfied.

ANNEX II

CHAPTER IV

RULES OF PROCEDURE AND LIMITATION OF ACTIONS

Article 19

If a claimant has not brought an action to enforce his claim or if notification of such claim has not been given to the operator within a period of six months from the date of the incident which gave rise to the damage, the claimant shall only be entitled to compensation out of the amount for which the operator remains liable after all claims made within that period have been met in full.

Article 20

1. Actions under the provisions of this Convention may be brought only before the courts of the Contracting State where the damage occurred. Nevertheless, by agreement between any one or more claimants and any one or more defendants, such claimants may take action before the courts of any other Contracting State, but no such proceedings shall have the effect of prejudicing in any way the rights of persons who bring actions in the State where the damage occurred. The parties may also agree to submit disputes to arbitration in any Contracting State.

2. Each Contracting State shall take all necessary measures to ensure that the defendant and all other parties interested are notified of any proceedings concerning them and have a fair and adequate opportunity to defend their interests.

3. Each Contracting State shall so far as possible ensure that all actions arising from a single incident and brought in accordance with paragraph 1 of this Article are consolidated for disposal in a single proceeding before the same court.

4. Where any final judgment, including a judgment by default, is pronounced by a court competent in conformity with this Convention, on which execution can be issued according to the procedural law of that court, the judgment shall be enforceable upon compliance with the formalities prescribed by the laws of the Contracting State, or of any territory, State or province thereof, where execution is applied for:

(*a*) in the Contracting State where the judgment debtor has his residence or principal place of business or,

(*b*) if the assets available in that State and in the State where the judgment was pronounced are insufficient to satisfy the judgment, in any other Contracting State where the judgment debtor has assets.

5. Notwithstanding the provisions of paragraph 4 of this Article, the court to which application is made for execution may refuse to issue execution if it is proved that any of the following circumstances exist:

(*a*) the judgment was given by default and the defendant did not acquire knowledge of the proceedings in sufficient time to act upon it;

(*b*) the defendant was not given a fair and adequate opportunity to defend his interests;

(*c*) the judgment is in respect of a cause of action which had already, as between the same parties, formed the subject of a judgment or an arbitral award which, under the law of the State where execution is sought, is recognized as final and conclusive;

(*d*) the judgment has been obtained by fraud of any of the parties;

(*e*) the right to enforce the judgment is not vested in the person by whom the application for execution is made.

6. The merits of the case may not be reopened in proceedings for execution under paragraph 4 of this Article.

7. The court to which application for execution is made may also refuse to issue execution if the judgment concerned is contrary to the public policy of the State in which execution is requested.

8. If, in proceedings brought according to paragraph 4 of this Article, execution of any judgment is refused on any of the grounds, referred to in subparagraphs (*a*), (*b*) or (*d*) of paragraph 5 or paragraph 7 of this Article, the claimant shall be entitled to bring a new action before the courts of the State where execution has been refused. The judgment rendered in such new action may not result in the total compensation awarded exceeding the limits applicable under the provisions of this Convention. In such new action the previous judgment shall be a defence only to the extent which it has been satisfied. The previous judgment shall cease to be enforceable as soon as the new action has been started.

The right to bring a new action under this paragraph shall, notwithstanding the provisions of Article 21, be subject to a period of limitation of one year from the date on which the claimant has received notification of the refusal to execute the judgment.

9. Notwithstanding the provisions of paragraph 4 of this Article, the court to which application for execution is made shall refuse execution of any judgment rendered by a court of a State other than that in which the damage occurred until all the judgments rendered in that State have been satisfied.

The court applied to shall also refuse to issue execution until final judgment has been given on all actions filed in the State where the damage occurred by those persons who have complied with the time limit referred to in Article 19, if the judgment debtor proves that the total amount of compensation which might be awarded by such judgments might exceed the applicable limit of liability under the provisions of this Convention.

Similarly such court shall not grant execution when, in the case of actions brought in the State where the damage occurred by those persons who have complied with the time limit referred to in Article 19, the aggregate of the judgments exceeds the applicable limit of liability, until such judgments have been reduced in accordance with Article 14.

10. Where a judgment is rendered enforceable under this Article, payment of costs recoverable under the judgment shall also be enforceable. Nevertheless the court applied to for execution may, on the application of the judgment debtor, limit the amount of such costs to a sum equal to ten *per centum* of the amount for which the judgment is rendered enforceable. The limits of liability prescribed by this Convention shall be exclusive of costs.

11. Interest not exceeding four *per centum* per annum may be allowed on the judgment debt from the date of the judgment in respect of which execution is granted.

12. An application for execution of a judgment to which paragraph 4 of this Article applies must be made within five years from the date when such judgment became final.

Article 21

1. Actions under this Convention shall be subject to a period of limitation of two years from the date of the incident which caused the damage.
2. The grounds for suspension or interruption of the period referred to in paragraph 1 of this Article shall be determined by the law of the court trying the action; but in any case the right to institute an action shall be extinguished on the expiration of three years from the date of the incident which caused the damage.

Article 22

In the event of the death of the person liable, an action in respect of liability under the provisions of this Convention shall lie against those legally responsible for his obligations.

CHAPTER V

APPLICATION OF THE CONVENTION AND GENERAL PROVISIONS

Article 23

1. This Convention applies to damage contemplated in Article 1 caused in the territory of a Contracting State by an aircraft registered in the territory of another Contracting State.
2. For the purpose of this Convention a ship or aircraft on the high seas shall be regarded as part of the territory of the State in which it is registered.

Article 24

This Convention shall not apply to damage caused to an aircraft in flight, or to persons or goods on board such aircraft.

Article 25

This Convention shall not apply to damage on the surface if liability for such damage is regulated either by a contract between the person who suffers such damage and the operator or the person entitled to use the aircraft at the time the damage occurred, or by the law relating to workmen's compensation applicable to a contract of employment between such persons.

Article 26

This Convention shall not apply to damage caused by military, customs or police aircraft.

Article 27

Contracting States will, as far as possible, facilitate payment of compensation under the provisions of this Convention in the currency of the State where the damage occurred.

Article 28

If legislative measures are necessary in any Contracting State to give effect to this Convention, the Secretary General of the International Civil

Aviation Organization shall be informed forthwith of the measures so taken.

ARTICLE 29

As between Contracting States which have also ratified the International Convention for the Unification of Certain Rules relating to Damage caused by Aircraft to Third Parties on the Surface opened for signature at Rome on the 29 May 1933, the present Convention upon its entry into force shall supersede the said Convention of Rome.

ARTICLE 30

For the purpose of this Convention:
– 'Person' means any natural or legal person, including a State.
– 'Contracting State' means any State which has ratified or adhered to this Convention and whose denunciation thereof has not become effective.
– 'Territory of a State' means the metropolitan territory of a State and all territories for the foreign relations of which that State is responsible, subject to the provisions of Article 36.

CHAPTER VI

FINAL PROVISIONS

ARTICLE 31

This Convention shall remain open for signature on behalf of any State until it comes into force in accordance with the provisions of Article 33.

ARTICLE 32

1. This Convention shall be subject to ratification by the signatory States.
2. The instruments of ratification shall be deposited with the International Civil Aviation Organization.

ARTICLE 33

1. As soon as five of the signatory States have deposited their instruments of ratification of this Convention, it shall come into force between them on the ninetieth day after the date of the deposit of the fifth instrument of ratification. It shall come into force, for each State which deposits its instrument of ratification after that date, on the ninetieth day after the deposit of its instrument of ratification.
2. As soon as this Convention comes into force, it shall be registered with the United Nations by the Secretary General of the International Civil Aviation Organization.

ARTICLE 34

1. This Convention shall, after it has come into force, be open for adherence by any non-signatory State.
2. The adherence of a State shall be effected by the deposit of an instrument of adherence with the International Civil Aviation Organization and shall take effect as from the ninetieth day after the date of the deposit.

ANNEX II

Article 35

1. Any Contracting State may denounce this Convention by notification of denunciation to the International Civil Aviation Organization.

2. Denunciation shall take effect six months after the date of receipt by the International Civil Aviation Organization of the notification of denunciation; nevertheless, in respect of damage contemplated in Article 1 arising from an incident which occurred before the expiration of the six months period, the Convention shall continue to apply as if the denunciation had not been made.

Article 36

1. This Convention shall apply to all territories for the foreign relations of which a Contracting State is responsible, with the exception of territories in respect of which a declaration has been made in accordance with paragraph 2 of this Article or paragraph 3 of Article 37.

2. Any State may at the time of deposit of its instrument of ratification or adherence, declare that its acceptance of this Convention does not apply to any one or more of the territories for the foreign relations of which such State is responsible.

3. Any Contracting State may subsequently, by notification to the International Civil Aviation Organization, extend the application of this Convention to any or all of the territories regarding which it has made a declaration in accordance with paragraph 2 of this Article or paragraph 3 of Article 37. The notification shall take effect as from the ninetieth day after its receipt by the Organization.

4. Any Contracting State may denounce this Convention, in accordance with the provisions of Article 35, separately for any or all of the territories for the foreign relations of which such State is responsible.

Article 37

1. When the whole or part of the territory of a Contracting State is transferred to a non-contracting State, this Convention shall cease to apply to the territory so transferred, as from the date of the transfer.

2. When part of the territory of a Contracting State becomes an independent State responsible for its own foreign relations, this Convention shall cease to apply to the territory which becomes an independent State, as from the date on which it becomes independent.

3. When the whole or part of the territory of another State is transfer- to a Contracting State, the Convention shall apply to the territory so transferred as from the date of the transfer; provided that, if the territory transferred does not become part of the metropolitan territory of the Contracting State concerned, that Contracting State may, before or at the time of the transfer, declare by notification to the International Civil Aviation Organization that the Convention shall not apply to the territory transferred unless a notification is made under paragraph 3 of Article 36.

Article 38

The Secretary General of the International Civil Aviation Organization shall give notice to all signatory and adhering States and to all States members of the Organization or of the United Nations:

(*a*) of the deposit of any instrument of ratification or adherence and the date thereof, within thirty days from the date of the deposit, and

(*b*) of the receipt of any denunciation or of any declaration or notification made under Article 36 or 37 and the date thereof, within thirty days from the date of the receipt.

The Secretary General of the Organization shall also notify these States of the date on which the Convention comes into force in accordance with paragraph 1 of Article 33.

ARTICLE 39

No reservations may be made to this Convention.

IN WITNESS WHEREOF the undersigned Plenipotentiaries, having been duly authorised, have signed this Convention.

DONE at Rome on the seventh day of the month of October of the year One Thousand Nine Hundred and Fifty Two in the English, French and Spanish languages, each text being of equal authenticity.

This Convention shall be deposited with the International Civil Aviation Organization where, in accordance with Article 31, it shall remain open for signature, and the Secretary General of the Organization shall send certified copies thereof to all signatory and adhering States and to all States members of the Organization or the United Nations.

The Convention has been signed, as of January 1, 1954, by: Argentina, Australia, Belgium, Brazil, Denmark, Dominican Republic, Egypt, France, Israel, Italy, Liberia, Luxembourg, Mexico, Netherlands, Philippines, Portugal, Spain, Switzerland, Thailand and the United Kingdom. It has been ratified by Egypt on the 23d of February 1954.

INDEX 1)

All references are to paragraphs and to the footnotes thereto

1) See also Table of Cases.

GPSR Compliance

The European Union's (EU) General Product Safety Regulation (GPSR) is a set of rules that requires consumer products to be safe and our obligations to ensure this.

If you have any concerns about our products, you can contact us on ProductSafety@springernature.com

In case Publisher is established outside the EU, the EU authorized representative is:

Springer Nature Customer Service Center GmbH
Europaplatz 3
69115 Heidelberg, Germany

Batch number: 10824476

Printed by Printforce, the Netherlands